ALLEGIANCES

To Connie

with much affection

Adelyn

2-20-96

ALLEGIANCES

ADELYN BONIN

Fithian Press
SANTA BARBARA
1993

Design & typography by Jim Cook

Published by Fithian Press
Post Office Box 1525
Santa Barbara, California 93120

LIBRARY OF CONGRESS CATALOGING-IN-PUBLICATION DATA

Bonin, Adelyn,
    Allegiances / Adelyn Bonin.
        p.   cm.
    ISBN 1-56474-036-6
    1. Bonin, Adelyn, 2. Jews—Germany—Biography.
3. Jews, German—Israel—Biography.   4. World War, 1939–1945–
Personal narratives, Jewish.   I. Title.
DS135.G5B6   1993
943.1'55004924—dc20   92-39139
                                                      CIP

ALLEGIANCES

(A section of photographs follows page 140)

FOREWORD

This book is not a novel and does not jump from highlight to highlight with the neat and logical conclusions we often expect of fiction. It is, rather, an exact recounting of the events in my life before I came to the United States. I was born into a momentous and often horrifying time and, though only a tiny part of it, I was typical of the multitudes whose lives were wrenched into unexpected patterns by the events of these years. Fortunately, I saved two records from this period without which I would not have been able to proceed—my parents' letters to me until the outbreak of World War II and the diaries I kept during the years I spent in the British Army, 1942-1946. I translated this material from the German in which it was originally written into English. My memory supplied the rest of the material concerning my early life in Berlin and my later experiences in Palestine.

In language I was sometimes hard put to decide whether to use British or American terms—the latter is now more natural to me, but during the period I write about, of course, it was not. I hope I have adopted an acceptable combination. I should note that the designation "Palestinian" as it is used here refers to Jews living in the British Mandate of Palestine before and during World War II. The State of Israel did not yet exist and the term "Israeli" was not used.

I wish to thank my good Army buddy, Edith Büchler, for the help she gave me in checking some details. Above all I am deeply grateful for the constant assistance and encouragement of my friend Mary McChesney, who prodded me along to finish the work. It now stands as a memorial to my parents, Otto and Lili Bonin—the only way I can honor their memory.

1. BERLIN

They were cheap little swastikas made out of metal. We had not paid more than twenty pfennige for them at the corner store. Proudly, Grete and I displayed them in our lapels and then spent the rest of the day running up and down Drakestrasse, raising our hands in the Nazi salute to every brown-shirt, every Hitler youth we met, and there were a lot of them around in the streets that day. They were celebrating the birth of the Third Reich. The date was January 31, 1933. The place was Berlin. And I was twelve years old. That afternoon was a turning point in my life because by evening my whole world had changed.

My coat was hanging in the hall, the swastika still in its lapel, when my father came home. He noticed it immediately, shook his head, sighed, and asked me to follow him into the library. He looked at me and did not say anything, then looked away as if he had forgotten me. I always had thought of him as calm and able to deal with anything, never at a loss for words as he seemed to be now. He lit a cigarette. His hands shook slightly. He did look tired. And then I realized that he was home much earlier than usual. I began to feel a tightness in my chest. Something serious had happened or was about to happen. "Yes, Vati?"

"Baby—" (that's what he always called me, although I had a sister nine years younger than I). "Baby, this is very difficult for me to explain to you, but the long and the short of it is that you can't wear a swastika. You are not one of them. They are scum, idiots, fanatics who will ruin our country, who will tear down our Republic. Their Hitler, our new Chancellor, will build a dictatorship which will spell the end for free expression, for free pursuit of ideas—oh, I could go on, but. . . ."

9

He did not finish his sentence. His eyes had left me again and I did not know how to call him back. Then, still not looking at me, he said, "Baby, we are Jews. You are a Jew. I had hoped to spare you this. I had you baptized a Christian, and neither your mother nor I belong to any congregation. I had thought that this would remove all difficulties for you. How could I foresee that the Nazi theory of Aryans versus non-Aryans would become the law of the land?" He shook his head as if he himself could not believe what he was telling me. "I don't know what will come of all this. I don't know what the future will bring. But for the moment you must know that all these celebrations of the birth of the Third Reich are a time of sadness for us. You must realize that you are not a part of their new Germany, that you have, though, a proud heritage of a different Germany, the one you learned about in school and in our home—the Germany of Goethe and Schiller and Bach." He kept on talking about the kind of Germany he believed in, the ideals he held dear, but I was not following him. My thoughts circled around the words, "We are Jews. *You* are a Jew."

But what was a Jew? I did not really know. There were no Jewish girls in my class. I did not know any Jews in our entire school or neighborhood. Were the friends of my parents Jews? I had no idea. The concept had no meaning for me and was not part of my experience. I had heard enough to understand that being Jewish, according to the Nazi theory, had nothing to do with religion, that it had become a racial designation. Anyone whose parents or grandparents were Jews was a non-Aryan, a Jew. I never had taken this seriously, nor had I felt that it had anything to do with me. Like all the other kids in school, I was a Protestant, a Lutheran, and no one ever mentioned religion in our home. Marie, our maid, was a Catholic, and when I was little she sometimes had taken me with her to her church. I had enjoyed the service and loved the little pictures of Mary and the Jesus child the priest would give us children after the service. My thoughts kept revolving around the religious aspect. I was not able to grasp this new idea of race, of being different from all my friends. In what way was I different? Why? I lay awake a long time that night trying to understand. The more I thought, the bigger the problem became. And then I thought of tomorrow and was overwhelmed with a new problem. Of course, I could not wear the swastika anymore, but how was I going to explain this to my classmates?

In the next weeks I tried to find out about my heritage but received little help from my parents. My father had, on rare occasions, mentioned that the Bonins were a very old German family. I had heard him remark laughingly that the "von" had gotten lost during the inflation, but I never knew quite what that meant, nor had I really cared. Vaguely, I also remember his talking about his grandfather on his mother's side, who had been a rather large landowner in East Prussia. The story went that he, my great grandfather, had lost a considerable fortune playing cards with his neighbors. Maybe this was the reason that he left East Prussia and came to settle in Berlin. But when I began to question my father about where his Jewish heritage or, as we all quickly got used to calling it, his non-Aryan blood came from, I suddenly was confronted with a totally new story. According to this story, his latest version, his father's family originally had been Sephardic Jews who had left Spain in the sixteenth century, then settled in Holland, and from there had migrated to the Rhineland where they had practiced the trade of silver and weaponsmiths. When, in the eighteenth century, Napoleon decreed that all Jews were to have a family name, this ancestor liked the name of the nobleman he worked for and asked permission to use it. Permission was granted, but with the proviso that he must spell the name Bonnin. How our name was later changed back to Bonin is another story. In later years, long after I had left home, my sister told me yet another story, namely, that our father had assured her that he was the descendant of a very old Prussian family who had settled in East Prussia. But maybe that was the gambling grandfather's line on his mother's side. It was hard to pin my father down. He was a clever man of much imagination who loved an audience, and I remember his telling me, "Never mind if a story is not one hundred percent true, as long as it's entertaining." Still another version dating back to pre-Hitler days pointed to the French origin of our family name, insisting that we were descendants of a Huguenot family who had fled to Germany. Maybe at that time my father had just re-read Goethe's "Hermann und Dorothea" or maybe his love and admiration for Napoleon had given the impetus to the idea that the weaponsmith chose our French name. Or maybe my aristocratic great grandfather, the von Bonin, had married a Jewish girl. In any case, as far as my father's forebears are concerned, I will never know whether I have Sephardic or Prussian blood running through my veins. I suspect a mixture of both, and as far as the Nazis were concerned, it was tainted, a concept that was too new and too confusing for me to understand.

I was on much firmer ground with my mother's family, though I never tried to go back farther than my grandparents. Apparently they both grew up in Silesia and the only episode I recall from that time is my grandmother's relating proudly that her name was entered in the "Golden Book" in Breslau for her outstanding scholarship. I am not sure what that "Goldene Buch" really represented, but it certainly must have been quite an achievement in those days to be recognized, not only as a girl but a Jewish girl, for outstanding intellectual accomplishment. Once again, I don't know what made my grandparents move to Berlin except that Berlin in the 1870s and 1880s was a vibrant, quickly growing city pulsing with pride as the capital of a new Germany, attracting all kinds of people from the more backward Eastern provinces, among them many Jews, drawn by the liberal policies of the city toward them.

Ever since I can remember, I differentiated between my grandparents by calling my mother's parents Opi and Omi and my father's Opa and Oma. Not very original but practical and simple. (As practical and simple as the name I gave the two birds that joined our household when I was five years old. They became Piepmatz 1 and Piepmatz 2, a "piepmatz" being an endearment for "peeper.") I never knew Opa and Oma. They died before I was born. Of Opi I have only one recollection and it is my very first childhood memory. I was two and a half years old and I see myself climbing up some very steep stairs. Considering my size, they may have been ordinary stairs, but I remember wondering why they were not carpeted. My mother holding my left and Omi my right hand, the three of us ascended these stairs and entered a room in which Opi seemed to live. The room did not have much furniture. I remember a bed and a chair. Opi was sitting in the chair in his pajamas and a dressing gown. He called me to him, took the tip of my nose between two of his fingers, turned them slightly and then showed me, smiling, the tip of his thumb. "Got your nose!" he said. Opi died a few days later in that hospital room, but I was too young to understand this.

My memories of Omi are most vivid and cover many years. She seemed the epitome of all grandmothers—small, plump, jolly, with wispy white hair. Omi was my dearest playmate and far more fun than most of the children in our neighborhood. My favorite game with her was playing school, I, of course, in the role of the teacher, she playing the part of a pupil to whom I had to explain the same material over and over. She never seemed to tire of her part as the "dumb Liselotte" and again and again I would double over with laughter at her feigned stupidity. Omi lived in the suburb of Friedenau, which was quite a distance from our house and required taking the streetcar for a forty-five minute ride and then another ten minute walk, yet Omi undertook this

12

trip at least two or three times a week. Regardless of whether or not she would visit us that day, mother talked to Omi on the phone every morning. To me these talks seemed endless, but they were a daily routine after breakfast. Omi would arrive around noon and then, as is typical in a German household, we ate our main meal at 1 P.M. In the afternoon mother and Omi would share a cup of coffee, after which Omi would depart for her flat in Friedenau. As glad as she was arriving, she always seemed eager to leave, afraid of meeting my father if she lingered too long. Vati and Omi did not get along. As a matter of fact, my father did not care much for any of my mother's relatives. Though he supported Omi and a few of mother's nephews, he did not wish to be involved with them.

When I was about seven, Omi bought me a book, the title of which I have long forgotten, but one of the stories in it was entitled "Oma and Omi." Oma, who was Father's mother, was pictured as wealthy, formal, and somewhat cold. Omi, Mother's mother, on the other hand, was not so well situated but was sweet and caring. When the story began the two Omas did not speak to each other, but then, of course, it all ended happily with the two grandmothers becoming good friends through the love of their common grandchild. Well, I could not bring Oma and Omi together because Oma had died long before I was born. Still, from all I had heard, I thought the characters were quite similar to those in our family.

My father came from a very well-to-do family. Grandfather, my Opa, owned a bicycle assembly plant, which my father, as the oldest son, eventually inherited. Vati's younger brother and his sister, my Uncle Hans and Aunt Trudchen, were silent partners in the business, but that suited them fine since neither one was interested in an active partnership, Uncle Hans being a practicing physician and Tante Trudchen a wealthy woman, not practicing anything. Thus my father became a businessman, a job he did not entirely enjoy. In later years, recalling how he loved to teach and to explain to anyone who would listen to him about anything that had just occurred to him, I often thought that he would have made an excellent university professor. Of course, I was always the most available listener, but I remember his asking Platsch, our chauffeur, to come out and view the night sky with us for a quick lecture on the stars, and how he would assemble us, my mother, me, and Marie from the kitchen, in his darkened study for a lesson in astronomy, using the new "planetarium" which he had given me for Christmas. And I remember all those rainy Sundays which were devoted to museum visits. He would choose a particular museum, then decide on a certain department of that museum, and on our way there he would introduce me to what I was going to see. I think that in those years my love for teaching and the study of different cultures and history was born. My father's knowledge seemed to me unlimited. Whenever I or anyone else asked a question, he knew the answer. Once, when I asked my mother why we did not have an encyclopedia in our library, she replied, quite earnestly, "Whatever for? We have Father!" This answer seemed totally satisfactory to me.

But it was not merely for his intellectual capabilities that my mother and, therefore, I, too, admired Vati. He was handsome, possessed all the social graces, and was excellent at sports. In the winter it was skiing, in the summer sailing, and during the year both my parents played quite a bit of tennis. His favorite sport was mountain climbing, the kind where you are roped together and climb precipitous rock faces. Before the great depression, during school vacations, I often would travel with my mother to one of the resorts on the Baltic or North Sea. She was a very good swimmer and preferred the sea to the mountains. Sometimes we did accompany my father to the Dolomites, where he did most of his climbing. He seemed without any physical fear, whatever the situation. Perhaps he had learned that as a student, when he was a member of a dueling society. The duels he fought then had left him with two long scars on his face, one on the chin leading into his lower lip, which gave him a little lopsided, rather charming smile, and the other starting over his left eyebrow and leading diagonally right up to his hairline. More than once my mother told me that she had fallen in love with those dueling scars when she first met him. He once told me that after the duels the young men had to stand at attention while a doctor sewed them up, without any anesthetic. This was meant to teach them complete disregard for pain. Thus those scars became a visible sign of bravery as well as status and position in the upper class. I saw some evidence of his courage one Christmas season when our Advents wreath caught fire and my father, in his quiet, deliberate way, grabbed the burning wreath and carefully carried it all the way out into the garden. Both of his hands got badly burned.

My father's favorite toy was our Protos, a big open touring roadster. Driving to and from the office, taking it out on weekends, and using it for business trips was a joy he often shared with me. In the early twenties a car in Germany was still a great luxury and few people had one. How I loved it when Vati took me on some of his business trips. He had bought me overalls, goggles and a soft helmet, an outfit reminiscent of World War I pilots, of which I was very proud. The two of us would be off for two or three day trips, visiting some of his customers in small towns all over northern Germany. When we were way out in the country he would take me on his lap and let me steer Protos. Sometimes he would take me with him to work and then he would drive over the Avus, a racetrack right in the city. I think today it is part of the autobahn, but in the twenties you could take your car out there, open it up, and see how fast it could go. I believe that in those days driving was a sport, not a necessity. We belonged to the BAC, the Berliner Automobil Klub. This was a real club with a very limited, rather exclusive membership who met for dinner dances and had special contests like following a balloon, with a prize for the first car that found where the balloon had landed. Usually four balloons would take off and each car was assigned a specific balloon to follow. One year my mother, who also was anything but timid, got it into her head to volunteer as a balloonist. Always ready for a bit of showmanship, she had a smart new outfit made for the occasion. I can still see the scene, one balloon after the other taking off with great fanfare. My mother was in the third one, waving happily from her basket, looking ever so elegant in her light beige three-piece ensemble plus hat and gloves—impressive, but not quite the appropriate garb for ballooning. We watched the balloons climb up high, then took a sighting on Mother's balloon and off we drove. The balloons were supposed to fly for a few hours and then land. At first my father and I kept track of "our" balloon, but then we lost sight of it. Since we knew the approximate direction in which it was heading, we kept asking villagers if they had seen a balloon landing anywhere near. Finally, after four hours of searching, we found the unfortunate balloon, its basket still half submerged in a muddy duck pond, the wet crew of four in a nearby farm house, sitting around the stove trying to get warm. The most pitiful sight of all was my mother, bedraggled, muddy, her expensive outfit ruined. That was the end of our experience with balloons. After that we returned to our ordinary Sunday occupations.

"Ordinary," however, is the wrong word to use for my family. As I grew older I could see how different my parents were from others, but when I was little I accepted it all as perfectly ordinary. Like the fact that my father spent much of his time and, as I found out later, most of his money, at the races. Many were the Sundays we spent at the race courses, where I occupied myself picking up the discarded betting tickets, which were highly valued by my playmates as playmoney for all kinds of games. I remember one particular day—I was about five at the time—it must have been Marie's day off and my father probably had given her a ride to the station on his way to the racetrack. Anyway, I saw the two of them drive off together. Later that afternoon my mother and I took a walk to the station and, as we often did, sat on a bench and waited for my father's car to come by and pick us up and drive us home. Two old ladies were sitting next to us on the bench and started a conversation with me. "Are you waiting for your daddy to come home from work?" they asked. "Oh, no," I answered. "My daddy doesn't work. He goes to the races with our maid while my mother and I stay home." The two old ladies responded with shocked silence. My mother yanked me up from the bench and gave the ladies an embarrassed smile. They turned their heads away from us. We did not wait for my father but walked home.

Even our Sunday picnics were not the run-of-the-mill outings where the family chooses a place at one of the many lakes which surround Berlin and settles down for a relaxing day. Not us! First my father would consult a map to find some remote destination. Then, once on our way, he would suddenly spot a side road, often nothing more than a sandy trail which, he was convinced, would lead us to some yet undiscovered, idyllic place. More than once we got stuck and he had to walk some distance to find a farmer who would come with his horses and pull us out. I should mention that by no means was my father's "adventurous" behavior swallowed with equanimity by my mother. My mother was a very vehement person, who never suffered in silence. She was never at a loss for words and was always ready to tell you exactly where she stood and where she thought you should stand.

My mother! These two words evoke such a flood of feelings that it is hard to sort them out, to separate them chronologically, because the total picture to which my feelings respond today could not possibly have been the same one a small child would have formed. It is difficult to recreate the impressions of a five year old. Yet there are very definite memories, and the pictures they resurrect are still vivid. They are even stronger than the memories I have of my father because my mother created the all-encompassing aura of my childhood. What fun she could be! She had a boundless fantasy and that, coupled with her theatrical talents (at one time she had wanted to become an actress), made her the best of storytellers. I never tired of listening to her inventing stories, especially the ones where she personalized all kinds of animals, gave them human characteristics, and made up voices for them. One of my favorites was the story in which several bugs and insects found refuge under a large mushroom during a downpour. Their conversations, always different in each consecutive retelling, charmed me each time anew. And she did not stop at just living creatures. She could make anything around us come alive. I remember that once, when I needed a new coat, she told me for days before we went to town for the purchase about that one special coat hanging on the rack in the department store, dreaming about what kind of child it would keep warm in the winter and how it wished for a little girl who would take good care of it and love it just as it would love her in return. Of course, I could hardly wait to get this wonderful coat, love it, and look after it. Yes, my mother understood how to make a wonderful adventure out of the most ordinary happenings and awakened in me a permanent delight at the simple events of everyday living.

Just before my sixth birthday and before I entered first grade, Mother had the idea of giving a big children's party celebrating the beginning of my school days and the end of the first carefree years of childhood. The theme of my, or rather *her* party, was "Schlaraffenland"—the fairytale place where nobody works, where food hangs from trees and drinks of all kinds flow by, where life is nothing but pleasure, mainly the pleasure of eating and drinking—a sort of glutton's paradise. My mother worked for weeks turning the entire house upside down in order to create such a revelry of feasting. When she finally had finished, it had become an extravaganza worthy of the name "Schlaraffenland." The guests, about thirty children, arrived at 4 P.M. and were greeted by two huge cardboard pigs which stood at both sides of the entrance, constantly bobbing their heads. I have no idea by what device this was made possible. The only thing I recall is that she had borrowed the pigs from our butcher. Once inside the door, the children had to crawl through a tiny opening which led them into a mountain, the guardian of the "promised land." This mountain was an intricate maze of steps, boards, and ladders which took up our entire hall, the study, and the living room. Scrambling up, down, and over these various obstacles was supposed to indicate the long trip to reach "Schlaraffenland," which, of course, was in the dining room. There all the furniture had been taken out so that the room seemed to be enormous. Crisscrossing it in every direction were strings from which dangled shorter strings and at the end of each of these was fastened a cookie or a candy. All this was at a child's eye level and we were supposed to eat these goodies without touching them, once again illustrating the fact that in this fantasy land everything simply dropped right into your mouth. I don't recall the rest of the party in detail. It probably resembled the other parties my mother had given for me, with much food, many games with prizes, and a lot of shrieking excitement. In the end I always had the feeling that *she* had more fun than I. She loved parties, and especially children's parties where her creative spirit was not confined by accepted social convention. The latter she followed as little as possible. Whereas the children of her friends all had a nanny, a "Kinderfräulein" in German, I heard her once say that she was glad to be well enough off *not* to have a nanny for me, meaning that she had all the time in the world to devote to me. In my early years I probably accepted this gladly, but I remember that later on, as her total absorption in me grew, it often felt like an inexplicable extra weight upon me.

My parents were both good-looking people. Of course, a child is no judge of that, but I had my mother's word for it as far as my father was concerned. And as for her, I had plenty of evidence. I could see that people looked at her, turned their heads, seemed always to treat her with some extra smile or courtesy. I don't believe she was beautiful in the classic sense, but she was elegant and charming. I have mentioned before that she and I often traveled alone together. I believe it was the summer of 1926 that we went to Italy. My father had taken us to the station and before bidding us goodbye had presented me with a box of calling cards. I was terribly proud of seeing my name in print. (Almost as proud as when the churchbells rang for me a year previously when I was baptized. I don't remember anything about that ceremony, but I never could get over the idea that the churchbells had rung just for me!) On this train trip we were taking the sleeper and would arrive at our destination, Merano, the following forenoon. I usually had the upper berth, but since the compartment was small, in the morning my mother got me ready and let me out so that she would have the roomette to herself. There I stood, in the gangway, looking out the window, my box of calling cards clutched in my hand. I noticed a very good-looking gentleman standing by the next window. He looked over, smiled at me, and I offered him one of my new cards. Very seriously he brought forth one of his own calling cards and the two of us carried on a lively conversation. As it appeared later, it must have been more of a monologue on my part, because when my mother finally came out and joined us, this nice gentleman bowed to her and said, "Madam, there is no need to tell me anything. I know everything."

I remember that he had told me he was on his way to Milan, but he got off with us in Merano! He even stayed at the same hotel as we did and became a fun companion of ours for a few days. At the time I thought he might have changed his plans because of me, but now, of course, I know better. I also know that my mother would never even have toyed with the idea of any kind of an affair. I am sure that the nice gentleman left unrewarded. My mother adored my father as long as she lived, though it was he who first fell in love with her. He was introduced to her by friends at a chance meeting in the tearoom of some department store. He was twenty-one then, a student of mathematics and engineering at the University in Berlin. She was eighteen, had just finished school, and was about to leave for England for a year's exchange, in order to learn English. With such imminent parting on the horizon, they soon met almost daily and made a commitment to each other before my mother left for London. I use the word commitment because it was not an official engagement. Such a formal announcement would have to wait until my father could make his parents accept his new love. His mother was absolutely opposed to the new girlfriend. Though my mother came from a good, middle-class home, her background could in no way match that of my father. His mother wanted a woman of at least equal status for her oldest son and, as I heard the story later, most adamantly declared that "that woman will never cross our threshold as long as I live." Today it is hard to imagine that two people so much in love would not simply pick up, get married, and settle down together. But in those days (the event I am describing took place in 1907) it would have been unthinkable for a young student to give up his inheritance, his entire future prospects, and set up house without being able to support his wife. That his future wife should work and perhaps help him finish his studies was totally inconceivable.

My father visited my mother twice during her stay in England. When she returned to Germany they spent five more years being secretly engaged. During that time my father finished his studies and began his apprenticeship in the family firm. My mother occupied herself with the usual activities of a young lady in those times. She helped at home, went shopping, played tennis and croquet, had singing lessons, even went so far as to consider the stage as a possible career. She took drama lessons and managed once to get a minor role in an operetta. I think she played a chambermaid and had two lines of dialogue. My father went to each performance and forced all his friends to sit through an entire performance just to see Lili on stage for three minutes. In the spring of 1914 my father's mother died and a few months later World War I broke out. My father then made two important decisions. He felt that it was his duty to volunteer immediately. He would not even wait for a commission, as his younger brother did, but enlisted in the Army. His second decision, or maybe it was the other way round and this was the first decision, was to marry my mother. They had a civil ceremony, and soon afterward he was sent to the Belgian front and later to the Eastern front, where he spent almost three years as a lorry driver, advancing in rank to Sergeant and in territory all the way to Istanbul, or, as it was then called, Constantinople. He never was in a battle and never killed anybody or anything except one pig that ran into his lorry. Nor was he ever wounded, but he got a hernia lifting some heavy supplies and was sent back to a hospital in East Germany. As soon as my mother found out where he was, she was on her way to him. When the nuns who were in charge of the hospital would not let her in because she was a civilian, my mother bribed them by volunteering herself for any job needed. With her usual charm and persistence, she succeeded. Soon she was sitting by my father's bedside, darning mountains of soldiers' socks. Their being together did not last long, however. He was sent back to the Eastern front.

My mother now got it into her head that she would win over her father-in-law. Upon returning from the hospital, she went straight to my grandfather's house and simply moved in and took over. Knowing my mother, this seems quite natural, yet I can imagine the astonished servants and my incredulous grandfather. I was not told any particulars of this episode, only that my Opa refused to talk to my mother, refused even to eat with her, and tried to ignore her totally. But little by little things changed, and by the time my father returned from the war, my grandfather loved his Lili like his own daughter. On his deathbed a year later—my mother was pregnant at the time—his last wish was directed to her. "Lili, if it's a daughter, call her Adeline after my wife. And forgive her. She did not know you."

My mother did deliver a girl, but the baby died at birth. A year later, in 1920, I was born and my birth certificate lists me as Adeline Ingeborg Bonin. Ingeborg, apparently, because I was born with blonde hair and blue eyes, which, my mother insisted, called for a Nordic name. I was born in a small private clinic, attended not only by two specialists (my mother was deathly afraid that she would lose me as she had lost her first child) but also by a nurse, who had been hired even before my arrival and stayed with my mother at the clinic. When I was brought home, Sister Anna came along and lived with us until I was six months old. Nine years later the same Sister Anna returned to us when my sister, Edith, was born. I got to know her well then. She seemed to me quite stern and stiff, but that may have been partly due to her highly starched uniform.

My mother told me that when she carried me home from the hospital, the first to greet her was our dog, Faust. Faust von Schlotheim was his full name, and he was a pure-blooded boxer. My father had bought him for my mother before he left for the front. Faust might have possessed a very aristocratic name, but his behavior was decidedly plebeian. He loved everyone who came to the house and showed it by getting up on his hind legs, putting his front paws on their shoulders, and slobbering all over them. When I say he loved everyone I should add that there was one exception—me. He must have known instinctively that the blanket my mother carried so carefully up the stairs held a rival for her affections, and he was jealous. The way my mother told it, he came rushing down the stairs, stopped suddenly, growled, and then leaped forward and bit right through the pillow I was lying on. He missed me by less than an inch! But gradually Faust accepted the fact that I was to be a permanent resident in the household.

My mother kept a "baby book" in which my weight, my size, my every utterance was recorded. I wonder, do mothers still do this sort of thing? Probably not. Today they record on videotape, where action and voice can be replayed on the big screen. I have no such tape and the baby book disappeared long ago with everything else my parents possessed. In my early teens, though, I used to take it out sometimes and leaf through it. Today I recall but a very few points from those pages. I apparently was a very happy baby, cried little and giggled a lot. My development seemed to have been normal as far as walking and talking were concerned, except that I did an awful lot of the latter, even though most of it was gibberish. As recorded in the book, there was only one unusual event during my first year. The doctor told my mother to stop breast-feeding me when I was nine months old. Apparently I did not take to this deprivation kindly and would not swallow any of the substitutes. In those days not much was known about formulas. In desperation my mother finally hit upon the idea of giving me goat's milk, and that was okay with me. But in order to have a regular supply of it—after all, this was the height of inflation and food supplies were uncertain and uneven—my parents bought a goat, the price of which in those days must have come close to the price of an automobile. The goat lived on our balcony, and it was Hedwig's duty to feed it, milk it, and clean up after it.

Hedwig! I must tell about Hedwig. When my mother first set up her household after my father's return from the war she looked for a maid. She did not want an experienced girl but one she could train herself. She interviewed several girls and finally decided on Hedwig, who had not brought along any references but just the phone number of her previous employer. When my mother called that number, the lady of the house would not say more than that Hedwig was honest but unsuitable for her household. My mother must have seen this as a challenge and hired Hedwig on the spot. Hedwig's home was a farm in the hinterland of Pomerania. When she came to us she could hardly read or write, but she was a willing pupil and soon adored my mother. She took every word my mother told her in its most literal sense, which led to endless misunderstandings or amusing incidents, like the one that happened when a very good friend of the family arrived earlier than expected at our house and my parents had not yet returned from their walk. Hedwig refused to let him in.

"But, Hedwig, you know me, don't you?"

"Yes, that I do."

"And you say the Bonins will be back within half an hour?"

"Yes, that's correct."

"But you won't let me in to wait for them?"

"That's right, sir."

"And why not, may I ask?"

"Because Madam told me not to let anyone in."

The poor man was too exasperated to argue further. It would not have helped him anyway. He had to wait outside.

My favorite story about Hedwig concerns Mother's first dinner party, not too long after Hedwig's arrival. The two of them had worked very hard shopping, cooking, setting an elaborate table. Hedwig had been instructed on how to greet the guests, how to serve the various dishes, and so on. Under my mother's watchful eye everything went fine. The party was a success. As was the custom in those days, on their way out the guests all left a tip for the maid. Hedwig looked first at all her new riches on the entrance-hall table, then at my mother. "Oh, Madam," she said, "I could not accept all that money. After all, Madam, you did half the work, so let's divide it!"

All these incidents I heard my mother relate at a later date. There is one event, however, that I do remember myself. I must have been about four years old and on this particular morning I was just finishing my breakfast when I heard my father call from the bedroom, "Hedwig, what time is it?" Hedwig, who had been clearing the table, looked up at our big grandfather clock and, after some hesitation, during which my father impatiently repeated the question, she answered, slowly, "Well, the big hand points to the five and the small hand is between the nine and the ten." That evening my father sat Hedwig and me down in front of the clock and taught both of us how to tell time.

Hedwig left us when I was five years old. She had received a letter from home, a few lines that her mother had dictated to someone in the village who could write. All the letter said was that she must return home immediately. Her mother had found a husband for her. She also should bring a few pots and pans from the city, enough to start her own home. And her new fiance sent his regards and would she be sure to see a dentist before they got married. He suggested a set of false teeth would be better than having cavities filled. In the long run such a set would be far cheaper and certainly less trouble. So, with a river of tears, Hedwig left us, though not before my mother had bought her an entire trousseau including all the pots and pans she would ever need, and, yes, she did leave with a set of perfect teeth. I don't remember if they were her own or false ones. I suspect the former.

This was 1925, and that year brought many changes into our house. My mother now needed someone more capable than Hedwig, someone who could make decisions and take charge of things. No longer was she looking for a maid, but rather a housekeeper. Next door, Reinicke's maid, Minna, had once introduced her friend, Marie, to my mother. Marie was working for an Army officer's widow who had a hard time making ends meet. My mother had taken a liking to Marie at first sight. Now she made up her mind to have her work for us. She went to see her and made her an offer. At first Marie refused to leave her employer, figuring that to look after one single woman was far easier than taking on an entire family. But then, Marie did not know my mother, who simply upped the ante until she had arrived at a figure that Marie could not refuse. And so she came to us, almost against her better judgment. I did not like Marie at all. She seemed bossy and cold and I resented her for taking my Hedwig's place. So I told all my playmates that our new maid was a very cruel woman who beat me and starved me when my mother was not at home. It made a very good story and was quickly picked up in the neighborhood. The next thing I knew there was a scene at our house where Marie cried and threatened to quit, my father tried to soothe her, my mother made me apologize to her, and, the worst humiliation, I had to stand in a corner all during dinner while, as I imagined, *she* was gloating over me.

It must have been around this time that my father fell in love with Lotte W. The W.s were part of my parents' circle, members of the same club, and I knew them as Uncle Kurt and Tante Lotte. Their son Joachim was a few years older than I. They had a summer place by a lake not too far from Berlin where we spent many weekends together. I have some snapshots from that time. As a matter of fact, they were given to me by Mrs. W. a few years ago when I looked her up on one of my visits to Berlin. Marie had found her address for me, and when I called on her she was somewhat embarrassed, but only at first. I found her a very attractive woman still and I also felt sorry for her. She told me that Uncle Kurt had died even before the war and Joachim had fallen on the Eastern Front, on the bloody battlefield of Stalingrad. I asked her if she had any pictures of my parents and she gave me all she had, most of them photos taken at the villa in Woltersdorf. There is Uncle Kurt, so Prussian-looking with his monocle, his arms around Lotte and Lili, both most attractive women. There is Joachim pushing me in a little wagon, and there is my father, good-looking, debonair, in his white flannels, his tennis racket held loosely in his hand. How long ago!

I don't really know how it all happened. Did my father first fall out of love with my mother and then meet Lotte W.? Or did he meet Lotte first and fall in love with her? Was it a sudden, passionate affair or did it develop slowly? I do know that it lasted for about three years, but my memory of those years is fragmentary. I don't remember seeing my father much at all during the week. He would be home on Sunday mornings and I began to hate those breakfasts we ate together. It became routine that my parents would fight. That is, my father never really fought—he hardly said anything. My mother, on the other hand, was strident in her accusations and highly emotional. All these Sunday breakfasts ended the same way, my father throwing down his napkin and leaving the house, my mother, totally undone, in tears, throwing her arms around me and telling me I was the only one who loved her, the only one she had left. I felt so sorry for her and resented that my father hurt her when he himself seemed not to suffer at all. On the other hand, I remember wishing that my mother would listen to him when he told her, "Li, please, not before the child!" These were, incidentally, the first English words I learned. My mother always seemed past listening, never able to stop herself. She grew worse and worse until she finally had a complete nervous breakdown and was, as customary in those days, packed off to a sanitarium at the Riviera.

During the first month of my mother's absence I was sent over to my Uncle Hans' house. Uncle Hans, as I mentioned before, was my father's younger brother. I loved the time I spent there, probably because his household was in many ways the absolute opposite of ours. First of all, there was a togetherness that was lacking in our home. Uncle Hans was a physician. His practice was in their home and his office hours, like those of most German doctors, took up three hours in the morning and a few hours twice a week in the afternoon. Of course, he also had to look after his patients in the hospital. Still, he was home most of the day and shared every meal with the family, whereas I was used to eating with only my mother, except for those dreadful Sunday breakfasts and an occasional Sunday dinner at which father always turned up late—he simply was incapable of arriving anywhere on time—and ruined all hope for a congenial meal together. I made up my mind right then and there that when I grew up I would marry a doctor because he could stay at home. As for Aunt Antoinette, she seemed a much more ordinary mother than mine. She was not as absorbed with her two children as mine was with me. Most of the time my cousins, Jean and Mimi, were left to their own games. During the weeks I spent there it was like having a brother and sister. The three of us would play undisturbed for hours. Even when we misbehaved the punishment meted out by Aunt Antoinette left me laughing rather than crying. She would grab "the whip" from its permanent place in the kitchen and dash after us, chasing us around the dining room table. I almost wanted to precipitate such episodes because the intended punishment always turned into a hilarious game, which ended with our being sent to the playroom, where we had wanted to be in the first place. My mother's punishments for me were very different. For a first offense her approach was one of logical explanation and fair warning. At the second offense the warning would be turned into action, like depriving me of my bike for a week or not allowing me to play outside with my friends for a couple of days, and no amount of begging or crying would reduce the sentence. It was not just in dealing out punishment that she was strict. She was very ambitious for me and often carried her goals to an almost ridiculous extreme, like the time I was supposed to get my fifteen-minute breaststroke certificate in swimming. I was only five years old then and had just finished my first swimming lessons. On the day set for the final examination the pool was rather crowded and the water a bit choppy. I remember the swimming master watching me and my mother watching the clock. After about ten minutes I had swallowed so much of the choppy water that I felt sick to my stomach and told my mother I had better get out of the pool. "Oh, no!" she said. "You have only five more minutes! Stay there and be sick if you have to. I'll have the pool drained and cleaned if necessary." Yes, with all her love and devotion to me, she was the strictest mother I have ever met.

In the afternoons at "the Doctor's," as Uncle Hans' household was always referred to, we would drive out to Pfaueninsel, not to the actual island but to a beautiful spot of sandy beach just opposite it. Here we would picnic, swim, and build a raft which we used to hide in the bushes for the next day's use. Then on the way home we three kids in the back seat of the car would play all kinds of games until we became so loud and unruly that Tante Antoinette would turn around and silence us with a torrent of French. She was French and the entire family was bilingual. It was a wonderful summer. I loved not being an only child. I loved being treated like a child. And as much as I longed for my mother, I felt the relief of not having to feel sorry for her, of not having to make up for her unhappiness.

Soon after I returned from my uncle's house my mother came home too. She seemed much better, calmer, and for a while our entire household ran smoothly. Every morning my mother walked me to school and at 1 P.M., when classes let out, she would be waiting for me. She said that she did it for her health, that walking was good for her, but I knew it was her anxiety that something could happen to me that made her want to be with me always. I got used to it and did not mind, especially since she was a great companion and soon became a favorite with a number of my classmates, who would be downright disappointed when, sometimes, Tante Li, as they called her, would not be there to walk a flock of us home and entertain us all the way with her marvelous tales. As far as I can recall, she was the only mother who visited the homeroom teacher to find out how her child was doing. Actually, I did very well that first year, so well that it was decided I should skip the second year. Obviously, this was something my mother and Fräulein Kruger had cooked up between them. I was never consulted and was most unhappy when confronted with the *fait accompli.* I had been one of the youngest and smallest in first grade. Now I was positively immature and diminutive in size compared to the rest of the third graders. I felt lonely without my friends and lost as far as school subjects were concerned. It took months until I had caught up. In physical education and games I never quite measured up to the rest of the class. Being so small and not yet as coordinated as most of the others, I was always the last to be chosen on a team, which humiliated me no end. I also had to tell my mother not to accompany me any more, to and from school, because my new classmates would see this as further evidence of my babyishness. I was afraid she might be hurt, but she understood. She had taken a great interest in helping underprivileged children and was busy collecting money, clothes, and food for needy families. So she did not need me quite as much. She continued, however, to oversee my daily homework, and only when she was one hundred percent satisfied could I go out and play. Those afternoon hours were the favorites of my day. I had many friends among the neighborhood children, and here I fit right in in age and size. Our choicest game, the one we liked best, was Trappers and Indians, inspired by our reading of Cooper's Leatherstocking stories and Karl May's books about Old Shatterhand and his friend Winnetou, the Apache chief. And then there were the games modeled on Robinson Crusoe where we'd set up a tent made of old blankets and the back yard became our "tropical island." My number one friend was Werner S. Both of us loved going to the movies, especially when there was a Tom Mix film showing. Tom Mix and Karl May represented America's Wild West to us. Of course, we had also heard of New York, where everyone was either very rich or a poor emigrant, and of Chicago, the gangster city. Then, too, I knew the American flag. Whenever I got a new bicycle, my father took me to the plant so that I could choose all the accessories for it. As a pennant I always picked the stars and stripes because I considered it the most beautiful. And that just about exhausted my knowledge and interest in America, a place mostly referred to as *da drüben* [over there].

Shortly after my eighth birthday, in 1928, my mother informed me that I would get a baby brother or sister. She asked me which I'd prefer. I was so shocked at first that I could not answer, but then my mother, in her usual imaginative fashion, drew such an appealing picture that I began to accept the new idea and even looked forward to having a brother or sister. I knew, of course, that she had no control over the gender of the baby and so I told her that whether it was a boy or girl, it was all the same to me. Every night, though, in my prayers I asked God to please, please make it a girl. The possibility of having a younger brother, who would tease me all the time, was most upsetting. During the remaining six months of my mother's pregnancy the two of us grew even closer, if that were possible. She would guide my hand over her growing belly, making me feel the new life. We'd speculate together about what part we could discern, what the baby was doing at any given moment, and, of course, I had my mother tell me in great detail what our future would look like once the baby arrived. She also promised me a totally refurnished room. After all, I had outgrown the kinderzimmer and now, as the older sister, was ready for something more like a study. My happy expectations were marred only by some fears regarding my mother's physical welfare. Her pregnancy was not an easy one and I was constantly worried about her. I had heard Fräulein Polk, her masseuse, tell her that she should not stand too much since she was suffering from varicose veins, and with the added weight she was carrying, this apparently could present problems. In my mind I already saw my mother collapsing from bursting veins. This became such a phobia with me that when we took the streetcar or bus and there was no vacant seat, I would approach the nearest man, call his attention to my mother's condition, and ask him to give her his seat. After I had done this a few times, my mother decided to forego public transportation and we took taxis instead, to my great relief.

When the baby finally was due, I was more nervous than my mother, but it all went well. My prayers had been answered. My mother delivered a baby girl in March of 1929. Two days later I saw my sister for the first time. She was born in the same private clinic where I had been born and there, too, was Schwester Anna, my old nurse, who had been rehired, attending her. In those days babies were put in a crib at the foot of the mother's bed. I was allowed to look at the baby, touch her smooth skin and the velvety fuzz of her hair, and hold her tiny little hands. I could not get over the perfection of each little fingernail, each tiny toe. A week later Mother, my new sister Edith, and Schwester Anna came home. The days following were nothing like what my mother had led me to believe. Sister Anna was extremely bossy. She and Marie did not get along at all, each guarding jealously her sphere of authority. My mother seemed to have fallen into a post-natal depression. My sister was developing strong lungs, screaming an inordinate amount of the time, and my father absented himself as usual. Eventually, though, things returned to normal. Sister Anna left, Mother and Marie shared the new duties, and I felt much relieved at not having to worry so much any more, or rather, my old worries were replaced with new ones.

One of these worries concerned school. My second year in elementary school had not been my favorite, but by the time I was in fourth grade all the hurdles had been overcome. I was not the best or second best in class, but I was in the top third, had made new friends, and played a passable game of Völker and Schlagball, something similar to softball. Yet there was really no time to relax. The pressure was on to get into the Lyzeum. After the fourth grade in elementary school, usually at the age of ten but in my case at the age of nine since I had skipped a class, a decision had to be made about what kind of further education a child would receive. At the time there were three choices. A child could continue in the basic school for another four years and then learn a trade. Or the child could transfer to a middle school for another six years and then go to art or business school to become a secretary, nurse, or other semi-professional. The third and most desired choice was the Gymnasium for boys, the Lyzeum for girls, a nineyear prep school for the university. A student had to have good grades and money for this last choice because tuition, though subsidized in part by the State, was not entirely free. There was no question but that I had to go to the Lyzeum. Since my grades were good, I had to take an oral examination only and after passing it was admitted for the fall of 1929 to the "Sexta" of the Goethe Lyzeum. Here the hours were longer, the subjects more demanding, and the homework seemed interminable. I especially resented the daily lists of English vocabulary I had to memorize. Of all the subjects I had to take (we had no electives) the learning of a foreign language at that time seemed to me the most useless. Where would I ever need to speak English? Surely I would live all of my life in Germany, marry a German, and have my children grow up in Germany. And why would I want to read in a foreign language when all good books were translated into German? Even all films coming from abroad were dubbed in German. But the curriculum called for not just one but eventually three foreign languages so I had to buckle down.

Since school took up most of the day and there was little time left for playing with my neighborhood friends, I saw less and less of Werner. He had been accepted at a Gymnasium. In addition, he was very busy with a Scout group he had joined. I envied him his smart uniform and would have loved to join too. But first of all, his was a boys' troop. After the age of ten the two sexes seemed to be officially separated everywhere. Secondly, my father had forbidden me to join any youth group with political overtones. Unfortunately, most of the organizations were leaning heavily to the Right, at least in the suburb of Lichterfelde where we lived. The Army had its barracks not far from us and many of its officers lived around us. The rest of the neighborhood consisted mostly of civil servants and good middle-class burghers who had little time for the unruly gangs of Communist youths and preferred to side with the well-disciplined boys of the Right. Since in Lichterfelde the latter were in the majority, we saw fewer fights between these two factions than in other parts of Berlin. In the industrial area especially, where most of the workers lived, street fights between the Right and Left truly had become gang warfare. The newspapers reported incidents of brutal beatings almost daily, but I was not much aware of all this. Among the girls in my class, a few had joined the BDM [League of German Girls], the female arm of the Hitler Youth. Others belonged to youth groups organized by the Church. I finally found my niche by joining the VDA, an innocuous group pledged to helping Germans living abroad. We wore a blue and white uniform, had regular meetings, and went for hikes on weekends.

Another worry I had was the deteriorating financial situation of our family. This was partly due to the general economic condition within Germany but also, to no small extent, to my father's addiction to betting at the racetrack. Things became so bad that one summer, after we returned from our vacation at the seashore (my father, as usual, had only come up for weekend visits), my mother found all three of her fur coats gone. There was an awful row, from which I understood that the furs had been pawned. At first that word meant little to me, but as time went on I heard it mentioned more and more. Much of my mother's jewelry finally went the way the furs had gone, and once again I saw my mother crying a lot, this time not about another woman but about money. When my mother was depressed and unhappy I, of course, worried. Yet to the outside, at least at first, nothing really changed. We continued to live in the same house. We were still the only people on our block who had a car. Platsch, the business chauffeur, was still available to us, and Marie continued to manage the household. The only compromise I saw was that Fräulein Polk, mother's masseuse, now came only once a week instead of making her previous daily visits. That was in 1930. Within the next two years the situation worsened very rapidly.

I wish I could say that I understood at the time the traumatic events that were happening in Germany during this period and finally led to the Nazi takeover, but I was too young to comprehend the political and economic forces which began to overshadow our daily lives. Yet all the events which followed cannot be understood without seeing them in their historical framework. The Wall Street crash of '29 had affected Germany immediately, and 1929-1933 was a period of economic crisis as Germany joined the rest of the world in a depression. Unemployment rose and many banks collapsed. 1931-1932 saw the economic crisis at its height—10 percent of the population were unemployed and only 50 percent were earning a large enough salary to live on. This economic crisis and the international tensions set the stage for Hitler and the National Socialists—the Nazis. The economic situation highlighted the fact that there was no one to exercise real authority. The Weimar Republic had failed to develop a governing class. In 1931 many of the Ruhr industrialists threw their support to Hitler, as did other parties of the Right, hoping to "use" him as a bastion against

Communism. This gave Hitler more political clout and "respectability." In April, 1932, Hindenburg, now eighty-five years old, was again elected President, but he was doddering, unable and unwilling to defend the Republic. In the election of July, 1932, the National Socialists, with 37.8 percent of the vote, were the strongest party in the Parliament. Within a few months, on January 30, 1933, Hindenburg named Hitler *Reichskanzler* [Chancellor] and parliamentary democracy in Germany was at an end. The ordinary citizen simply saw in Hitler someone who could prevent the Red scare of the Communists and thought the parliamentary system too weak to govern effectively.

It was on the day of this transfer of authority that I learned of my Jewish background. Yet as I grappled with this new knowledge, nothing much really changed in my life, at least not right away. Berlin was still Berlin. Mutti and I went downtown shopping, albeit just window shopping most of the time. After tramping through our favorite store, the KDW, we would stop at Telschow's to have our traditional *Nusstorte* and then would take the train home to peaceful Lichterfelde. True, downtown we saw a lot of Brownshirts on the streets, troops with or without bands, marching everywhere and always bearing the new flag, the swastika. It had become law for every citizen to honor the flag with stretched-out arm, the new salute of the Third Reich. Usually my mother tried to find a side street when such a troop approached, but on my way to and from school, as strange as it may sound, I simply joined my friends in saluting the flag, not thinking much about it one way or another. What seems even more incomprehensible now was my participation in the huge May Day parade (Labor Day in Germany). On that day every school, every labor union, every business and social organization, every member of the SA and SS marched to the Tempelhofer Feld, where Hitler was to address the masses. All students wore their uniforms, mostly those of the Hitler Youth. My entire school marched, and I admit that I felt quite proud in my blue and white VDA outfit. It was a terribly hot day. People stood all along the roads of our march, giving us water. Most of the streets were so blocked with marchers that we often had to wait until the groups ahead proceeded. It took us half a day to get to the Tempelhofer Feld, and by the time Hitler addressed us, most of us were too tired to listen closely to what he was saying. We also stood too far away to see him well, and all I remember of the rest of that day was coming home hungry, thirsty, and with painful blisters on my feet.

A month previously, on April 1, a boycott of Jewish stores and businesses had been declared, but since there were none in our neighborhood, I did not see any evidence of this boycott, a word, incidentally, that I had never heard before. My father did not go to the plant that day but drove over to Uncle Hans' place to see how he was faring. True enough, there were two Brownshirts marching in front of his house, each carrying a placard stating: "Germans! Defend yourselves! Don't patronize Jewish businesses!" They approached my father, telling him that the doctor practicing there was a Jew, but when my father identified himself as the doctor's brother, they just shrugged and continued their picketing. One might wonder how, in view of this boycott, I could have taken part in the May Day celebration, but during those early days of the new regime, one simply tried not to stand out. Had I not participated in the parade, I would have been the only girl out of the several hundred pupils in the Goethe Lyzeum not to do so, and this certainly would have drawn special attention to me and therefore would have endangered my family. There was another reason, as far as I was concerned, for attending the May Day celebration. Though I had been told that I was different from my friends and schoolmates and understood this theoretically, I had not yet accepted it. It was too sudden, and since nothing yet had really changed for me in my immediate surroundings, I found it appropriate and quite natural to continue in all school affairs. Neither my name nor my looks identified me racially and, since there were no other Jewish girls in my school, it did not occur to any of my classmates that I might be a "non-Aryan." Like any thirteen-year-olds, we all had quite different things on our minds, like boys, clothes, and movies, and we could not have cared less about government, politics, or racial laws. My father's attitude remained optimistic. He was sure that the present regime could not last long and would give one logical reason after another to prove his point.

On November 12, 1933, the first *Reichstagswahlen* [Parliamentary election] of the Third Reich took place. These elections were quite different from any we had had before. Gone was the multiparty voting sheet. Instead, it was a simple "yes" or "no" vote, showing either confidence in the new system or disagreement with it. The Nazis were determined to show the whole world that the Third Reich ruled with the mandate of *all* the German people. For this they needed more than just a simple majority of "yes" votes. To achieve their goal they first of all let it be known that votes might not be as confidential as they are supposed to be. Rumors were spread that there were ways to identify a "no" voter, and fear of retaliation began to spread. Secondly, every effort was made to get everyone out to vote. Booths were set up at train stations to catch the traveler, at hospitals to catch the sick, at sanatoriums to catch the recuperating. Transportation was provided for the elderly and for invalids. All this was carried out in an orderly and festive atmosphere. Gone were the awful street fights, the beatings and confrontations between groups of the far Left and the far Right. The reason I remember this election day so well has to do with my grandmother and her friend, the SS officer, a story which seems quite unbelievable.

Omi had a large flat in Friedenau. After Opi's death she rented out two rooms to supplement her income. A few months prior to the November election she had lost her tenant and had advertised for a new one. The first person to look at her rooms was a very nice young man to whom she took an immediate liking. The feeling apparently was mutual and all was set for him to move in. There remained only the required filling out of papers for the new tenant, which then had to be signed by the landlady and taken to the official or local authority who dealt with such things. This document was a lengthy questionnaire requesting not only name and new address but also age, religion, occupation, income, family status, etc., and now the new form mentioned "race" also. This form had to be filled out whenever a person moved so that the government knew at all times where anyone was. Under "occupation" Omi's new tenant filled out *"SS Sturmbannführer"* [Major in the SS]. My grandmother immediately informed him that, to her regret, he could not move in after all because she was Jewish. He brushed that fact aside with a big bear hug. "Grandma, I like you. I like the rooms and I'm staying," he said. "We just won't tell anyone." Omi said that he was a very nice tenant but admitted that she felt a bit uncomfortable with his friends coming and going, mostly dressed in their uniforms, always greeting her, entering and leaving the house with their noisy clicking heels and outstretched hands, smiling "Heil Hitler!" at her.

On that Sunday of the elections, after my parents had voted, we all went over to Grandma's house and arrived just in time to see a huge black limousine with the official swastika pennants draw up in front of her house. Two SS men jumped out, saluted us, and then told Omi that they had come to escort her to the voting booth. She made them wait in the parlor until she got dressed for the occasion. A half hour later, here was my round little Jewish grandmother, dressed in her Sunday best, helped most courteously by two SS soldiers into the car that her renter, the *Sturmbannführer*, had sent for her. Anxiously we waited for her return. When the limousine came back, again the SS men

33

helped her up the stairs and saluted her, in answer to which she just nodded her head. "Well," my father said, "so you could not escape voting 'yes' after all!"

"What do you mean?" Omi answered. "Of course not! I voted 'no'." My parents looked at her in horror, thinking of all kinds of possible consequences. Luckily, though, her ballot must not have been tampered with. There were no further consequences. After all, who could have guessed that the SS Major's beloved "Granny" would be one of the few who dared a "no" vote. When all ballots had been counted, the result was 92 percent "yes." One wonders who the courageous 8 percent "no's" were. Proudly, I thought that Omi was one of them.

Christmas, 1933, was our last one in Lichterfelde. We still celebrated it in our traditional fashion. First there was the Advent's wreath with its four candles, each to be lit on the four consecutive Sundays before Christmas. About two weeks before Christmas my father and I always went shopping for the Christmas tree. I looked forward to that evening and could hardly stand the wait until Vati came home. Of course, it was already dark by then. We drove to the train station, where the usually half-empty parking lot now looked like a little forest surrounded by vendors' booths selling ornaments of all kinds, candles, Christmas candies, and cookies. Usually the weather had turned cold by then and quite a bit of snow had fallen. The vendors had little iron stoves in their booths, over which they warmed their hands. The smell of the wood burning, the fragrance of the evergreens, the aroma of spices and nuts, were all part of the enchantment of that evening. We had always chosen a very tall tree that would reach from the floor to the high ceiling in the livingroom. This was the first time my father decided on a smaller tree, and we skipped the usual stop at the *Nürnberger Lebkuchen* stand, those delicious cakes that have no equal anywhere. The tree would be kept outside until the morning of the 24th. Then Herr Lempke, our doorman, would help us carry it up and place it in its stand. After that, the living room was out-of-bounds for me and, now, for my sister too. While Mother did the trimming, Omi, who arrived early on that day, helped Marie in the kitchen, baking and cooking. Sometimes, too, she helped me put the finishing touches to my present for Mother. Mutti insisted that the only gift she valued was one *made* by me rather than purchased. Year after year, whether I embroidered, crocheted, or knitted, I never seemed to be quite ready on time. I remember how, as the afternoon progressed, I would be almost sick with excitement. It wasn't just the anticipation of all the presents. Rather, it was stage fright. Year after year our teachers gave us a list of Christmas poems. Each of us had to choose one and memorize it so that we could recite it at home on Christmas Eve. It seemed to me that every year the poems grew longer and I was scared to death that I would get stuck or forget a line. So there I sat, confined to my room, repeating over and over again the verses until, finally, I heard my father drive up. That meant the festivities were about to begin. My mother then rang a little bell, the signal for me to come out. The victrola played "Stille Nacht, Heilige Nacht" ["Silent Night, Holy Night"]. The doors to the living room were opened wide.

How can I describe the pleasure that ran through me when I entered? There stood the Christmas tree in all its splendor, lit up with candles and bedecked with shining ornaments, tinsel reflecting the flickering lights. For each family member a table had been set up with gifts. My sister's gifts were under the tree and mine were on the table in the alcove. There stood my family, Father in a dark suit, Mother and Omi all dressed up too, Marie in her black and white uniform, my sister holding onto Father's hand, all waiting for my recital. Well, I always made it without getting stuck and Mother always had tears in her eyes. After that everyone got busy admiring their presents. Since all our gifts were laid out unwrapped, we all walked from table to table telling which presents we had given. I think that mine was always the biggest table. After we had thanked each other for the gifts, we sat down to eat our traditional Christmas Eve dinner, first a bouillon, then roast goose, red cabbage, and mashed potatoes. For dessert we had Stollen, a yeast bread filled with fruit, ginger, nuts, and marzipan. I don't remember what everyone did after dinner because I was busy with my presents until bedtime. The same probably was true of my sister, Edith. Omi went home soon after we had eaten. I assume that my father returned to his study and mother helped Marie clean up.

Christmas Day was "extended-family" day. Uncles, aunts, and cousins went to the home of my Great Uncle August and Great Aunt Grete, also Great Uncle Bernhard and Great Aunt Ella. There I would meet all my uncles, aunts, first, second, and third cousins, and we would admire each other's favorite Christmas presents, which we had brought along, while the grown-ups spent a few hours in lively conversation. This year, 1933, the discussion revolved around one theme only—what was going to happen to all of us under the Nazis? How would the new regime deal with us? Some began to talk about emigrating, perhaps to the United States or South America. My father argued vehemently for staying put, insisting that this government was doomed, that the German people would soon come to their senses and things would return to normal. He felt that it was his duty to remain and see this difficult but abnormal time through. We all departed rather subdued.

The year 1934 brought many changes. Our financial situation had gone from bad to worse. My father apparently had, over a period of time, incurred heavy debts, which he now was unable to repay. After having mortgaged the house, furniture, jewelry, and fur coats, he still was not able to satisfy his creditors so he had to sell his interest in the bicycle plant. In other words, he lost everything and overnight our entire lifestyle changed. We had to give up our home and move to a small apartment. Marie had to leave us, as did the chauffeur, the masseuse, and the extra help in the house. From now on mother would do all the cleaning and cooking. The car was sold, the furniture auctioned off. All we had left were our beds and a few odds and ends, enough to furnish the new apartment. This consisted of one and a half rooms plus kitchen and bathroom. No longer did I have my own room. Edith and I slept, together with mother, in the small room and my father on a couch in the larger room, which served as a living room. Actually, our new apartment was located in a rather nice area, closer to town, but it was far from Lichterfelde and I felt I had lost not only my home but all my friends too. I did not see anyone my age in the neighborhood, nor was it easy to find friends in my new school. Within a few weeks after our move my grandmother died suddenly of a stroke. My mother and I felt this loss most keenly. It seemed to me that with Omi's death my childhood truly had ended.

Our life had altered so rapidly that none of us had had time to contemplate these changes. My father was busy trying to find a new livelihood. My mother was occupied making our place livable. As for me, even before I had time to adjust to my new school, a more dramatic event occurred. I was called to the Rector's office and informed that my "non-Aryan" presence in a public school was no longer desirable. In other words, I was kicked out of school. This was the first time the Nazis had a direct impact on me personally and it became another turning point in my life. My first reaction was one of relief because I did not like my new Lyzeum. This relief, however, changed quickly to resentment and a mood of defiance. If "they" did not want me, then I certainly did not want to be any part of "them." I rejected my former allegiances. It immediately occurred to me that since "they" had now marked me as a Jew, it was time that I became one. But how to go about it? I knew that I could not expect support from my parents in this endeavor, nor did I know anyone to whom I could turn. I needed to talk to a rabbi, but how could I get in touch with one? I finally hit on the idea of going to a Jewish bookstore and looking at some of the titles and authors of books dealing with current events. I found what I was looking for right away. There apparently were two outstanding rabbis in Berlin, a Dr. Prinz and a Dr. Swarsensky. I decided on the latter, looked him up in the phone book, and made an appointment. At the given hour I arrived at his office, expecting to meet an old man with a long white beard, clad in a black gown. But Dr. Swarsensky was nothing like that. He was good-looking, young, and dressed like any businessman. I was almost shocked, but then, so was he, to judge by his surprised expression and his hesitant question, "Fräulein Bonin?" Probably he had expected some grown-up young lady, not a thirteen-year-old girl in kneesocks, short skirt, and sweater-pullover. When I told him that I had come to find out how to go about becoming a Jew, he shook his head. Why would anyone under the present circumstances be crazy enough to take on such a burden? I explained to him that racially I was a non-Aryan, that my parents were totally assimilated and opposed to any Jewish affiliation, and that I knew no other Jews. I told him that I had been expelled from school, that I really needed to belong somewhere, and that maybe I could find my place in the Jewish community.

Rabbi Swarsensky listened, nodded, and smiled in a kindly way, but what he said seemed most unsatisfactory to me. According to Jewish law, he explained, I had remained a Jew even though I was baptized a Christian, since my mother was Jewish when I was born, as was her mother and so on. On the other hand, I certainly was not a practicing Jew. If I wished to become a member of the congregation, I would have to take instructions. These lessons would consume much time, but if I was serious he would arrange them for me. He also advised me to find a Jewish school, join a Jewish youth group, and so create a new circle for myself. Such suggestions were easy to make but hard to carry out. Jewish schools—and they were the only ones open to me now—either were very orthodox or, if more modern, leaned toward Zionism, the movement aimed at reestablishing a Jewish national homeland in Palestine. The same was true of any Jewish youth group. Since my father was absolutely opposed to Zionism, he refused to send me to such institutions. He wanted me to attend a school which would not indoctrinate its pupils with Zionism but rather would stress their *German-*Jewish heritage. He believed it was our duty not to run away but to remain in Germany and keep alive this proud history. His ideals stood in direct contrast to the opinions of most people at the time. So did his optimism, with which he tried to convince everyone that, if not tomorrow, at least soon, things would change and this temporary insanity would pass.

The result of all this was that at the age of thirteen I found myself without school, without friends, and with nothing to do. So I sat and read. I read voraciously for eight hours a day. I devoured Dostoevsky's *Crime and Punishment* and *The Idiot,* Tolstoy's *Anna Karenina* and *War and Peace.* I read Selma Lagerloff, Knut Hamsun, Thomas Mann, Feuchtwanger—anything I could lay my hands on. I tried to submerge myself and live vicariously through the characters of these books. The more I read, the more depressed I became. Most of the literature I was reading was anything but uplifting, and much of it was above my head. I should have been outdoors playing or doing some useful work, but my mother did not have the heart to make me do anything. She felt sorry for me but had little time to sympathize. Much of her time was taken up looking for work. The only kind available was housekeeping. So she, who had been served left and right, now had to clean other people's houses. I think the very thought of this appalled me more than anything that had happened to us so far. I began to blame my father. Here he was, out of work and apparently unable to support us, yet taking it in his stride, being quite cheerful and optimistic about future prospects, which never seemed to materialize. At the time it did not occur to me that his good spirits in the face of adversity showed as much courage as my mother's ability to confront a situation and immediately act upon it. Her first job as a part-time housekeeper did not last long. She soon found a better one, looking after two children while their parents were away trying to find a place abroad to which they could emigrate. This new job had the advantage that she could take my sister with her to work, which left me even more alone. Within a month her employers returned. I don't recall what the result of their search was, but I do remember that they recommended my mother to another Jewish family who needed someone to watch over their house until they were settled in their new homeland. In this way my mother became a specialist in looking after homes and apartments of absentee owners, often supervising the packing of all possessions and taking charge of sending off the entire household to the owners' new addresses abroad. I think she even began to enjoy this new job of hers.

In the spring of 1934, when my mother had been working for more than two months, she came home one day with the name of a newly opened Jewish private school. She had heard of it through a friend of her employers. According to this friend, the school was exactly what my parents had had in mind for me but had given up hope of finding. Dr. Vera Lachmann was the owner, director, and principal teacher. She, too, like my father, had felt the need for a school that stressed the German-Jewish heritage rather than Zionism. In fact, she was so much opposed to the latter that she required of her students a pledge to leave her school if they became Zionists. At first we were only six students of various ages. The classes, if you could call them that, were held in Dr. Lachmann's beautiful large home. Instruction was really individual tutoring, designed to our various levels and abilities. Tuition was figured according to the parents' ability to pay. I paid nothing because nothing was what we could afford. There were several other part-time instructors. One was Dr. Lachmann's own retired former tutor, Mrs. Herrmann. Of the others, I especially remember Dr. Clare, who taught music. He was the only Aryan among the small faculty and must have risked his entire career by teaching in a Jewish school. He looked very English and I quickly developed a crush on him. From the first day that I attended Dr. Lachmann's school I was happy. It seemed to me that within a month I learned more German, history, geography, math, art, and music than I had learned in a year at the Lyzeum. We did not have physical education classes or physics or chemistry because there were no facilities for these subjects. By May our number had increased to about fifteen students and it was obvious that we had to find a bigger place. One of Dr. Lachmann's relatives, a wealthy banker, donated the smaller of his two adjacent villas in the Grunewald for the school, so before summer vacation we moved to our new quarters. All of us helped, painting walls, cleaning floors, and washing windows. Now there was plenty of room to grow in. The garden provided ample space for physical education activities and outdoor games. Tables, chairs, books—everything was donated by friends and relatives. In fact, we got more than we could use because so many Jewish families were emigrating, leaving behind all they could spare. Sometimes I wished I could acquire one of the discarded pieces of furniture for our bare little apartment, but I was too ashamed to let anyone know how poor we now had become.

It is always hard to be poor, but it is even harder when poverty comes upon you suddenly and when you feel that it has happened just to you. True enough, many Jewish families around us were forced to change their living standards, but whereas theirs was a slow decline, we had, so it seemed to me, already landed at the bottom. With all my schoolmates well-dressed, I felt ashamed of my one and only dress. I was too embarrassed to invite anyone to my home. This problem, however, was soon solved by our move to Grünau. My father had not been able to find work and my mother's earnings were not enough to feed us and pay the rent. Luckily, my father had found someone who wanted to rent our apartment for a few months so we sublet it and moved into the country. Our new abode was a little summer cabin consisting of two tiny rooms, a small veranda and an alcove containing a campstove and a few pots and pans. With some imagination you could call it a kitchen. There was no running water. We had to use an outside pump and carry the water in to heat it up for washing and cooking. The toilet was an outhouse. All this sounds pretty awful, yet, when one looked at the beautiful piece of land surrounding the shack, one could forget how primitive and uncomfortable it was. The entrance to the property was a long arbor covered with wild roses. Currant bushes flanked its sides. There was a lawn in front of the cabin where we spent most of our time when the weather was good. A huge orchard had been planted all around the grass. There were cherry and apple and plum trees. Behind the orchard was an entire strawberry field and, to my sister's delight, there was a rabbit hutch at the very back of the property. The couple that owned the land came regularly to harvest the fruit, but we could take as much as we wanted for our own use. It was a wonderful place for a weekend retreat, but to live there on a more permanent basis was not easy, especially for my mother. Yet, during those summer months, all of us felt a bit freer, a bit more relaxed. The rent was cheap, and it did seem as if we were on vacation. A ten-minute walk brought us to the Langersee, where we could picnic and swim, and during the week the beach was completely empty.

Shortly after our move my father found a job selling insurance so he and I commuted to town. It took me over an hour to get to school, first a twenty-minute walk through the woods to the train station, then forty minutes by train and then another walk to Jagowstrasse in Grunewald. Mother had, of course, stopped working and soon summer vacation began for me, too. Then we went swimming every day, lay on the sand or grass, and got a good suntan. Once again my mother had time for us. I wanted her to play our old game—reading the future. It really was nothing else but Mother's wishful thinking about what life held in store for us. Her picture of me was always the same. I would be a professional woman, elegant but quite tailored in a trenchcoat, gloves, carrying a leather briefcase, either just leaving for or returning from some business trip. There never was any mention of a husband or children. I did not mind. I rather liked her image of me and wanted her to go on and on. But my sister was too young to be interested in the future and my mother's mind was now more occupied with trying to understand the present.

It was during my summer vacation, on August 2, 1934, that President Hindenburg died. Hitler immediately combined his office as Chancellor with that of the president and from that day on was called "the Führer." It was around this time that we first heard of concentration camps. The official version held that their purpose was re-education of political dissidents. According to rumor, a number of inmates, mostly Communists but more recently also a few Jews, had been mistreated and even tortured there. But wherever there is dictatorship and the press is censored, rumors abound, so we did not pay much attention to them.

As the summer drew to its end I was impatient to return to school. By September many new students had enrolled. We were now about thirty. More part-time teachers had joined the staff as well. If I was happy when I first entered Dr. Lachmann's school, I was now even more content. Studying had become fun. The classes I enjoyed most were those taught by Dr. Lachmann herself—German literature, history, and art appreciation. Goethe, Schiller, Nietzsche and Hölderlin, the painters and sculptors of the Middle Ages, Church history, Jewish history, the Greek drama—these were her favorite themes. She believed in the classic Greek ideals of duty, honor, and perseverance, which had been handed down to us over the ages to preserve and perpetuate. "Time ennobles" was one of her mottoes. Self control and moderation combined with German romanticism made for a rather odd mixture in her personality. Yet I saw no contradiction in all of this, took it in, digested it, and became a faithful disciple. My admiration for Dr. Lachmann in no way interfered with my crush on Dr. Clare. A little later, though, when my girlfriend Rachel and I began to notice the new boys around us in school, Dr. Clare receded into the background.

Some time during that year our school acquired a new neighbor. The villa next to us, empty since our own move to the Grunewald, now was occupied by none other than Heinrich Himmler, head of the SS. One might expect that this would lead to unpleasant confrontations, even our eviction, but the contacts between our Jewish school and Himmler's SS guards remained downright neighborly! When off duty they often watched our games, cheering on one team or another and kicking the ball back good-naturedly when it had flown over the fence between the two villas. Only once do I recall that a platoon of six soldiers came marching over to us. When we saw them goose-stepping through our gate, we were sure that this would be the end of our school. After much stomping and saluting, all they did was deliver a message from the Herr Reichsführer: Would we please pipe down between the hours of 1 P.M. and 3 P.M. because the Herr Reichsführer liked to nap during that time! In retrospect, it seems incredible that we Jewish children were living peacefully side by side with the highest commander of the SS, but there were many such incongruous incidents during the beginning of the Hitler regime. I remember, for instance, my little sister—she must have been all of five years old—falling for the newspaper vendor on the street corner opposite Omi's house. Whenever we visited there, Edith would stand at the window looking adoringly at the toothless old man who was shouting out, *"Der Angriff! Der Völkische Beobachter!"* These were the two most popular Nazi newspapers. Then one day she must have slipped out of the house unnoticed. The next thing we knew, there she was, standing beside the vendor, one hand holding his, the other holding a paper, and the two of them shouting in unison, *"Der Angriff! Der Völkische Beobachter!"*

In October, to my mother's great relief, we moved back into our apartment on the Hohenzollerndamm and I no longer had to spend hours commuting. My mother began to work again, taking my sister with her. Most of her work still consisted of packing up households. Sometimes she would bring home clothes or other useful articles that were left behind when the families migrated. Food, however, was not always plentiful. Still, I was by now so occupied with school and friends that I hardly noticed. Christmas, 1934, held a big surprise for me. Somehow, my father had managed through his previous connections to get a bicycle for me. I knew that he could not have paid for it and hoped that it would not be repossessed some time in the future. In the meantime, I was overjoyed. The bike gave me many advantages. It saved me the long streetcar ride to and from school and the daily worry that there might not be money for the fare. It allowed me to meet my friends after school and on Sundays, but above all it made me feel more independent. I now could leave home whenever I felt like it, and that was most of the time. Unaware of the fact that I had come to that awkward teen-age stage where home was a place you hated, where everything your parents said and did seemed stupid and wrong, I was baffled by my own attitude. What had happened to my deep attachment to my mother and my respect for my father? Why did my parents irritate me so and why was I so unable to control myself? Every morning I woke up vowing not to contradict them, not to argue, and not to break out in tears, but by evening I usually had broken all my resolutions. My father tried to talk to me, but I would not listen. My mother was hurt by my behavior, which made me feel guilty and only reinforced my desire to get away. I began to see my parents in a different light. My mother became for me the epitome of suffering. Once she had been a beautiful young woman for whom the world held nothing but great promise. And then what happened? Her husband had rejected her for another woman. She was living in poverty. Sorrow had begun to play havoc with her looks, and she must have worried herself sick about our future. And my father? What was wrong with him? Why couldn't he learn some trade and support us? Why didn't he try to get his family out of Germany and find a new existence somewhere abroad as so many men now were doing? Why didn't he at least make some plans? Sitting and waiting it out suddenly seemed a cowardly thing to do.

I even began to question some of Dr. Lachmann's values. Her "time ennobles" now held little attraction for me. I wanted action and longed for change, for something that would break the routine of what I considered a hopeless, dead-end street. No more could I see a relationship between what I learned at school and what was happening outside. Why were we delving into German history and literature when the present government burned the very books we were supposed to study? Why did we spend time trying to understand ideas that were condemned to silence, who knows for how long—perhaps forever? What was the point of dwelling on the history of past empires when we were becoming stateless in our own country?

Into this mood of dissatisfaction, bordering at times, with typical teen-age volatility, on despair, like a fresh breeze came the idea of Zionism. I don't recall how it started. Probably some of the new students, not as yet intimidated by Dr. Lachmann's strict taboo on the subject, had introduced us to some of the principles of Zionism. Here, finally, was an idea that promised a future, was optimistic, and was ready to put theory into practice. Best of all, following its premises, we could leave our dreary present in a country that despised us and start a new life in a new land, building on our own ideals with the work of our own hands. Instead of waiting for better times while trying to avoid being noticed, we could be proud again and carry our heads high. For me this breeze became a wind that finally would blow me into entirely new directions and allegiances.

I knew that it would be very difficult if not impossible to convince my parents that my future lay in Palestine. When I first brought up the subject, my father was so horrified that he angrily asked me not to pursue the subject. But I would not let loose. Fortified with my new arguments, which I had acquired by burrowing into Zionist literature, again and again I insisted that there was nothing for me to look forward to in Germany, that I wanted to leave before it was too late, and that the only way to do so was for me to become a Zionist and go to Palestine. We argued almost daily, my father still insisting that the Nazis were only a temporary aberration, that by the time I finished school Germany would be back on track, and that I would be able to continue studying at a university. Both my parents saw me, eventually, practicing some kind of profession. I, contradicting them at every step of the argument, maintained that the Nazis might be in power forever, that I had to get out while I could, and since they did not have the means to send me to school abroad, I saw no other way out than to join all my friends and, with the help of the Jewish Agency, make my way to Palestine.

"All your friends?" said my father. "I thought that Dr. Lachmann shared my views with regard to Zionism and that you had to leave her school if you became a Zionist. If you are really serious, you must tell her." Leaving Dr. Lachmann's school so far had seemed a rather remote consequence of my plans. I had hoped to stay there until all hurdles had been cleared and emigration had become a reality. Now my father had confronted me with a choice, and I did not like it. Up until now my mother had made all decisions for me, even the most minute ones. She had told me what to wear, what to eat, when to sleep. When I was little and we had company, I even had to ask her permission to speak. If she acquiesced, I had my say and then fell back into silence. Of course, in the last few years I had been left more to my own devices. Still, I never did have to make choices. Now, suddenly, I was confronted with having to tell Dr. Lachmann of my new plans and, as a result, I would have to leave her school and face a very uncertain future. I spent much time visiting various Jewish agencies in order to get a clearer picture of what my options were if I decided to emigrate to Palestine. What I finally came up with was the Youth Aliyah. [Aliyah —Hebrew, meaning "ascent"—the expression used for immigration to the "Promised Land."] This was an organization, founded only a few years before by Recha Freyer and sponsored by Henrietta Szold and the Hadassah, a women's Zionist organization in America. Youth Aliyah was designed for boys and girls aged about sixteen who would be sent to a kibbutz for a period of two years. There they would work half a day and study the other half, learning Ivrit [modern Hebrew], the goals of Zionism, and the history of the labor movement and the kibbutz. Apart from parents' agreement, which everyone except myself took for granted, there were several other steps to be taken before final Aliyah. I would have to attend a different kind of Jewish school, one that offered Ivrit and an introduction to the history of Zionism, its basic premises, goals, etc. Next, I had to go on *Hachsharah,* a four weeks' stay on a farm, where a group of us would work and learn together. This probationary period served several purposes. First, we were supposed to get an idea about what our life would be like in a kibbutz. Second, this was a weeding-out process. We would be watched and judged on our suitability for communal life, agricultural work, and general ability to adapt to new surroundings. I was told that it would take, roughly, a year from the time I signed up for the program until the departure from Germany. The more input I received, the more I became convinced that this was the right road to follow. And once I was convinced, I began to act. First, I went to see Dr. Lachmann. She was *very* upset and kept telling me how much she hated to lose me, not just as a friend but as a follower of her ideals. I had a hard time not to cry, but I knew that her code of honor did not permit tears. That evening, though, when I thought about how I had loved the school, the teachers, my friends there and the entire atmosphere of the place, doubts began to assail me. Had I made the right decision or had I embarked on a foolish and dangerous course? I tossed and turned late into the night, trying to foresee the future. However, waking up the next morning, I felt that I had made my choice, that I was not going to look back, that I would go forward to a new life.

The next step was my parents' signature on the Youth Aliyah application. I had been right in going to Dr. Lachmann first because my father simply could not believe that I would go through with it. When I confronted him with the accomplished fact, he began to waver, to consider. He read all the brochures I had brought home and finally the three of us, my father, my mother, and I, sat together and discussed my future in the light of these new circumstances. I did not convince my parents overnight. I don't recall exactly how long it took until my father finally signed the papers, but two events helped to persuade him. The first was, once again, our financial situation. My father just did not seem very able to sell insurance. Who knows whether he was not a good salesman or whether times were not propitious. After all, it seemed futile, even ridiculous, to try to sell insurance to Jews, and his contacts with Aryans were growing fewer and fewer. My mother's income could not even cover our basic necessities. The only expense we could reduce was our rent. So, we had to give up our little apartment and move to a furnished room. Our new landlady was an old woman who rented out rooms, just as Omi had done. We shared the kitchen and bathroom with her, and I was given a tiny cubbyhole off the kitchen. It was only large enough for a bed and a nightstand, but I was happy to have my own place. It made up a little for having to give up my beloved bicycle, which had been sold, along with most of the little we had left in the small apartment. I am sure that this downward progression in our lives was a factor which helped to overcome my parents' resistance to my plans. The second event that contributed to their change of mind came with the announcement of the Nuremberg Laws. On September 15, 1935, at the *Parteitag der Freiheit* [the Party Day of Freedom] for the "protection of German blood and German honor," all Jews were deprived of their citizenship. Marriage between Jews and Aryans was now forbidden, and Aryan women under the age of thirty-five were not allowed to work for Jews. Jews were excluded from working in the civil service, journalism, radio, farming, teaching, and theatre. They were forbidden to hold public office or work in the stock exchange, and there were restrictions on their practice of professions and their engaging in business. Thus, most Jews now had lost their livelihood and all discrimination against them had official sanction. So it was that, shortly after our move and within days of the promulgation of the Nuremberg Laws, my parents agreed to let me go. I had to promise, however, to return after my two years in the kibbutz were up and we would then re-evaluate my future plans.

In the fall of 1935, I enrolled at the high school which had been recommended for students intending to emigrate to Palestine. What a contrast to Dr. Lachmann's school! Her private school was located in the Grunewald, Berlin's wealthiest and most beautiful suburb. My new school was an hour's subway ride from home and was located in one of the poorest areas of the city. I always felt as if I were in a different country when I emerged from that ride. Around the school I saw tenement houses, factories, and warehouses, but no trees or gardens. For the first time I saw a few Jews—I assumed they were Polish—wearing long black caftans, wide-brimmed fur hats, and sidelocks. The building the school occupied was not too bad. It was large and accommodated several hundred pupils. I had never seen so many Jewish children in one place and kept wondering and looking, trying to discover what we had in common. Not much, I thought. As for the subjects taught, I disliked most of them, too. Instruction in Hebrew was difficult and very foreign. The history of Zionism I found only moderately interesting. The other subjects were not challenging so I was bored and watched the clock. Unlike Dr. Lachmann's school, but in tune with all public schools, we finished classes by 1 P.M. Then came the long subway ride home. Since I didn't have much to do in the afternoon, my homework was quickly finished, I tried to find a part-time job. Through my uncle's recommendation I was hired as a doctor's assistant for an ear, nose, and throat specialist. I worked there four times a week, from 3 P.M. to 6 P.M., and really enjoyed my first employment. I was paid bi-weekly and from the beginning I tried to figure out how best to spend my first few marks. I finally decided on a new slip for my mother and for myself a pair of grey leather shoes that I had admired in a shop window every day on my way to Dr. Hirschmann's office. It was all spoiled, though, when I came home with my purchases. Apparently my father had expected me to contribute my earnings to the household funds and meant to pay part of our rent with them. In retrospect it seems to me that he was quite right, but at the time I could not see his point of view and was angry. I would not return the shoes and insisted that my mother accept the slip, which she did, albeit tearfully. What a brat I must have been and how often did I wish in later years that I could undo all the hurt I ever inflicted on my parents!

Christmas, 1935, was the saddest of all the Christmases we had ever spent. We could not afford a tree and there were very few gifts to exchange. My father tried valiantly to get us into a good mood, but my mother's spirits remained low. I knew that she was thinking that this probably was the last Christmas I would be with them. Luckily my little sister was totally unaware of our depressed spirits. She played with her new puzzle and told her two imaginary friends, Josef Sturki and Ellie Zanty, about school, which she had started a few months before. I must be honest and admit that I was not really so despondent either. Part of me looked forward to the coming year, knowing it would bring great changes. Anticipating the adventure in far-away places, I already felt a little disconnected from my present surroundings. If it had not been for mother's dejected face, I could have been quite happy.

The year 1936 began very much as 1935 had ended. I continued going to school and disliked it as much as I did in the beginning. But since I knew it would not be for long, I could take it. My job at Dr. Hirschmann's office was fun. I learned a lot and felt comfortable with my employer and his patients. Our financial situation did not improve.

My father still tried, unsuccessfully, to earn some money. My mother's jobs were not regular so she had taken to cleaning houses when nothing else was available. To me this indicated that we had sunk even lower than I had thought possible. I could not bear looking at her chapped red hands, at her tired face, noting the loss of all her exuberance and enthusiasm for life. There were other changes around us as well. Friends, relatives, and acquaintances began to depart for wherever they had some connection, to whatever country would take them. An entrance visa to some South American country, a certificate for Palestine, an affidavit from America—these were the most highly prized possessions and hoped-for life savers. The major topic of any conversation became who had left recently, who was going to leave, and where to. How had they gotten their papers? Who had helped? How much did they have to pay? It was around this time that Uncle Hans received an affidavit from an American cousin to go to the United States. He was going to take a residency at a hospital there, and as soon as he qualified he would open a practice and then have Aunt Antoinette and my cousins Jean and Mimi follow him. I think that by now, if my father had been offered a refuge and the means to take advantage of it, he, too, might have considered leaving Germany. As it was, he neither had the money nor knew the right people who could provide him with exit papers, entry visas, or the like. There were only two ways left open—an illegal one, which he would never agree to take, or immigration to Palestine, for which the Jewish Agency provided money, but this for him was also out of the question. It seemed amazing to me that under these circumstances he could continue to be optimistic, never complain, and in a cheerful mood still maintain that things would change and the future soon would be bright again. I did not realize what courage such an attitude must have indicated. As for myself, I valued action only. But knowing that my mother always had believed and still did believe in anything my father said, I was thankful that she shared his vision of better times to come. She might be tired and worn, but tomorrow things would change—how, she did not know, but change they would. Father said so.

That my parents did not perceive the seriousness of the situation was due partly to the fact that we lived in Berlin and partly to the approach of the Olympic Games. No one quite understood what a concentration camp was. Gas ovens and mass extermination still were in the future, as was the compulsory wearing of the yellow star, and unless one was unlucky enough to resemble the ridiculous caricatures of Jews which the *Stürmer* published, it was impossible to identify a Jew on the street. And as Berlin prepared for the summer Olympics of 1936, every German, every Nazi (after all, had not 99 percent of the electorate, at the latest poll, declared itself in agreement with Hitler's policies?), wished to impress the world with the achievements of the Third Reich. Many signs, *Juden unerwünscht* [Jews not welcome], or "Jews enter this place at their own risk," or "Jews strictly forbidden," came down, though not all of them, and I had an opportunity later that summer to see that in towns outside Berlin anti-Jewish slogans abounded. But then, Berlin always had been more liberal, though the choice of this word was not quite appropriate any more.

In March I was informed that I was to report for my four weeks' training in preparation for the two years of kibbutz life. Our training farm was located near Rüdnitz, a village about two hours by train from Berlin. I was very excited. Things were moving. I was going to leave home for a while, forget about all the daily worries, and live among kids my own age. If I was a little apprehensive about how well I would stand up to physical labor and get along with the other participants, I need not have worried. All of us arrived by train from every part of Germany. I should not say 'all' because one future *chaluz* [pioneer-worker] was driven up in a chauffeured car. Those of us who had already checked in looked in utter astonishment at the long limousine and watched the liveried driver as he climbed out, opened the door for his passenger, carried his suitcase up to the office, and announced, "I have the honor to introduce Mister Hans Leob to the Camp Commandant." Poor Hans. Everyone howled with laughter. To his credit I must say that Hans turned out to be such a likable fellow that his grand, if not ridiculous, entrance was soon forgotten.

After registering, we were assigned to our dorms. I shared mine with nine other girls. We slept in bunk beds and had communal showers with hot water available only once a week. There were no special laundry facilities, and since the weather was cold and often rainy, keeping clean became a bit of a problem. The food was rather poor, too, but we always had plenty of potatoes and bread. I did not mind any of this and loved every day of the entire four weeks. I had never been to a summer camp, and except for the few weeks I had spent with my cousins during my mother's nervous breakdown, I had never been away from home without her supervision. So this was like a great vacation. We had to get up early, usually at 5 A.M., and after a quick wash and breakfast we assembled in the yard where our counselors would read out the day's assignments for each one of us. Most of the time we worked in fields belonging to our own farm, but sometimes small groups of us were sent to some of the nearby farms to help out. We usually put in a six- to eight-hour day. The work consisted mainly of hoeing, weeding, digging, and cleaning out sheds. The boys helped in repairing and cleaning barns. The girls had kitchen duty. I don't remember much about our work, but I don't believe it was very hard. What I do recall distinctly were the hours after work. When we had washed up, changed, and eaten our dinner, we met in the large front room where we listened to lectures about Erez Israel [the land of Israel] as it was then called. We would sing together, accompanied by a few guitars or an accordion. It was Ruth who played the accordion. She and I had very quickly become inseparable. There were boyfriends too. The dating game took place after the evening meeting. Boy would approach girl with the usual opening, "Would you like to go for a walk?" Two or three walks with the same boy and you were considered a steady pair. That, in turn, would lead to holding hands and eventually to a very innocent kiss. How young we were! For me there were Peter and Rudi and Hans. I had a hard time making up my mind, but finally it was Hans, the boy who had been chauffeured to the camp, and Peter for Ruth.

The second Sunday of our stay was visiting day. My mother came for a couple of hours, bringing me a welcome change of underwear. She thought I had never looked scruffier or happier. All too soon judgment day arrived, meaning the eve of our departure, when our counselors would read the names of those who had 'made it.' Out of the fifty in camp, about thirty would go together to the same kibbutz in Erez Israel. Peter, Ruth, Hans, and I were among them. Apparently we had been considered the right material, physically and mentally able to become pioneers, adaptable and capable of relating easily to communal life. I was never able to figure out why some of the others had not measured up to these criteria. I was especially sorry that Hans S. (not my boyfriend Hans) would not be coming with us. I liked him a lot and admired his ability to stand up for his opinions, which often ran contrary to the accepted Zionist theory. Apparently such individualism was undesirable here. All this weeding out did not mean that the other twenty would not make *aliyah*. For many of them other ways would be found to go to Erez Israel. For some, further training was suggested. As for our group of thirty, we were told that as soon as our certificates came through, which usually took nine to twelve months, we would depart. This would leave us plenty of time to get ready. We packed and left Rüdnitz happily, promising to keep in touch until we would meet again. My boyfriend, Hans, left for Munich—by train this time. Ruth left for Salzwedel. Home, when I got there, I found just as depressing as ever. I still was as angry with my father for not being able to support us and still felt sorry for my mother. I also had a vague feeling of unease—perhaps it was guilt—that I was unable to improve the situation, guilt because I was longing to leave. The only one untouched by all this was my sister Edith. Whereas I was ashamed of being poor, she could not remember being anything else and accepted our reduced circumstances as normal.

During the following months Hans S. and I became good friends. He lived very close to us, and since neither of us went to school (I never did go back to that hateful high school at the other end of the city), we had a lot of time on our hands. Hans was an amateur philatelist and introduced me to this fascinating hobby. He presented me with one of his albums which he had outgrown and got me started on my own collection. We spent hours pouring over catalogues, washing and sorting stamps, and visiting dealers to exchange our doubles. I acquired quite a nice collection without investing a penny. Hans did not seem at all disturbed that he had not been among the forty 'chosen' ones. Apparently his parents were emigrating to Erez Israel anyway and he would just go with them. In May I received a letter from Ruth, inviting me to spend a week at her home in Salzwedel. Since I had no money for a train ticket (Salzwedel was several hours by rail from Berlin), I thought of hitchhiking. Of course, a girl could not hitchhike alone, so first I had to talk Hans into coming along. That was easy. He was all for it. The next hurdle was my parents. To my surprise, they agreed readily after talking to Hans about our proposed trip. My father really liked Hans. He thought him mature and responsible and did not anticipate any difficulties for us, especially since Hans looked like an advertisement for the Hitler youth, tall, blond, and blue-eyed. I wrote Ruth about our plans and she answered that she looked forward to seeing both of us. Hitchhiking in 1936 was almost as safe as taking the train, and since traffic once out of Berlin was light, that presented little danger. But it was precisely that lack of traffic which upset our plan to arrive in Salzwedel by nightfall. We got stuck in a little village about two hours from Salzwedel, with no further transportation in sight and no train or bus station near. There was a small country inn with rooms for rent. We hated to spend our entire pocket money for two rooms so we decided to say that we were brother and sister and take one room only. It was the first time that either of us had shared a room with the opposite sex. We stayed as far apart from each other as possible in the big double bed and neither of us slept very soundly. Since that night, though, I have always referred to Hans as the first man I ever slept with!

The next morning we did get a lift and arrived in Salzwedel before noon. Ruth lived with her parents and a younger sister in a beautiful, large country villa. Her father was a banker and had, to all outward appearances at least, not yet suffered financially. The only change the B.s had experienced concerned their help. The Nuremberg Laws had decreed that no Aryans were to work in Jewish households, and since there were no Jewish cooks or maids available in Salzwedel, Mrs. B. and her two daughters did all the cooking and cleaning themselves. In the morning I helped with the household tasks. Afterwards we took bicycles and rode around the neighborhood. I was fascinated with small town life. It was here, too, that I repeatedly saw the signs, "Jews not welcome." Ruth must have been used to it because she took no notice, and when I mentioned the signs, she just shrugged her shoulders. The townspeople all greeted her in a friendly fashion and I could not see any overt animosity. We spent much time talking about our future, trying to guess what life in the kibbutz would be like. Of course, we discussed our new boyfriends and the other kids from camp, with whom we would live for the coming two years. I don't believe Hans liked it so well in Salzwedel. He felt left out by our girlish talk and in his fearless but often confrontational manner he had antagonized Ruth's father, who was very authoritarian and not used to being contradicted, especially by a mere teenager. Anyway, Hans decided to leave early and take the train home. When Ruth asked me to stay another week, I accepted with alacrity. Hans would tell my parents that I was staying on and I knew they would not mind. I did have just enough money left for a one-way train ticket home.

A week later on my return trip to Berlin I played a little game to amuse myself. Pretending to be a foreigner and speaking broken German, I started a conversation with the other passengers in the compartment. I was quite good at this because mother and I had often played a similar game in public. We would consider our role-playing a real success if someone finally turned to us and asked where we were from. We came from wherever was our fancy at that moment. My fancy this time was to be an American, here for the Olympics. The other passengers were delighted to talk to me and, of course, their first question was, how did I like Germany. Instead of remaining on safe ground, I began to question them about conditions that foreigners were not supposed to know about, like the inflationary prices of dairy products, vegetables, and meat. They denied it. I then moved to even more dangerous ground, telling them that I had heard rumors about the confiscation of Jewish property and even mistreatment of Jews. They told me that only those Jews who were active enemies of the Reich were punished. The majority of Jews were still living undisturbed among them. They insisted that Hitler was a saint, that he had provided jobs for everyone, that he had made every German proud again to be a German, that things had never been better, and that anything negative I might have heard was nothing but rumor, spread by Communists and the like. I was getting bored. My game had turned sour. After all, what had I expected them to say? I was, however, taken aback when I related my little adventure at home. My father was very angry and reminded me that if by any chance I had been found out, my game might have had serious consequences for all of us. I think he was worried that I did not seem to realize the seriousness of our situation, where the smallest false step in any direction could draw attention to us and jeopardize our safety. My exuberant mood over what I had considered a clever and daring performance plummeted. He was right. I just did not sense the danger, nor did I comprehend the implications of the momentous changes occurring around us. But does one ever, especially when one lives right in the middle of them, is young, and lacks experience and judgment? Our lives are changed by the tides of history, yet most of us are involved in our everyday living and lose the wider picture. No one in our family really saw the water gathering into a tidal wave.

I continued to work for Dr. Hirschmann three times a week, in the afternoons, and saved my small salary to pay for some of the clothes I would need in the kibbutz. All of us had received a list of what we were to take with us. Now I worried about Ruth's visit to Berlin. Her parents wanted to buy her entire outfit in the city and I wanted to return her invitation and invite her to stay with us for a few days. But how could I ask her to stay in our one-room furnished place? I would have died of shame. Then my mother had a wonderful idea. Her present job was that of a housekeeper in a beautiful villa in Charlottenburg. The owners, like so many still wealthy Jews, were some place abroad, trying to find a new livelihood. My mother was looking after the house and their two small children. Both my mother and sister were living in this fine home, and since there was plenty of room, my mother suggested that I invite Ruth to stay with us there. She was quite ready to pretend that this was our home. So Ruth came to stay at 'our villa' and we had a wonderful week. I remember that one afternoon we went to see a film that everyone had been talking about,

Broadway Melody, an American musical. Never had I seen anything like it. The music, the dancing—what a fantastic spectacle! Both of us were so enchanted that we remained in our seats after the performance and sat through the entire show a second time. At the end of the week Ruth's parents came to Berlin and she moved into a hotel with them. They spent two days buying her all the clothes on the list. The one item Ruth was the proudest of was a gorgeous three-quarter length leather jacket, which I envied her no end. The price of it probably amounted to more than what we paid in two months for food and rent. Yet when my mother saw my face, she somehow managed to buy such a jacket for me. I was so happy that I never did inquire about what sacrifices she must have made in order to get it.

In August, a few weeks after Ruth's departure, I received a letter from the Jewish Agency informing me that the kibbutz where my Youth Aliyah group was going to spend the next two years was called Tel-Josef. The letter also stated that, because of fears that Great Britain might once again close or limit immigration to their Palestine Mandate, the Jewish Agency was attempting to distribute as many certificates as they could and was mobilizing all available transportation in order to get as many Jews as possible out of Germany and into Palestine. Therefore, I should immediately request my exit visa and passport and be ready to leave at a moment's notice. I was stunned. Originally we had been told that we would leave approximately eight to ten months after we had returned from camp and that was less than four months previous. Two days later I received another communication: On September 1st our group was to leave by train from Berlin to Marseilles and would take ship from there to Haifa. I had less than a week to get ready! Actually that was a blessing because it shortened the prolonged, painful goodbyes. My mother took those days off to help me get my wardrobe ready. I still see her sitting for hours, sewing nametags in my clothes, tears running down her cheeks. I could not stand it, and if it had not been for all the running around I had to do, I think I might have backed out at the last moment. On the second day of the five I had left, it looked for a while as if I really would have to give up the whole thing. I had gone to the police station to fill out the necessary forms for a passport, only to be told that such applications had to be cleared by the Gestapo, which would take at least three weeks. No explanation about the urgency of my case moved the official. I was desperate. It was in such emergencies that my father was at his best. He decided that we had to take the initiative and brave the lion's den. In other words, we would go directly to the Gestapo headquarters and ask for approval of my application. A Jew going to the Gestapo, voluntarily drawing attention to himself? It seemed insane, and very courageous. My father planned this undertaking like a strategic mission. He wanted us to be at the Gestapo office before the official in charge arrived. Once behind their desks, such bureaucrats were more aware of their power and therefore less approachable, he explained. He put in his lapel his World War I ribbon, which indicated that he held the Iron Cross, and hoped that his dueling scars would establish some rapport between the official and himself. After all, they identified him most visibly as having been part of the German elite. I am sure that they did help.

When the official we were to see arrived and saw us already waiting in front of his office, he asked us to enter, in quite a friendly fashion. My father explained to him that I needed a passport and could not wait for the usual three weeks. Would the officer be able to expedite the procedure? The officer apparently could do so. He found a form and unscrewed his fountain pen. Name of applicant? Bonin, an old German name. The official smiled at my father. Address, occupation, age, race. The official looked up, not smiling any more. The entire picture now had changed for him. Still, he did not say anything and after a short hesitation continued with his questionnaire. Finally he turned to my father and told him that he would now check the records. If anything questionable whatsoever was found there, my application would be denied. We were told to wait outside. I was sure that they would not find anything against my father in their records. And then my heart jumped. I remembered that, about a year before, he had been questioned about his habit of reading foreign newspapers in a coffee house he used to frequent. Someone must have reported that as suspicious. At the time he had told the interrogating clerk that he wanted to keep up his fluency in English, French, and Spanish. He never did hear anything further about this and apparently none of it had reached the Gestapo because, an hour later, we were called in again and with a short nod and the usual "Heil Hitler!" we were given the clearance paper and dismissed. How I loved my father at that moment! He had dared and he had won. And he had done that for me and my future, in spite of his deep disagreement with my plans.

But the story is not finished yet. By the time we were back at the police station, ready to hand in the Gestapo clearance, which then would enable the official there to issue me a passport, it was growing late, and the line in front of the appropriate window was long. Just before it was the turn of the man in front of us, the clock showed 4 P.M. and the policeman behind the counter slammed down his window. He was through for the day, and the next day was Saturday with everything closed and no passports issued. Sunday everything was closed, too, and I was supposed to leave on Monday. Had our visit to Gestapo headquarters after all been for nothing? I looked at the other clerk behind the next window, but he, too, was just finishing with his last customer. Then suddenly he looked up and saw my distress, my eyes filling with tears at the helplessness I felt in the face of German bureaucracy. He smiled, motioned me to wait, and, before pulling down his window, he put his finger to his lips, indicating that I should keep quiet. I hoped fervently that I had interpreted his meaning correctly. And I had. When the office had emptied and his nasty colleague had left, my smiling friend opened his window again and, after receiving the Gestapo clearance, issued me my passport. I could have fallen around his neck. As it was, I thanked him and we just smiled at each other. He would never know that he probably had saved my life.

I now must describe the last weekend I spent at home, but I find that I can't recall it. To this day I have trouble remembering endings—endings of books I read, of movies and plays I see, endings of anything, and I wonder if it all started with those last days in Berlin. As much as I try to evoke pictures, my mind draws a blank. Then I look at my father's letter. He must have written it before we left home, the day they took me to the station. I had a hard time translating it into English. The ink had blurred from the tears I had shed reading it. The paper, too, shows wear from being folded and refolded many times. I remember taking the letter out of my leather jacket pocket and reading it over and over. Now that I try to translate it I think I do see my mother crying, my father trying hard not to cry. Two old people standing at the station, waving, growing smaller and smaller as the train gathered speed, until all I had left was this letter:

My dear Adeline,

Just a few lines as a goodbye, but you may wish to read them over again later. Not one superfluous word will they contain, and you must remember them always. You know that I love you very much. Any harsh words that have passed between us, from either side, have never changed that for me. So, my best thoughts go with you, and I wish from the bottom of my heart that all your hopes will be fulfilled. But you should also know one more thing. When a father loves his child as I love you, then even though he may already be old and gray, he still understands her and all that might happen to her. She can always look at him as a true friend. You must know that even if one day not all your blossom-dreams should ripen, you can come to me without hesitation. My dear child, you can always confide in me your hopes and fears, your joys and sorrows. Though I hope you will never need it, I assure you that there will also be a *place* of refuge for you with me, always. You must remember this forever. And now, don't be downhearted but rather, be optimistic! I wish you a happy journey into your new homeland.

Your father

2. KIBBUTZ TEL-JOSEF

The train journey seemed endless. We crossed Germany into France, our final destination, Marseilles. At first the mood in our compartment was subdued, but soon our two counselors, the Ickelheimers, the couple whom we had gotten to know at the preparation-camp and who now were in charge of us until we arrived in Tel-Josef, moved from compartment to compartment and made us mix and get acquainted with those we had not met before. There were thirty boys and ten girls in our group. The Ickels, as we called them for short, organized us into small groups and gave us numerous projects to do that related to our new life in the kibbutz. One of these was to find a good Hebrew name for those of us who did not have a Jewish name. Ruth, of course, could remain Ruth, but the name Adeline had to go. I studied the list very carefully and finally decided on Nurit. It meant 'red poppy,' a flower which apparently was quite common in Palestine. Everyone agreed that the name fit me and so my new life began as Nurit.

After we crossed the border into France, a new sense of freedom took hold of us. We began to sing the pioneer songs in German and in Hebrew, and we leaned out of the train windows waving, shouting, and behaving like a bunch of teenagers suddenly freed of all constraints. By the time the train finally reached Marseilles we were so tired that we followed our guides in a daze from the station to the ship. What awaited us there, however, woke us up in a hurry. Most transports to Palestine were ships on their regular run from Trieste to Haifa but, as I mentioned, due to the possible restriction of legal immigration, the Jewish Agency had mobilized all available ships from whatever harbor they could. Our ship, the *Patria,* was a French ship and it was almost full of soldiers from the French Foreign Legion, most of them blacks and Moroccans. There also were Arabs in long gowns and turbans, surrounded by their women and children, and poor emigrants whose nationality I could not identify. We were led down to the hold of the ship into huge dormitory-like halls. Most of the bunks were already occupied by grinning soldiers of the Legion. We took one look at their leering faces and scrambled back up the ladder as fast as we could. We were scared and nothing on earth could make us share quarters with them. Instead we decided to sleep on deck. Someone suggested that we might fall overboard so Hans had the brilliant idea of tying us together, ankle to ankle. I was sure I was drowning anyway when I woke up the next morning, soaked with water—the crew was washing down the decks! The Ickels must have talked to the purser because after lunch we were given a separate section in one of the holds, and after a while the previously frightening Legionnaires seemed quite human and harmless, though we actually had little contact with them. Our passage was uneventful, the weather beautiful, the sea calm. We spent most of our time on deck, busy with all kinds of activities. Hebrew lessons were one of these. I also wrote long, detailed reports to my parents, which I would mail to them on arrival at Haifa.

Our ship docked for almost six hours in Alexandria, Egypt. We were not allowed to disembark, but we hung over the ship's railing and watched with fascination the exotic panorama unfolding below us on the pier. My first impression of the Middle East was a din of noise far louder than any I had ever experienced. Everyone was shouting, at each other, at us, at nobody in particular. Porters clad in strange white pantaloons ran up and down planks, first unloading, then loading countless sacks and boxes, some so large and heavy that I could hardly believe one human being could carry such weight. Vendors clad in long white gowns were trying to sell souvenirs, hats, and shirts. For hours on end they held up their wares, never taking 'no' for an answer. Men in business suits, with their red fezzes, endlessly gliding a string of beads through their fingers; women clad in black, sitting along the wall with a child in one arm, stretching out the other arm to beg. Strange smells assaulted us, a mixture of musty, spicy, and smoky. I very much wanted to own a fez but was told that this was Arab garb and never was worn by Jews. Oh, well . . .

The next day was the most exciting of the entire journey. After breakfast we all rushed on deck, eager to catch our first glance of the promised land. After searching the horizon for a couple of hours, squinting into the bright sunlight, we finally made out the shoreline. Another four hours and the *Patria* had anchored at her Haifa dock. Here the harbor seemed even busier than Alexandria. There were more people around, not so many fezzes but more Europeans, that is to say Jews, most of them dressed very informally in khaki shorts and short-sleeved shirts, with no ties or jackets. The shouting was the same as in Egypt, only this time it was in many different languages, Hebrew, Arabic, English, and German. I was impressed with the beautiful site Haifa occupied. The city stretched from the shore up the hills. White houses surrounded by cypresses and pines dotted the slopes. Someone explained to us that the lower part of Haifa, the harbor area, was inhabited mostly by Arabs while the new Jewish settlers had built their homes and businesses on the hills, all the way up Mount Carmel. What a beautiful view these houses must enjoy looking down on the blue Mediterranean and the white shoreline, all of it framed by an equally blue and cloudless sky. However, I didn't have much time to contemplate the scenery because we were ready to disembark. More shouting, pushing, and waiting in line for passport controls. We became aware of a lot of English soldiers and policemen, many wearing shorts and tropical helmets. Our group was herded here and there, waiting for more formalities to be completed and papers to be stamped. And now for the first time we also began to experience real heat. I tried to shield my head by covering it with my leather jacket, but that only made me feel more suffocated. How I envied the people around us in their shorts and loose-fitting overblouses. By mid afternoon we proceeded to the train station. The train was already in and as soon as we had boarded, it left. This three-hour trip through the Emek [the Valley of Israel] was like something out of a Wild West movie. All along the corridors British soldiers were posted, each one holding his rifle, loaded and cocked, out of the open windows, and as we passed villages, settlements, and the small town of Afula, everywhere we saw soldiers on rooftops, usually behind sandbags, their rifles at the ready. The countryside was flat with hills rising on both sides, green fields alternating with arid strips of land. We passed *chaluzim* [Jewish pioneers] working the soil, waving to us. We saw Bedouin tents and mounted policemen. It seemed to me that we not only were covering distance in miles but also in years. The Arabs with their sheep, and their donkeys and camels, belonged to the country of Abraham and Jacob; the *chaluzim*, the soldiers, and the trucks were of the present. This was a country of contrasts where the old and the new were confronting each other, where Arab and Jew claimed a homeland and the English ruled, albeit uneasily.

Tel-Josef, September 15, 1936

Dear Vati, Mutti, and Edith,

I've been here for a week now and am beginning to settle in. It's too soon to say whether I really like kibbutz life. There certainly is a lot to get used to, but let me tell you about our immediate surroundings first. Tel-Josef is not a new kibbutz but one of the older ones. There are about four hundred people living here, which includes the children. Most of the kibbuzniks are of Polish or Russian origin and speak to us in Yiddish. At first we had a little difficulty understanding, but now it has become our *lingua franca,* though, of course, our Hebrew, or as it's called here, Ivrit, is improving daily. Well, to get back to Tel-Josef. Our fields, orchards and vegetable gardens stretch out for miles all through the valley, and our vineyards climb up the foot of Mount Gilboa, opposite us in the distance. The main crops are corn, alfalfa, grapefruit, grapes, olives, different kinds of fruit and all kinds of vegetables like eggplant, tomatoes, cucumbers and carrots. Tel-Josef is known for its dairy cows and the kibbutz produces and sells a lot of butter, milk and cheese. We have a huge chicken farm as well as goats and sheep. Except for the children, we all eat together in a big dining hall, a large, modern building, one of the few that has electric lights. (The children's houses do too). I know you'll be interested in the food, Mutti. The bread is good and there's plenty of it. Sometimes we get eggs, goat cheese, cream, plenty of olives, eggplant, which is a new vegetable for us, and cucumbers and tomatoes, which we mix with oil and vinegar. For each table there is usually a tureen of fruit soup, to which you help yourself. If it were not for the fact that it's lukewarm and always has flies in it, it would be quite good. Meat is served daily, but it's always the same—two boiled meatballs accompanied by a dish called kasha, a crushed buckwheat. Someone said that the meat comes from cows that are slaughtered just before they die of old age. I think I'll opt for vegetarian food. Several in our group have already done so and their food looks far more appetizing. Last Saturday we got a piece of halva for breakfast. It's a delicious sort of Turkish sweet dish made of sesame seeds, chocolate and honey. Desserts are either fruit or pudding. If we get hungry between meals, when the kitchen is closed, they always put out baskets of fresh bread and bowls of used cooking oil. I love dunking the bread into this and I eat a lot of it. Now about our living accommodations. The children live in very comfortable modern houses whereas the rest of the kibbutzniks live in wooden barracks, little bungalows, or tents. Our quarters are better than theirs. We occupy four small but brand new tile-roofed stone buildings. Each has two large and one small room with a little balcony in the middle. I share a room with Ruth and two other girls, Erika and Sonya. We sleep on iron cot-beds. The only other furniture is a chest of drawers, which we share, and a little table by the window. Our light comes from a kerosene lamp, which has to be cleaned and filled daily. Our work clothes, boots, etc., we keep in a big cupboard outside on the covered balcony. The rest of our laundry we collect every day from the *machsan*. This is a room all lined with shelves, where each one of us has a cupboard with our name on it. Here our dirty laundry is collected and then delivered in big sacks, sorted, folded (not ironed), and placed in the cubbyholes. The system works very well. Genia, who is in charge here, always has two of us to help her. It's easy work, sorting, folding, sewing on buttons, mending socks, so it usually goes to whoever does not feel too well or has been sick and is recuperating. And there are quite a few of us under the weather. I guess it's due mostly to the difference in food and climate. As for me, I'm holding up, though the heat bothers me a lot and the physical labor is hard. In another letter I'll write in more detail about the kind of work we're doing. But before I close I must mention our sanitary facilities! The showers and toilets are, for me, the hardest thing to get used to. They're housed in a little building about a block down the hill from our rooms. It isn't the distance that I mind, though I imagine when the rainy season starts it won't be too pleasant to have to walk all that way in the mud to use a bathroom. What I do mind, first of all, are the toilets themselves. There are two ordinary ones and one kind I've never seen before. It's just a hole in the ground with two hewn-out places to put your feet on. Someone called it a French toilet, but I rather think it must be an Arab contraption because they seem to squat a great deal anyway. All three toilets are water closets, but—and this is what disturbs me—no paper must be thrown in. Instead it has to be put into open canisters, which stand next to the toilets. The toilet paper, by the way, is nothing but old newspaper. Can you imagine the smell and the flies, not to speak of the sight?

Then there are the showers, right next to the toilets. There are five showerheads, all in one area with no partition for privacy. The first day I went in there I just sat on the bench in the little anteroom, too embarrassed to move. Women came and went, women of all sizes, shapes and ages. All I could think of was, I can't do this, yet I'll have to, and not just today and tomorrow but for two years! I know you'll probably smile when you read this and think me too finicky. The other girls don't seem to mind as much as I do so I simply must get over my embarrassment. I shall not mention this again, but you did want me to tell you everything. It's late and my roommates are long asleep so I'd better close now because the wake-up gong rings at 5:30 A.M.

Love and kisses, as always, yours,
Adi-Nurit

Our days are fairly routine now. Wake-up call at 5:30. We get dressed and then walk down to the toilets and take care of our morning wash-up. From 6 to 6:30 A.M. is breakfast, and then we are off to whatever work we are assigned for the day. The first four weeks we are being shifted around, working everywhere, so that we can get an idea about which of all the different branches of agriculture appeals to us most. After this trial period we're supposed to choose our preferred specialty, which will then become our permanent workplace. So far we have worked in the *pardesim* [grapefruit groves], the vineyards, and the fruit orchards. Most of the work is back-breaking, weeding with a *turia*, a short-handled hoe. It's especially hard in the vineyards since the ground is covered with stones. As we work our way down each row, two on each side of the vines, as hard as I try I keep falling behind. Yesterday Hans was my partner, and every time he finished a row he came back to help me on my side so we could finish with the rest of the workers. But I don't always have such a great guy with me and slowly I'm getting a complex about my ability to keep up, especially since the other kibbutzniks judge you by your work output. It's a new and very unpleasant experience for me to be at the bottom of the heap instead of at the top. Working in the carrot fields, thinning the rows, was easier, but then we harvested cucumbers, tomatoes, and eggplants. They had to be collected in big tin cans and then carried to the packing shed. I thought my shoulders would break. Why is all this physical work so hard for me? I'm beginning to dread each working day and find myself wishing for some slight illness, a broken finger or a sprained ankle, anything to get me off for a little while from the daily anxiety over my inadequacy. But about this I shall not write home. All I wrote them was a general description of the work we are doing.

Tel-Josef, September 22, 1936

My dearest Parents and dear little Edith,

Thank you so much for all the mail I've received. Mutti, it's wonderful that you write to me every day, but please don't spend all your free time keeping a diary. You need some rest too, especially with all the overtime you put in. And, Vati, special thanks to you for all the running around you had to do to get my big trunk off. All of us are looking forward to getting our things. In the meantime, we make do with what we brought along. Also, the kibbutz has issued us some khaki shorts and workshirts as well as a couple of blue shirts for after work, which make us look like real kibbutzniks. Mutti, you asked about the children here, how many there are, how old they are, and why they don't eat with us, or, rather, with their parents. There must be about seventy children here, a few almost our age but many more little ones, toddlers and babies. It's a joy to watch them because they look so happy. Unfortunately, we can't communicate too well yet with the older ones since they speak Hebrew only, but that will change as soon as our Ivrit becomes more fluent. All the children live in the two children's houses, two, three or four to a room. We were shown around and I marveled at the light, clean and charmingly furnished rooms and at all the toys, games, and play equipment they have at their disposal. Any child must be happy in these cheerful surroundings. The women who look after the children all wear white smocks and some are special kindergarten teachers. Others deal with the infants only. The parents come after work to collect their kids and take them to their bungalows or play with them outdoors until it's bedtime, when they deliver them again to the children's houses. Some people have criticized the kibbutzim for such a strange family life, but I find this an admirable system. I don't believe that anywhere in the whole world a child could grow up with more care and love than it receives here. On top of it, the parents are always relaxed and able to devote themselves totally to their kids during the hours they spend together. There is never any impatience or anger because children don't interfere with adults here. All live their own lives and then look forward to their shared hours. By the way, the older children have a three-room schoolhouse here and two teachers in charge of it. From what I hear, they get a good, all-around education including playing musical instruments, physical education and art. And talking about education brings me to our own. Every day after work and after eating we shower, change our clothes, and from 3 P.M. to 5:30 P.M. we have classes. Actually they're not classes but small group studies of Hebrew as well as lectures and discussions of the history of the kibbutz movement in general and Tel-Josef in particular, about other kinds of agricultural settlements, about the early history of Erez Israel, its pioneers and the present state of the *Histadrut* [General Federation of Jewish Labor]. We learn about the country's economy and its agriculture. The main emphasis is on a quick integration into kibbutz life, to make us into productive workers whose goal will be to perpetuate the ideals of our teachers and one day found our own kibbutz in new territory. Hebrew, or Ivrit, does not come as easy for me as did French and English. Reading it is especially hard since almost everything is printed without vowels. We have two teachers, Nechemia and Judith. Both are old pioneers and well versed in the country's history. Like many of the other Tel-Josefers, they came here in their early twenties when the valley was nothing but a swamp infested with malaria. They drained the land, built roads, enriched the soil, and founded settlements. Most of them suffered malaria, malnutrition and other diseases. They had to contend with hostile Arabs, yet they never gave up, and now they are a self-sufficient breed who proudly look back on their achievement. I'm telling you this so that you get a feeling for what kind of ideals Nechemia and Judith wish to instill in us. Though everything they tell us is new and interesting, I have a hard time to keep awake. After five or six hours of work in the fields it's hard to study, especially in this unrelenting heat. It does cool off a bit in the evening, and after dinner we enjoy our time off. About that in my next letter. In the meantime, I love you all and wish you were here to share all these new experiences with me.

Love and kisses,
Your Nurit

Tel-Josef, September 30, 1936

Dear Vati, Mutti, and Edith,

We just got our mail and there again was another letter from you. Congratulations, Edith, on having received the best grades of the entire class. Vati, I was very much moved to hear about all you have been doing for me. I can imagine all the red tape you had to go through to send the trunk. It must have kept you busy for days. And, Mutti, you shouldn't have bought so many additional gifts for me, though of course I will enjoy the candy and the photo album. But you must not spend every spare penny on me. Please remember, I'm fine and well taken care of. We have everything we need here, though there is no money exchanged anywhere. Everyone simply gets what he needs. Once a week we go to a kind of store where we receive whatever we ask for—soap, toothpaste, combs, brushes, razor blades for the men. None of the women use make-up. That is frowned on as capitalistic luxury.

Two days ago we had quite a bit of excitement here. It was dinner time and most of us were in the dining hall when suddenly we heard shots and then all the lights went out and we were told to take cover under the tables. It was an Arab attack and lasted only a few minutes. As soon as our *shomrim* [armed guards] returned the fire, the attackers fled. No casualties, no damage. Apparently such attacks have happened before, ever since the outbreak of the riots last April. After the lights came back on everyone returned to their seats and finished dinner as if nothing had happened.

Since I wrote last I've been busy harvesting, first olives and then grapefruit. The orchards are quite a distance from the settlement. A truck takes us to and from work, and since we start our work before breakfast, a horsedrawn wagon delivers our food around 8 A.M. It's fun picnicking under the trees. The air is still relatively cool then and the break is most welcome. Around 1 P.M. the truck comes back for us. The real kibbutzniks, of course, work the entire day. Our half day consists of about five to six hours. Their full day means anything from nine to twelve hours, six days a week. Several in our group have already decided where they want to work. Ruth likes the orchards and eventually will become a specialist in the growing of fruit trees. Hans is going to become a milker and looks forward to being a dairy farmer. Chawa, one of the other girls, has been accepted in the children's house. I'm still being sent here, there and everywhere because I can't make up my mind. Last week we harvested olives, which was fun, sort of, but I can't imagine a life as an olive grower or, right now, as any kind of farmer. Well, more next week.

With love and kisses from,
Your Nurit

Though I promised to write home about everything that happens here, I didn't mention that every morning when the truck takes us to work, two or three of our *shomrim* ride with us, their guns ready, and as we turn into the road leading up into the orchards, they climb down, rifles cocked, and walk ahead of our truck, scanning the road for boobytraps that may have been placed there by the Arabs the night before. Agriculture always had seemed to me such a peaceful occupation, but here it often feels like working under siege. I also did not tell my parents how unhappy I still am about work. I have the feeling that I don't really fit in. Worse, even, I suspect that I've chosen a future that does not suit me at all. My father wrote in his last letter, "Don't let small annoyances get you down. One is plagued with those all his life. Are you getting along with your group? That is the main thing. Hold up your head and be positive." So, obviously, some of my doubts must have come through in my letters, but, except for the showers and toilets, which I shall never get used to, it isn't the small things that bother me, nor is it our group. I do get along very well with all of them. Ruth and I have become very close, and since there are thirty boys for ten girls, it's easy to be popular. To tell the truth, Ruth and I are the most sought after. What bothers me is the realization that I don't really like kibbutz life. No doubt it's a wonderful way of life for *chaluzim*, but I don't feel that is what I want to be for the rest of my life. I have not discussed this with anyone, not even Ruth or Hans, because, quite rightly, they would ask me what I was thinking about when I signed up. What had I expected? And I don't know the answer to that except that I was seduced by the idea of adventure.

Tel-Josef, October 16, 1936

Dear Vati, Mutti, and Edith,
It is late in the evening. My three roommates are already asleep and I'm writing this by the light of the kerosene lamp. It's

very dark outside and I hear the jackals howling. It sounds like what I imagine a night on the prairie or maybe in Alaska would be like. Mutti, you say you envy me the heat. How I wish we could change places for a little while, although here too it's getting a bit cooler now and the last few nights have been downright chilly. Now to answer some of your questions. No, I'm not getting fat from eating all that bread and oil. I work and sweat it all off. Yes, I'm very tanned from working outside. Hans has taken some pictures but we have to wait until someone travels to Haifa to get them developed. Then I'll mail them to you. You ask if I lack for anything, if there is something you can send me. No, I don't really need anything, except I wish we had toilet paper, but that is hardly anything you could mail.

Now I must tell you about the high holidays. You would think, since this is a Jewish country, that Rosh Hashanah and Yom Kippur are faithfully observed. But, as I mentioned to you before, the kibbutzniks here are socialists and have no interest in religious traditions. We did have a day off on both holidays, but there was no special celebration or fasting. On Rosh Hashanah a few of us went visiting an area of Tel-Josef I had not been to before. It is where some of the parents of our *chaluzim* live, who have come to Palestine from Poland, sponsored by the kibbutz. There are about forty of them. The men were all dressed in their traditional long, black coats, wore fur or felt hats, and had sidelocks. They were singing and dancing joyfully while we joined the womenfolk in the outer circle, clapping our hands to the increasing rhythm of the dancers. On Yom Kippur I went again to the old people's quarters, but this time I was not met by the exuberant joy they had exhibited before. Now the men were praying loudly, mournfully, bobbing their heads and upper torsos, back and forth, back and forth, their white prayer shawls hiding their faces. How different they are from anything I have ever seen before and how strange that our free-thinking kibbutzniks are only a generation removed from them!

Last week was Succoth, the feast to celebrate the end of the harvest, and that was celebrated in a big way. Everyone participated. The day before, the whole kibbutz prepared for the big parade in which we would exhibit the fruits of our labor. I wish you could have seen the procession. First came the children, most of the girls in white robes, waving palm branches. Then each group of workers carried samples of their produce on litters decorated with flowers. Since I've been working mostly in the vegetable fields, I carried a kind of stretcher with three others in our group. It was laden with carrots, green peppers, tomatoes, cucumbers, and eggplant. Ruth and Shulamit carried a pole with a huge cluster of grapes made up from hundreds of small clusters. All of us wore garlands over our shoulders and flowers on our caps. We went around the entire kibbutz and finally arranged the offering of our harvest on the lawn in front of the dining hall. Afterwards everyone danced the *hora* and a kind of polka, on and on to the point of exhaustion. When some were too tired to continue, they would drop out and others would take their places. Our group joined in too, and I danced until I was drenched with perspiration. When most of us finally left for bed, we could still hear the music and the pounding feet. Once again it's after midnight so I'll close.

All my love and kisses,
Your Nurit

Tel-Josef, November 3, 1936

My dearest Parents,

The last two days it has rained on and off, the first rain of the season, rather gentle showers, yet it has totally changed the soil. We all are wearing rubber boots now. The earth sticks to them in big clumps until eventually these clay-like globs fall off, only to accumulate again after a few steps. This mud is called *botz* and we all hate it. Walking becomes a slow and difficult process, each leg carrying an extra weight of many pounds. Several times, when I was trying to pull my leg from this gooey clay, I came away without my boot, landing on my hands deep in the mud, my boot standing empty behind me. When this happens, you need someone to pull you out. What a mess! The rain, though, makes everything smell very fresh. The dust has been washed off so that everywhere you look the colors seem brighter. Just before the rain started we had an entire day of house-cleaning, under Genia's supervision. We emptied our rooms of all furniture, washed the bedsteads with paraffin, and squirted the cupboards with a spraygun to get rid of ants, spiders, or any other little beasties. Our floors are tiled and we take turns washing them daily, but this was the big, once-a-month clean-up. Genia also warned us of scorpions, which like to hide in damp cleaning rags, and told us to be sure to shake out the rags carefully before using them. Well, house-cleaning is not my favorite occupation, but it's more fun than working in the fields. Actually, lately I've been detailed for all kinds of other jobs. I spent two days washing socks on the washboards. When the skin was about ready to peel off my hands, I was sent to another part of the laundry, hanging up sheets to dry. Staring at the white cloth in the brilliant sunlight almost blinds a person. I guess they gave me all these duties to make me appreciate field work again! We have a new teacher. She, too, is from Germany and has a degree from Heidelberg. Like us, she works six hours and then instructs us. She also leads voluntary discussion in the evening about art and literature. Our group has elected me to organize these meetings. It seems I do better at this sort of thing than I do at field work. Oh, I almost forgot! Our trunks have finally arrived! They had never been unloaded from the ship and had gone back to Marseilles! Now all is unpacked and I can't thank you enough for all you have sent on top of the required list. Please, please don't spend any more on me. I don't want you to deny yourselves because of me. The candy was still delicious and much appreciated by my roommates too. I'm enclosing the film Hans took. The pictures came out quite well and will give you an idea of what our life is like here.

There is some commotion outside. Boys and girls are lining up for a haircut, the first since we arrived here. I must close and take my place in the line.

With all my love and a thousand kisses, yours,

Adi (Nurit)

P.S. I'm enclosing a separate note for Edith.

P.P.S. Vati, you asked if we have religious services here and if some of the kibbutzniks eat kosher. The answer is 'no' to both questions. The old parents who live in separate quarters way down toward the dairy installation do their own cooking and live by the same conservative traditions they followed in their *shtetl* back in Poland or Russia. As I told you before, religion and *chaluz* are at opposite poles. However, there are conservative kibbutzim in which all the laws are observed, but these are very few and there are none here in the Emek (Valley).

The day after I mailed the above letter I began to feel quite sick. First I had a headache, then my eyes and all my limbs hurt when I moved, and by noon the following day I ran a high temperature. The doctor came and diagnosed it as sandfly fever or, as it is called here, *pappataci*. It lasted four days. Now I'm up again but feel very weak. I must admit, though, that I like this stage of recuperation. I get all kinds of extra food like butter, cream, double egg rations and halva to build me up. Best of all, I don't have to work in the fields for a week. So I help Genia in our *machsan*. I distribute the clean clothes, sew buttons on, and mend socks. How pleasant this work is compared with the back-breaking field labor. Incidentally, I'm not the first to suffer from *pappataci*. It is quite common here and several in our group had come down with it before me.

Tel-Josef, November 28, 1936

My dearest Vati, Mutti, and little Edith,

We, our group and our teacher, Nechemia, are back from a five-day trip which took us up to the Galilee and as far north as Tiberias. We saw the Jordan River, which is surprisingly small for such an important stream, and visited several kibbutzim, among them Degania, the first kibbutz, founded in 1909. Now it's a beautiful place with many trees and gardens. The Sea of Galilee, called *Yam Kinneret* in Hebrew, which means "the lute" because it's shaped like one, is about thirteen miles long and seven miles wide. It's 686 feet below sea level. The water is fresh, not like the Dead Sea (which I haven't seen yet). Vati, I'm sure you'll be interested to know that we visited the tomb of Maimonides in Tiberias. Though he died in Egypt, he wanted to be buried here. We walked our feet off, herded along by Nechemia from one famous old site to another. We also saw the hot springs at Tiberias, but I found the communal bathing there pretty unappetizing and didn't try it. In the cool evening we sat on the shore of the Sea of Galilee, sang songs, and thought about the centuries of historical events that had touched this place. I wish you all could have shared these days with me.

Today I was supposed to go back to field work, but I've developed a boil on my left hand so I decided to see the doctor. The dispensary is located between the two kibbutzim of Ein-Harod and Tel-Josef. In order to get there you have to cross a wadi, which during the summer is completely dry but now has become a pleasant little river. I'm told that when the really heavy rains begin it can become a raging torrent. The nurse put some salve on my hand to draw out the infection. I think I'll be able to go to work tomorrow.

All my love,
Your Adi (Nurit)

The last few letters I received from home held quite a few surprises. There was the news that my parents had officially joined the Jewish congregation and had been duly registered as being of the Jewish faith. I asked my father why he thought this step necessary. Here is what he replied:

"No, it was not necessary at all. But, as correct as I formerly found it to renounce the Jewish faith officially, in order not to espouse externally that which I no longer felt any connection with internally, so I find it just as correct today not to hinder but to promote a solidarity which, after all, has been forced upon us. In other words, I will not stand on the sidelines. That is all—no more and no less."

I do admire my father for this strong stand.

The other news concerned their move from the Uhlandstrasse to Pariserstrasse. Apparently they found a much nicer room in a large flat. Mother, especially, seems to be tickled fixing it up. I am grateful for any little pleasure she has because her life seems so sad to me. She works very hard, does not seem too well, and on top of it she's taking my absence very hard. She writes to me every day and tries to fulfill any wish I may have. Yet she hardly makes enough to pay their rent and food. She never complains, only asks if there is anything she can send me. And Vati, poor Vati. How he must hate it that he can't contribute to their living expenses. He's still trying to sell insurance. Meanwhile, Mother is already trying to find a way how they could send me the money for a visit home after my two years are up here. Two years. That seems such a long time. Yet the three months since our arrival here have passed quickly. If only I could find the right work! Everyone seems to think that the vegetable fields are going to be my permanent workplace. I still don't care for farm labor at all, but what else is there?

I got two more boils on my arms, and I go to the nurse every day. It's very painful. I'm not the only one suffering from this complaint. Some are worse off than I, like poor Hanoch. He's so covered with boils that he can't work at all and the kibbutz feels they'll have to send him away from here. I think our diet is at least partly at fault. I won't say anything more about this in my letters. It worries my mother so much when I'm sick while I'm far away from her.

There is something else I hesitate to write about, not so much because it might worry my parents but because the entire matter is not clear to me but rather vague and leaves me with a feeling of unease. Paradoxically, it concerns the only thing that makes me, in spite of all my troubles here, very happy—my close relationship with Ruth. I have written home and told them how much we mean to each other, and my parents seem to share my happiness in such a wonderful friendship. Yet I doubt that even they understand the intensity of our feelings. And maybe in the exuberance of our new love we have been too absorbed with each other to leave room for anybody else. In a group of thirty boys and ten girls, when you remove two girls from the 'dating game' the boys are bound to become jealous, and I'm beginning to hear some unkind remarks about us. But I hate to give up this closeness. I love the hours in the evening when, after dinner, everyone pairs up under a blanket on the big lawn in front of the dining hall. Then Ruth and I lie together, watching the stars, and dream about some far-off future. Maybe we should be less obvious about our attachment, not hold hands or always sit together, but why not? What's wrong with a friendship as deep as ours? I think a lot about this.

Tel-Josef, December 17, 1936

My dearest Parents,

By the time you receive this letter it will be Christmas. What wonderful memories are connected with those days, yet I see that you have given up celebrating it. Now it is Chanuka instead. As I read in your letters, that is due to Edith and what she learns at school, and I suppose this is as it should be. I feel in myself a certain revolt against a new way of life being forced upon all of us, but, Vati, you are so right—one has to declare one's solidarity, and in the end it is most important to belong somewhere and to something. How inventive of you, Mutti, to make a Chanuka candelabra out of clothespins and how wonderful that Edith is invited to so many parties and receives gifts from her friends. Don't worry, she won't even realize that for now you're not in a position to buy her anything. I was so pleased with her last letter and enclose a little letter just for her.

Here the winter season has really arrived. Rain is pouring

down in sheets almost every day. The ground is soaked and the walkways (we have no real sidewalks) are as slippery as ice. All along these footpaths wires have been stretched so that we can hang on to them as we walk. Work in the fields is often interrupted when one has to run for shelter from the torrents of water coming down, and many are the days when outdoor work is not even attempted. Then we are detailed to mend sacks in preparation for the harvest and help out in the sewing rooms, which are usually the domain of women in the more advanced stages of pregnancy. Most of these jobs are easy, and I'm very happy not to have to face the burning sun with bent back or bended knees hour after hour, day after day. I don't even mind the damp cold, which creeps in everywhere. We don't have any heating in our rooms and the stone floors, without any covering, make it seem even chillier and quite *ungemütlich* [uncomfortable]. The strange thing is that after a few days of such downpours the sun will come again and immediately it gets warm enough for us to shed coats and jackets. Winter has brought me another benefit. During the cold months only one of the two shower facilities is being heated, so that the shower closest to us has only cold water available. The result is that hardly anyone uses it and once again I can wash in privacy. It's very chilly but I don't mind. I'm going to close this letter now and, even though you don't celebrate it any more, wish you as merry a Christmas as is possible under the circumstances. And for the New Year, may 1937 be our last year of separation.

All my love and a thousand kisses,
Your Adi

Tel-Josef, January 8, 1937

My dearest Vati and Mutti,

I can't believe this! First it was *pappataci*, then the boils, and now I am down with, of all things, scarlet fever! It started with a sore throat and within twenty-four hours I developed a high fever. By the time the doctor came to see me, red rashes had begun to show up on my arms. No doubt, he said, it was scarlet fever. Then he asked my three roommates if they had ever had this disease. "No" from Sonya and Ruth, "yes" from Erika. Well, he told Sonya and Ruth to move out, declared our room an isolation ward, and appointed Erika as my nurse. Poor Erika!

75

Both of us will live together for at least four weeks, and since I can't go to the toilets, she has to empty out my bedpan, bring water for washing, get food—in short, she has to wait on me hand and foot. I feel awful about it, but she says it's really not a hard job. I don't know. I would hate it. My fever is down, but I'm not allowed to get up yet. Ruth has been sending me little letters every day, and Erika keeps me abreast of all that is happening. She stands outside on the balcony for hours, talking to all who pass by.

This is a short letter. It's hard to write while lying down, and I get tired very quickly, but I don't want you to be without my weekly letter, and I promised to tell you everything. Don't worry, I'm already much better. Soon I'll be out and about.

Love and kisses, yours,
Adi

Tel-Josef, January 15, 1937

The doctor has just been here. He is satisfied with my progress. The fever is gone and the rash, which had finally covered my entire body, is subsiding too, but he does not want me to get up yet. Maybe next week. The days pass very slowly and the high points in my life are my daily notes from Ruth and mail from home. Mother writes me twice a week now so that I won't get too lonely and bored. I am so touched by this, especially since I know that air mail is very expensive and must make quite a dent in their budget. My father plans to take a refresher course in land surveying. He believes that this would be a profession he could practice abroad. He is finally exploring possibilities of emigration, maybe to Australia or South America. But it is very hard, first to find a place that will accept Jewish refugees, and then to get the money to pay for visas, travel tickets, and have enough left over to afford a roof over your head until you find a job. Of course, they can't leave Berlin until they have paid all they owe. So far, as Mother says, these are only dreams.

Tel-Josef, January 27, 1937

Today is my first day up. I feel a bit shaky on my legs and, wonder of wonders, I have grown a whole inch! My clothes feel a bit loose, which must mean that I lost some weight too. Well, that's all right with me. Erika, on the other hand, is getting fatter all the time. I have little appetite and she eats for the two of us. It really is a bad thing to be cooped up like this, and though I know it must be as hard for her as it is for me, I resent her constant presence, am irritated at almost everything she says and does, and find it harder every day not to give way to screaming fits. The only relief now are Ruth's daily visits. She has managed to get hold of a ladder, which she has placed against the back wall of our building, and though it does not quite reach the window, we can now talk to each other.

In today's mail was a letter from my parents to Erika. In it they thank her for all she is doing for me. When she read it to me, I had to admit that the last three weeks must have been very hard for her. After all, through no fault of her own, she has been confined in one room with one person, removed from all her friends, could not attend classes, missed out on a concert, and all that because of me. I should be more understanding of her bad temper and just overlook her sulkiness, which seems to increase from day to day.

Tel-Josef, February 2, 1937

The doctor was here yesterday. He said that I could get out of quarantine in another three days, that is, day after tomorrow, and that is not a minute too soon because neither Erika nor I can stand each other's company any more. We have been yelling at each other and today almost came to blows. It started with her practically throwing the food at me and then my telling her that she ate like a pig and how glad I was to be soon rid of her, whereupon she slammed out of the room, vowing not to return. So, now I am alone, but I feel awful. Why is it that I have so little control over my feelings? I wish I could apologize for losing my temper.

Tel-Josef, February 7, 1937

These last few days were the worst I have ever gone through, yet to a great extent I have only myself to blame for what has happened. The day Erika left I watched her from the window, talking excitedly to any passerby. I wondered what she was telling them. The next day I found out. Before going to work Ruth climbed the ladder to my window and, without looking at me, she said, "It's over between us. I want to finish a relationship which I now think is abnormal. You have influenced me into directions I don't want to go. So I don't want to see you or be around you any more."

I was so stunned that I could not find an answer. I just broke the pencil I was holding in two. Though my isolation was supposed to last another day, I rushed out of the room and ran down to Genia's workshop, where I burst into tears and told her the whole story. She comforted me as best she could, but I felt sure she did not understand how heartbroken I was at the collapse of my first love. I don't remember much about the next few days, but I do know that the quarantine came to an abrupt end and I moved in with three other girls. Hans, dear Hans, came to accompany me to the dining room. I didn't want to go at all because I was scared to face the rest of the group. If Erika had succeeded in turning Ruth away from me, how much more then would the others consider me an abnormal monster! To my relief, we were late to the dining room and the few fellows and girls around didn't pay much attention to me. Maybe not everyone had yet heard Erika's accusation, or maybe not everyone believed her. Hans didn't. Neither did the three girls I now share a room with. They thought Erika was simply taking revenge by spreading rumors and that Shalom and Rudi, who had wanted to date Ruth for a long time, now saw their chance to get me out of the way. Was that really all there was to it? Or was there just a little bit of truth in what Erika called my 'abnormal tendencies'? Surely she was wrong in telling everyone that I was a danger to the group. But was my attachment to Ruth abnormal? Had it been wrong that I loved her more than anyone else in the group, that I preferred her company to that of any of the boys? Was I abnormal because their kisses and their petting left me cold and I would rather not? I found some relief in writing my parents all about it. I knew that they would understand and be able to answer some of my questions.

Genia, who was wiser than I gave her credit for at the time, arranged for me to have a week's vacation, ostensibly to recoup my strength after my illness but, in truth, to give me time to pull myself together as well as time for the entire episode to recede into proper perspective. I decided to visit Sam and Hedden G. in Tel-Aviv. They were old friends from Berlin, younger than my parents but, of course, much older than I. Both of them had written to me several times, inviting me to stay with them whenever and as along as I wanted. I had not visited them before because of the continuing Arab riots which made travel, especially between Haifa and Tel-Aviv, unsafe. Almost daily the newspapers reported busses ambushed, travelers shot at by snipers, even stoned by mobs. Also, we were not supposed to get any vacation until we had been in the kibbutz for at least a year.

Haifa, February 16, 1937

My dearest Folks,

I have an hour's wait until the bus leaves for Afula, from where I'm sure to catch a lift back to Tel-Josef. Last week I sent you only a postcard from Tel-Aviv, but now I'll use the time to write you in more detail about my vacation. The trip to Tel-Aviv was very interesting, even a bit dangerous. On the first leg of our journey through the Valley of Israel, the Emek as it is called here, the driver stopped several times, got out of the bus and carefully inspected, once a stone in the middle of the road, then a hole he must not have noticed on his previous trip, and finally some branches left on the highway. Every time he returned to his seat we breathed a sigh of relief that it had not been a planted bomb or a mine. In Haifa I changed busses. First the road led along the coast but then turned inland. We passed a lot of Arab villages, some nomads on donkeys, others leading camels, followed by their families, women in black, children somewhat reminiscent of gypsy children I've seen in Germany. Looking at these Arabs in their long flowing gowns, with their proud faces, dark eyes and hooked noses, sitting majestically on their camels, I felt sure that thus Abraham and the rest of the Old Testament Israelites must have looked. In just a few hours we arrived safely in Tel-Aviv, but in that short time we traversed millennia.

It was late afternoon when I showed up at the Grossmann's and after midnight by the time we went to bed. There was so much to tell, so much to catch up with. The Grossmanns have a lovely apartment on Dizengoff Square, a beautiful plaza with a fountain in the middle of it which, as soon as it grows dark, plays in all the colors of the rainbow. We watched it every night while we sat on their large balcony talking and talking. I had to tell them all about life in the kibbutz, and they in turn acquainted me with city life. At first I felt like a country bumpkin, still indoctrinated with the values of the commune. But already on the second day I found that I preferred Tel-Aviv. Its elegant population and downright cosmopolitan atmosphere, at least compared with Tel-Josef, seemed most attractive. I loved the clean white city by the blue Mediterranean. It all looked so new, so clean. The weather, too, was fantastic. The sun, of course, was shining just the same as in Tel-Josef, but here there was always a fresh sea breeze blowing. We—that is Hedden and

I and, when he had time, her husband, Sam—spent almost every morning at the beach. Then we went home for lunch and a rest. Afternoons we strolled along Allenby or Ben Yehuda, window shopping, and eventually we would end up at one of the many coffee houses, where we sat outside, people-watching. Twice we went to the cinema, the Mugrabi. When the movie starts the roof rolls back so that the theater is pleasantly cool. One film was English, the other German with English subtitles, and on the right and left of the screen translations in Hebrew and Arabic were rolling off. I found this fascinating.

I loved Hedden's home-cooked food, which was reminiscent of yours, Mutti, but best of all was the privacy and cleanliness of the bathroom! After three days I was sold on the lifestyle here and wished that I didn't have to go back to Tel-Josef. Though I didn't even want to think about it, I followed your advice and did tell Hedden and Sam all that had happened there with Ruth. Both of them thought even the suggestion that I was 'different' was absolutely ridiculous. My problems seemed very remote here anyway. I am grateful for that. All together, this vacation did me good. Physically, at least, I feel well again and ready to work. So don't worry about me. Sometimes I think that telling you absolutely everything that is happening to me may not be the best idea, but I promised not to keep anything from you. I miss you.

Your loving daughter,
Adi

Tel-Josef, February 20, 1937

I just received my parents' answer to my disturbed letter of February 5, in which I told them all about my fight with Erika, her defamation of my character, and the ensuing break-up with Ruth. I am much moved by what they had to say. Here are their letters, translated word for word as they wrote them:

Berlin, February 13, 1937

My dear, dearest child—

Your letter arrived today, as punctually as usual. Little one, be strong. Don't take what has happened so tragically. If only I could be with you now to take you in my arms and help ease these moments for you. About the affair itself, my dearest, Vati will write you. Read his lines several times and you will see that his comments will help you a lot. Of course, I can see only your side of the matter. You were sick for so long and are physically all run down. Now you must go out into the sun again. Try to eat, even though you have no appetite. Maybe it would be best if you could get a vacation and visit the Grossmanns in Tel-Aviv. There you would find understanding and friends who could help you physically and mentally. My little one, don't be downcast. Don't take any rash steps and above all, just get well and strong for all that lies ahead of you. After all, you are so very young. Surely much that is beautiful still lies in your future.

Unfortunately, I cannot protect you from disappointments. No one is spared these, but you're right—they do change a person. Please, please, try not to be so sad. In my thoughts I kiss all your tears away.

Always yours,
Mother

And this from my father:

My dear little daughter—

If your father did not have such a tranquil nature, which often drove you up the wall and perhaps is doing so even now, then he would lose heart the same as you do. Instead he says, "It could have been much worse." Then he looks at the actual damage to see what can be glued together and straightened out so that the car will, in spite of the breakdown, pull out of the ditch and get onto the straight road again, with only a few scratches showing. Yours will heal completely or leave, as a memoir, only little scars which will not hurt at all. If I study carefully what you write, I see that the fault lies in exaggeration, on all sides. You yourself, dear Adeline, have recognized clearly your own share of the blame. Your actions were not exactly selfish, but you were thinking only of yourself and Ruth. Ruth is the passive one in this affair, first under your influence and now under Erika's. (I may be wrong in some of what I put down here, my child. Such things are often not as clear from a distance, for a third party, but in the final analysis I think I'm correct.) So—Erika is your opponent. I am not blaming her. She is young, enthusiastic, and sees herself as savior and guardian of the group. She saw how important your personal attachment to Ruth was and, exaggerating as, after all, youth always does, she sees dangers where there are none. And the others? The same. So they make a mountain out of a molehill. That's understandable. Youth is stormy and intolerant. After all, an old judge whose own heart has known sorrow is wiser and more just than a hot-shot young magistrate.

I reconstruct the entire episode this way. Everyone looked on the friendship between the two of you smilingly. Then Adeline, irritated by her long isolation, fretted and grumbled to Erika, who, after all, had made quite a sacrifice for her, so that finally Erika lost patience. Your fight released the tension, and Erika has now stepped out as the warner and rescuer of the group. Adeline, I don't believe that you have unnatural tendencies. You may think so, but these are passing stages of adolescence. With some people they are hardly noticeable, with others more persistent and longer lasting. You already recognize some of this clearly yourself since you write, "Not all that is beautiful and comfortable is right." And with that, one could actually close the book, but I want to help you and advise you.

First of all there is a big hurdle to overcome. Ruth blames you. She advises you to leave the kibbutz. My dear child, these are emotional fits. She hides behind them because she is afraid of a relapse on your part as well as on her own. But don't take it too hard. It will set itself right. Speak openly with Erika, with the Ickels, with Schalom and with Rudi. Tell them quietly about your intention to prove yourself. They cannot carry the responsibility of judging and condemning intolerantly. You are not coming to them pleading but as a member of your community, to which you are responsible, just as much as each of them is. You must have the opportunity and time to prove yourself. When you get to Tel-Aviv, talk it over with Dr. Grossmann. He is a sensible man and a good friend. Above all, hold up your head. Don't despair or do anything rash, like staying in Tel-Aviv and looking for a job there. Dear Adeline, Tel-Josef is your place and you have the duty to continue working on yourself and for your group, to conquer for yourself the place that is due you according to your intelligence and abilities. You will succeed and you will calm down, and one day you will be able to write us that you are happy again because you do have the stuff for that, little one. Just don't throw yourself completely into your emotions, and don't carry your heart on your sleeve. Wait. The day will come when you will smile at the young Adeline. Above all, look after yourself so you will recuperate. When the body is weak, the nerves break down, and when the nerves break down a little thunderstorm looks like a catastrophe. You yourself have recognized the right way to go, so walk then. Only the first few steps are hard. I can do no more than strengthen your self-confidence with the few little pieces of advice I have given.

In my mind I caress your troubled brow, as you so often did for me, and tell you a hundred stories of people, beginning with old Odysseus and King Solomon, and Napoleon and Heine, Spinoza, Rembrandt and Goethe, all of whom were at one time driven to despair by their wild hearts. For all of them the heart at last grew calm and, for some, even happy. So it will for you.

A kiss,
Your father

And this is the man I often had accused of not understanding me, with whom I argued and fought, whom I even accused of insensitivity! How could I?

Tel-Josef, February 27, 1937

Dear Parents,

Thank you so very much for your understanding, your support and advice. It helps me a lot, and as you have seen from my last letter, the days in Tel-Aviv also have served to put things more into perspective. Still, I was a bit uncomfortable about my return to Tel-Josef. I need not have been. During my illness Ruth's parents had made their final move to Israel and settled in Haifa. Ruth left a few days ago to visit them in their new home. So I have not had to confront her. Nobody seems to be interested in Erika's fabrication any more, and I try my best to ignore her.

Last night our group was asked to choose two representatives to participate in a three-day educational conference at Tel-Haj, up in the Galilee, and to my surprise and delight I was one of them. We are to leave day after tomorrow so in my next letter I'll write you about that trip. One more thing. A few days ago Genia said, apropos of nothing, that I would be quite an attractive girl if it were not for my two protruding front teeth.

She told me that several of the children here were having their teeth straightened by a very good orthodontist who came once a month to Ein-Charod to take care of all the kids from these two kibbutzim. She would talk to her about me. I hope something will come of it.

I started working again in the vegetable gardens. The work is hard, but now that I feel good again it seems easier.

Until next week, with much love and many kisses,

Your grateful daughter,
Adi

Tel-Josef, March 3, 1937

Dear Ones,

I have just returned from Tel-Haj. If you look on a map you'll see that it's situated near Metulla, the northernmost outpost of Erez Israel. The area in this Upper Galilee is called Hula and once was nothing but a malaria-infested swamp. Now, thanks to the hard work of the pioneers, the land has been drained and you can see cultivated fields everywhere. The lectures we listened to were designed to fill us with the same spirit that inspired the early pioneers of the Zionist movement. We visited the little cemetery where Trumpeldor and some of the other *shomrim* who lost their lives fighting for these ideals are buried. On the lighter side, it was fun to meet the representatives from all the other Youth Aliyah groups. I even met a girl who was in my class at that awful school I attended in Berlin, just before I went to camp, remember?

But what stands out most for me about this trip was the incident that took place on our return trip, when we had to change busses in Tiberias. We had an hour's wait for our connection, and most of us walked along main street, looking at shops. All of a sudden I heard a commotion, shouting and screaming, and then the sound of shots fired. Within seconds I saw a crowd of Arabs coming toward us. Everyone ducked into the open stalls along the street. I, too, threw myself on the ground, covering my head with my arms, not daring to look up. The rioting Arabs passed by, shooting indiscriminately. I felt some plaster trickling down on my hands. A bullet must have hit the wall above me. Then the sound of more bullets close by. I was sure that we had had it. What did I think in those few seconds? Nothing very dramatic. I remember worrying about what would become of my stamp collection if I died! Isn't that stupid? The sound of the crowd receded and I raised my head. Looking at the other five or six people lying on the ground, my first thought was: "My God! They're all dead!" But in a moment they too got up. None of us was harmed, just a bit shaken up. The Arab disturbances, their rioting against Jewish settlers and English policies, is increasing.

Tonight I'm very tired so I'll close now.

With much love and kisses, yours,

Adi

Tel-Josef, March 19, 1937

After sending this last letter I began to doubt the wisdom of having told my parents about those dangerous moments in Tiberias. I knew that they would worry about my safety, but two weeks later, when I received their answer, I was glad that I had told them because they mentioned that they had read about the incident in the paper. One thing, though, I won't write about is that, due to the increasing number of attacks by Arabs against Jews, we—that is our Youth Aliyah group—are now being trained by some of the kibbutzniks who are also officers in the Haganah, the secret Jewish Defense Force. Three times a week we practice handling a gun and shooting at targets. The cache of rifles which the kibbutz owns, illegally, of course, is well hidden in dug-outs under the ground. Every time we come for practice the weapons are taken out and unwrapped. What a collection they are—Turkish and German rifles from World War I, French and English of a later variety. We learn to handle them all, and to shoot either standing, kneeling or lying down. We learn to take the rifles apart, clean them, and, above all, respect them. After our two weeks' training we, too, will take part in guard duty, in which all kibbutz members participate.

Ruth is back and things are not too easy for me. It's hard to be completely ignored by her, especially when I remember how close we used to be. She and Shalom spend all their free time together. I am seeing more of Hans, who is very supportive of me. I don't believe, though, that he has any inkling of how I feel toward Ruth and, of course, I can't discuss it with him or, for that matter, with anyone else here. My parents are the only ones with whom I can be totally honest.

Tel-Josef, April 5, 1937

My dearest Parents and Edith,

Now Easter and Passover have passed. Your last letter stated that you had snow at Easter while here it's getting very warm again. The rainy season is definitely over. We had an extra day off on Pesach, as it's called in Hebrew, but otherwise there was no special celebration. Once again, though, the older folks (remember, I told you about the parents of some of the kibbutzniks here) observed the holidays with their old traditions.

Lately I've had to put some extra hours in to catch up on my Hebrew studies. Then we finished our Haganah course and now, once every ten days, it's my turn to stand guard during the night. I had my first guard duty two nights ago. I had looked forward to this new experience, but now I dread it. The night seems endless and very dark. I sit in an observation post. It is just a seat surrounded by a three-foot-high brick wall. My job is to keep my eyes peeled for any sound or movement which might indicate approaching Arabs. Then I should fire my rifle, not so much at the enemy but to warn our Shomrim as well as everybody else. I am not afraid, though it is a very strange feeling to have a loaded gun in your hands. It's just that the hours stretched forever and my eyes kept wanting to close. As far as movement and noises were concerned, the night was pitch black and the jackals were howling so loudly that I never would have heard any rustling in the underbrush. Hans, who starts milking at 5:30 A.M., got up an hour earlier to keep me company. Now *that* is more than friendship! I think he's in love with me.

I've also had a few lessons in horseback riding. Peter, another fellow in our group, and I have made friends with two of the mounted policemen from Bet She'an who visit Tel-Josef regularly on their patrol. They invited any of us to come and see them, but so far only the two of us have taken advantage of the invitation. I find I really like horseback riding and intend to see our new friends often. The kibbutz, though, does not approve of such fraternization with the police. To be sure, our new friends, Mike and David, are both Jews, but the other four policemen, including the sergeant in charge, are British, and the few other employees at the station are Arabs. The kibbutzniks have no time for either of these groups, but as long as they don't outright forbid us to go, I'll continue with my riding lessons. Does that sound a bit rebellious? Well, maybe it is. It seems our group is now split into three sections. There are Shalom, Mordechai and Ruth, who lead the conformists. They do everything they are supposed to do and are already looked upon as the new generation of idealistic *chaluzim*. Then there's the second group, to which Hans and I belong. We do some of the things that good pioneers frown upon, like playing popular music, dancing cheek to cheek, talking about city life, and admitting to a longing for something other than the monotonous kibbutz fare. The third group are vacillating followers.

It's time for dinner so I'll close for today. Much love and many kisses.

Yours,

Adi

Tel-Josef, April 15, 1937

The news from home is a mixed bag. My mother works far too much, and I don't believe she's too well. She has a recurrent infection under her fingernails and has had to have several of her fingers lanced. As soon as one heals, another starts. Now the same thing is happening to her toenails. She also cannot make her peace with my being gone. Her letters are still so full of pain about our separation that it hurts me to read them. My father has been brushing up on his engineering skills. He feels theoretically caught up but wishes he could get some practical experience. However, there seems to be no opportunity for this, even if he volunteered his services. So it is all the more remarkable that he did find a job! The firm that hired him sells radium products all over Germany. His job is to lecture, show slides and explain the benefits of radium treatments. The firm pays all his travel expenses and in addition he'll get a percentage of the sales. It is good for his self-esteem to be able to contribute again to the household expenses. Also, he loves traveling and since he lectures only once a day, he has time to wander around the beautiful medieval towns of southern Germany. Mother feels very lonely without him, but from what she writes I can clearly see that both of them have come much closer to each other of late, which makes me happy. I also get the feeling from their letters that they are finally thinking in terms of emigrating. My father's efforts to renew his engineering skills show that he is preparing for a future somewhere else in the world. I know it won't be Palestine. Just to be sure, I asked him in one of my letters what he now thought about Zionism. His answer was pretty much what I had expected. "I see Zionism as a great blessing—a refuge for Jews who could no longer live in their Eastern homelands, Poland, Russia, etc. That it will succeed politically, as some groups wish it to do, I don't believe. Also it seems to me that the population distribution in Palestine is wrong, when I read that of 430,000 Jews living in Palestine, 270,000 live in the big cities. What you people do in Tel-Josef, Ein-Harod, and the three hundred other settlements is surely splendid. What has been done in the Hula area is even heroic. On the other hand, one might be a bit more doubtful about the value of the population on Mount Carmel or in Tel-Aviv. But this I only know through hearsay. Maybe it looks different closer at hand."

There is one more piece of news from home that I have consistently ignored. Several months ago my father wrote that the Economic Assistance of the Jewish Agency, which pays the kibbutz a monthly stipend for me, has been informed that I am not listed in the Jewish Registry. Therefore, they cannot continue to make further payments until they receive evidence of my registration as a Jew. Knowing that I had talked to Rabbi Swarsensky, my father contacted him. Doctor Swarsensky told him that I had seen him only once, had not participated in any religious instruction, and never had been officially accepted into the Jewish community. Therefore, he could not testify that I was Jewish. He recommended that I get such a statement from a rabbi in Palestine. For months now my father has asked me to send him such a statement. So far I have simply ignored his requests, hoping that the entire matter would resolve itself or simply go away. I can't think of anything more embarrassing than going to the kibbutz Council and telling them that I am not really a Jew, at least not officially, and that I'll have to see a rabbi about becoming one! In my parents' last letter my father sounded very upset because the Youth Help informed him that they no longer could be responsible for my upkeep. So I guess I really must do something about this problem. If only I had followed Rabbi Swarsensky's advice I would not be in this predicament now!

Tel-Josef, April 26, 1937

My Dear Ones,
Today, Vati, is your 51st birthday. I hope my birthday wishes arrived on time. How I wish we could celebrate all together, but maybe, if not next year, the year after. This, then, is my main wish for all of us—that we will be reunited in 1939.
Now for the news from here. We have had a few *khamsins*.

These are the hot winds that blow from an easterly direction. They bring the hot, dry air from Arabia and are terribly enervating. They are called *khamsin*, meaning 'fifty,' since they blow about fifty days out of the year. Everyone hates them because they make a person nervous and on edge. They kick up a lot of dust and cover everything with sand. It's hateful to have to work outdoors during one of these winds, but my outdoor career soon may come to an end. I have something else in mind, but I won't tell you until I know more.

Vati, you will be pleased. I finally went to Shmuel, the present chief administrator of our kibbutz. He has made an appointment with the rabbi in Afula. I'm to see him next Wednesday. Last Monday the orthodontist was in Ein-Harod. I went over to see her and had impressions made of my teeth. On her next visit, in May, I'll get my braces. The entire procedure will last between three and four years. I do know that the monthly payments for this are an enormous sacrifice for you and cannot thank you enough for making the treatment possible for me.

Continued on Wednesday

I just came from Afula. We saw the rabbi and Shmuel asked him to write out a declaration attesting to the fact that I am a Jew. The rabbi stroked his beard (he is an Orthodox Jew, the only rabbi available here), shook his head, and finally gave his verdict: "If she was a boy, I could find out very simply, but since she is a girl, how can I tell if she is a Jewish daughter? Now, if you want me to sign such a paper, she has to go into the *mikvah* [ritual bath] and be baptized to make sure she is a Jew." I looked at him in horror. Mind you, he never looked at me. He addressed himself to Shmuel only, and I got my first taste of what it means to be a woman among Orthodox Jews and therefore of secondary importance. Shmuel tried to argue with him, but to no avail. We are to come back next week. By then the rabbi will have prepared all that is necessary for the ceremony. I can't tell you how I hate all this, but by next week I'll be able to enclose the desired affidavit. In the meantime, all my love,

Your loving and grateful daughter,
Adi

Tel-Josef, May 8, 1937

My dearest Family,

   You would never believe what I had to go through to become a Jew! If I were not so embarrassed in front of my group, I would have found the entire procedure hilarious. And a real procedure it was! Let me start at the beginning. Once more Shmuel and I took the train to Afula. Afula is more a village than a town, with just a couple of dirt roads. From the station I could already see the smoke from the *mikvah*, the religious bathhouse. They were heating the water for my baptism. We proceeded to the rabbi's house, where I was handed over to a woman who took me to the *mikvah*, a huge indoor pool, white-tiled all the way up to just below the ceiling. The water was steaming. I was ordered to undress completely and then walk into the pool. I thought it was enough to be covered up to my neck, but no, the woman insisted that I duck under all the way. Three times I had to do this before she let me out. After I had dressed again she led me back to the rabbi, who was praying with three other elders, rocking back and forth, and in between the woman was reporting the success of my immersion and conversion, while I stood there dripping. Nobody had thought of towels. My hair was soaking wet and my clothes stuck to me. I felt better when Shmuel winked at me. He had as little patience with all this rigmarole as I did and was impatient to leave. After considerable praying and headbobbing, the rabbi finally wrote out a letter, which was witnessed by the other three elders and then ceremoniously given to Shmuel, who looked at it in disgust since it was written in Yiddish. He had expected it to be in Hebrew, our official language. There followed quite an argument, but the rabbi would not budge, so we finally had to accept the document, which by this time, having been pulled angrily from hand to hand, looked like anything but an official proclamation. When we left the rabbi we found that a small crowd had gathered in front of his house. They had been speculating about what had happened in the *mikvah* and at the rabbi's. Everyone wanted to see the "new Jewess." Shmuel took me by the hand and we raced as fast as we could to the station. My hair was still wet when we got back to Tel-Josef, and everyone wanted to know how come. No one believed my story. I can understand that. Would you have believed it? Anyway, the enclosed funny-looking letter states that I am now officially a member of the Jewish community. I hope someone can translate it and that the Jewish Agency will be satisfied.

Love and kisses, yours,
Adi

Tel-Josef, May 15, 1937

My dearest Folks,

In my last letter I was so busy telling about my "conversion" that I forgot to mention our May 1 celebration. Of course, everyone had the day off, and the Youth Aliyah groups from both kibbutzim (Ein-Harod and Tel-Josef) paraded and stood together listening to endless speeches. Ben Gurion was supposed to give an address as well, but at the last moment he must have been called away. I did see him, though, on the previous evening in the dining hall at Ein-Harod. He was discussing something very animatedly with a number of kibbutzniks. I guess they, like everyone else, were discussing the Peel Plan, the British proposal to partition Palestine, of which Ben Gurion seems to be in favor, yet many in the Labor Party oppose it. I'm sure you, too, have read about it and, Vati, I'd like to hear your thoughts about this matter. Please write me about it.

Now to the news here. I hinted to you before about a possible change in my occupation. It all started last month when I had to take my work shoes to the shoemaker for new soles. Here I came out of the broiling sun into a pleasant workshop where four men, one of them a trainee from our Youth Aliyah group, sat around a low table, hammering and sewing away. I have always been fascinated watching people work with their hands, and I asked the man in charge if he would mind my watching them a bit. No, of course not. We began to talk, and the longer I stayed, the more I liked what I saw. I began to wonder what it would be like to work here, to learn this trade. That evening I talked with Werner, the cobbler-apprentice. He told me that he had learned a lot in those few months from Dan, the master shoemaker, who was a real great guy, and he advised me to talk to Dan frankly if I really wanted to become a shoemaker. He thought that they had more than enough work to justify employing another helper, but a girl? That he was not sure of. The next day, when I came for my shoes, I broached the subject.

91

Dan, who appears to be a rather deliberate and quiet man, promised to think over my request. He did not seem to doubt that a girl could do the work. He just wanted to be sure that I was serious and would stick with it. I hoped I had convinced him because by that time I had become enthralled with the idea of becoming a shoemaker and was positive that I had finally found my place. I waited impatiently for a decision. Then, three days later, Dan told me that he had made up his mind and would be glad to accept me as a trainee, but I would have to work in rotating shifts with Werner, one week from 8 A.M. to 1 P.M., the next week from 1 P.M. to 6 P.M. I was ecstatic, but Dan warned me that we still had to win the vote of several committees. Oh, how I hate these various councils who sit and decide about every phase of your life! It's the one aspect of communal life that I find hardest to take. Every time you want to make even the smallest change, like getting a different roommate or asking for another room, or job, or even getting married, your request will be studied by a committee which, after due deliberation, will render its verdict. In my case, they didn't come to a quick decision. Most of them didn't believe that being a cobbler or shoemaker was a trade for women, and some of them apparently doubted the seriousness of my request. But Dan, who is one of the older and most respected members of the kibbutz, finally was able to get the committee to agree to a one month's trial period for me. I am to start this coming Monday. So, what do you say to your daughter's becoming a shoemaker? I'm very excited about it.

Lots of love, yours,
Adi

Tel-Josef, May 27, 1937

My dear ones,

I still don't know how you feel about my becoming a shoemaker, but I must tell you, I love it! No more the back-breaking work in the fields with the sun shining on you unrelentingly, no more the feeling of physical inadequacy, no more watching the time, being relieved when work is over and dreading the next day's labor. On the contrary, now I find the clock moves too quickly, and every day I look forward to the next day. I think Dan is quite happy with me. He says I am learning quickly and apparently am good with my hands. The first couple of days I learned to make the heavy, waxed thread used to sew double soles, and I started to use different files for finishing work, etc. Besides Dan and Werner, there are two other men working here. One, Joshua, is a journeyman. He and Dan make up all the new boots, shoes, and sandals for the entire kibbutz. The third man, Rudi, is an old Bavarian who, before he came here, had been a cobbler in some remote little village in the mountains. He speaks the funniest German dialect and not a word of Hebrew. Joshua and he don't like each other and never address each other. Dan tells Rudi what to do in Yiddish, which is not always a success. I'm not sure whether this is due to language difficulties or to Rudi's stubbornness. I suspect the latter because Rudi seems to have difficulty understanding Dan only when it concerns something he doesn't want to do. Dan can't understand any of Rudi's mutterings, but since most of them are not too complimentary, I don't try to translate. Anyway, Rudi, being a cobbler, does all the repair work. Werner and I will eventually learn both repairing and making shoes. Our workshop makes at least one pair of workshoes and one pair of sandals per year, plus one pair of after-work shoes every other year for everyone in the kibbutz. That must come to about eighty new pairs a month. So you can see, we are very busy. Making sandals goes very fast, but all other shoes are made on an individual basis. Dan takes the orders, the measurements, distributes the work, teaches us, and on top of it is the fastest and best worker.

Mutti, don't be afraid that I'll ruin my hands. I've made myself little leather protectors that fit over my thumbs and index fingers. And talking about things that fit, maybe even too tightly, reminds me about my braces. As if I could forget them! Since last Wednesday my mouth is full of wires, one upper and one lower inside brace and one upper outside brace. The inside ones are to widen my jaws to give the teeth more room, and the upper one outside is to push the teeth in. At first I couldn't chew at all and every tooth hurt, but it's already getting better, though I still talk funny, but I'm so glad that my teeth are getting fixed and I do want to thank you again for doing all this for me.

This letter, then, has nothing but good news. I know that will make you very happy too.

Lots of love and kisses, yours,

Adi

Tel-Josef, June 7, 1937

Dear Vati, Mutti, and Edith,

Today, Mutti, is your birthday. I hope my birthday letter reached you in time. I was so sorry to hear that your cold developed into a nasty bronchitis but hope that by now you feel much better and won't go back to work until you feel one hundred percent well. Relapses are even harder to get over. This is your first birthday that we're not celebrating together. I wonder what you will be doing. Are you having friends over for *Kaffee und Kuchen*? Are you going to a movie? What did you get from Vati and Edith? I want to know every little detail so that I can imagine being there.

Now to your last letter. Both of you question the wisdom of my having exchanged agriculture for a trade, and, for a woman, in an unheard-of field. But look at it this way. I never liked field work and I really love what I'm doing now. You doubt that there is a future in it for me. Well, probably not, but at the moment I'm thinking only of my time here. Three quarters of a year has already passed. I have another year and a quarter to go, and the time will pass much faster for me doing something that makes me happy. After all, who knows what I will be doing when the two years are up. The only thing I do know for sure is that I won't stay on in a kibbutz. So the work in the vegetable gardens would have prepared me as little as shoemaking will for my future.

Last week I was on the afternoon shift and so had to miss my classes. I don't really mind because I learn more from Dan than I do from our teachers. Dan is originally from Poland. He is entirely self-educated but knows more about Jewish and Russian literature than anyone I have ever met. He also edits Tel-Josef's weekly newspaper, and all during the day people come in to ask him for advice or discuss current problems with him.

I wish I were with you today, but don't be downhearted, Mutti. Soon we'll all be together again.

All my love,
Adi

P.S. Mutti, you wrote in your last letter that I must be the one in our group who is getting sick most often. No, not at all. Two in our group have had typhus and were sick for many weeks. Quite a few had *pappataci,* and one boy had to be sent away from here because his whole body became covered with boils. We have had broken arms, fingers, pulled tendons, and much more. So, you see, I'm just average.

From my father's letter of June 8, 1937:

"The local Jewish newspapers write a great deal about the Peel Report and the probable partition of Palestine, and how they snap at each other! History repeats itself. Now we have England's 'astute' statesmanship and the intolerance of the Jewish parties, on the one side Weizmann, on the other side Jabotinski. Two thousand years ago the 'astute' statesmanship was Rome's, and in the burning Jerusalem the same bigoted splinter groups fought each other. Well, you'll probably say, I don't understand the problem, being so far away from the events. But I do understand one thing: There is no such thing as one hundred percent perfect solutions. All there can be, always, is compromise. If partition should come now, it would be a bitter pill for many, but it would be a shrewd move and, probably, the right one. As the report states: It is unthinkable that 400,000 Jews should be handed over to Arab domination, and it is equally untenable to deliver one million Arabs over to Jewish control. Whether an autonomous Jewish state is permanently in the interest of worldwide Jewry, or whether an extensive settlement under the English protectorate or within the British Dominion is preferable—about these options one can be of divided opinion."

Last week was so busy that my letters home were very short. The reason is the grape harvest, when all available hands are needed. Werner and I had to join the happy crowd too. I say happy because everyone is in a holiday mood during this harvest. The trucks take us out at 5 A.M. and we arrive at our vineyards at the foot of Mount Gilboa a half hour later. Though the sun is up, the air still feels deliciously cool and fresh. Each of us is given a pair of garden scissors and assigned a row. Then we begin cutting the clusters of grapes. We must be careful to clip only the ripe ones. We are supposed to taste the bottom grape of each cluster and then spit it out because too much grape eating gives you the runs. Most of us, though, consume quite a quantity of these sweet, luscious grapes, especially first thing in the morning before the breakfast wagon comes. I love these first few hours when the grapes are still covered with dew and the heat is not yet unpleasant. The grapes are put in large tin cans, which we take back to the end of the row where they are picked up by another team who carry them to the packing shed. There they are packed into wooden crates, sealed, and eventually picked up by trucks for shipment. The pickers, the runners, the packers, the crate makers, the truck loaders, each team depends on the other and everyone has a good time doing his share. At first I resented being taken away from the shoemakery, but soon I was caught up in the general elation. The breakfast wagon arrives between 7 and 8 A.M. and we take about a half hour off. By 9:30 it is getting hot, but the tempo does not slacken. We usually work until 1 P.M., when the truck comes with the midday meal and takes our group back on its return trip. The others work until late afternoon. Still, we put in seven hours every day. Tomorrow will be our last day, and I'm looking forward to getting back to the shoemaker's last.

Tel-Josef, June 19, 1937

My birthday, and punctually the afternoon mail brought congratulations from home. I was very moved by their lines. Some even brought tears to my eyes, as when my mother wrote, "I can go back from year to year and recall each one of your birthdays until your hour of birth, which made Vati and me so very happy since finally my most ardent desire was fulfilled through you. And in all these years you have been the realization of my wishes and you still are and will remain so."

And then I had to smile when my father wrote, "Seventeen years ago I had imagined the future very differently, and if someone had told me that I, at my present age, would sit in a furnished room and you would till the soil in the land of milk and honey, I would have told him to take a cold shower." Then he continued in his usual optimistic way that, "though everything turned out differently than planned, the unexpected also has its charm." For the first time he mentioned that perhaps, for me, the way things turned out might be for the best. How wonderful they both are and how I miss them! I must try, though, to be more careful and not mention any wishes because they try to fulfill them all, at I don't know what sacrifice to themselves.

After dinner we had quite a party. Everyone came with some little gift. Hans brought his record player and we danced and sang until way after midnight.

Tel-Josef, August 3, 1937

I just received a letter from my father in answer to my inquiry about his thoughts regarding the future of Palestine. It was dated Berlin, July 27, 1937. He writes:

"You asked me what I think of the future of Palestine. I see very dark for it. In the first place, I foresee an economic recession. Investors will fear that their capital will be endangered because of the continual riots in the country. In the second place, I fear that eventually England will give up its mandate and withdraw from Palestine. How did I come to these conclusions? It's very simple. The hate between the Arabs and Jews is not new but age old. You can find its mythical origin already mentioned in the Bible when the old sheik Abraham casts out Hagar and her son Ishmael in favor of his son Isaac. A people always remembers the wrongs suffered by its ancestors.

"Furthermore, today England sees the impossibility of a peaceful agreement between Jews and Arabs, farmers and nomads, and, like a physician, she makes the painful incision, because the operation is urgent. However, whether the operation will save the patient, even a good physician cannot predict. Aware of the necessity to forcefully and conclusively end a situation which has become unbearable, England is looking in two directions. She wants to keep the sympathies of the world, mainly the American world with its influential Jewish population, as well as those of a few million Muslims living in her dominions. The result is a solution which will please neither: an autonomous Jewish state, albeit a very small one, and an Arab Palestine, but not all of Palestine! All the yelling, all the protests and proclamations will not change England's mind, but I fear the Jews don't comprehend that yet. They seem to have little understanding for realistic political necessities. They live in ideologies, and their history is a chain of missed opportunities, from Cyrus to Alexander to Augustus, always. A French proverb states, 'Chacun à les défauts de ses qualités' [One has the faults based on one's good qualities.] The good Jewish qualities—intellect, critical ability, the faculty to reason abstractly—have misled them into isolating themselves, again and again, from other cultures and into being intolerant and overbearing. Over time, millions have split off and assimilated into other cultures, fertilizing them. The rest remained in tragic isolation. It is the

97

old struggle between Flavius Josephus, who fervently wishes that his compatriots become good Roman citizens of Jewish persuasion, and Dr. Jochanan, who asks Titus for 'just a very small but independent university.'

"I feel that the Jews lack political sense and their strength is now being dissipated through quarreling among the different parties. Assuming that the Peel Report will, with perhaps a few changes, become a reality, what will be its consequences? Immigration to the extent envisioned by the Zionists will be impossible since much of the land will go to the Arabs. Thus, investment opportunities will shrink and new money will not be easily available. The economic outlook will not be encouraging."

My father's pessimistic evaluation of the present situation was a surprise to me, especially since he is usually such an optimist. Also, his opinions are very different from those we get here, which had led me to believe that the poor Arab *fellahin* are being exploited by their absentee landowners. Once we help them to become educated, they will see how much better off they would be in peaceful co-existence with the Palestinian Jews, who have dried the swamps, made the desert bloom, introduced industry, and brought a higher living standard to the land, from which the Arabs, too, would profit. As far as England is concerned, we feel that her sympathies lie entirely with the Arabs and we can expect little from her sense of justice.

Tel-Josef, August 10, 1937

My dearest Folks,

Thank you so much for the snapshots from your last outing and the enlargement from the little portrait of the three of you. I'll ask Hans to make me a frame for it.

We had quite a bit of excitement here. Golda Meir was in Ein-Harod and made a quick visit over to Tel-Josef. And do you know what they showed her here, among, of course, other things? A brand new field of work for women—shoemakery! And who was the shining example of this innovation? Me! I was so surprised by the sudden pride with which the very same people who only a short time ago told me that this trade is not for girls now introduced me to Golda that I was totally tongue-tied and only grinned inanely at her. Incidentally, we are very busy now. We have finished almost all the new sandals and are now starting on work boots. Dan says that we must finish three hundred pairs of these before the rainy season sets in. As before, I love the work and am learning a lot.

You ask me how my Ivrit (Hebrew) is coming along. I am quite fluent in speaking now. Writing is coming along, too, but reading is still very hard because newspapers and books are all printed without vowels. You also ask about my braces. I am quite used to them by now. The only time my teeth hurt is after Dr. H.'s monthly visits, when she tightens the braces. Then it hurts for a day or two, but I don't mind. I'm so glad to have this done. Won't you be surprised when you see me with straight teeth, a few inches taller, suntanned and slimmed down! But I'll still be your same loving daughter.

Adi

Tel-Josef, December, 1937

During the next few months my letters did not contain any memorable news. Life in the kibbutz had become routine. I was happy in my work. Our afternoon instruction had become a bit monotonous. I still avoided Ruth but was busy with other friends in our group. My riding lessons in Bet She'an stopped because once again the country was going through a period of intensified riots and we left the kibbutz as little as possible. It must have been the beginning of September when I began to suffer from an itchy rash between my toes. The nurse treated it with a salve which, if anything, made it worse. Finally it became so bad that I could neither work nor sleep and my toes were one open, oozing sore. The itching was so bad that I often attacked my toes with the rasp I used at work. Once again it was Genia who talked to the doctor and he made a series of appointments for X-ray treatments for me in Haifa. I did not write home about any of this, not only because my mother always worries so about my health, but also because this time there would have been the additional fear of the Arabs, whose attacks were increasing daily. All in all, I had to make six trips to Haifa. The busses were never attacked directly, but the driver had to proceed very cautiously, watching the road for any irregularity which might indicate a hidden fuse or bomb. Twice it probably was one or the other because we all had to get off the bus, which then made a detour and picked us up at a point further down the road, to which we had walked. Two passengers stayed behind to warn all traffic about the unexploded device until it could be defused.

The X-ray treatments were a wondrous thing—the dark room with the enormous machine that descends, zeroing in on such a small part of your anatomy, the very short exposure, the brevity of the entire treatment, and the miraculous results that were very evident after a few weeks. Within two months my feet were completely healed.

I am now well into my second year at Tel-Josef and the group is beginning to talk about future plans. The major objective of our education here has always been the preparation for founding a new kibbutz. The usual outcome of a youth group such as ours is that a nucleus of sixty to seventy percent of the original group moves out to found a new community. The remaining thirty percent have either formed attachments to other kibbutzim or prefer to live on a *moshav*, where they farm their own piece of land, or they leave the land to try their luck in the city. I have no plans yet. All I know is that I don't want to go with this or any other group to found a new settlement. If I continue to live in Palestine, it will be in the city. But much depends on my parents. They still don't seem to search aggressively for a new home outside of Germany. Though I hear of many people leaving there, our entire family continues to live much as they used to. Things have even been looking up a bit for my parents. Since my father is now making some money, Mother works only part time. He seems to enjoy his new job traveling around the country, giving speeches. They have time for leisure, take little day trips, go to the movies, the zoo, and the botanical gardens, and, of course, spend much time playing with Edith. Uncle Hans bought himself a new car and often the two families go on picnics together. Vati proposed that my mother come to visit me, but she writes that she'll be strong and work another nine months until I come back to see them. So all is on hold until my two years are up and I'll return home. Should this not be possible, my parents write that we'll meet some other place, like Italy or Switzerland. Apparently if one has the money, this is not difficult. Uncle Hans and Aunt Antoinette visit my cousin Jean, who studies in Italy, regularly. Tante Trudchen, Father's sister, just returned from a vacation on the Riviera, and Hedden Grossmann has been back to Germany twice during the last year and a half to visit her sisters in Berlin. Sometimes I wonder if people here don't exaggerate the danger for Jews living in Nazi Germany. There is one more thing that continues to please me. Apparently my mother and father really have found their way back to each other. My mother writes that if it were not for missing me so much, she could be one hundred percent happy again, that her long years of unhappiness and waiting are over. I am so glad for them.

Tel-Josef, March, 1938

The new year has not brought many changes to Tel-Josef. The political situation is about the same. Arab riots continue and we are still called on to do guard duty. Though I feel more comfortable now handling a gun, I still hate the lonely nights when every little sound magnifies itself against the surrounding silence and time fools you again and again. You are sure that half an hour has passed, and when you finally look at your watch, not more than four or five minutes have elapsed. So far we have not had any further attacks on our kibbutz. As a matter of fact, some of the bedouins have returned and pitched their tents just above our water tower. As is their habit every year, they immediately extended an invitation to any of us who would like to visit them. Of course, they expect some present in return for their hospitality. Our teacher, Nechemia, who speaks Arabic fluently and knows this particular nomad family from previous years, took several of us to call on them. Apparently they had seen us climbing up and were expecting us because the entire family was there to greet us. We were ushered into the tent and seated on a rather dirty carpet. Actually, it was more than just one tent, more like several adjoining ones, so that it gave the impression of several rooms, but since the tents extended toward the back, where it was dark inside, all I could make out were blankets and rolled-up carpets. It was difficult to say how many belonged to the family because there was much coming and going, but I believe there were five or six men, even more women, and at least a dozen children. The women served us some kind of sweet tea, then went to sit by the entrance to the tent, surrounded by their children. They were not veiled but wore black robes. We were fascinated by their tattooed faces and silver jewelry hanging in many strands from their ears and noses. They, in turn, pointed at our short hair. They giggled a lot but did not speak to us. The men wore loose brown caftans and the usual *keffiyah*. Our new neighbors were very friendly. We gave the men the cigarettes we had brought along, smiled at each other, laughed about jokes we did not understand, and felt awkward but not uncomfortable. After several cups of tea and many salaams, we left. These are not the Arabs we fear. The latter are shadowy figures who attack at night, probably inhabitants of the neighboring towns and villages who, incited by fanatics, want us off the land at any cost.

In February we had quite a scare. Shalom, who is Ruth's present boyfriend, caught typhus. Within the next ten days two more in our group fell ill, but this time I was spared. They are all three on the mend now, though Chawa lost all her hair, but that, too, is growing back. We have finished our winter quota of working shoes. The last few weeks we have been making 'good' shoes. I have been learning the cobbler's trade, putting new soles and heels on old shoes, mending and patching uppers. I don't mind this at all. I rather enjoy giving an old pair of shoes a new life and making it shine. While life continues peacefully here in its daily monotony, I do worry about my parents. Not that anything definite has happened to them, and maybe it's only my imagination, but the tone of their letters seems to be changing. There is no more mention of the pleasant little outings, the visits to the movies, to the zoo, etc. Instead, my mother writes, the topic of conversation everywhere they go is—so and so has left for the States or South America. So and so is about to leave for Palestine or Shanghai. This one has just received his immigration papers to Australia, while another family is still waiting. And for the first time she asks, "What will become of us?" My father keeps studying and reviewing his old textbooks, trying to refresh his knowledge of engineering. Two months ago all Jewish doctors were informed that they no longer could treat patients on insurance or welfare. This means that most Jewish physicians no longer can make a living from their profession. Uncle Hans had been corresponding with a cousin of ours in New York and is expecting an affidavit soon. Once in the States he will have to go through a two-year internship, and then he can open a practice. My father believes that for himself there are no openings in the US. "America employs young people only, and at age fifty you are considered old and over the hill," he writes. I don't know whether or not this is true. In any case, it's the first time I heard him consider emigration. In spite of all this, my mother mentions my homecoming, if even for just a visit, and counts the weeks until my two years are up. My little sister, though, seems to be perfectly happy. She loves her school, is always the best in her class, and has many friends. I was very touched when my mother described her birthday celebration. She was nine years old this month, and Mutti put on a show for her similar to what she used to do for me in the 'good years.' In order to have enough play room, my father moved out most of the furniture from their one-room living quarters. My mother took a day off from work. Twelve of Edith's classmates were invited, games were played, little prizes distributed, ice cream consumed.

Many of the families of Edith's classmates seem to be very wealthy. Mother tells of Edith's being invited to an estate outside of the city or a chauffeured limousine calling for her. I marvel that there are still Jewish families of such wealth living in Germany, and what is even more puzzling, that they continue their lifestyle as before. As far as

Edith is concerned, she does not seem to be impressed by such outer trappings. From her letters she appears to be a healthy and happy child. Since she has been left alone often, when my mother works, she has become very self-reliant and also quite a help to my mother in their household.

My own thoughts go round in circles. Will I go home in September? Will I be allowed to return to Germany? What will I do with my future? To be a shoemaker here in Tel-Josef is one thing, but it is still not a trade accepted for women outside and, anyway, I don't believe I could earn a decent living with it. And what about my parents? Are they considering leaving? Will they be able to leave? Where would they go? Would we all go together—to wherever? I must be patient, which is hard for me. I suddenly feel quite insecure. I must try to concentrate more on my daily tasks instead of trying to decipher the uncertain future.

Tel-Josef, May, 1938

I am very worried about my parents. The change that I had felt only vaguely now has become an obvious and urgent search for refuge anywhere in the world. Every letter talks about another possibility. My father mentions Persia and Turkey, then Chile, Shanghai, Australia. In his last letter he even wonders if there are any possibilities for him in Palestine. I immediately made inquiries but was told that, since I am still a non-self-supporting minor, I cannot sponsor them. It breaks my heart to read my mother's lines. She is beginning to realize that I may not see them in a few months, but she consoles herself with the thought that there will be a place where all of us will live together, some time in the future. And my father now leaves no stone unturned. He has made connections with a Jewish engineering society. They advised him to concentrate on roadbuilding and feel sure that he can get a visa to Chile as an engineer. He has reestablished a connection with cousins who have lived in Australia for two generations. He has approached our cousin in America. Surely one of these avenues will work out. I had to smile at my mother's remark. She says she is confused about which foreign language to learn. One day it's English, then Spanish, then English again. Both at once are impossible for her to learn, she says. So, for the moment, she'll wait until she knows for sure where they'll go. God, I hope we'll all know soon.

On the lighter side. It's been about a year since I was baptized into the Jewish faith and the rabbi of Afula wrote out an affidavit to that effect. I had postponed and postponed this step, procrastinating for weeks until finally, upon my father's urgent appeals, I had acted. Well, now it seems that none at the Jewish Agency could decipher the rabbi's Yiddish handwriting! They shook their heads, filed the paper, the contents of which no one quite understood, nodded, and seemed satisfied. And for this I had to go through all that trouble and bother!

Tel-Josef, July, 1938

Beginning in June I had a week's vacation, which once again I spent in Tel-Aviv with the Grossmanns. I did not feel too well after my arrival and, sure enough, on the second day I woke up with a high fever and aching all over. Doctor G. diagnosed it as an attack of *pappataci* fever. I was really out of it for a few days, and when finally my temperature was normal again, I felt very weak. Doctor G. called Tel-Josef and asked them to leave me in their care for another two weeks, or at least until I had regained my strength. The kibbutz agreed and I began a wonderful period of recuperation. Every morning Hedden and I went to the beach. We swam and sunned until noon. Then home for lunch and a rest, sitting on the balcony, reading or talking. We drank iced coffee by the liter and I consumed pounds of my favorite food— halva. I was back in Tel-Josef in time for my birthday, my eighteenth. As usual my friends gave me a great party. Even Nechemia and Genia as well as Judith and Ruth, our other two teachers, came visiting. At the stroke of midnight four of the fellows began to serenade under my bedroom window. I could not quite get into the spirit of it all. My usual birthday letter from home had arrived a day early and in it my father stated quite definitely that he did not think it wise for me to come home in September. Since he did not go into any further detail, I assume that circumstances there have deteriorated and he would be afraid for me if I returned. Still, he is hopeful to find a new home for all of us, somewhere, soon.

Tel-Josef, August, 1938

Only five more weeks and our two-year Youth Aliyah will be over. Our group has now decided to go a third year on *Hachsharah* to Kibbutz Raanana. There they will be full-fledged members of the kibbutz and learn all the additional skills needed to start a new settlement. Of course, not everyone will go. Several will join their parents in Haifa, Jerusalem, and other places in this country. One boy will emigrate to the United States. Hans Loeb will share a farm with his older brother, not far from Haifa. Ruth is marrying a fellow from our neighboring kibbutz, Bet Hashita, and is going to live there. All in all, twenty-eight are going to Raanana. I have decided to join them, for the following reasons: Raanana is not far from Tel-Aviv. This will give me the opportunity to look around there for a job. Also, the shoemaker in Raanana sent word that he has enough work for a helper so there would be a job for me. I still have much to learn and maybe I could complete my apprenticeship there. And one more reason: I don't really know how to proceed on my own, having no money, no place to live, and no job. It will be easier all around if I stay with my group, at least for a few months. Sonya and Reni, my present roommates, have decided much the same. So we hope we can stay together.

The news from home is depressing. My mother writes again how everyone talks about nothing but emigration—where, when, how. Visas, affidavits, and passports are the main topics. Uncle Hans has received his affidavit and quota number and will be leaving for the USA on October 8. Aunt Antoinette and Mimi will follow him later. My father is working hard on some drawings which he intends to submit with his application for a job in his old field as a civil engineer. He is quite hopeful. At the moment he does not have a job so, once again, Mutti works overtime to make ends meet. Oh, how I wish that a way would open and they could get out!

Raanana, September 23, 1938

Ten days ago we moved to Raanana and my first impression of this kibbutz is not favorable. The people in Tel-Josef were far friendlier and everyone was always ready to help us. Here we are treated like a bunch of newcomers that nobody really wanted. Most of our group work in a nearby factory. The money they earn goes, of course, to the kibbutz or is being set aside for their future homestead. I am working in the shoemakery. Actually that is far too fancy a word to describe this tiny hole in the wall in which David and I work. We don't make any new shoes but repair old ones so I'm not learning anything. Still, from what I hear, it's more pleasant to work here than in the factory. I don't have to leave at 6 A.M. in the truck and come home at 5 P.M. My hours are from 7:30 A.M. to 3:30 P.M., and I eat in our dining hall instead of having to take sandwiches to work. Our lodging is quite a problem. We are being moved around all the time. First I shared a tent with two others, then a room with three women I didn't know. Now, thank goodness, I'm in a room with Sonya, Reni, and Shulamit. Last Saturday I spent in Tel-Aviv visiting the Grossmanns. I had no money for the bus so I hitchhiked into town. It's only a twenty-minute drive and very easy to get a ride. Next time I'll try to get a day off during the week so that I can start looking around for a job.

Raanana, November 12, 1938

The whole country is beside itself over the fate of the Jews in Germany. The newspapers are full of reports about the pogrom. The headlines shout: *Reichskristallnacht,* "Every synagogue in the country burned down or damaged," "Jewish store windows smashed, businesses plundered," "Thousands of Jews killed!" The ostensible cause of this outbreak was the act of a young Jew who killed a German official in Paris. (His parents had been deported to Poland.) In retaliation the Nazi government provoked and orchestrated these terrible acts. All this happened on the night of the ninth of November. I am terribly worried and am waiting more anxiously than ever for mail. It is ironic that only a few weeks ago my mother wrote that they were all breathing easier now that the Munich agreement had been signed and war had been averted.

Raanana, November 21, 1938

A letter from home, dated November 14! Thank goodness, my parents are all right. But, as relieved as I am to hear from them, I'm also frustrated because they say nothing about the terrible events of 'Crystal Night.' All my father says is that he is now happy that long ago I decided to go to Palestine. He still hopes to see us all reunited, but in any case he will try everything he can to get my sister Edith out. He also mentions that, though his engineering drawings are finished, there is now no point in taking them to the employment office. As usual, he closes with a positive note, but between the lines I read a resignation that I did not find there before. What worries me even more, there was not the usual long letter from my mother but just a short, though, of course, very loving note.

Raanana, December 14, 1938

I like it less and less here in Raanana, but my thoughts now are not primarily about my job or even my future, but rather about my parents. Since *Kristallnacht* I have had regular mail, but their letters give few specific details. My mother does mention that she is very sad because she can no longer go to the movies since this was the only diversion she could afford. It had allowed her to escape the present and, for a few hours each week, live in a pleasant fantasy world. From what we hear and read here, the Nazis are issuing one decree after another, each one designed to humiliate and restrict Jewish lives. Jews are forbidden to go to theaters, concerts, museums, libraries, amusement parks. They cannot use swimming pools, ice rinks, beaches. They are not allowed to walk on certain streets. All their driver's licenses have been confiscated, and on and on. What will be next? There must be a way to get my parents out, and as quickly as possible! But what can I do ? I wrote to them that I'm sure they could find jobs in either Haifa or Tel-Aviv, but the difficulty, of course, is getting a certificate. The British are maintaining a very tight quota and are not about to open the doors any wider.

The next letters from my parents showed an increasing sense of urgency. The following are excerpts from their letters:

Berlin, December, 1938

Vati: "If I could get an affidavit to the USA, it would still take two years because there is such a long waiting list. So I have to try to go somewhere else first for those two years. But where? One hopes that at least some countries will open their gates a little."

Mutti: "We are leaving no stone unturned to get Edith out. Maybe she could go to a children's home abroad or to a family. I would try to get a job, maybe near her, as a housekeeper or looking after children. If only I don't have to separate from Edith! Though I cannot stand the thought of having to separate from Vati either. I don't know how to live without him."

Vati: "The most important thing now is to get Mutti and Edith out. Maybe there will be, there *must* be, another way than the one into the ghetto. What do you think about Palestine? How could we get Edith there?"

Vati: (a week later) "That Mutti wrote to Dr. J. in England, you know already. He answered that it will be very difficult to find a position for her because there now is an over-supply of household help and governesses. He will, however, try hard and asked us to send him her references. Edith has been registered for emigration to England. Your ideas about getting her into a home in either Haifa or Tel-Aviv appeal to us very much. Keep trying and whatever comes up first, we'll do. Edith, who was very enthusiastic about England, is now just as excited about your plans. She is, after all, a real child and whatever is mentioned last has the charm of the new for her. First she cried that she had to leave home. Now she can hardly wait to go. So much for the plans for Mutti and Edith. I myself have registered for the French colonies. I think of Madagascar. Further in progress is our application to Australia. Uncle Hans is trying for an affidavit for us to the USA, but that will, as I wrote you before, take two years before your place on the quota comes up. If you can come up with anything there, try it. Somewhere in the world there ought to be some possibility for me, working in my former profession as an engineer on bridges, roads, railroads, or dams and locks."

On December 20, I had the usual detailed letter from my mother. She sounds sad because once again there will be a Christmas without me. Still, she is trying to face the uncertain future valiantly, keeping up her spirits for Edith's sake. Apparently she now has more time to spend with Edith because suddenly everyone who can is leaving. Of her three work-places, one family left last week, and one will be leaving shortly so that she'll have to look for new employment. Vati added only two sentences: "Cousin Katz from New York answered that he can give no more affidavits. Furthermore, he does not think I could find a job in the USA."

But then, when it all seemed to look hopeless, I received this news from home, dated December 30, 1938:

"We had a letter from our cousin in Australia, who says that he's very happy to sponsor us and give the necessary guarantees for us. I'll answer him today and will fill out all the forms he mailed us. He writes he has no doubt I can find a job there and he looks forward to welcoming us with open arms. Naturally, we are continuing to follow up on the other possibilities too—my application for a visa to France and its colonies, and your efforts for us in Palestine, and Edith's and possibly Mother's emigration to England."

I could not have wished for a better Christmas or New Year's present. It is not just that a new door has been opened, but this seems more hopeful than all the other avenues, and the tone of our Australian relatives sounds warm, even eager to have us. Above all, we could all be together there.

3. TEL-AVIV

Tel-Aviv, January, 1939

During my last two visits I have talked a lot to the Grossmanns about moving to Tel-Aviv. They said that I could stay at their apartment until I found a job and could support myself. I had planned to find a job first and then move, but it was impossible to look for work during the few hours I got off from Raanana. So I moved to Tel-Aviv right after New Year's and spent the first week of 1939 trying to find a job. I followed ads in the paper, but there were very few. I applied as household help, salesgirl, as a maid in hotels, and as a waitress in restaurants. Everywhere it was the same—sorry, we have no openings. Here you have to know someone who has a friend or relative who knows of someone who needs someone. This system is called "protect-cia" and, without it, it's impossible to get anywhere. At the end of my second week in town, through one of the Grossmann's neighbors, I got a job as a general assistant in a child care center. Unfortunately, it was only for a week while the permanent girl was on vacation. Then, yesterday, when I went to the grocery store, the owner was talking to a customer and I heard him mention that he needed some help. I immediately offered my services and was told to report this morning. So today was my first working day at the Wager's store. My hours are from 8 A.M. to 7 P.M., with one hour off for lunch. It's a ten-hour day and not an easy one at that. The grocery store is brand-new, light, and clean, like everything here in Tel-Aviv. Mr. and Mrs. Wager, immigrants from Germany, do most of the serving behind the counter. If they have any difficulty with Ivrit then I have to translate, but about seventy-five percent of the clientele in this area are German Jews. My job, at least for the moment, consists of running and cleaning. Fetch the can from over there! Bring in another case of rice! Fill the sack with flour! Clean the cheese knives! Wash the shelves! Throw out the trash! Take the old leaves off the lettuce! Wash the carrots! I don't have time to catch my breath, but I hope that, once I get used to the job, it will be easier.

The news from home is, at the moment, more cheerful. My parents had another letter from the Australian cousin, who states that, if all goes well, they should have their entrance permission in about six to eight weeks. As soon as the papers arrive, my father will apply for their passports and book passage. This may take another couple of months, but they are confident that by May or June they will be on their way. My mother is looking forward to the long, exciting trip and all the opportunities in that new land. She is sure I'll be happy there, too, and writes about nothing but the wonderful future we'll soon be sharing together. The three of them now are eagerly learning English.

Australia! What a strange thought. Somehow I had always pictured us united somewhere in Europe or America. I had not even known that we had relatives in Australia. I'm trying to read as much as I can about this, to me, at least, totally unknown continent. Our relatives live in Brisbane, and from what I've found out so far, it must be a very nice city. Opportunities for young people apparently are limitless. Everything I'm finding out about Australia I like. It's just that I don't see us there yet. I don't know why not.

Tel-Aviv, February, 1939

I hate my job as a grocery clerk. Mister W. is a terrible boss. He resents every second I am not fully occupied. The moment I stop for a drink of water or to use the toilet he yells for me. The work itself is very tiring too. Besides cleaning, shelving, wrapping, etc., I now also have to deliver goods when the boy whose job it is gets too busy. The hours are so long that I'm exhausted when I finally get home. And 'home' is not much of a place to relax in either. When I first arrived here I slept in the den, but last week a relative of Dr. Grossmann's arrived from Lithuania and since she is much older than I, I had to give up my couch and am now sleeping on a mattress on the floor in the living room. This means that I can't go "to bed" just any time but have to wait until everyone is ready to retire. I must find other living arrangements and a different job, but both at the same time will be impossible because how can I pay rent if I don't have a regular income? In other words, if I move I must continue at the Wagers and I don't believe I can stand that very much longer. Besides, as long as I work such long hours, how can I look for another job?

No further news from Australia, but something amazing has happened as far as Edith is concerned. I must go back a long way to ex-

110

plain it. In 1910 my mother, who was then twenty-one, spent a year in England. At that time a year abroad was considered a kind of 'finishing school' for young ladies. She lived in London with a family by the name of Frank. Mr. Frank was German, his wife English. After my mother returned to Germany, they kept in touch with each other until World War I. After the war—my mother had married in the meantime—a letter arrived from Mrs. Frank telling that her husband had been interned during the war and because he was German, they had lost everything and were having a very hard time. Could my parents help them in some way? My father agreed to get Mr. Frank started in Berlin. The family came over and, with my father's help, they soon prospered again. (I remember visiting them when I was a little girl.) Some time during the Depression the Franks decided to go back to England and my mother lost touch with them. Two weeks ago my mother wrote me that she had received a phone call from Mrs. Frank, who was in Berlin for a few days. She wanted to know if there was anything she could do to help getting, if not my parents, at least the children out of Germany. My mother told her that I was already in Palestine and my sister had been registered for the children's transport to England, but that they had not heard anything further and assumed that it took some time to find a suitable place for Edith in England. Mrs. Frank told mother that she herself was too old to take a ten-year-old to live with her, but that, immediately upon her return, she would try to find a family willing to take my sister. My father welcomes the idea. He believes it will be summer before they can leave for Australia, so this will give Edith a good chance to learn English. He writes that most mothers would be relieved to have this opportunity for their child, but not Mutti! She cannot bear the thought of separating from her little one too, even if only for a few months. I feel so sorry for Mother and I wonder if this separation is really necessary. On the other hand, what if the Australian plans don't materialize? Then it would be better to know that Edith is safely out of Germany.

Tel-Aviv, March, 1939

A lot has happened to me during the past few weeks. The last day of February I quit my job. I had had it with Mr. W. I had charged a customer twenty-five cents too little, whereupon Mr. W. screamed at me in front of several customers. This was the last straw. I took off my apron and walked out. When I told Hedden Grossmann about it, her only response was, "And how are you going to pay for your food now?" Well, I was in the mood for walkouts. I would leave her house-

111

hold too, as soon as I could. I was tired of sleeping on the floor and having every slice of bread I consumed counted. So the next few days I pounded the pavement. I went from store to store along Ben-Yehuda Street. Nothing. No help needed anywhere. But at Mugrabi Square I ran into Sonya, my old roommate from Tel-Josef and Raanana. Since I had left there two months ago, I had not been in touch with any of my group. Sonya brought me up to date about some of the others. She herself had left Raanana two weeks after I did. Her move had been precipitated by hearing from a former classmate who was now living in Tel-Aviv. She had visited this classmate and at her house had met a young fellow with whom it was love at first sight. He had found a job for her in a household as well as a room not far from where I had met her. She insisted that I come and see it and meet her new boyfriend. I did so the next day. Gideon (he used to be Georg) is a very nice guy. I was a bit down after my futile search for work, but his good mood, his open face with its happy smile, was infectious. It turned out to be a lovely evening. The next day Sonya and I met again for a cup of coffee. She told me that she and Gideon had talked over my situation and they both felt that I should move in with her. All I had to do was agree and Gideon would look for a bed or couch for me. As for rent, we could settle that when I had a job. Could I have asked for more? This was the answer to all my problems. Gideon did find a couch for me—he didn't say where—and after a few days I discovered it had some bedbugs, but we took care of that. Anyway, I was happy to have my own bed and to be with friends my own age again, because Sonya and Gideon had, as I soon found out, a whole circle of friends.

My luck seemed to have turned around altogether. The day after my move, as I trudged down Allenby Street, I noticed a delivery van in front of one of the new stores. They were putting up a sign: Dr. Scholl's Foot Comfort Service. I walked in. Workmen were setting up cubicles for treatment rooms, counters, and shelving. I introduced myself to Mr. Rotholz, the owner of the place, and asked him if he might have an opening. He wanted to know, in very broken Ivrit, if I could speak German and seemed much relieved when I replied, *"Ja, natürlich."* Yes, he did need someone who could speak these two languages fluently and could translate for him and his wife. He was going to do the selling of all Scholl products and his wife would do pedicures and other foot treatments. I would be the receptionist, making appointments, answering the telephone, and being available at all times to translate between the R.s and their customers. Since they were just starting out, they could not afford to pay much, but if I'd be satisfied with their offer, I could start the following week. My salary would be even less than what I had made in the grocery store, but it would pay my rent, and since so far I hadn't found anything better, I agreed.

On opening day, I reported at 8 A.M. The workmen had finished and the store was ready for its first customers. Everything looked sparkling clean and very modern. I met Mrs. Rotholz and later in the day Dr. Kahn, the podiatrist, who also was part of the establishment. Everyone, including me, wears a white lab coat. Since there were no customers yet, Mrs. R. and Dr. Kahn left after a while, and I helped Mr. R. unpack cases of Dr. Scholl's foot supplies, price them, and shelve them. The first day passed uneventfully. We had no more than two or three customers. During the next few days a few more showed up, and I began to set up appointments. The work is not demanding at all. I rather enjoy it. My hours are from 8 A.M. to noon and from 2 P.M. to 6 P.M. We close for lunch, like most stores here, for two hours. After the first week Mr. R. gave me the keys to open the store. First in is the Yeminite cleaning woman who washes the floors. I asked Mr. R. why I couldn't do that and in this way augment my salary. He didn't think it quite fitting for a receptionist to wash floors, but I promised to do it before I officially opened the doors. He agreed, and I am now earning enough money to support myself.

The letters from home contain little news. Mother's mood swings between elation at the prospect of living in Australia, where there are no cruel winters, where the sun seems to shine always, where there is no unemployment and the opportunities are unlimited, and, on the other hand, depression over the thought of Edith's leaving. She has much less work than before because most of her employers are leaving Germany. Mostly she is busy now helping to dismantle households and pack containers ready for shipment. This work is not as hard, and she makes more money for fewer hours. All my father writes is that we must wait patiently and keep on trying every possible avenue. He feels that whatever one does should be done sensibly and thoughtfully. The way some people dash off to Shanghai, for instance, without any proper preparation, without knowing what they will be doing and where they'll be living—one hears that they aren't even allowed to live in the European quarter—such emigration seems senseless, he says. Well, maybe he's right, but sometimes it's better to make a move, even if it's not a perfect one.

Tel-Aviv, April, 1939

Business at Dr. Scholl's Foot Comfort Service is picking up. Doctor Kahn and Mrs. R. are doing quite a few pedicures, treating ingrown toenails, and prescribing arch-supports and all kinds of other Scholl products. Mr. R. does most of the selling. I help out wherever I am needed. It's an easy job. The customers are pleasant and the atmosphere in the shop is professional, very different from that at the Wager's grocery store. My salary covers rent and food but does not leave me anything over for other expenses. So the other day I hit on an idea about how to save lunch money. Next door to Scholl's is a Viennese Bakery Shop, and every morning, while I am washing the floors, I see the salesgirl from the bakery dumping yesterday's left-over pastries into the garbage. Of course, I would have been far too embarrassed to ask her for them, but as soon as I come to work I now line their garbage can with nice fresh paper, and then after I have finished cleaning, I check the can. Most days I'm lucky and have enough pastry for lunch and even take some home to Sonya. I don't think all this rich stuff is a very good diet, but as long as I don't gain weight, I don't mind, and the lunch money I save I really need for other necessities. I also have decided to get money somehow for a second-hand bicycle. It's too costly to pay bus fare every day, and walking makes my ten-hour day into a twelve-hour day. Maybe I can sell or trade my camera, or even my stamp collection.

I was anxiously awaiting news from home, hoping to hear something definite about my parents' emigration. Finally there was a letter, but the news was not what I had hoped for. The Australian Immigration Department had refused my father's application. They have more requests than they can take care of and apparently prefer younger people. "Well," my father writes, "of course we are disappointed, but you know that nothing gets me down. I will just keep on trying." Still, I worry so much about them. Ever since the pogrom in November of last year we hear of increasing harassment of Jews, arrests, and official decrees to restrict their ability to function. For instance, Jews are no longer allowed to own any object of gold, silver, platinum, precious stones, and pearls. I asked my father in my last letter to let me know how their daily life has been affected by all this, but I'm not sure that he will be able to tell me the truth. So far their letters mention no fear for themselves, only worry about me when they read in the newspapers about the increasing Arab unrest and disturbances. But as yet there has been no trouble here in Tel-Aviv.

Tel-Aviv, May, 1939

Everyone is up in arms about the White Paper on Palestine, in which England declares that Jewish land purchases in Palestine are to end and Jewish immigration will be limited to 75,000 Jews during the next five years and then no more. This means that here, too, the door will be shut to most of those who want to escape Hitler and the Nazis. And, of course, any attempt of mine to get my parents to Palestine is now impossible. The few available certificates to enter the country have long been spoken for. It is just as my father said it would be—England has given in to the wishes of the Arabs. All over the country there are protests and strikes and manifestoes against the White Paper. In the midst of all this, attacks on Jewish businesses continue, even in Tel-Aviv. Scholl's Foot Comfort Service was hit one night. When I came to work in the morning the police were there, assessing the damage. The show-window had been shattered, but except for broken glass all over the place, no harm was done. It was just another act of Arab violence against Jewish property.

I am now the owner of a bicycle, albeit a very decrepit one, but that was all I could get in exchange for my camera. Still, I love the old thing. It propels me to and from work and gives me a chance to do errands during my lunch hour. It also saves me time and the money for bus fare because the weather has turned very hot again and walking in the heat of day is no pleasure.

As for the news from home, it is incredible how optimistic my parents sound. My father tried to get a job in an office as an assistant in an engineering department, but apparently the only available job is construction labor. However, he was offered a job as a landscape worker. This job, too, is hard physical labor. From 7 A.M. to 4 P.M. he, with two other much younger men, has to clear the rubble left after new construction, level the ground, and landscape around the new buildings. Vati says that the first few days were very hard for him, but now he enjoys the physical labor and is proud that he can keep up with his young co-workers. And Mother is even prouder of him. She writes that, seeing how Vati can hold up his end and knowing that I, too, have learned to work, she has no doubt that the three of us together, as soon as we are reunited, will make it up the ladder again. In answer to my question about how their lives have changed, all they mention is that the streets still look the same, but their free time is now spent with nice walks if the weather is good. Otherwise, they stay at home. They no longer can visit the cinema or restaurants or cafes. The beaches, too, are out-of-bounds for Jews. For Mutti, who loved the movies and looked forward every weekend to swimming at the different lakes, this must be very hard. Even harder must be the realization that they now are openly considered outcasts in their own country and must live in permanent fear of what may happen to them next.

Tel-Aviv, June, 1939

It is really getting hot now. To cool off I spend most of my Saturdays at the beach, but the water, too, is getting quite warm, not as refreshing as it was in the spring. Often I meet Hedden Grossmann there and after a couple of hours swimming and suntanning together, I spend the evening at their house or meet Sonya, Gideon, and some of their friends. We stroll down the Ben-Yehuda and usually end up in some outdoor cafe, where we watch all of Tel-Aviv pass by. On a Friday or Saturday night every Tel-Avivian sooner or later will walk by your table. There is a delightful atmosphere of meeting, greeting and exchanging the latest news.

My latest news is that I received my first marriage proposal! This is the way it came about. A few weeks ago I received a letter from Hans L., which had been forwarded to me from Raanana. He invited me to visit him and see his farm. Since his place is not far from Tel-Aviv and I was curious to see how he was getting along, I agreed to come and spend a day with him. From the moment I got off the bus, nothing went right. Hans was not there but had sent a neighbor to pick me up. This fellow informed me that Hans could not leave the farm because he was expecting the Vet. "Why the Vet?" I asked. Well, it seemed that one of Hans' cows was about to calve and Hans, in his older brother's absence, was very anxious that nothing should go wrong.

When the neighbor let me off at Hans' house, again there was no one around. I walked over to the stables and there was Hans, trying to calm his cow. I thought he needed more calming than his cow! His first words to me were not very complimentary either: "Oh, I hoped it was the Vet!" But then he did take me to the house and I could see that he had expected me. The table was set for two—white tablecloth, silver and china, wineglasses, and candles! It looked quite festive and a little too formal for a luncheon, I thought. However, we never did eat lunch. We ate dinner and that hours later and in a hurry because I had to catch the last bus back to Tel-Aviv. Hans had spent the entire afternoon with his cow, which was having a hard time giving birth to a calf. The Vet never showed up and I was not much help. I didn't know for which one I felt sorriest—Hans, his cow, or the calf. But everything came out all right at last, except that Hans, instead of being relieved, seemed even more fidgety than before. Then suddenly, during our rushed dinner, with much blushing and stuttering, he asked me to marry him! The proposal was completely unexpected and entirely out of character with the whole afternoon. I told him that he had caught me by surprise and that I would have to think it over, but I already knew I could never be a farmer's wife. All the way home I had to smile at the thought of having to compete with a cow.

Sonya, however, is seriously thinking of getting married soon, which means I'll have to move. I can't afford the room all by myself. Besides, I have never lived alone and would find it lonely. I miss being part of a group and knowing I belong. On my way to work, as I pedal along King George Street, I pass by a very attractive building surrounded by beautiful grounds. On its large veranda, facing the street, I usually see quite a few girls, all about my age, relaxing on lounge chairs. I must stop there and find out what kind of place this is. Perhaps it's a young women's hostel, and maybe I could live there.

On the 19th was my nineteenth birthday. The congratulations from home arrived on time and made me homesick. Vati and Mutti as well as Edith each wrote a separate letter, and all three wished for nothing more than that this should be the last birthday we are celebrating apart. Mutti says that next year, when the four-leaf clover will be whole again, she'll make up for all that we missed this year. Vati, upon advice from the Australian cousins, has again applied for a visa to Australia, this time as a surveyor because apparently there is a demand for those. Maybe they'll consider older applicants for this job. He is also exploring the possibility of going to Chile, and the latest idea is the Philippines, where engineers are needed.

The news in their next letter was depressing. My father's landscaping job is over and the new job he now holds sounds much too hard for a man of his age. He has to get up every morning at 4:30 A.M. in order to get to work at 7:30. He has a long train ride and then a forty-minute walk through woods until he reaches his work place. Then for ten hours he pushes a wheelbarrow up and down a hill, until the entire mountain of earth is leveled. Sometimes he's on night duty as a switchman at the railroad track there. That work is a little easier. My father, as usual, makes the best of this situation, and I find his attitude admirable. He writes:

"The work agrees with me splendidly. We work at the sand hills of Falkensee. There's not an inch of shade. We are dried out like Foreign Legionnaires. I keep everyone entertained with tunes from musicals and operettas, and I sing them entire arias in Italian. They say, 'If we didn't have that *Meschuggener* [crazy guy] we'd all be nuts by now.' During the break I teach them English and learn Yiddish from them. I also converse fluently with our two deaf-mutes and am mastering sign language."

The other news concerned my sister, Edith. Mrs. Frank, true to her word, has found a suitable family and all the guarantees from England have been received so that Edith will be able to leave within the next few weeks. I feel my mother's suffering when she writes:

> "You cannot imagine my emotions. It is incredibly difficult for me. I can still hear your comforting words, which you voiced before *your* emigration: 'Look, Mutti, you still have your little one.' But what will I have left now? 'Vati,' you will say, and that is true, but my emotions tell me that I am first of all a mother and no logic or common sense will convince me that it is necessary to give up one's children at such an early age. When the applications arrived I had already decided to say 'no' to the entire scheme. Then we had a discussion among the three of us, two against one, and, of course, Vati won out with his logical reasoning. The next morning on her way to school (three times a week we go together) little Edith said to me, 'Mutti, I thought it over, and I believe that the two of us must be reasonable. You pull yourself together and I'll pull myself together. Then everything will turn out all right. You'll try to follow me to England as quickly as possible. I'll ask around there about a position for you as a household help, and if they say you are too old, I'll tell them that they don't know my mother. She works like a twenty-year-old.' Well, with that I felt beaten, and now, at least outwardly, I have to resign myself to my fate. My only hope is that the separation will not last too long, that something will work out for us and I'll get both of you back to join us wherever we'll find a place together."

Tel-Aviv, July, 1939

The next letter from my mother was written at the beginning of this month.

> My dearest Daughter,
> Now Edith's departure is coming as quickly and unexpectedly as yours did. I am still dazed, but I must not show Edith and Vati how I feel inside. On Tuesday, when I came home from

work, there was a telegram that Edith's permit from England had arrived and she is to be ready for the children's transport on July 11. During these last days we have been wildly busy. Since Vati was working nights, for two days he didn't get to sleep at all during the daytime. I had to stop work and go to all kinds of different offices and agencies to deliver papers, get signatures, etc. Once again I had second thoughts about letting her go, but I was informed that if she didn't go with this transport, she would never get another permit. Now everything is in order and we're just waiting for the call to tell us when and where we have to take her. There's still much to do—washing, sewing, ironing, but somehow I'll get it done on time. Day before yesterday I gave a children's farewell party—games with little prizes, cake, and ice cream donated by one of the ladies at our pension. In the evening we had a picnic on paper plates—potato salad, hot dogs, raspberry and orange juice. We played games, had a candy 'rain,' and all the kids brought Edith little gifts. You know how good I am at arranging this kind of thing. As a farewell present Edith gave me an umbrella and Dad a tie.

First Edith cried, but now she is excited and looking forward to the trip. But I worry so. She needs so much love. Will she find it there? Who will tell her to brush her teeth, dress warmly, and a thousand other things? You were sixteen when you left, still young and inexperienced, but Edith is hardly more than a baby. And how empty it will be when she is gone! My thoughts return to this constantly. When I come home there will be no childish smiles to greet me, no little hands stretched out to me, no endless chatter and laughter—only my old furniture and junk will stare at me. Even her little bed won't be there any more. I'll work hard, but nothing will fill this emptiness. It's a long way to Golgotha! Well, enough of this. I embrace you and kiss you lovingly.

Your sorrowful Mutti

Edith's transport was postponed from the 11th to the 13th of July. On July 14th my mother copied Edith's first card, written on the train and mailed enroute from Holland:

Dearest Mutti and Vati:

It's only 11 A.M., but I want to write to you. We are riding without a break. I see beautiful fields, fat cows, and

119

hardworking farmers. I ate some cold chicken and pretzels. My new doll, Gaby, has cried so much she has used up an entire hanky. We passed Hanover, then Bentheim, and soon we'll be in Holland. Many regards to everyone in our pension. To you endless kisses,

Your not sad Edith

My mother adds, "If she gets to people who really *love* her, and I underline the word *love*, she'll soon settle down and miss me less. I, though, will not get over it. It is too much—first you and then she. I knew it would be hard, but I was not prepared for this much pain. It follows me everywhere."

How I wish I could be with my mother now to help her over this difficult time! But what can I say to her other than repeat again and again that we must hold on to the thought that all these separations won't last long and somewhere soon we'll all be together again. In the meantime, I'll have to go on with my life here.

I have found out that the attractive house on King George Avenue is called Beth Hachaluzoth [House of Women Pioneers] and belongs to the WIZO, the Women's International Zionist Organization. Last week I peddled over there on my lunch hour to see whoever was in charge. I was ushered into a reception room and a very pleasant woman asked how she could help me. I told her that I had been passing by on my way to work, that I had been attracted by the atmosphere of the house, and that I had been wondering if there was any vacancy, any possibility for me to move in. She did not think so and explained that the girls living here had come to Erez Israel, to this house, to go through a two-year apprenticeship, much as I had gone to Tel-Josef. However, whereas our *hachsharah* [apprenticeship] was for the sixteen- to eighteen-year-old group and was designed to make us into farmers, these girls are usually eighteen when they begin the program. Their two-year training prepares them more for life in the city by teaching them various trades, like dressmaking, weaving, hair dressing, typing, and shorthand, and some are in nurse's training. There were no girls living in the house who did not belong in the program. Still, I insisted that I would like to speak to the woman in charge and was given an appointment for the following day. The next day I met the Directress, R.B., who impressed me as a very formidable lady. In her early fifties, standing tall and very straight, her graying hair combed back severely into a bun and her eyes seeming to bore right into you, she appeared reserved and distant. Once again I explained how much I would like to live in the Beth Hachaluzoth. She told me, with slightly raised eyebrows, that she understood I had been informed by her administrative assistant that this would be impossible. Why, then, had I insisted on this appointment? Well, because I felt that perhaps she could make an exception. But why should she? This was not a boarding house but a live-in training school. And who was I, anyway? What made me think that I would fit in? So I told her about my background, my two years' Youth Aliyah, my apprenticeship as a shoemaker, my present job, my longing to live again among people my own age. She asked me more questions and seemed, suddenly, interested in what I told her. There was even the beginning of a smile on her firm face. Then, when I had answered all her questions, she told me to come back in a week. She had to think things over and also make some inquiries about the legality of such a step. So, apparently, my living in the Beth Hachaluzoth is not impossible after all. I am very excited at the prospect.

Tel-Aviv, August, 1939

I have moved, and I still can't believe my luck! It has been only ten days since I had my first interview with R.B. and was told that there was no possibility for an outsider to live here. But at our second meeting she informed me that she had liked my determination and what had impressed her even more was my fluency in Hebrew and my training in the kibbutz. I obviously represented the kind of young person she hoped her girls would become. By living among them, speaking Hebrew with them, and instilling in them a bit of the pioneer spirit, I could help to wean them away from their old ways. She felt that, though the girls were manually preparing for the new land by learning a trade, spiritually they were still a long way off from integration. For this reason she would make an exception and take me in. I was not so sure that I really represented the pioneer spirit, but I would try my best to fulfill her expectations.

My new room, which I share with two other girls, is bright and airy, decorated in light colors. The bedspreads and drapes are handwoven on the looms downstairs. The whole house is spacious and cool. The showers, the washrooms, sparkle. Everything is new and clean. I eat breakfast and dinner with the girls in the dining hall, the food prepared by the girls who study home economics. We have several beautifully furnished common rooms where we spend most of our time after dinner. The atmosphere is like what I imagine a young women's club would resemble. I love it. And for this paradisical life I pay less than what I paid for that tiny cubbyhole I shared with Sonya! My monthly fee includes all my meals as well, and for the first time since I left Tel-Josef I'll be able to buy some clothes and have money left over for a few luxuries. Maybe I'll even be able to save a little. But it's not the monetary advantage that matters most. It's the entire atmosphere in the house. I did not know until now how much I had missed being among young people again, sharing common interests, laughing, talking late into the night. This and the luxury of space, cleanliness, and order make me happy. Somehow, though, thinking of what my parents are going through, I feel almost guilty for being so happy.

My father's letters continue to sound calm and are basically optimistic. He never mentions, though, what is actually going on in Berlin. All he writes is that he enjoys his physical labor, but he admits that it is very hard. Mutti says she hardly recognizes him, he has become so lean and suntanned. No news from Australia, Chile, Manila, and wherever else they applied. My mother, unlike my father, does not seem to be able to rouse herself from her depression. She says that she can't even go to work. Unfortunately, since my father is gone all day long and goes to sleep as soon as he gets home, she cannot share her grief with him. Our letters are her only consolation, especially Edith's, who is having a wonderful time and writes enthusiastically about how good everyone is to her. At the moment she is at the seashore on summer vacation with her new family. In spite of her depression, Mother has bought lightweight materials for a wardrobe suitable in a warmer climate. How typical of her that in her deepest sorrow she already is anticipating a brighter future, which at the moment is Brisbane. She is also taking an English class twice a week. Vati has asked me repeatedly if I am now fluent in English. The only people who speak English here are Englishmen sent out to administer their mandate. Most of their offices are in Jerusalem, and few Jews have contact with them. In the kibbutz only Ivrit was spoken. Here in Tel-Aviv you hear about as much German as Ivrit, and in between a little Yiddish. So where would I pick up English?

Sonya married Gideon last week. It was a small ceremony with only a handful of relatives and friends. I wrote a long letter to Hans telling him how moved I was by his proposal but that I was not yet ready to get married. I added that I hoped we could stay friends. The truth is that I am not ready to marry *anybody* right now. As uncertain as my future is, I feel that so much is still waiting for me. If my parents succeed in emigrating, I want to join them and help them. If ever there is a chance that I might learn a real profession, I want to be free to take that chance. I want to find out who I am, what I can do, and not depend on someone else or attach myself to someone else's life, at least not yet.

Tel-Aviv, September-December, 1939

WAR! We are at war—have been for three weeks now and I still can't believe it! On September 1st German armed forces marched into Poland. Two days later Great Britain and France declared war on Germany. The *Yishuv* [the Jewish population in Palestine], in spite of its grievances with regard to the British White Paper, threw its full support behind the British. President Weizmann declared that, "Their war is our war," and Ben Gurion's words expressed the general sentiment when he said: "We shall fight the war as if there were no White Paper, and the White Paper as if there were no war." Every day, every hour, we heard on the radio and read in the newspaper of the lightning German advance called "Blitzkrieg." Within a week they stood before Warsaw. On September 17 the Russians invaded Poland from the East, and by the end of the month Poland had ceased to exist.

What does it all mean to us—to the *Yishuv* in general and more particularly to my family and to me? What will happen to my parents and all their plans? Now they won't be able to get out. So what is to become of them? How will I find out? How will we stay in contact? It's a good thing that my sister got out, and just in time. As frightening as is the thought of total war, I hope it signifies the beginning of the end of the terrible Hitler regime.

All during September I had no word from my parents. Then in October I received two letters, one dated September 10, the other September 26. Both had been forwarded to me by my great-uncle August, who had emigrated to Sweden. Amazingly, neither letter made any mention of the war. Instead, my mother told about the lonely celebration of their silver wedding anniversary. She worries about us but wrote that they are well. The letters were quite different in tone from previous ones and obviously were written with an eye to the censor. I immediately wrote to Sweden, but when Uncle August sent me another letter, dated October 7, my parents said they had not heard from me. However, Mother wrote that she had received several postcards from Edith. I realized then that, as long as this war would last, contact between my parents and us would be every limited, if possible at all. Still, I kept sending letters to Sweden. Quite a few of the girls in the Beth Hachaluzoth were in the same position as I. They, too, had families who still were living in Germany or in German-occupied Czechoslovakia. We could share our anxieties and support each other. I was very grateful to have been accepted into the house and congratulated myself over and over again that I had taken the initiative to effect this move. Still, as long as I worked outside I was not quite a full-fledged member of the group, and more and more I wanted to belong totally. I began to mull over the problem. There was no way I could become a trainee learning a trade, but why couldn't I become a member of the staff? My best friend in the house was Fanny L., the instructor for dressmaking. Why couldn't I also become an instructor, teaching shoemaking? I would have to convince our Directress that shoemaking was an acceptable profession for women, not only in the kibbutz but also in the city, that we could open a shoemakery and repair-shop on the premises, offer a two-year training course and make money at the same time, exactly as Fanny's dressmaking class, or the weaving group did. As soon as it became clear to me what I wanted, I acted. I laid out my plan to R.B., hoping to convince her immediately with my enthusiasm. I did not bowl her over right away, but she did not reject the whole idea either. She promised to think about it and let me know. A week later she called me into her office. She had found out that the Beth Hachaluzoth in Haifa, our sister institution, had just begun to operate such a workshop. There a shoemaker was instructing several girls. I was flabbergasted. I had thought I was the first to introduce shoemaking as a women's trade, and now they already were teaching it to girls in the city! But before I had time to dwell on having lost the advantage of being first, the Directress continued. Since a precedent had been set, she was in favor of opening a similar workshop at our house. Furthermore, she was willing to give me a try as instructor, providing that I would first go to Haifa and spend some time in the shoemakery there until the master shoemaker would certify me as capable of teaching the trade. During this apprenticeship, which with my background should not take more than six months, I would live in the Beth Hachaluzoth in Haifa and get my room and board, but no salary. I agreed immediately. Not only would I eventually be a permanent member of an institution I liked to work for and belong to, but as an instructor I would also make a decent salary. R.B. made all the arrangements for me in Haifa. I quit my job at Dr. Scholl's and, at the end of December, I moved to Haifa.

1940

It took me four months to receive my certification. I cannot say that I enjoyed this time because I felt lonely and longed for my friends in Tel-Aviv. Often I hitchhiked back there, not having enough money for a bus ticket, and spent Saturday with Fanny, who had moved out of the Beth Hachaluzoth and now had her own apartment. Sometimes one or another of my friends came to visit me. Some Saturdays I went to the beach or explored Haifa and its surroundings. Still, I counted the days until I could go 'home.' I did return to Tel-Aviv in April, ready to start the shoemakery. The shop we would use was part of the Beth Hachaluzoth, opening to the street so that customers could step right in. My first assignment was to buy the necessary equipment, tools, leather, work benches, and other supplies. One of the girls who had not been too happy with her training in the kitchen asked R.B. if she could become my first apprentice. The Directress, now my boss, agreed. This girl, Aviva, was a few years older than I. She took to the trade quickly and soon became my right hand. Since the outbreak of the war, there had, of course, not been any further Aliyah. The WIZO was now putting its efforts into training young girls from poorer families who needed to acquire skills in order to earn a living. Thus, two teen-age *Sabras* [those born in Palestine] became my other apprentices. R.B. had made arrangements with some Jewish welfare institutions from whom we got sacks of shoes in need of repair. Right from the beginning we had more work than we could take care of. It did not take long until we had some walk-in trade as well, so that soon the shoe repair shop of the Beth Hachaluzoth was a going concern. This was a very happy time for me. I liked my work, enjoyed instructing the girls and seeing their progress. The shop did well and R.B. seemed satisfied. I had made many new friends in the house and finally experienced a sense of security. For the first time since I had left my family I felt as if I had a home again. It seemed almost incredible to me that on top of all this I was being paid a good monthly salary. My only sorrow in the midst of my good fortune was that I had so little contact with my parents.

In March I did receive one letter, via Sweden, a single typewritten sheet from my father. In this letter he did mention that they had heard from both Edith and me. He wrote that they were well but that Mutti suffered from not being in regular contact with us. He still had his old job which, though hard, gave him the satisfaction of being able to support both of them and the knowledge that he was not too old to hold his own anywhere in the world.

He wrote: "With this expression of incorrigible optimism I will close my letter." This was the last real message I received until summer, when it became possible to send twenty-five words via the Red Cross in Switzerland. I received such messages every few months from then on and, of course, mailed the same to them. All we could say was that we were well and missed each other. Still, as long as I received these notes, I knew that my parents were alive.

In the spring the so-called *"Sitzkrieg"* suddenly came to an end. On May 10 Germany invaded Holland, Belgium, and Luxembourg. On May 12 the Germans invaded France. By the end of May what was left of the British forces in France was evacuated at Dunkirk. And when it began to look as if Hitler was conquering all of Europe, Italy decided to join the Germans. On June 10 she declared war on the Allies. On September 6, literally out of the clear blue sky, at three in the afternoon, five Italian planes appeared and bombed the totally defenseless city of Tel-Aviv. There were neither military targets anywhere nearby nor any anti-aircraft defenses. The only purpose of the air-raid must have been to frighten the civilian population. That day I had gone with Fanny to the *souk* to buy some food for the weekend, which I was going to spend at her flat. We were walking through the stands of the butchers when suddenly the entire street exploded. We dived into the nearest stall and hit the floor. Within seconds fires erupted around us. I heard people screaming. Someone pointed to the sky and there I saw a few planes climbing high and turning westward. Then came the sirens of ambulances and fire engines. Fanny and I were not injured, but around us we saw a number of people who were. Like everyone else we rushed 'home'—for us that was the Beth Hachaluzoth. A bomb had fallen near it and a number of wounded were being treated in our reception hall, which had been quickly converted into an emergency first aid station. There were in all about 117 casualties. After this attack, air-raid shelters were built, air-raid drills took place day and night, and blackouts were strictly enforced. We felt that the war had come close. However, no more air-raids occurred, and for the rest of the year life continued much as before.

1941-1942

I finally carried out my father's wish and contacted an aunt of his who lived in Tel-Aviv. I had hesitated before because I did not want to show up as the poor relative she would feel sorry for and obligated to invite, from time to time, for a hot meal. I was determined not to call on her until I was well enough off to feel independent and in no need of charity. Now I was ready. Armed with a bunch of flowers, I called on Tante Else, and much to my surprise I spent a delightful evening with her and her friend, Professor Zondek. I had to promise to come back again soon to meet her daughter, Lotte, my second cousin. I did so and soon became a regular visitor at Professor Zondek's Friday night dinners. The atmosphere at his house reminded me of days long-gone-by in our own home. After dinner other guests often arrived and the rest of the evening would be spent in lively conversation. Sometimes we would listen to a 'concert' made up of records, mostly classical, which had been carefully selected for that particular evening.

The discussion these days mostly concerned the progress of the war, which seemed to be coming closer all the time. Fighting was breaking out all around the Mediterranean. In the Western Desert in Egypt, the British troops under General Wavell, though much outnumbered, had captured 130,000 Italians, and we rejoiced over that good news. But in March, 1941, Hitler sent General Rommel to Africa and the picture began to change. In October of 1940 Mussolini had tried to take Greece and failed, but in February of 1941 Greece had asked Britain for assistance against the Axis. British troops arrived in Greece in March of 1941 but were driven out by April. And then, at the end of May, Crete, to which the British troops had been evacuated, after fierce fighting also was taken by the Germans.

It must have been early in 1941 that Britain evacuated a number of civilians from Cyprus, most of them refugees who had fled there from Nazi-occupied territories. Upon their arrival in Palestine several of the women were temporarily put up in the Beth Hachaluzoth. And that is the way I met Mimi and, through her, Laszlo, events which ultimately changed the course of my life. Mimi was about eight years older than I. She seemed the essence of sophistication, so well-groomed and dressed, so assured of herself. I was fascinated by all she told me of their life in Nicosea. Many of these Cypriots were in the entertainment field, a life of little work and much pleasure. Now this life had been interrupted by the war, but neither she nor any of her companions appeared worried. They were, for the time being at least, wards of the British government, which had not yet decided what to do with them. In the meantime they were to stay in Palestine, at the expense of the British, from whom they received a monthly stipend to cover their living expenses. Mimi took me under her wing. She had her sister, who had been on the same transport, make me my first elegant dress, a two-piece outfit in royal blue. Under Mimi's guidance I put on my first make-up. She went with me to buy my first high heels. She took me to a hairdresser and insisted on a new, more fashionable haircut. Under her tutelage I had my first cigarette and my first drink. In short, she changed me from an awkward girl into a young lady.

Mimi and her compatriots, whom we all called "the Cypriots," though most of them originally were Czechs and Hungarians, did not stay long at the Beth Hachaluzoth. As soon as they received their first government checks, they rented places in town and settled in. Mimi took a room just across the street from my 'shop' so we visited often, and many evenings I went with her and her friends to a cafe-house, sometimes even to a nightclub, which again was a new adventure for me. Then Mimi introduced me to Laszlo. My first impression of him was that he looked like Jose Iturbi, only younger. I guessed him to be in his early thirties. I liked Laszlo from the beginning, his suntanned looks, his smiling eyes, his sturdy physique. I liked the way he treated me, with consideration, charm, and no small amount of flattery.

Mimi seemed to feel that it was about time I had a steady boy friend, and not a boy but a *man*. I thought so, too, but, to be frank, this was one time when I very quickly lost control of the situation. I was too inexperienced to know how to deal with Laszlo's advances and, of course, I was afraid that if I refused him he quickly would choose some other girl. So I experienced my first 'love affair.' Laszlo was not unkind, but he was much more interested in his own satisfaction than in mine. I soon thought to myself, "If this is all there is to sex, then what's all the fuss about?" I found it neither very exciting nor very satisfying. Still, I continued to find Laszlo's lifestyle intriguing, and I enjoyed being with him and Mimi and their friends. Laszlo was a trumpet player and, since he was a very good one, he had found a job right away in a well-known nightclub. Working evenings only, he usually spent his mornings at the beach and his afternoons meeting friends in one of our many outdoor cafes. His life was so casual, so carefree! When we were together we did not discuss the frightening course the war was taking or our worries about our families, still left behind in Europe. Instead we laughed, we had fun, and I felt more mature, a young woman beginning to be experienced and knowing that she was desired. At the back of my mind was also the feeling that everything would be even better if we were married. (My mother had assured me years ago that men don't stay with women unless marriage forces them to.) Is it surprising, then, that when two months later Laszlo did ask me to marry him, I agreed immediately?

Since all the 'Cypriots' were under British protection and Laszlo, though Hungarian by birth, had no real passport but only a paper that designated him as 'stateless,' we had to go to Jerusalem to see whoever was in charge of his group and ask how to go about getting a legal and official marriage license. So we traveled to Jerusalem and saw a British official, to whom we explained our situation. He listened, seemed sympathetic, but was quite adamant in his objection to our marriage plans. Turning to me he explained that if I married Laszlo now, I would lose my British/Palestinian citizenship, which I had acquired by virtue of having lived five years in a British mandate, and all the advantages that came with it. I would become stateless, the same as Laszlo. Furthermore, if Britain decided to end the 'Cypriots'' sojourn in Palestine and transport them somewhere else, I would then have to go with them. Surely I would not like to live out the rest of the war in some camp, God knows where. No, in all good conscience he could not leave me to such a fate. He felt sure that if our love was strong enough, we could get together after the war.

Of course, I could not have disagreed more with everything the man said. After all, what did British citizenship mean to me? Nor did he scare me with the idea of having to leave Palestine and live out the war somewhere else under the protection of the British government. On the contrary! That sounded adventurous to me. I was all for arguing it out with the little red-headed Englishman and was most surprised when Laszlo got up, took me by the hand, thanked the official politely, and before I had any chance to protest, led me out of the office. I was angry. What had happened? Had he changed his mind? Did he agree that we should wait until the war was over to get married? Was he just giving in to that pompous little official? Why had we not argued with him? When I finally paused in my tirade, I noticed how quiet and thoughtful Laszlo had become. He asked me if I really had listened well to what the Englishman had said. Of course I had! Had I heard him say, "What if you were shipped away from Palestine?" Yes, so what? Maybe we would live in Kenya or South Africa. Did I not catch his remark about living in some camp for however long the war might last? A camp? What kind of a camp and for how many years? No, I had not paid any attention to the word 'camp' and I still didn't put much credence in it. After all, the 'Cypriots' had enjoyed a free life in Palestine and even were paid for doing nothing. Why should this not continue either right here or in some other place?

Laszlo was not convinced. He seemed troubled and remained thoughtful. He asked me to be patient. Things would work themselves out.

Patience, however, was never my long suit. I always preferred to act, and soon I would have a chance to do so, though not in the way I had expected. Our interview in Jerusalem took place in early September. Less than a month later Mimi rushed into my shop. She was so excited and upset that she could hardly speak. She waved an official-looking document at me, and when I read it I, too, was stunned. It was a short notice, a copy of which had gone to all 'Cypriot' refugees in transit in Palestine. It ordered them to be packed and ready for continuation of their voyage. Departure date: October 5. Meeting place: train station, Tel-Aviv, 5 A.M. There was no mention of their final destination. Why, that was only three days away! I threw down my shoemaker's apron, told Aviva to take over, and rushed over to Laszlo's place, while Mimi went to see her sister. We all would meet that evening to discuss any strategies we could think of with regard to my coming along. But as far as Laszlo was concerned, there could not be any such plans. He vetoed any scheme that would involve illegal action, like smuggling me on board the train. He maintained that not only was this wrong, but also he was convinced that we could never succeed. All his arguments sounded weak to me. He did not seem very decisive. I told him that if he loved me, he should at least try to keep me with him. He just shook his head. I left feeling depressed but not defeated. My mood changed, though, when I met Mimi, her sister, and her brother-in-law. The three of them were all for attempting to get me on the train. They remembered how they had boarded the ship in Cyprus, where control had been very lax. At that time a few British soldiers in charge of the embarkation had separated the women from the men and had several times attempted a head count, but in the final confusion of boarding, anyone could have joined either group undetected. At least, that was Mimi's version, supported by her relatives. The three of them suggested that I pack a rucksack and one small suitcase, exactly as they would do, meet Mimi at 4 A.M., proceed by taxi to the train station, board the train with the rest of them, act nonchalant, and, when asked for my name, maintain that I was Mimi's *other* sister. It would not be my fault that I was not on the list. Someone must have made a mistake at headquarters back in Jerusalem. My two 'sisters' and my 'brother-in-law' would back me up in all of this. It seemed a feasible scheme. I now had a plan to act on, but I would not tell Laszlo about it until I saw him at the station, when any objection he had would be too late.

That night I could hardly sleep. My mind went around in circles. I tried to decide what I would take with me, what I would leave behind, whom of my friends I would tell, to whom I would and would not say goodbye. I tried to picture my future. Where would we land? What new country would I live in? What new adventures waited for me? Would I be Mrs. Fenish soon, or maybe not marry so quickly after all? A couple of nagging questions tried to intervene. Why had that official in Jerusalem been so set against my marrying Laszlo? And what was all that about a camp? Did he perhaps know more than he had let on? But

I pushed back any negative thoughts and concentrated on carrying out the plan that would open a new life for me.

The next day I took Aviva and my two roommates into my confidence, Aviva because I wanted her to take over my work and there were many things she had to know in order to be in charge of the shop. My two roommates because I could not hide my preparations from them and also I needed their help for my 'escape.' Our house was always locked from midnight to 6 A.M. That day after work I did my packing and in the evening, after it grew dark, I hid my suitcase in the bushes under the balcony. Then, after a few hours of restless tossing and turning, I got dressed, threw my rucksack over the railing, and with the help of my roommates climbed down from the balcony, retrieved my suitcase, crossed the backyard, and climbed over the wooden gate to the street. As soon as I reached Mimi's place she called a taxi. Punctually at 5 A.M. we arrived at the train station. Just as Mimi had predicted, there was quite a bit of confusion, but only at first. British soldiers were cordoning off the entire station. No one but the 'Cypriots' was allowed near the train. The taxis that had brought us had to turn back immediately. All in all there must have been several hundred passengers. A British sergeant directed us to the different coaches, separating the men from the women. Each one had to show the transit order they all had received two days before. Mimi's sister quickly gave me hers and then insisted that her husband had both of their copies. He, of course, was at the other end of the train. The sergeant waved her on. Mimi, her sister, three other women, and I were given a very nice compartment. We stowed our baggage and sat down. I had passed the first hurdle, but my heart was still beating a mile a minute. I looked out the window. The entire platform now had been cleared. Only bored soldiers were standing guard all along the platform. I heard doors closing. The train was ready to leave. I began to breathe a little easier.

From several compartments away I heard the short, clipped accents of British officials, probably the last control. Now they were in the compartment next to ours. They were checking names against a list, just as Mimi had told me they would do. This was the last hurdle. I was ready, and here they came, one Army officer, a Sergeant, and a civilian. The civilian glanced down at his list and then, since I was first by the window, he looked up at me. I was so shocked my heart skipped several beats. This was the little red-haired official from Jerusalem, the one who had objected to our request for a marriage license! For a second I hoped he would not recognize me, but he did.

131

What followed I considered, at the time, the most humiliating moments I had ever lived through. Yet, I must admit, the situation was handled in a most gentlemanly fashion, so very English. My red-haired 'adversary,' who apparently was in charge of the entire operation, handed me over to the CID officers who took me and my luggage off the train. He then gave orders to find my 'young man' in the men's section of the train. We were given a few minutes to say goodbye, with the CID officers discreetly stepping back and turning their heads away. I was so choked up that I could not say one word to Laszlo, and I don't remember what he said to me. All I do remember were the redhead's last orders: "Take her to the police station and keep her there for about two hours, long enough so that she won't be able to take a taxi and try to board the train at Kantara." Kantara, explained one of the CID officers later, was the border town between Palestine and Egypt. He explained much more to me during those two hours at the police station—that my scheme never could have succeeded, that if I had not been discovered in Palestine, I surely would have been pulled off the train in Egypt since the control anywhere near the Suez Canal was very strict, that I then might have landed in an Egyptian prison. Had I ever been in Egypt? He could not think of a worse place for a young girl than an Egyptian prison. I heard him, but I really did not take in what he was saying. (Though later, quite a bit later, I found out how right he had been.) For the moment I could think only of my dashed plans.

Freddy, as this CID man introduced himself, could not have been kinder. He drowned me in countless cups of tea, lent me his large, snow-white handkerchief to wipe away my tears, which I was trying very hard to suppress, and for two hours tried to entertain me with amusing anecdotes of his overseas service. Then he drove me back to the Beth Hachaluzoth. I entered through the shoemakery. My two apprentices were on their lunch hour. Only Aviva was there, her face one big question mark when she saw me, but she would have to wait for an explanation until later. I wanted to use the mid-day break, when everyone was either eating in the dining room or relaxing on the balcony, to stow away my luggage and change into my working clothes. I was lucky. Nobody saw me, and Aviva told me later that the Directress had not yet visited our shop on her daily round of inspection. When she did so, later in the afternoon, we were all hammering and sewing away as if nothing unusual had taken place. Nobody had even missed me!

The next two weeks were very hard. Though I thought my foiled escape had not been noticed, somehow almost everyone in the house knew about it, except, of course, the administrators. All the girls wanted to know every detail about what they referred to as my 'romantic interlude.' I hated their constant inquiries and spent as little time as possible in the house. Instead, I visited more and more with Professor Zondek and Tante Else. Though they maintained separate households, she took charge of his and spent most of her time at his home. In their tranquil life, their ordered surroundings, I found the calm I needed. They, in turn, seemed to enjoy having me around and treated me very much like a newly found member of the family. Within two weeks Aunt Else suggested that I move into the apartment which she shared with her daughter, Lotte. She had a third, unoccupied bedroom, to which I was welcome. I moved in at the end of the month. By leaving my old surroundings and getting away from everyone who knew Laszlo and me, I hoped to distance myself from the entire episode, put it behind me. However, this was not yet to be.

I had missed my period at the beginning of the month but attributed this to the strain I had been under. When, in November, I missed my period again, I felt sure that I was pregnant. I went immediately to the *Kupat Holim*, the health plan that covered us all, and made an appointment with a gynecologist. After the examination she told me that, in order to be sure that I was pregnant, I would have to be checked again in four weeks.

How can I describe my feelings during those four weeks? I wanted to believe that it was all a bad dream, yet I felt absolutely sure that I was pregnant. I felt angry at myself for not having known anything about birth control. Why had I not asked Mimi to enlighten me? Why had I been so trusting and left all precautions to Laszlo? I was angry at him too. He must have been aware how little I knew about all matters concerning sex. But what good was it to mull over how the situation could have been prevented? I had to face it. The one thing I knew with certainty was that I did not want a child at this time of my life. I was alone. I was not ready to accept the responsibility for another life all by myself. I felt trapped. How I wished that I could talk to my parents. I needed their advice, their understanding and compassion. But now the decision had to be mine alone.

Just as I expected, at my next visit the gynecologist confirmed the fact that I was indeed pregnant. As for terminating a pregnancy, I would have to see a committee which dealt with these decisions. Two days later I confronted this committee, which consisted of six doctors, one or two of them probably psychologists or psychiatrists. They asked me why I did not want to bear this child. I told them that I was not married, that Laszlo had been shipped to a camp at an unknown destination, far away, for the duration of the war, and that I did not wish to bring a child into the world without a father. I was alone, with no means to support two people. One doctor after another tried to convince me that all my objections could be overcome. Had I thought of seeking financial aid? Had I considered putting the child into a home until ways could be found to maintain both of us? Had I thought of putting it up for adoption? Furthermore, did I realize that abortions usually were recommended only for health reasons or for women who already had had a number of children, in order to relieve economic hardship? Of course, I had considered all these possibilities. I had thought about hardly anything else. But I did not want a child of mine to grow up in an orphanage, and I knew how difficult it was to place a child for adoption. Most people were barely able to support themselves and their own children. I told the committee I was deeply convinced that to bring an unwanted child into the world was wrong. I was determined to have an abortion and I would much prefer to have it done legally, in a hospital, than in some quack's kitchen, but I would do even that if I had to. I was dead serious and no argument could persuade me otherwise. The doctors asked me to wait outside. After ten minutes I was called back in and informed that they had granted my request and that I was to report to the hospital on the following Tuesday at 6 A.M. The abortion would be performed some time before noon and I would have to stay at least one night in the hospital. After this I should rest for another two or three days at home.

One problem still remained, though a much smaller one. I needed someone to pick me up after the operation and a place where I could recuperate for a few days. I was reluctant to go back to my room at Aunt Else's because I did not want her to know anything about my condition and if, by any chance, there were complications, she was bound to find out. The Grossmanns also were out of the question. We had not been very close for quite a while. Fanny would have been a solution, but she was on vacation in Jerusalem, celebrating her engagement to Richard. All my other friends lived in the Beth Hachaluzoth and going there was, of course, impossible. Well, this was Wednesday so I had five days until I had to report to the hospital. I was fortunate. Friday afternoon, after work, I ran into Sonya at Woolworth's, my old friend Sonya. Why hadn't I thought of her right away? Over a cup of coffee we exchanged news. She told me how happy she was with Gideon, how well their marriage had worked out. They had moved to a larger apartment and had his sister, Betty, living with them now. I brought her up-to-date on all that had happened to me in the last few months, ending with the latest problem I faced. She did not hesitate a moment. Not only would she get me from the hospital, but she also insisted on taking me there and told me I could stay at her place as long as I needed to. I felt very lucky to have such a wonderful friend. As it turned out, Gideon's sister Betty became just as fine a friend as Sonya was.

I made arrangements at the Beth Hachaluzoth to take a few days off and told my aunt that I would be spending those vacation days with some friends. On Monday evening, the day before the operation, I spent the night at Sonya's. We had a lovely dinner, drank some wine, and they did everything possible to make me forget my coming ordeal. Early the next morning Sonya and Betty accompanied me to the hospital. Both of them tried hard to make conversation, but all I could think of was that I wanted it to be over. The waiting seemed endless. Finally an orderly took me to a four-bed ward. I was given a hospital gown and told to undress and once again I had to wait, sitting on my assigned bed. I listened to the other three women who were there for the same purpose as I. They all were much older than I. All of them had three or more children, and one apparently had had an abortion before. It was she who was taken first. Forty-five minutes later she was brought back on a stretcher and dumped unceremoniously on her bed. She kept moaning that she was hurting and that they had not given her any anesthetic. Up until then I had not been afraid, but now I began to be scared. Soon the second woman was called, then the third, and all of them came back crying, complaining, and swearing. Then I was called and told to go upstairs to surgery. Two surgeons were having a cup of coffee outside the surgery. I asked them if they were the ones who would perform the abortion. Yes, they were. I told them how scared I was after having watched the other three women and how I wished they would "put me out." They smiled and reassured me that, since I had never given birth, they certainly would use ether so that I would not feel anything. And I did not. When I woke up, I was back in my bed and Sonya and Betty both were there, with a bunch of flowers for me, which seemed a bit inappropriate, but I was very touched. The next day I was discharged from the hospital. I have heard people say that women often fall into a depression after an abortion. I did not experience such a depression, yet there was still a lot of anger left in me with which I had to deal. I did some soul-searching and realized that whatever I thought about Laszlo, in the end I could blame only myself for having been swept away by what seemed glamorous and exciting. I would have to learn to evaluate people more perceptively and not be seduced by flattery and outer trappings. If in this way I could benefit from this experience, then it was not all bad. As for now, I must be grateful to be given the chance to start anew. During the time that I had been so preoccupied with my own problems, momentous events had taken place. On December 7th the Japanese had attacked Pearl Harbor and the United States entered the war. The Germans had invaded Russia and had advanced to the outskirts of Leningrad. The RAF was hitting Germany hard, while the German Air Force continued their Blitz of England. Nearer to us, in the Western Desert, the new German general, Rommel, was outside Tobruk. The British were recruiting Palestinian Jews into their Middle East Forces and more and more young men began to join up. How I wished I could join too! I did not have to wait long. About two weeks later, in the middle of January, I saw a big billboard going up on Allenby Road. It said: "Women, join the Army! Become a member of the ATS! (His Majesty's Auxiliary Territorial Services.) There was a picture of a woman in uniform, her hands resting on a steering wheel. I knew immediately that here was my chance to participate in the war, to do my bit, however small it might be, in the battle against the evil forces of the Third Reich. The very next day I went to the Recruiting Office. I was given numerous pamphlets to read and forms to fill out. The recruiting officer suggested that I take them home and study them carefully. Furthermore, Chief Commander Chitty, the head of the Women's Services in Britain, was coming to Palestine. She would address all prospective recruits. I was advised to go to the meeting, and if after that I was still interested in joining up, I should bring back all the forms, filled out and properly signed. Though I was sure that nothing could change my mind, I did as I was told.

The brochures did not contain any specific information other than to state that joining the Army meant for the duration of the war and that, as soldiers, we would have to perform whatever duty we were assigned, wherever it might be. That was fine with me. Miss Chitty's talk was more enlightening. She explained the need for women to take part in the struggle to win the war, that the ATS, the Women's Territorial Services, was the women's branch of the Army 'at home' and she was delighted that now we here in Palestine were given a chance to serve as well. She announced that the first fifty young women would begin their training as soon as the facilities were ready in Sarafand, the big training camp not far from Tel-Aviv. This first group would be a small one and from this group NCOs (non-commissioned officers) as well as trainees for officer's school would be chosen. Six weeks later, in March of 1942, the second group, a much larger one of five hundred new recruits, would begin their training and, she hoped, every six weeks thereafter a new group would follow. She told us that most of the jobs would be in offices, as typists, telephone operators, clerks, etc. Some would be needed in food services, as messengers, as all kinds of administrative assistants, and a few as drivers. Drivers! That's what I wanted to be, a driver, just like the girl pictured on the billboards. I already saw myself behind the wheel of a staff car, in some foreign country. And who knows, one day I might get as far as Berlin and then I would find my parents. Although it did not look like it at the moment, I never doubted that England would win this war and that my parents would live through it unharmed.

At the beginning of the following week I went back to the recruiting office and delivered all the requested forms. I was told that the first group of fifty women already had been chosen and that I would be part of the next group of five hundred, who would begin their training about March 10. The next step was a medical examination, and when I passed that satisfactorily I was, for all practical purposes, "in the Army." Since I didn't have to pay rent at Aunt Else's and my future soon would be taken care of, I wanted to quit my job immediately. To my surprise the Directress did not mind at all. She said she was very proud of me for having joined up and wished me all the best. As for 'my shop,' Aviva could take over for the time being, perhaps even for the duration.

All this occurred in January of 1942. I was free until March 15—a two months' vacation. Never before had I had such a long vacation. Now I had time to do anything I wished. First on my list was learning how to drive. Thinking of the ATS girl on the recruiting poster, I felt sure that almost all the new recruits would want to be in her shoes. However, Miss Chitty had said that only "a few" drivers would be needed so there would probably be little driver training in camp and only those who already could drive would be chosen. Since hardly anyone owned a car in Palestine, girls who knew how to drive were very few. I figured I would have a good chance to be chosen as a driver if I had a driver's license. Therefore, I spent almost all the money I had saved on driving lessons. Then, after I had learned all about handling an ordinary car, I decided my chances would be even better if I also knew how to drive a truck, and I spent the little money I had left on additional lessons to learn how to double clutch and handle a three-ton lorry.

I remember the thrill when I first sat behind the wheel, actually driving a car. I could hardly wait for the next day's lesson and regretted when the hour was over.

Aunt Else's daughter Lotte, my second or maybe she was my third cousin (because she was quite a bit older than I, she seemed more like an aunt), had opened a confectioner's shop and sometimes asked me to help out, selling candies, chocolates, etc. It was she, too, who introduced me to Rolf. She had asked him to have coffee with her at our apartment. Then she called me in, introduced us, and not more than five minutes later excused herself, saying she had forgotten about some business meeting. How obvious could one be? But instead of being embarrassed, Rolf and I broke out laughing.

The two of us then spent a pleasant afternoon and later both of us were grateful to Lotte for having brought us together. Rolf was the best thing that could have happened to me at this time. He became a very close friend and we spent much time together. He came from very much the same kind of family I did and had a great sense of humor. I did not tell him anything about the 'Cypriot Chapter' of my life. I considered it closed and was grateful to him for helping me forget it. Yet, had it not been for that episode and its traumatic consequences I might have fallen in love with Rolf, but I had been badly burned and was not ready for any kind of commitment. A close friendship was all that I had to offer.

Only once did I receive a postcard from Laszlo. All it said was that they were in a camp on a tropical island, that he was well and hoped I was the same. I suppose he was not allowed to tell where they were. Rumor had it in Tel-Aviv that the island was Mauritius on the East coast of Africa, in the Indian Ocean. In February I received a more detailed letter from Mimi. She was sure I must have had a guardian angel who had prevented me from going with them. She did not like it at all in the camp. Of Laszlo she said little except that he had a new girlfriend. None of them had a real job. Life was hot, confined, and boring. All she hoped for was that the war soon would be over and she could leave there. I did not answer. As I said before, this chapter of my life was closed.

The rest of the time I spent sorting my few possessions. Though Tante Else told me that I would always have a place in her apartment, I wanted to leave things all tidied up.

I packed away my books, my parents' letters, my photo albums, and clothes. Then I made one small but very important purchase. I bought a diary. For the last two years I had not been able to correspond with my parents. All I could write were those twenty-five words via the Red Cross in Switzerland. I decided that from now on I would keep a journal of all that was going to happen to me and one day, when this war was over, they could read all about their daughter's experiences in the Army.

The night of March 14th I could hardly sleep. On the 15th I got up early—but that is already part of my new diary.

PHOTOGRAPHS

1923

Vatti, Mutti, and Adeline.

1924

1928

Adi at Kibbutz
Tel-Josef, 1937.

(Below left:) Working as a
shoemaker at Kibbutz
Tel-Josef, 1938.

(Below:) Passport photo,
leaving Germany, 1936.

In the British Army, 1942.

Ambulance
maintenance,
Alexandria, Egypt,
1942.

Penny Otto with Pamela.

Adi in uniform.

(Above:) The "Desert Rats"—Rowna, Jane, myself, and Pat.
(Below:) Our camp on the Western Desert, 1943.

(From the top:) Near Perugia, Italy, January 1945.
Evacuating wounded at airport outside Rome,
February 1945. Convoy duty in Italy, 1945.

Esther and I, last leave in Rome,
March 1946.

Just before leaving Palestine,
June 1947.

4. THE ARMY

Sarafand, March 16, 1942

At 8 A.M. we had to assemble at the recruiting office in Tel-Aviv. What excitement—the first 500 ATS* recruits! Busses took us to the training depot in Sarafand. We all were in high spirits and sang during the entire trip. We arrived at 9:30 A.M. I never would have believed that an Army camp could be so big and so beautifully laid out, with broad streets, tree-lined avenues, gardens and greenbelts. First came the formalities of registering, filling out forms, and receiving pay-books. A soldier's Service Book, usually referred to as Paybook, is the most important thing he or she owns. It must at all times be carried in the left breast pocket of the shirt, jacket, or battledress. The Paybook is a soldier's identification, without which he or she cannot be paid or get leave. It contains all medical and service-related records, names of next of kin, and even has a place for a last will. My Paybook contained an additional surprise. It stated that my parents' nationality was Ottoman! It was explained to those of us who had German parents that we would be safer with a Turkish background in case we were taken prisoner. (Palestine had been under Turkish rule before World War I.) After these preliminaries, we were led to our billets. I share a room with three other girls. We sleep in bunk beds. I'm very satisfied with my first day in the Army.

Sarafand, March 17, 1942

Today we received inoculations and shots. Also we were issued our metal kits of eating utensils. We begin to live like soldiers, marching left-right, left-right.

---

*For a list of all military initials, see Glossary on page 351.

Sarafand, March 19, 1942

I felt awful yesterday, as most of us did. I had a fever from the shots, and the food does not agree with me, but I'm sure I'll get used to it. The nights are very cold and we have a hard time falling asleep. Also, I can feel every iron bar through my thin straw mattress.

Sarafand, March 20, 1942

Our camp begins to look more and more like a training depot. Almost everyone is in uniform. We are being drilled and have lessons every day. We march, singing this ditty:

> Left and right and left and right!
> Swing your arms and *sheket!* Quiet! [*Sheket* is the
> Hebrew word for "quiet."]
> Keep your head up straight! You are on parade!

Today we had our first pay parade.

Sarafand, March 21, 1942

An exciting day—the first great 'hut' inspection. For hours we scrubbed walls, cupboards, beds and floors with soap and water. The result of all this labor—we were confined to barracks! Why? Apparently this morning some idiot had used the WC, which was designated as night toilet only. That was the cause of much laughter and amusement for everyone except the girls in our hut. And so we received our first military punishment: two days no leave and stand on parade every hour on the hour from 6 P.M. to 11 P.M.

The second great event of the day: we went through our driving tests. When the sergeants arrived to test us, they first asked which ones among the 150 hopeful future drivers actually had a civilian driving license. There were only ten of us who had such a license. We ten were then tested on staff cars. Next we were asked if there were any who had ever driven a truck or could double clutch. Just as I had anticipated, I was the only one who could do that, so I was tested on a big five-ton lorry. It all went fine. I passed both tests with an "A." My driving lessons really had paid off!

About being confined to barracks in the evening, we all were terribly upset because this was to have been our very first leave to Tel-Aviv. Instead, we had to stand parade in the cold and rain every hour. Yet, by the fifth parade at 11 P.M., we were rather enjoying ourselves. We even danced a bit and made up a few songs.

Sarafand, March 25, 1942

Things are moving along quite routinely now. We have a schedule which mostly looks like this:

6:30	Reveille
7:15	Breakfast Parade
8:00	Morning Parade
8-9:00	Drill
9-12:00	Lessons
12:30	Dinner Parade

Then siesta until 2 P.M. Afterwards again lessons, which end with PT (Physical Training) and finally a Shower Parade. Evenings are free but are taken up with polishing buttons, buckles, badges, shining shoes, etc. Some of the things I like best are the morning and evening bugle calls, especially the latter. It is so sad, yet beautiful.

Sarafand, Tel-Aviv, March 26, 1942

My first pass—from after duty until 22 hours. We took the bus into Tel-Aviv. Everywhere people stared at us since we were the first girls in uniform they had ever seen.

Sarafand, March 27, 1942

I had a very sore throat and decided to go on Sick Parade. After three hours of waiting to see the doctor, I received the verdict—suspicion of diptheria. Hospital and isolation!

Sarafand, March 30, 1942

My fourth day in the hospital. It's a small building, more like a sanitarium, and if I were not in isolation it would not be too bad. The first two days I had to stay in bed, but now I am allowed up since the doctors have decided that the sore throat is not diptheria but some other kind of infection. However, since that, too, might be contagious, I have to stay in isolation. I spend my time sitting in the garden, reading, washing dishes, bringing food to the sick, and translating for the doctor. One wonders at the Army's logic. I am not allowed out, but I am allowed to touch the dishes of the other patients!

Sarafand, April 2, 1942

Thank goodness, I am out of the hospital. Because of an outbreak of typhoid, every bed was needed, including mine. Although the doctor still was in doubt about what caused my fever, I was released. Back in camp everyone was glad to see me again. I, too, am happy to return to duty.

Sarafand, April 4, 1942

This afternoon we had a big sport field day. Every platoon had to take part. Our platoon won second prize. We now have regular leave—Wednesday and Saturday from 6 P.M. to 11:30 P.M. and Sunday from 2 P.M. to 10 P.M. I spend most of this time with Rolf, who also is thinking of joining up.

Sarafand, Tel-Aviv, April 6, 1942

We are terribly excited. Right after breakfast an endless row of busses arrived to take us to Tel-Aviv for the big Recruiting Day Parade. We had polished our shoes and shined our buttons to a sparkle. Vicount Samuel and Mrs. Edwin Samuel reviewed our parade. The *Palestine Post* said, "This second Jewish Soldiers Day in Tel-Aviv once again has shown the public the military value of these men and women in uniform."

Sarafand, Tel-Aviv, April 7, 1942

I have two days' leave, the last before we are posted. I wonder where? I really enjoyed the training weeks, but I'm looking forward to the future because then I will finally become a real driver.

Sarafand, Tel-Aviv, April 16, 1942

Over a week has passed and much has happened. When I went on leave I already did not feel too well. The next morning I knew I was running a fever. All day long I spent in bed, but when my fever climbed to 39.6, I was very concerned. The next day Aunt Else's friend, Professor Zondek, diagnosed my illness as the flu. My fever kept climbing, and, since we had been told that in case of illness we must report back to camp, we ordered a taxi and I was taken, half unconscious, to the hospital in Sarafand. It was a different building from the one I had been in before. I was put in an enormous ward with about sixty beds. A few of my acquaintances from my last hospital stay were there, but I was much too sick to take notice. The doctors and nurses all were very kind, and after three days I was allowed to get up for an hour, but I felt so weak that I took no pleasure in it. Today I am allowed to be up all day, but what good does it do me? My company left yesterday for Egypt! I have been promised that I will be sent after them, but I don't quite believe that. I'm really depressed. What bad luck to have been sick twice within such a short period of time, especially when basically I am a very healthy person.

Sarafand, April 22, 1942

Today I was discharged after thirteen days in the hospital. I stood around for a couple of hours before anyone could decide what to do with me. Apparently it is out of the question to send me to my unit. For the time being I've been attached to Headquarters. Until Headquarters is issued a lorry, which I am supposed to drive, I have to pitch in wherever help is needed. So I am to wash dishes and scrub floors! Naturally I'm in a very bad mood. The girls are all new recruits, I don't know anyone, my pals are all gone, and I dislike the awful jobs I have to do.

Sarafand, May 1, 1942

My lorry has arrived, a two-ton very second-class Fordson. Lady Francis, our Transport Officer, tested me again and seemed well-satisfied with my driving. I'm overjoyed that I now have my own car. Everyone in camp stares at me as if I were the eighth wonder of the world. Unfortunately, I had to move again and leave my nice room. At the moment I am attached to "A" Company and am billeted in a huge hut with the new driver-recruits.

Sarafand, May 8, 1942

I have been working for a week with my lorry and remain quite a sensation—the first woman driver in uniform! When I have to drive into Tel Aviv or Jaffa, people stop walking or driving as soon as they see me. The *Palestine Post* printed my picture on the front page. My lorry is being used as staff car and I drive any ATS officer wherever she wishes to go. I love this job and believe that I have never been as satisfied with any work I have done as with this driving. I have also gotten used to the big hut and, although I'm not crazy about most of the new girls, I did find a new friend among them, Irene.

Sarafand, May 14, 1942

The four weeks' training of the second group of recruits, to which Irene and all the girls in my hut belong, is almost over. Irene put in an application to remain in Sarafand and drive the second Fordson, which Headquarters has just received. Her application was approved, and now we are both permanent drivers and are posted back to Headquarters. Irene has to drive rations, laundry and whatever is necessary within the camp, and I drive the officers outside of the camp. Sometimes we also have to take the newly turned out driver-trainees to Lydda station, from where they usually go to the huge depots near and around Ismalia and Tel-el-Kebir in Egypt.

Since I named my car "Rhett," Irene, of course, had to call her car "Scarlett."

Sarafand, May 18, 1942

Irene and I moved out of the big hut into a comfortable bungalow surrounded by gardens and white gravel walks. We have our own bath and toilet. The room has four beds, but so far we haven't seen any other occupants. Today I drove for the first time to Jerusalem, not an easy drive with the old lorry. Both Irene and I have a lot of trouble with our cars. They are really second-class vehicles and spend more time in the workshop than on the road. Also, neither of us has any idea about maintenance. Most days I work twelve or thirteen hours, but much of this time is spent sitting around waiting, which is just as tiring as driving. All in all, though, I am glad that I was not sent with my original company, especially since I have learned that they all landed in Egypt, driving lorries in big depots, from one workshop to the next, or delivering them to different units nearby. Not one of them has her own car.

Sarafand, May 19, 1942

Once again there is great excitement in camp. Everyone washes, irons, polishes, and brushes. We are being drilled for another great parade. This time His Royal Highness, the Duke of Gloucester, is to inspect the ATS and the Palestine Recruit Training Depot. I wanted very much to stand on parade and see the Duke, but my officer was of the opinion that it had been too long since I had participated in any drill training. As if I could not march as well as most of the new recruits! So I sneaked into the hospital where I could see the entire parade grounds from the windows. It was such a hot day that two girls fainted. I was fortunate, after all, that I could watch the ceremony from the cool hospital corridor.

Sarafand, June 9, 1942

Now I have been working for more than a month with my staff-car lorry, and I love it. I have now learned to change the oil, grease the car, and pump the tires. I wash Rhett regularly and fill him with petrol.

Everyone says that I'm a good driver, and I feel that I'm improving all the time. My officer has asked me if I would like a promotion, in which case I would have to give up driving. Of course, I refused the promotion.

Sarafand, June 16, 1942

Irene is in the hospital. She got an inflammation of the nerves in her arm from turning the heavy steering wheel. So now I have to take over her duties and drive rations, laundry, etc. One drives half a mile, waits two hours, drives two miles, waits another hour. I certainly prefer my 'staff car' driving.

Sarafand, June 19, 1942

Though today is my 22nd birthday, I am not in a good mood. Irene is still in the hospital and I've been doing her awful job for two days. I would have liked to celebrate my birthday with her. She did give me a pretty cigarette holder. From Aunt Else a pair of hose and sunglasses, and from Lotte chocolate and cigarettes. Rolf bought me a leather writing case, which I'll get the next time we see each other. Still, the day seemed bleak with no one offering birthday congratulations. Just a day like any other day. But the worst is not receiving a word from my parents. It's been a long time since I've had any message from them via the Red Cross.

Sarafand, Tel-Aviv, June 20, 1942

I have a forty-eight hour leave to Tel-Aviv. Neither Aunt Else nor Lotte are at home and I have the run of the flat. I spend the time sleeping late, going to the beach, visiting old friends, and going out with Rolf. This will be the last time I'll see him in mufti. He, too, has joined the British Army.

Sarafand, July 18, 1942

There is very little work for me here. Daily I am expecting a posting. Will it be as staff car driver or will it be a promotion as driving instructor? I am now working as instructor for new driver-trainees.

Sarafand, July 21, 1942

Today I had an accident, but not through my fault. An ATS driver came in from Gaza. I jumped on the running board of her truck and just wanted a lift for a couple of blocks to the hospital. About one hundred meters away another truck was parked. She passed it so close that, had I stayed on the running board, I would have been crushed between the two vehicles. I jumped at the last moment and sprained my ankle.

Sarafand, July 22, 1942

I had a long talk with Subaltern Cole. She wanted to post me to Tel-El-Kebir in Egypt, where my former unit had gone, and recommended corporal's stripes for me, but I am not enthusiastic about it. I told her that, of course, I would go wherever I was sent but that I am not keen on promotion but rather on interesting work. I don't know what will happen.

Sarafand, July 24, 1942

A few girls left today with orders for 504 Company in Tel-el-Kebir. My sprained ankle saved me from being one of them. Perhaps this is just a delay, but maybe I'll get something more to my liking. I must lie down almost all the time to get the swelling down in my ankle. Rhett, my lorry, has been dumped. Our officers are using a staff car provided by the motor pool. There is no need for a special ATS driver. Irene is going to stay here to carry rations.

Sarafand, August 1, 1942

Hurrah! Tomorrow I am finally leaving, as an ambulance driver, to Alexandria. Because of my greater driving experience I am being posted to 502 Company in Alexandria. This unit is supposed to be the best and most elite company of the ATS. They're all English girls and Subaltern Cole asked me yesterday if I thought my English was good enough for this assignment. "Of course!" I answered. Well, I'll just have to learn fast! I have a thousand things to do, beginning with packing.

In transit to Egypt, Sunday, August 2, 1942

There are about one hundred girls being posted to Egypt; ten of them are going with me to Alexandria. I don't know any of them since they're all from the last bunch of recruits. Lorries took us to Lydda. It's now 4 P.M. and awfully hot. We are sitting surrounded by our kit-bags, haversacks, and steel helmets, waiting for the train. We're all grouchy since we've been waiting in the hot sun for over an hour and a half. Palestine railroads never run on time. Nothing seems to run on time in the Middle East and no one seems to care. *"Malesh!"* ["It does not matter"—one of the first Arabic words I learned.] *Malesh* the waiting! *Malesh* the heat! *Malesh* the flies! What does it matter? Finally the train arrived. The compartments were jammed, hot and smelly, but I didn't mind too much since I was on my way and each mile would bring me closer to action.

Slowly we traveled southward. Outside it was growing dark. The countryside was changing, the rolling hills of Palestine leveling off to a vast, flat wasteland. Gone was the lush green. Only barren desert remained, stretching endlessly. Since blackout regulations were strictly enforced, there was nothing to do but try to sleep.

In transit to Egypt, Monday, August 3, 1942

We had an awful night. Everyone slept wherever she could find a little room, some on the floor, some on the benches. I found a place among our kitbags and had the feeling that they were all filled with steel helmets. I kept waking up as the train slowed down or came to a complete stop waiting for trains coming the other way, most of them Red Cross trains. Sometimes I caught a glimpse, through a hastily raised shade, of stretchers with wounded, casualties from the fighting in the Western Desert. The front is moving closer.

The train stopped in Kantarah, the border town between Palestine and Egypt. We were glad to get out and stretch. The two-hour stopover meant a hot meal and a few drops of warm water. We tried hard, but not too successfully, to wash the mixture of sand and dirt off our faces. Dawn crept up quickly and with the rising sun our spirits also rose. Tonight would see us at our new posts.

It is only a short stretch from Kantarah to Benha, where we changed trains for Alexandria. A fast train in peacetime makes this trip crossing the Suez, the Egyptian desert and part of the Nile Valley in three hours, but this is not a fast train and this is not peacetime. Besides, the eastern side of the Nile is densely populated with soldiers' camps and at each one we have to stop to discharge more men. We passed Tel-El-Kebir, where my old outfit is now stationed. I felt no regrets but rather thought myself lucky not to be there. My siege in the hospital and then my sprained ankle had spared me from another boring camp life. As far as I could see, Tel-El-Kebir looked exactly like Sarafand, like any camp. It was here that the ATS officer in charge got off with the remaining girls, advising me that from now on I would be in charge of the ten girls bound for Alexandria. She gave me the movement orders and quickly disappeared. Soon the train stopped again. The door was pushed open and a dirty face grinned at us, babbling unintelligible guttural words of which I understood only "Benha."

Apparently this was where we had to get off. The dirty face was the railroad official. To prove it, he energetically helped us with our baggage. After piling it on the platform, he stood motionless, with outstretched hand. We gave him his *baksheesh* for which, he said, Allah would bless us till our dying day. Someone told us to hurry over to the other platform because the train from Cairo to Alexandria would leave in five minutes. Hurry! How can one hurry with kitbag, rations, and gasmask, while trying not to lose any of the girls in the midst of hundreds of shouting, gesticulating natives who are trying to hang on to your jacket, arms and legs?

"*Baksheesh!*"

"Sister! You want to buy eggs?"

"George! Shoeshine?"

It was several weeks before I understood that male and female alike are addressed as George, Sister, Joe and Captain! Arriving on the other platform, we found ourselves waiting again. No train in sight. I felt more and more uncomfortable. The number of natives around us increased. They sat in groups, the women apart from the men. They discussed us, and, judging from their loud laughter, they found us most comical. They squatted there, chewing and spitting, oblivious to the flies settling on them. Children, whose hair had never seen a comb, were covered with sores all over their bodies. The babies' eyes were so covered with flies that they couldn't open them. I felt disgust mingled with pity. Carefully I watched my belongings so that they would not be touched by any of the crowd.

A Corporal came out of the station office, looking bewildered at the sight of girls in uniform. Waving his arms and shouting, "Yallah, Yallah!" he cleared a path for himself. "The train will be here in ten minutes. Where are you girls going?"

"Up to Alexandria."

"Alexandria? Are you nurses?"

"No, ambulance drivers."

"Ah, you're joining 502, Captain Otto's outfit."

"Do you know it?"

"Of course. Everyone does."

Before he could give us more details, the train arrived. For a change the first and second class compartments were almost empty. We settled back to enjoy the views of fertile, flat green land bordering the Nile, the Delta—natives guiding their blindfolded donkeys walking round and round, turning water wheels, camels laden with goods, walking along the train track on the way to the market, men and boys working with ox-drawn plows. The Egyptian native, unlike the Palestinian Arab, who wears a tight-fitting robe, is clad in a long, flowing garment, the *gellabiah*. Instead of the head-scarf or *keffiyah*, he wears a scull cap. His appearance is not as impressive as that of the nomads I have seen in Palestine. Although we were moving along quite swiftly, no breeze found its way into our compartment. Our uniforms were soaked with sweat. A layer of fine sand covered everything, and our parched throats found no relief in the luke-warm drinking water. My first sight of the Nile was disappointing. Was this sluggish, muddy, yellow river the same that had swept along the royal barges of Cleopatra, Anthony, and Caeser? Had they, too, passed the countless washing, spitting, drinking natives and their oxen, who use its waters for bathing, urinating, and bowel movements? Every drop of water here means disease and sometimes death. The English, I learned later, had posted warnings every few feet along the banks, that any soldier who so much as got his hands wet with this water had to report to the nearest medical officer!

An Egyptian train official entered our compartment. He was wearing an old, grimy khaki uniform that had seen much better days. His wide feet were bare, his fez set at an angle on his head. He twirled his mustache with importance and padded in our direction. "Cheerio, George," he announced to everyone in general and followed this with an amazing series of gyrations of the right hand as a show of manners and sign of respect. What a queer salute it was!

"Salaam, Sister! Papers please, Sister."

I extended our movement orders. "Thank you!" He bowed low over my hand and took the papers, then stood silent for a moment, savoring the importance of his position. I watched quietly as a beetle climbed up his foot. Balancing on one leg he squashed the beetle between his toes. Then he pronounced darkly, *"No koyes!"* He regarded us with angry eyes. *"No koyes!* Only for *ten!"*

Though our knowledge of Arabic was sketchy, we all knew the meaning of *"No koyes."* It meant "no good."

I gestured impatiently for the papers and immediately saw the trouble. We were eleven girls with movement orders for ten. My name had been omitted! The conductor saw his duty and was about to do it. *"No koyes!"* he bellowed with finality. "Go back! Get out of train! Sisters better get out!"

Chances looked slight, but I began to talk, to persuade, to cajole, to threaten. At last, a speculative look crept into his face. He asked softly, "You got bully beef?" (This was canned beef, the common army ration.)

"Yes, sure, we have bully beef," I replied.

"You got *three?*"

We looked at each other in silent understanding. Yes, we most certainly had three tins. "Yes, we have three. Three whole bully beef."

With extended hand the Egyptian official proclaimed, "*Koyes! Koyes!* You go to Alexandria!" I nodded. The transaction was concluded on the spot.

It was late evening when we arrived in Alexandria—the trip had taken thirty hours. We stumbled blindly off the train, eyes bloodshot from lack of sleep, faces in need of a good scrubbing. Our uniforms were a wrinkled mess since we hadn't changed them in two days. Our only thoughts were of hot food, hot baths and a soft army bunk. But there were surprises waiting for us. Two drivers from 502 Company were waiting for us at the train station. In their tailored uniforms, silk stockings (the regulation issue, which we wore, were of Khaki-colored cotton) and perfect make-up, they looked like officers, yet they wore no pips. Was this what the 502 privates looked like? They loaded us into a huge ambulance and after a short drive we arrived at our new billets. This was no camp, no army barracks, but two elegant apartment houses on a tree-lined avenue. Turbaned servants whisked our luggage away. Another member of 502, just as nattily dressed, led us to our rooms, rooms with wallpaper, carpets, comfortable beds. We couldn't believe it. Dinner would be served in half an hour. Quickly we freshened up and went down to the mess, but mess is the wrong word for this lovely dining room: tables laid with white linen, dark-skinned turbaned servants placing and removing delicious-looking food. Intimidated, we stood in the doorway listening to the easy laughter, looking at the well-tailored backs. Achmed (we came to know this lord of the servants very quickly) acknowledged us with a slight bow of his slim shoulders. We followed his white-gowned figure to the far end of the dining room to a little hidden corner, and we breathed again. We were among ourselves. The English girls did not bother us; in fact, they ignored us. We were excused immediately after our meal. Some of the girls appear to be depressed, but I feel a challenge. The obvious and absolute self-assuredness of these British girls is something I have never run across before, and I am very impressed by it. It's way past midnight and I'm completely exhausted.

Alexandria, August 4, 1942

Our first day at 502 MAC is immediately full of new work and new impressions. Breakfast had no resemblance to what we had been used to at camp. Again we were served by Egyptian waiters in long white robes with red sashes and fezzes. The atmosphere is rather one of an elegant, expensive *pension* than of army billets. After breakfast we were shown around our quarters. 502 Company occupies three floors in two adjacent apartment houses on the fashionable Rue Fouad. In the first building, on the ground floor, there is a large kitchen, a dining room (no separate Sergeant's Mess—all NCOs and other ranks eat together), a sitting room, and a most luxurious bar called the Rotor Arms. Most of the bedrooms, each accommodating two or three girls, are on the second floor. In the next building are the officers' quarters, the Transport Offices, and Quartermaster Stores. We were taken to the carpark across the street and introduced to the three fitters. I never before had seen women mechanics and these three, even in their dirty overalls, managed to look like ladies. They showed us the different kinds of ambulances the unit uses: large Austins, capable of carrying four, in emergencies even five, stretcher cases or ten sitters; a few Dodges, which carry only two stretchers and some older Fords, which also carry four stretcher cases.

After lunch we new arrivals were summoned to a meeting, held in the 'sitting room.' When the commanding officer walked in, we jumped to our feet. She motioned us to sit down, took off her hat and gloves, and stepped to the platform. I could not believe my eyes. So this was Captain Otto! I knew her! She had once visited Sarafand and I had been assigned to drive her around. Even then I had been impressed by her dignity and charm.

"Girls!" Captain Otto's voice was a quiet but firm request for attention. Our eyes focused on her expectantly.

"I imagine," she said, "or rather I *know* that you're all anxious to hear the order of the day, so I won't waste time with tedious formalities. I hope," she added with a quick, friendly smile, "that the accommodations are to your liking."

We thought back to our barracks in Palestine, the strict regimentation, made a brief comparison, and smiled back.

"Let me tell you," she continued, "the purpose of your posting to Alexandria. You will be given four additional weeks of driver training here, after which you will be re-assigned to other camps."

Her words "re-assigned—four weeks training" were the only words we heard. Our faces fell. Captain Otto noticed but did not comment. She continued, "Re-assigned to other camps, camps in great need of good drivers. Frankly, I can't tell you much about the Army's plans for you, but, in any case," and again she reassured us with that quick, disarming smile, "by the time the four weeks have passed, you'll be the best bunch of drivers the Army's ever had." She had sensed our keen disappointment and was trying to help us accept it. Then she glanced in my direction.

"Wait! I know you!" she exclaimed. She had recognized me in this crowd of girls, after such a long time. "Aren't you B-B-Bo . . ."

"Bonin, M'am," I said.

"Yes, certainly. You were staff driver at Sarafand, weren't you? But what are you doing among these trainees? You *are* already a driver and, as I remember, quite a good one!"

"Yes, M'am."

"Would you like to remain with our company, Bonin?"

"I'd love to, M'am."

She turned to the Sergeant-Major. "Pat, take her out this afternoon for a test run." She nodded and once again gave her attention to the rest of the group. I was too excited to hear the rest of her speech. Here was my chance to become part of this extraordinary outfit!

"All right, Bonin. Start her up," said Sergeant-Major Curlewis. My driving test began. First, I had to drive through some of Alexandria's city traffic, stopping and starting on various inclines and parking in narrow spaces, all the time getting the feel of the heavy ambulance with its huge, waist-high desert wheels. Then back at the yard I had to drive between cans placed as far apart as the width of the car, backing between them without knocking over a single one. After that, as a final test, a pail of water was placed in the rear of the ambulance. I had to drive over and around a number of potholes without spilling a drop! A badly wounded soldier, I was told, feels every pebble in the road, especially if he is a stretcher case, and 502 has always prided itself on the fact that it has driven wounded soldiers thousands of miles, over the worst roads, with a minimum of discomfort to its patients. Then the test was over. I had passed and now I was really 'in'! I would be a member of 502, and that was reason to be proud.

Alexandria, August 5, 1942

I am sharing a nice room with three of my travel companions. All of us feel rather strange, at times almost uncomfortable, in our new surroundings since everything is so very different from Sarafand. All the 502 girls—there are about thirty of them—are dressed like officers and we never know who is an NCO. Instead of the sewed-on regulation stripes, they sometimes wear little pins, at other times not even those. On their off-days they all prefer to wear mufti within quarters. Of course, only English is spoken. Everyone is extremely well-mannered, well-groomed, and smiles at us politely but distantly. This atmosphere of genteel superiority pervades the entire establishment and intimidates us. It is my first introduction to the English upper class.

As I found out later, 502 Company originally had been part of the MTC (Mechanized Transport Corps), which had its origin long before the war. Since this was a voluntary organization, all drivers had to furnish their own uniforms, received no pay, and put their own cars at the government's disposal. They drove all kinds of vehicles all over England. In World War II their first unit to leave for France was an ambulance unit. Captain Otto and Lieutenant Angus are the only two in the present 502 Company left from that group. During the evacuation at Dunkirk, Penny Otto had been captured while driving an ambulance full of wounded soldiers, but she succeeded in a daring escape, saving her ambulance and her patients. For this exploit she received the Croix de Guerre. After the fall of France the remnants of the unit were re-equipped and reinforced to twenty-five girls with twelve ambulances. In July of 1940 they were sent to Kenya to serve with South African troops. They shipped out at Glasgow and after eighteen days arrived in Capetown, from where they were sent to Durban. Finally a troopship took them to Mombassa, the main port of Kenya. They had hoped to be sent into the mountains to help the South Africans, who were fighting the Italians, but instead they stayed in Mombassa, mostly doing staff-car driving and transporting nursing sisters. In March, 1941, they received orders to move to Cairo, where they were to join a second MTC unit which had been sent out from England. By now only seventeen of the original twenty-five were left. The others had preferred to join the South Africans or go back to England. Those seventeen went by ship to Port Said and from there drove their ambulances in convoy to Cairo. Sixty other MTC girls awaited them there. In March of 1941 both groups joined and became the 11th MTC. They worked as ambulance drivers for almost a year, when a great change took place. General Headquarters, probably under the influence of Miss Chitty, the Middle East Commander of the ATS, had decided that the unofficial status of the MTC would have to be changed. They were presented with several choices: They could sign on as officers in the ATS, or WAAF, they could take civilian jobs in the Middle East, or they could return home to England. Twenty-nine of the girls opted to stay together and form an ATS unit. Eight of these were of the original group of twenty-five who had left England for South Africa. Penny Otto, as the new commander of 502 Company, did some hard negotiating as a condition for joining the ATS. These girls were not to be transferred from their unit without their consent. They would be allowed to continue wearing their MTC uniforms but with the ATS insignia. They could enter officers' clubs when off duty and no one other than privates could be posted to their unit. On the 9th of November, 1941, the 11th MTC ceased to exist and became 502 MAC—ATS.

In December the unit moved to Alexandria. Here they were kept extremely busy. Rommel was advancing in North Africa. Wounded were shipped from Tobruk to Alexandria and had to be taken to the 8th and 64th General Hospitals in town. Trains bound for Suez and Palestine had to be loaded with evacuees from these two hospitals. Several ambulances had to be on duty twenty-four hours a day at each hospital. Convoys transferred casualties to Indian and Australian hospitals further out from Alexandria. Each week, 502 carried several hundred patients, logging in thousands of miles. By the spring of 1942 the fighting in the Western Desert had come closer and 502 soon found themselves shorthanded. They looked for new drivers who, they hoped, would fit into their kind of outfit. Local recruiting added four drivers. One, the daughter of one of the wealthiest local families, became a part-time driver. Three others were English girls living in Egypt. In March, 1942, recruiting for the ATS in Palestine had begun. It was to this group that 502 looked for reinforcements, but very few of the girls had any driving experience. I was the third Palestinian driver to be accepted into 502. The shortage of drivers was not limited to ambulance drivers. Lorry drivers and staff-car drivers were needed in camps all over the Middle East and 502 Company from now on was to train small groups of Palestinian ATS girls, who were sent to 502 after their basic training in Sarafand. My ten travel companions were the first arrivals to receive such driving instructions. In the future, 502 would pick, here and there, a promising girl to become a member of their, or I could now say, *our* company.

I must mention one more important member of 502—Pandora, a beautiful, black, standard French poodle. She is actually Miss Otto's dog, but the entire unit looks upon her as its mascot. Yet Pandora does not seem spoiled, albeit she's a bit snobbish, rather like the rest of the outfit. At least, that is my first impression.

Alexandria, August 6, 1942

I have been told that I'll have to move out of my room since I do not belong to the trainees and soon will begin my real work as an ambulance driver. In the meantime, we have been driving all over Alexandria and its surroundings to get acquainted with the layout, the hospitals, the harbor, the train station, and so on. I find the city exciting. In some respects it strikes me as more mid-Eastern, in other ways as more European than Palestinian cities, the latter because it is far larger than either Haifa, Tel-Aviv, or Jerusalem. Many streetcar lines cross the wide boulevards. The buildings are higher, older, and grayer than those in Palestine and, to judge from our own building, contain large apartments with high windows, high ceilings, and elevators. I am impressed with some of the spacious homes surrounded by well-groomed gardens. Beautiful parks make Alexandria appear greener than all of Palestine together. On the other hand, the many natives in their long, white gowns, who fill the streets and hang onto streetcars and busses like bees on a honeycomb, give the city a very mid-Eastern appearance. Most of these natives understand no English but, whenever possible, try to catch your attention with their eternal plea for 'Baksheesh.'

After the morning drive we have theoretical and practical lectures concerning the maintenance of cars. Not only do we have to keep the inside spotless and check oil, water, tire pressure, battery, etc., but also at least once a week every driver is expected to clean the engine and for workshop inspection even the undercarriage has to sparkle. I am not particularly fond of all this cleaning and polishing, but I suppose that ambulances have to shine, at least 502's do. I don't believe that there is a single outfit in the entire army that keeps its cars in such excellent condition as 502 does. No wonder that this unit has such an outstanding reputation. This is one more reason for being proud to be one of them.

Alexandria, August 8, 1942

We had our first day off and went swimming at Sidi Bishr beach, about six miles out of town. The beach is very clean and almost deserted except for a few families who rent or own little cabins, some of them quite beautifully outfitted with comfortable deck chairs, couches, even bars. Our Company has rented two such beach cottages, which are at the disposal of anyone in 502 at any time. They are very comfortable and allow us to spend the entire day at the beach. Swimming was excellent, the water clear and clean. The waves were not as high as those on Tel-Aviv beaches so that we could swim out far.

In the afternoon we hailed a cab to take us into the heart of the city. This may seem like an ordinary procedure, but here it is more like taking one's life into one's hands. The drivers appear totally unaware of road courtesy or defensive driving. Leaning on their horns, they proceed at breakneck speed, with shouts of "Yallah! Yallah!," never yielding, missing cars and pedestrians by inches.

Our first stop was the Cafe Beaudroux, located at a busy corner in the downtown section of Alexandria. Here the European world meets, and chauffeurs in big limousines drop expensive-smelling ladies who, after their shopping, idle away their hours chatting, nibbling on French pastries, and drinking countless cups of coffee. We, too, sat there relaxing, lounging back in our chairs, sipping our iced coffee, and absorbing the atmosphere around us. Hawkers in long, white gowns shrieked out their wares. Children raced up and down the street accosting passersby, begging for *baksheesh,* or trying to sell dirty pictures to soldiers. Arabs in western dress, with a touch of East, their fez, passed by, arm in arm, gesturing eloquently, swatting or pushing aside diseased beggars. The sun melted the passing scene. Flies settled on the crumb-spread table. We flicked them away with our newly-acquired horse-tail switches. My energy began to ooze away, and we agreed to postpone our shopping for another day. For our return trip we decided on a *garry.* This horse-drawn carriage, with its moderate speed, was a far safer, though slower, method of transportation than the taxi.

Alexandria, August 11, 1942

Four days ago I started working as a full-fledged member of 502, most of the time on detail at one of the big hospitals. Our duty hours on detail are from 7 A.M. to 5:30 P.M. or from 8 A.M. to 6:30 P.M. Added to this is the trip to our duty stations and return home and the cleaning and maintenance of the ambulance before calling it a day. This means that we work a twelve-hour day. However, between calls we often sit and wait, so there is time for a little reading, letter writing, knitting, and talking.

When we are at 'stand-by' the day begins at 8 A.M. The drivers on stand-by work in the parking lot opposite our flats, doing maintenance or helping our three fitters in the workshop. This is a dirty job, for which we wear overalls, but we must be ready within minutes in our proper uniforms when we get the order for 'convoy.' Convoy duty involves either unloading whole trains of wounded and taking them to hospitals, or driving to the harbor for loading or unloading of hospital ships, emptying our local hospitals and evacuating patients to hospitals farther away from the fighting, and again filling up emptied wards with new casualties. For details I have been assigned my own car, a Dodge. It accommodates two stretcher cases. It's new and has rather hard springs—probably it was originally designed to be a van. But whatever its faults, it's mine and I'm very proud of it. Many of the girls have given their ambulances names and mottos, which they have painted inside the cab on the dashboard. For instance: A squirrel with "Get cracking!" A turtle with "Slow but sure." A frog with "Berlin or bust!" I decided on Pinocchio with "Keep smiling!"

For convoy duty we use only the big Austin ambulances. These are built to accommodate four stretcher cases or even five if we use the floor too. The two top stretcher racks can be wound down, the stretchers folded underneath, and leather cushions placed over the lower benches. With this arrangement the ambulance can accommodate at least five sitting cases on each side. There is room to store drinking water, blankets, first-aid kit, and bedpans. The driver sits in an open cab, high above the huge desert wheels. The cab itself is equipped with canvas side screens, but these we seldom use.

Strange, even though I have now moved away from the trainees and live with the regular 502 girls, even though I have passed the driving test with flying colors, with it all, I feel a certain depression. The English, especially those of the upper class, have the faculty for making a foreigner feel inferior. It takes a long time to change their attitude—a little less long to get used to it. How fortunate that I share a room with Dora and Edith. These two Palestinian girls joined 502 several weeks before I did. They are both a bit older than I. Dora is originally from Hungary and Edith from Czechoslovakia. Among ourselves we usually speak German. With the trainees we speak Hebrew and, of course, English at work and with the other 502 members, so that my English is rapidly improving.

Alexandria, Sunday, August 23, 1942

For the last two weeks I have really been working hard. We work five days, then have the sixth day free. The work itself also is rotated. One day a driver is 'on detail,' the next day at 'stand-by.' 'On detail' means to be on call at either the 64th or 8th General Hospital. For each hospital three ambulances are needed. We take discharged patients to the station or back to their camps. We transfer patients from one hospital to another and are generally on call for the hospital. I prefer working at the 64th General Hospital since all trips from there involve a drive of at least ten miles. Also, our ready-room there is comfortable, with a large covered veranda.

Incidentally, I have been measured for trousers, had my fitting at an officer's tailor shop, and am now the proud possessor of two pairs of dark green gabardine slacks. Up until now I had to work in the issued skirts, which, when one climbs up into the driver's seat of the big Austins, are really impossible. The poor trainees are mostly working in their overalls, but the Army is supposed to come out with a woman's issue of trousers soon. Of course, they won't look anything like 502's tailored gabardines.

Alexandria, August 27, 1942

The news from the Western Desert continues to be grave. Rommel with his Africa Corps and the Italians are still advancing. They are now about one hundred miles from Alexandria. General Alexander has replaced General Auchinleck, and General Montgomery is now in command of the 8th Army. Reinforcements are pouring in—tanks, guns, men. Alexandria resembles a city under siege. During dark nights the sky is alight with searchlights looking for enemy planes. As soon as there is some moonlight, the attacks begin and the anti-aircraft batteries thunder incessantly. When I first heard the guns boom I would rush out into the street to watch this spectacular sight. Now I am used to it, and since during full moon nights seventy percent of our unit have to be on stand-by, ready to go on duty, we all go early to bed to catch a few hours of sleep, never mind the air attacks. The wounded are pouring into Alexandria, a ceaseless stream, but we do not have time to reflect on the huge numbers of bleeding, dying men. Our workload has increased. We are up at 7 A.M. Twelve hours of hospital duty. Then back before dark, in time to clean the ambulances thoroughly. Up again at 7 A.M. Eighth General, Fifth General, 64th General Hospital. Enter cases here, evacuate them there. Carloads transported to hospital ships for England. About twenty cars are always out on convoy duty, sometimes bringing in new casualties, sometimes evacuating men farther east. We don't mind the hard work, and sometimes we feel rewarded when we see relief in the eyes of a badly wounded patient as he recognizes the 'Blue Devil' insignia of our company and breathes, "502! Thank God!" and falls asleep, perhaps for the first time in days.

Alexandria, September 1, 1942

I have been here for four weeks. The first trainees have finished their course and will be sent to Cairo or to camps east of Alexandria as staff-car or lorry drivers. Three are staying here, driving lorries for Mustapha Barracks. They (Sasha, Teddi and Deborah) have been dubbed the 'milk girls' since their loads consist mainly of milk cans. Ten new girls have arrived, but since their quarters are separate and their hours different from ours, we have little contact with them.

Alexandria to Damanhur, September 2, 1942

I have just returned from my first convoy. Last night the schedule on the roster read as follows: "Roll call, 7 A.M. Each driver to take one trainee. Lunches will be distributed at breakfast. Sgt. Hall in charge. Twenty ambulances. 7:15 A.M. at Eighth General Hospital." There followed a list of names and cars. And there it was: "Bonin, Ambulance #1207450." This was the real thing!

We were going to Damanhur, which lies fifty miles south on the way to Cairo, a hundred-mile round trip. At the Eighth General Hospital we were loaded with four stretchers to an ambulance. Most of the patients were amputees, who had to be transferred to hospitals farther east. All available space in Alexandria hospitals is now needed for the daily casualties that are being brought in from the Western Desert. I was seventh in convoy. Arriving at the hospital, we jumped out, opened the back doors of our cars, and then, one after the other, backed them into spaces designated by Sgt. Hall. Italian prisoners, working as stretcher bearers, hurried over and took blankets and stretchers from our cars. In a few minutes they were back with patients.

I waited by the side of my ambulance and while it was being loaded, jumped inside to make the wounded men as comfortable for the journey as possible. "Would you like a cigarette? A drink of water? All comfortable?" Then at last we were on our way, one straight line of Red Crosses, winding through the city, then spreading out, the distance between cars widening as we met the open country. The patients were serious cases, so our speed did not exceed twenty miles per hour. We rolled along. The day became hotter. The patients slept. After an hour of slow progress, I too began to feel sleepy. The route led us along a canal of the Delta, its flat, green country broken only by a palm tree now and then. Then a piece of desert road. Dust, sand, heat. My trainee, who was to have learned something on this trip, was fast asleep.

Slowly, carefully, the convoy crept along, one strong chain and I a link in the chain. This was not glamorous but serious, and it made me feel good. The ambulance, not built for the driver's comfort but for the patient's, was steady and solid, with excellent springs to soften any bumps for the wounded. It was not streamlined, since it was not meant for speed, but rather cumbersome, square, and somewhat top-heavy.

The road again became greener on both sides. Little rivers marked our entry into the Delta again. The water was gray and sluggish, like that of the Nile. Cattle, up to their shoulders, rested in the coolness of the water. Natives slept under date palms while their women worked in the fields. Ox-driven water pumps became more and more frequent. By noon the heat had reached its peak. My shirt was soaked, my hair wet. We would get water and a cigarette in Damanhur. Finally, the last two miles, then the outskirts of the town. Natives gaped at us. Dirty, smelly streets, then through another part of town with well-kept gardens and beautiful villas—as ever, the contrast of very rich and very poor. At last, the General Hospital.

Unloading was faster than anticipated. All the drivers were exhausted from the slow journey, so we decided to break up and drive back in groups of three, which would allow for greater speed. On the way home there was no necessity to stop for patients' needs. Not every hole in the road had to be carefully avoided. I drove along at forty-five miles per hour. (All our ambulances have a governor set at forty-five m.p.h. and cannot be driven any faster.) A cool breeze blew my hair about my face, and because there were no patients along, I could sing, which is the best way to stay awake. We were home by 4 P.M. I felt in such great spirits that I didn't even mind going through the usual routine of cleaning the car and checking it.

Alexandria, Saturday, September 12, 1942

Last night was the beginning of the Jewish New Year, and I am still impressed with how nicely the English girls behaved. It began when I came home late last night from duty at 64th General Hospital. Sergeant-Major Curlewis was blaming herself for having put me on late duty, so that I had not been able to join the other Palestinians for a special dinner at the Jewish Club. Well, I did not really care. For me the New Year still begins on January 1. The next surprise was the timetable, which listed me for a day off. I thought that it must be a mistake, but Lieutenant Stewart explained that they had tried to let off as many of us Palestinians as possible. Then this morning as I woke up the first thing I saw was a little powder box with a card from Captain Otto: "To Bonin, with best wishes from all of us." We had all received either cigarettes or powder. And at breakfast we had an extra portion of honey, and all the English girls came to our table wishing us "Happy New Year, kids!" In the afternoon we were invited to the homes of different Jewish families of Alexandria. I went with three of our trainees to the home of a Squadron leader and his wife. The dinner was so posh and elegant that we were glad when it was over. The evening we spent at the Jewish Club having a good time, meeting friends and dancing. Actually, this was the first occasion since my days in the kibbutz that I had really celebrated the event of the Jewish New Year.

Alexandria, Monday, September 14, 1942

I had just finished work, showered and dressed, ready to go to dinner, when I was told "Convoy"! Two ships, after an unsuccessful raid on Tobruk, had arrived at the harbor. We were to get the casualties from the ships and take them to the 64th General Hospital—Sergeant Hall, Hayes, myself, Ladyman, and Brown. When we left our depot it was still light, but by the time we arrived in Ras-El-Tin it was dark. We drove through endless gates, narrow streets, and across unguarded railroad tracks. After we had driven around for about an hour, turning and reversing again and again in the tightest spots, we were finally informed that the two destroyers were anchored at the other end of the docks. By now it was pitch dark. One could not see the hand in front of one's face, and, of course, the headlights were no help since they are permanently covered with masks.

Nerves taut, we continued our search. Cumbersome, in low gear, our five large Austin ambulances rocked through the narrow alleys of the harbor until we arrived at a quay. The road, if one could call it that, must have been bombed because the sheds and warehouses on both sides had been demolished and the rubble was piled high. Some of the scrap iron had been pushed to the side so that perhaps a small car could get through in the daytime, but it is still a miracle to me how we got through at night without ripping the canvas sides of our wide ambulances. We finally arrived at the designated quay but saw no ships. Kay Brown distributed a few dry bisquits, which we swallowed gratefully since we had missed dinner. Then a navy officer appeared and explained that again we had been given wrong information and were at the wrong quay. Reversing would have been impossible so we had to turn the ambulances around. Sergeant Hall guided each of us with a flashlight or we would have landed in the water. It was impossible to distinguish land, sky, or water. Then back through that nasty scrap alley and to the other end of the port where, finally, loomed the outline of a destroyer. No other ambulance was in evidence. Had I lost the others? That did not matter; the only thing of importance was to get the wounded off the ship. The masts of the ship stood out blacker against its black background, the sky or the water. Men clustered around a single lamp on deck, men who had undertaken a raid on Tobruk with unbelievable courage but had been repulsed by superior enemy strength. Unshaven, silent, black they stood there, black from their beards and the smoke of gunfire, in uniforms burned black. They stared at me dully. I felt very small facing them and ashamed of my clean uniform. Since I was the first ambulance to take off their wounded, I received the most critical cases. As much as I could see in the darkness, they did not have even the most necessary bandages, only a few rags torn from a sheet or some other piece of cloth. They were terribly burned and covered with dried blood. By the time my four stretcher cases had been loaded, Molly's and Pat Hall's ambulances appeared out of the darkness. They had been loading at a second destroyer, about fifty yards farther on, and I had not even been aware that another ship was so close, it was that dark. The three of us started off. We drove the entire way between five and fifteen miles per hour. My stretcher cases moaned and cried. One hallucinated. I could not look after them. I had to find the way, to avoid potholes and shocks. A medical orderly would have been a great help to the wounded, but those seem to be sent only when they are totally superfluous.

At 10:30 P.M. we arrived at 64th General Hospital. Finally, while waiting for the stretcher bearers, we could look after our men. I turned on the light in my ambulance and saw what war really looks like. Four boys. One was unconscious. The second turned in agonized pain. One had his face burned beyond recognition. The fourth appeared to have splinters of metal in his legs and back and bled profusely. The blanket had adhered to his back, causing him excruciating pain. I gave them water, lit cigarettes and held them while the men inhaled. Their hands were too badly burned to be of any use. And I tried to comfort them. They were as thankful as if I had saved their lives.

Brown and Ladyman also had arrived and everyone was busy with the stretcher cases. Then it was my turn to be unloaded. The unconscious soldier was the first. I had not paid too much attention to him since the other three had claimed my time, but now I looked at him more closely. So did the stretcher-bearers, who already had half-pulled out the stretcher. I realized that I was looking into the open eyes of a dead man. While the other three were unloaded a Medical Officer came out to look at the first soldier. After a short examination he covered him up. He must have died from loss of blood. The blankets, his stretcher, and the stretcher below were covered with it. The chaplain came out, closed his eyes, and said a short prayer. Then I drove him to the mortuary. Another hour of waiting because no one could find the right key for the door!

Two MPs waited with me. They were telling jokes and laughing, but I could not join them, not after what I had experienced that night and with the dead soldier still in my car. When I arrived home it was midnight. After the five of us had left that evening, all drivers had been called out with all available ambulances, even the small cars, to unload the ships. But by then we had taken the worst cases and their wounded were not as serious, nor did they have to wander around the docks searching for the right ships.

Alexandria, September 19, 1942

Today I was stand-by at the 64th General Hospital when Dora drove up to the MI room. I walked over to her ambulance. "What's your load? How many cases?" I asked.

"Just one," she replied, laconically. "Dead."

We had a cigarette while waiting for the MO to certify the death, and we watched as the stretcher-bearers opened her ambulance. Out of it bounced a head. It rolled grotesquely into the gutter, where it stopped, open-mouthed and staring. The stretcher-bearers began to giggle.

"My God! Don't just stand there! Pick it up quickly!" someone said. The head must have been almost severed from the body by a shell fragment and the bouncing of the car had loosened it completely. There is still a lot about ambulance work I have trouble getting used to.

Alexandria to Bucelli, September 20, 1942

Now I am driving almost every day to Bucelli, where an Australian hospital, all in tents, and a South African Convalescent Depot are located. Sometimes we take patients there, at other times we evacuate them from Bucelli to trains or hospital ships. The trip, about thirty-five miles from Alexandria, usually takes from an hour to an hour and a half. I become acquainted with another part of Egypt. First the road leads through green fields tended by the natives. I am always impressed by the extent of these green acres, a landscape much more open and less confined than in Palestine. At irrigation wells the water is pulled up by cows, donkeys, or old, worn-out camels that go round and round the well, their eyes covered with sacks so that they cannot see how they keep circling. I am disturbed at this cruel treatment of the animals. Sometimes the road leads through a little village of mud hovels, filled with dirty children. After a bit the road cuts across Lake Idku, which appears quite shallow because I can see fishermen standing in the water almost a mile from shore, casting out their nets. At some places there is salt water, with its mineral deposits, on one side of the road, and on the other side the fresh water of the Nile. I enjoy watching the sailboats, called *Felukahs,* carrying their loads, mostly cotton bales, down the Nile. The road is very narrow, really only wide enough for one car. Fortunately, there is not much traffic. The natives, too, are a permanent danger to the driver. They sometimes jump without warning directly into the path of the car, oblivious to any honking. Or it is the children, donkeys, chickens, or dogs that appear suddenly right in the path of the ambulance. Another hazard is weather. When it rains, the oil which has collected on the asphalt surface makes the road perilously slick, especially for our Austin ambulances with their wide tires. We must slow to ten miles per hour or we would land in the ditch. Driving in the rain, altogether, is no fun in the open Austins, with the rain coming in the sides.

Alexandria, September 27, 1942

Our second group of trainees has left and the third group has arrived, among them, to my great joy, Irene, my pal from Sarafand. We have much to catch up on, but very little time. Our schedules are so different that we don't see much of each other. In addition to my regular duties, I am now learning to ride a motorcycle. It is something I have wanted to do for a long time, and now Pat Curlewis received permission from Captain Otto to teach me. I am on my way to becoming a dispatch rider.

It is exhilarating to ride a motorcycle, the wind blowing cool in my face. I am aware of the skill necessary in maneuvering and of speed, which one never experiences with the ambulances. Sometimes I ride behind a lorry loaded with soldiers. Bored, they look down at the helmeted, begoggled motorcycle rider following them. Then suddenly one soldier notices my lipstick and points it out to the others. The entire load of men starts to smile and wave to me. This is fun!

Alexandria, October 19, 1942

Much has changed during the last three weeks. With the steady advance of Rommel, our work load has become even heavier. More and more wounded are pouring in from the Western Desert. Then suddenly we received orders to evacuate all patients because a major battle was expected and the beds will be needed for incoming casualties. More trains, more hospital ships, and a steady stream of convoys to Damanhur and Bucelli. Our trainees have been sent away, to Cairo, Ismailiya, or back to Palestine. There is no time now for motorcycle lessons. All leaves have been canceled. Captain Otto asked us Palestinian drivers if we would like to leave also. If the Germans were to take prisoners, we Palestinians might be in greater danger than the others. Of course, we refused. Speculation is running high. Is the expected battle finally the attack we have all been hoping for? Are we going to make a stand and turn Jerry and the Eyeties back?

Alexandria, October 24, 1942

All day long we heard the booming of guns. There was no clear news all day. We know only that the battle of El-Alamein has begun.

El-Alamein, October 25, 1942

Up at dawn. Fully dressed in driving outfit, gas masks, and steel helmets, we all went down to the Mess for an early cup of tea. I am one of the drivers assigned for convoy. This time the direction is not south or east, as usual, but west. We are heading directly to the front, now only about forty miles away. It is hard to convey the excitement that filled me. We moved along, the familiar long row of red crosses, overtaking large convoys of tanks and heavy equipment, being passed by countless lorries full of soldiers who shouted and waved happily.

"Hi! Off we go! It's started!"

"The fun's ahead!"

"Those blokes'll know us when we get there!"

"Take good care of us when we come back, girls!"

The lorries were heavy with supplies, all moving in one direction on the one road leading to the front. Our progress was slow. Toward us ambulances rumbled slowly, filled with the first casualties of battle. Empty trucks hurried back to Alexandria for more equipment. Dust-covered dispatch riders and here and there a staff car sped by us in both directions. On we drove, becoming more and more aware of the stifling heat, the dust, and the increasing noise of gunfire. Suddenly, when the traffic congestion was at its height, there in the middle of the road, not even a mile from the front line, stood a military policeman, directing traffic as calmly as if he were standing in the middle of London! He separated our convoy, waving us toward different tents off the main highway. There were no roads. We had left the road and were driving inland. Surrounded by clouds of dust, I could make out some Red Cross tents ahead of me. An orderly jumped into my path, directing me to one of them. Stretcher-bearers were running to and fro. Blood-drenched stretchers were piling up outside the tents filled with casualties waiting to be treated. The number of wounded made any real treatment impossible. These tents were nothing but dressing stations where emergency dressings, mostly plaster of paris, were put over bleeding wounds, over stumps of arms and legs, over shell-shattered bodies. There was a mixed stench of blood, sand, and sweat.

I had hardly come to a halt, jumped out and opened the back doors of my ambulance, when the stretcher-bearers were there loading in five cases, then hurrying me away. In front of me another 502 driver, Scottie, had just received her five cases. We decided to stick together on our way home but had barely covered a mile when one of those sudden desert sandstorms came up, decreasing our visibility to zero. I was engulfed in a cloud of yellow sand, impenetrable as a wall. I honked my horn for Scottie to stop. Fortunately the storm lasted only a few minutes, but when the sand and dust had cleared we could not see the tents we had left behind nor the main road leading back to Alexandria. Worse still, our two ambulances now pointed in different directions! Who had turned? We did not know. Where were we? Far in the distance we could hear guns. Where were they? Whose guns were they? If we chose the wrong direction now, we would be headed toward the German lines or, even worse, into the minefields separating the German and English lines. We set out again. Nothing on the horizon but sand and silence, burst open intermittently by the thunder of the guns. At last, in the far distance, we saw trucks and an ambulance—not ours. We had no choice but to head for them. As we approached, Free French soldiers rushed to meet us. "What are you girls doing here?" they shouted.

"Looking for Alexandria!"

"You're a good many miles from there, but take this road and it will put you on the main highway."

Scotty and I had driven straight south instead of back east. After giving our patients water, we immediately headed on, to the disappointment of the French, who were so delighted to see girls that they wanted us to stop and dine with them!

Progress was slow, but three and a half hours later we delivered our soldiers to the 64th General Hospital in Alexandria, all of them alive, thank God. Scotty and I were the last of the 502 drivers to come in. The others had feared that we were missing in action!

Alexandria, October 26, 1942

Today is actually my day off, but that is out of the question. There are no days off, not even evenings off. All of us are on stand-by. Overnight our entire life has changed. All drivers are divided into day and night shifts. Each of us takes her food with her, since we never know how long we will be on the road. We are not driving any more to the actual battle zone. Since the front line is so close, the field ambulances are now bringing the wounded directly from the First Aid Dressing Stations to the 8th General Hospital in Alexandria. There they are quickly unloaded and checked by medical officers, who decide what hospital they will be taken to. It is our duty to deliver them to the assigned hospitals. However, most of our trips are to the Australian Hospital in Bucelli, thirty miles from Alexandria. The Commanding Officer there has requested and been granted the services of 502 because we have the reputation of taking especially good care of our charges. Some days we make three round-trips to Bucelli. The road at night is quite dangerous and at times I feel I must have a guardian angel who is protecting me from accidents.

I am very gratified that I had the chance to participate in the one convoy of 502 that went to the front line, but the work we are doing now is just as important. It is a good feeling to be useful, but how can I use the word "good" at all when daily I see hundreds of young men mutilated and maimed? Though we have been transporting wounded all along, the sheer number of casualties coming in now is staggering.

Alexandria, October 27, 1942

My turn for details at the 64th. I was disappointed at first since these days stand-by work is far more demanding, but details have to be done just the same. For this work we now use the smaller Dodge ambulances, leaving the big Austins for the more serious runs to Bucelli. The day, however, turned out to be quite interesting. Many of the wounded Germans are brought to the 64th, and it is part of our job to drive them to the POW camp as soon as they are well enough to travel. Today I got my first five German prisoners. How strange to hear real Bavarian and Berlin dialects again! At first I did not want to let them know that I spoke German. I thought I might learn something interesting from their talk among themselves, but seeing a woman ambulance driver so near the front appeared to have struck them dumb. Finally, I took the initiative and asked them, in German, if they, too, had women in uniform. "Of course!" they answered.

"Also ambulance drivers?"

"Of course!"

It was amazing with what arrogance they spoke. When we arrived at our destination one asked me, cockily, how much they owed for the taxi ride. I assured them, "You will pay for all of it as soon as the war is over!"

After I delivered my charges, an officer showed me around the entire POW camp. Hundreds of German and Italian prisoners squatted on the ground in two separate groups. They were probably the latest arrivals. Others were marched around in smaller groups, some were putting up tents, building latrines, or just waiting in long rows, I don't know for what. Their uniforms torn and filthy, their faces unshaven, haggard and dirty, they stared at me. No smiles, no cockiness or arrogance here. Watching them, I felt depressed and could not enjoy any sense of victory. The face of defeat left me with dejected rather than soaring spirits.

Alexandria, October 31, 1942

The newspapers state that the enemy is really on the run and soldiers returning from the front line tell us that Jerry and the Italians are in panic. Endless rows of prisoners are coming in from the desert. We are as busy as ever and during this, our busiest time, Miss Chitty, the ATS Chief Commander of the Middle East, has announced one of her sporadic visits to 502. What awful timing! Once again she probably wants to try to talk a few of the original 502 members into accepting commissions and leaving the unit. She is badly in need of NCOs and officers.

I just heard that Miss Chitty has already left. She must have spent less than an hour at our depot. Captain Otto explained to her that every driver is needed right here and no one is willing to leave her post, regardless of any promise of promotion. Maybe we won't see her again for a while.

Alexandria, November 1, 1942

Joe, a friend of mine in the RAF, whose hobby is radios, had promised me for a long time that if he could ever get his hands on an old radio, he would try to fix it up for me. Well, today he came with a beautiful big five-tube Phillips wireless. Lieutenant Steward gave me permission to connect it right away, though I will have to pay five piasters a week for the use of electricity. Now we can go to bed and get up listening to music. We can get London, and sometimes even New York. It is really a first-class set and surely must be worth at least fifty pounds.

Alexandria, November 7, 1942

Today churchbells were ringing all over England to announce the victory in Egypt. We heard the broadcast this evening. Listening, I got goosebumps and was overcome with a feeling of homesickness—but for what? For where? Germany? That's now enemy territory. England? Why, I don't know it. I've never even been there. Palestine? No, I never really felt at home there. Strange how sad the sound of bells can make one feel.

Alexandria, November 20, 1942

It rains and rains and rains. At noon I took four stretcher cases to Bucelli and came home drenched to the skin. The rain drips through the canvas roof of the ambulance and the wheels part big puddles in the uneven road, splashing the water up into the open driver's cab so that one gets soaked from above and below at the same time. One can't drive faster than fifteen miles per hour because the road is as slick as a dance floor and the slightest use of brakes would get the top-heavy ambulance skidding and landing in the canal, which runs parallel to the 'highway' on both sides. On the way back I saw exactly that. A native bus a few miles ahead of me lost control, turned over, and landed in the canal. I did not stop because we were strictly forbidden to intervene in civilian affairs. Later in the evening I heard on the radio that in this accident there were fourteen dead and many injured. To get into a better mood I try to find some music, but the wireless crackles so that I finally turn it off. I am lying on my bed getting more and more depressed. Perhaps it's the weather, perhaps it's the terrible accident I saw today, or perhaps it's just a general letdown after the strenuous work of the last few days. After all, this is the first day that I have a little time to think, and my thoughts don't move in a very positive direction. When Chief Commander Chitty was here three weeks ago and had to leave without obtaining her goal, we all had hoped for a respite from her visits, but no! As soon as the emergency was over, she called Captain Otto to Cairo. Miss Otto has just returned and there is a meeting of all the original 502 members. From what I understand, they want to draw up a statement making it clear once and for all that none of them wishes to accept a commission and leave 502, and that one of the conditions under which they had joined the ATS was the guarantee that they would not be posted against their will. Miss Chitty will have to give in. But what of us few latecomers? (There are now twelve of us.) We have no such guarantees and will have to go wherever the Army sends us. I would hate to have to leave here and would gladly forego any promotion for the privilege of belonging to 502. I do hope that Captain Otto will fight for us.

Alexandria, November 29, 1942

Rommel is retreating so fast that there is no need now for the hospitals in Alexandria to serve as first aid stations. Instead, things are returning to normal routine. Again we enjoy days off and even leaves are granted. I will begin mine tomorrow, together with Deborah, one of the other Palestinian drivers—seven days plus two days travel time to and from Tel-Aviv.

Alexandria, December 8, 1942

I'm back home again. At 502 that is! It's a gray and rainy day, but I'm so happy to be back. Everyone greeted Deborah and me warmly, and the best thing is that I consider 502 MAC my real home now, that this is where I belong, whereas all through my leave I felt that I was on a visit. The week passed quickly, seeing friends, going window shopping, and taking daily riding lessons. (Since most of the girls in 502 spend their free time playing golf or horseback riding, I want to be able to join them.) Wherever I went I had to tell about the war in the Western Desert. Though in miles Palestine is not that far removed, it now seems like another world to me. I have lost contact with the people there, with their daily concerns over money, clothes, family, and high prices. But then suddenly I realized that in some respects I have been more isolated from the world events than the Jewish population of Palestine. On my third day in Tel-Aviv all the stores, coffee houses, and cinemas were closed. Black flags hung on every building and long funeral processions crossed the city. The Jews of Palestine were demonstrating their sorrow at the terrible persecution of the Jews in Poland and Russia. I had heard nothing in Alexandria about the pogroms, deportations, concentration camps, slaughters and mass murder. It is impossible to comprehend, and I simply can't imagine that this also might be happening in Germany. I am fearful for my parents. I hope another Red Cross letter from them will reach me soon.

My return trip was an unexpected surprise. Felix, the fiance of one of my roommates at 502, called me from the Café Pilz on the day of my departure and told me that he was having a drink with a few American pilots who would be leaving for Ismalia in an hour. They would be happy to take me along. What about Deborah? O.K., she could come too. I called her, told her the good news, and packed hastily. Good old Felix came and got me, we picked up Deborah, and then off we went in

172

a lorry together with the Americans. This was my very first flight. The plane was a huge bomber. We could feel hardly any motion at all, and in an hour and ten minutes we arrived in Ismalia. (By train the trip takes about sixteen hours.) We took a comfortable room at the ATS hostel and I immediately called Rolf, who is now stationed here, looking forward to spending an unscheduled evening with him, but my surprise did not work. He had gone out for the evening. I left a message and saw him the next morning. We had only a few hours together until Deborah and I had to board the train for the short trip 'home.'

Alexandria, December 9, 1942

As I said yesterday, I am elated to be 'home,' but at the same time I can't shake a feeling of anxiety. The demonstration in Tel-Aviv against the persecution of Jews in Nazi-occupied countries has brought renewed fears about my parents. It's been so long since I heard from them. I don't dare to imagine what might have happened and try to block it all out of my mind. And I can't help harboring a certain resentment toward all the English girls in the outfit who talk of home as the most wonderful, unchanging place, waiting for their return. What will I return to? What and where will my home be? I must not dwell on these useless speculations.

Alexandria, December 10, 1942

With the quick advance of the 8th Army in North Africa and Rommel's retreat, the picture is changing for 502. We had hoped that less work here might mean a posting, bringing us again closer to the action. Instead, we received a bunch of new driver-trainees from Sarafand, which can only mean back to the routine of last summer. Everyone is disappointed. Since many of us now on stand-by are seldom called out, we have regular instructions in auto mechanics. We are all on our way to becoming fitters. Those of us who are called out, often have to drive wounded POWs, mostly Italians but also some Germans.

Alexandria, December 17, 1942

Rolf spent an unexpected five days in Alexandria. He had brought some POWs back and was waiting for a new transport to arrive in Alexandria. We spent almost every evening together.

Alexandria, December 26, 1942

My first Christmas in the Army. We celebrated in grand style. On Christmas Eve 502 held a great reception for all the senior officers and

173

civilian officials connected with the services. It was a most elegant affair with a hired dance band and buffets with so much food and so many delicacies that it did not seem like wartime but was rather reminiscent of a movie set. Yesterday we celebrated among ourselves. Cook brought in the traditional plum pudding and we toasted: "Ladies, the King!" After that there was a special toast for Captain Otto. We sang "For she's a jolly good fellow" and then there were presents under the tree. We all gathered round. In one corner, somewhat shy and bewildered, stood Achmed, Cook, and the rest of our servants. This was probably their first Christmas party. Their long white robes with sash and turban, next to our artificial Christmas tree with palm fronds in the background, looked most picturesque.

Today was boxing day and again we entertained in the evening. This time we invited all other ranks with whom we work together—personnel from the 64th and 8th General Hospitals, the fitters from the workshops, etc. It was a very different affair from the previous one. Most of the men were rather shy at first, but as the drinks, this time mainly beer, began to flow freely, the party made up in rambunctiousness what it lacked in elegance. By midnight we were glad it was over.

Cairo, January 23, 1943

When I came home last night, Pat Curlewis told me that I would be on special duty to drive Captain Otto to Cairo. I was terribly pleased and excited. The only fly in the car-grease was that I had to drive her in our small utility van, a car I was not very fond of. Since we had to leave at 5 A.M., I set my alarm at 4 A.M. because I had to wake Miss Otto, make tea, and check the car once more. Everything went as planned and at 5 A.M. we were on our way, including Pandora, who probably was looking forward to the trip as much as I was.

When I think of the first hour of that trip I am still angry. It was, of course, pitch dark, and since I did not know the road, I lost my way several times. Miss Otto had to direct me since I seemed to have been cursed with blindness. Though she tried to find excuses for me—that I sat so low in the car, that my vision was hampered, that the masked headlights did not shed enough light, I was simply furious with myself. Finally, dawn came. With increased vision we made good time and arrived at the ATS camp outside Mina at 8 A.M. While Miss Otto was busy there for an hour, I saw a few old acquaintances from the training camp in Sarafand, all of them quite jealous that I was a member of 502. From Mina it is only a fifteen-minute drive into Cairo. The road passes the famous Cheops pyramid. I found my first view of it a bit disappointing. The Sphinx cannot be seen from the road, and the pyramid appears so suddenly around a curve in the highway that one simply is not prepared for it.

We arrived in Cairo a little after 9 A.M. My first impression was that of an enormous and busy city, less European in character than Alexandria, more Arabic, noisier, more congested. I really did not see enough to make any judgment. We first drove to the Sporting Club at Gesirah. Miss Otto ordered breakfast and had hot baths prepared for us. We bathed, changed into skirts and jackets, and then breakfasted. The British really know how to live 'in the Colonies'! I then drove Miss Otto to a number of offices, to Headquarters, etc. From 12:30 to 3 P.M. I was free, but I was too tired to do any sightseeing. So I drove back to my old friends at the ATS camp outside Mina and after some more conversation with them, Pandora and I lay down on a bunk and slept for an hour. At 3 P.M. Pandora and I met Miss Otto at the Sporting Club, changed our clothes back to pants and battle jackets, and headed home. The first hour was uneventful. We made good time. Then all of a sudden the highway was covered with sand, blown from the desert that stretched on either side of the road as far as one could see. The small car began to swerve, turned three or four times, mostly on two wheels. It seemed to take minutes before I could bring it to a stop. Both of us were as white as sheets since neither of us had believed that we would get out of this unscathed. But the only damage was one tire blown out. I changed it quickly. By this time it had grown dark again and I dreaded the drive back through Alexandria's worst quarters, remembering the mishaps of the morning. I got us home without any further incident, however, but I felt really frustrated because surely I must have ruined Captain Otto's good opinion of my driving.

Alexandria, January 23, 1943

Tripoli has fallen! The 8th Army is marching on! The Americans have landed in North Africa. This afternoon's edition of the newspaper says:

> The Union Jack is now flying over Tripoli, which was occupied by the Eighth Army at daybreak yesterday after a 92-day campaign, during which it covered 1,300 miles.
>
> Forward elements of General Montgomery's forces entered the pride of Mussolini's now defunct empire at 5 A.M., after advancing all through the night.
>
> The Eighth Army's achievement has thrilled the Allied World

and has already been described by Mr. Cordell Hull as "one of the most overwhelming, outstanding and important victories of the war."

If the Americans advance as quickly as our 8th Army, all of North Africa will be liberated in no time. And then Europe? Italy? Greece?

Of course we are elated with the news. We only wish that we had been part of the advance. Penny Otto has tried everything to get us moved, to follow the Army, but the General Staff refused. We are needed here. Alexandria is still the base for the big General Hospitals. Red Cross ships arrive continuously. We are again busy day and night, unloading and transporting patients. Most of the trips are short distances to the 8th and 64th General Hospitals, or the longer trips to the Australian Hospital thirty miles out of Alexandria. We have a constant stream of ambulances coming and going. Sometimes we have to wait for hours at the harbor until the hospital ships come in. When they finally arrive, such vast numbers of wounded are unloaded that we can't hope to transport them all at once. It is now a common sight to arrive at a pier completely filled with row upon row of stretchers, hundreds of them, waiting to be lifted into ambulances. Again the hospitals are overcrowded and patients are being transferred by train further east, to the Canal Zone. Loading trains with patients has also become one of our regular duties.

We average about two to three hundred miles of driving a day. It is a good feeling to be useful again. Even waiting at the docks is interesting. It is exciting to watch the arrival of freight boats, unloading of ammunition, loading of materials for the advancing army, the coming and going of destroyers, corvettes, troop ships, minesweepers, at times even a battleship. We watch ships at dry-dock being repaired. We listen to the sailors tell stories of German and Italian retreats through Libya and Tunisia. Of this we also have enough evidence in our work. The hospital ships not only unload our own soldiers but scores of wounded German and Italian prisoners as well.

Alexandria, January 29, 1943

Today I was on duty at the 64th General Hospital. I had come home and was having a drink in our bar when the awful news came through that Miss Otto is dangerously ill, unconscious and diagnosed as having meningitis. She was on her way to Syria for a long-deserved leave when she was suddenly taken ill in Jerusalem. Her condition is very serious. A hush has fallen over all of us.

Alexandria, January 30, 1943

Every few hours, all through the night, we have been calling the hospital in Jerusalem. Miss Otto is still unconscious. I am stand-by today and so I run every few minutes into the office to find out if there is any news. I am quite beside myself with worry and realize that I care as much about her as if she were my own mother. The telephone rings constantly. Every five minutes someone comes to find out if there has been any change. Officers, civilians, churchmen—all of Alexandria is concerned. But then, Penny Otto is really a very special person. The best of human qualities are harmoniously combined in her.

Alexandria, January 31, 1943

Miss Otto regained consciousness. She is still on the critical list, but at least there is hope.

Alexandria, February 3, 1942

Just heard that Miss Otto is off the critical list. The doctors feel that she may be back at work in two months. Now life looks up again.

Alexandria, February 7, 1943

Today after work I had high tea at the Sporting Club where I had the honor of seeing His Highness King Farouk, who was also having high tea there. I was disappointed with the way he looks—small, fat, bearded, with little pig eyes, not a bit like his portrait, which comes on the screen at the end of any movie—always first his picture and the Egyptian anthem, then King George's picture and the British anthem.

Alexandria, March 17, 1943

So the winter passed—drives to and from the harbor, convoys to Kantarah, trips to the Australian Hospital at Bucelli, drives to the prisoner camps, loading and unloading hospital ships and trains. Winter meant the rainy season and battle dress instead of khaki uniforms. It meant greasy, slippery roads, slower driving, dirtier cars and, therefore, more maintenance. I had a four weeks' course in work-shops, after which I was turned out a 'driver-mechanic.' I hated every day of that dirty course, but learned plenty about motors, springs, brakes, etc.

After passing the final test, which consisted of an engine overhaul and a complete brake job, I received the 'wheel,' which is worn on the lower part of the left sleeve. In spare time Wendy Brooks checked me out on the motorcycle (which I had also learned to repair). I learned how to handle the bike in sand, how to fall and throw the bike aside so that it would not land on top of me.

One day I put a notice on our bulletin board that I was willing to teach the girls German, and six volunteered. They seemed to enjoy my lessons, but the work increased again and I was able to teach German only sporadically, but the little I did, I enjoyed a lot.

In March twenty of us were taken on a day's trip to the battlefield of El-Alamein, where we had been in the midst of the push last year. Now the whole battle plan was explained to us. At the time it had all been too confusing, too immediate to understand and, of course, we had been too busy in action to attempt to understand it, but we had been one tiny cog in the giant, advancing wheel. Now we observed the burned-out tanks and guns, the forward German entrenchments, the booby traps the Germans had constructed from unexploded English bombs. In the sand I picked up a penciled letter from a young German girl to her soldier boyfriend. Where was he now? Dead probably—a prisoner of war, possibly.

On March 16th six of our girls left for Daba, ninety miles from Alexandria in the Western Desert, where they joined the 32nd Indian Field Ambulance. Those of us left behind are envious of their move forward. Once again we are busier than ever and have to take turns at night duty as well, sleeping in the Orderly Room to relieve the NCOs.

Alexandria to Ras-El-Tin, March 23, 1943

Today, for the second time, I had to drive an officer of the Royal Engineers on an inspection tour. This really is not the work for an ambulance driver, but lately we have had to do a number of different duty-jobs and today's was a most enjoyable one. Our first stop was at an installation way past Ras-El-Tin. There I had to wait for over an hour for my officer. It was a truly magnificent spring day with the sun shining warmly, not hot yet, a fresh breeze coming in from the sea, the light blue sky sinking in the far distance into the deep blue of the Mediterranean. I stretched out on the sandy beach, soaking in the serenity of the place. I closed my eyes so that I could not see the ack-ack guns pointing skyward in the background and just listened to the lapping of the little waves hitting the shore, the monotonous Arabic sing-song of some workers in the distance, and sometimes the motor of a passing car. How peaceful it all seemed. For a short time the war, the casualties, the wounded, the prisoners had ceased to exist.

We made several more stops later, on each of which the behavior of my officer seemed more and more puzzling. Around noon he asked me if I still did not want to powder my nose. I took that as a most inappropriate criticism and my answer must have shown my irritation because he blushed deeply. Again later he asked me if I did not want to spend a penny. A penny in the land of piasters, and whatever for? He seemed resigned, but uncomfortable for some reason. It was only later that evening when I related the day's events to the girls that, amidst their peals of laughter, I learned the meaning of these expressions. Apparently my officer had been asking me, in accepted English colloquialisms, if I would not like to use the ladies' room. What a long way I still have to go to master idiomatic English!

Alexandria, April 4, 1943

Work has increased a lot in the last few days. The Allies are now menacing the last Axis stronghold in Tunisia. Many hospital ships are coming from Tripoli. Again we are taking some of the wounded to the 8th and 64th General Hospitals. However, most cases we transfer onto Red Cross trains to Cairo, Suez, and Palestine. Here in our billets everyone is very excited because tomorrow Miss Otto is coming back.

Alexandria, April 6, 1943

This morning at breakfast I saw Kay and Monica, who had come in late last night from Daba. They are leaving again at noon. Both of them look wonderful, deeply tanned from the desert sun. From what they tell us, they have plenty of work, day and night trips. Life on the desert is very primitive and offers little variety, but they like it and hope to stay there. I saw Miss Otto when I signed out today. She looks fine and was very cheerful. Her row of medals has grown by a new decoration, the MBE—Member of the British Empire. I am really proud that she is our commanding officer and equally happy that she has finally returned.

Alexandria, April 7-13, 1943

I was on stand-by duty at the 8th General Hospital when an orderly told me to report to the MO on duty.

"Roll up your sleeve," the doctor said. "I'm going to give you an inoculation against smallpox."

"But I'm not due for another one yet, Sir."

"Well, you're going to drive a rather bad case out to Amariyah."

"A smallpox case?"

He nodded while scratching in the vaccine.

179

"But, Sir," I objected, "an inoculation takes at least several days to be effective." He did not respond.

I was scared. I have a horror of skin diseases and bemoaned my bad luck that, of all our ambulance drivers, it was my turn to take this infectious case to Amariyah. When they brought the stretcher out to my car, the orderly lifted the blanket from the sailor's face to see if he required anything before we left. I could not help looking and was terrified. His face was covered with horrible boils, bloody pus, unrecognizable features, swollen to distortion. The smell of him was revolting, rotten and foul. I have seen men mutilated, burned, dying, but this was something different, so horrifying that I was afraid, afraid to be near this disease, to drive my car, to breathe the same air!

The trip to Amariyah, where infectious cases are kept, takes only forty-five minutes from Alexandria but these were the only minutes so far in my Army career when I really wished I were anything but an ambulance driver. After they removed the patient from my ambulance, I thoroughly disinfected everything and exchanged all the blankets I had in the car for new ones. That evening I called several doctors I had become acquainted with at work and bombarded them with questions. How long does it take to catch smallpox after being exposed to it? What are the symptoms? It takes about twelve days after exposure. First symptoms—light temperature, headaches. I marked off the day on my calendar. I was really terrified. What would I do if I caught this dreadful disease?

The next day things got worse. The 8th General Hospital called, asking for the driver who had transported yesterday's smallpox case. Another case had been brought in from the same ship. He, too, would have to be taken to the infectious disease ward at Amariyah, and since there was no need to expose other drivers, they wanted me again! I had no choice. After the second trip I marked my calendar again. By afternoon two more cases came in and the next day another. Alexandria seemed to be hit by an outbreak of smallpox and I had become the stand-by driver for all cases. My calendar showed a whole series of crosses. Where did the last twelve days leave off and the next series begin? I was ashamed of my fears, yet could not master them. Finally I went to Miss Otto and tried to beg off. She said that she understood, but, after all, this, too, was part of being an ambulance driver, and would I really want someone else to be exposed too? I said no more. I shuttled back and forth with cases and when, after five days, the epidemic was finally checked, I was a nervous wreck.

Alexandria, April 15, 1943

We were awakened at 4 A.M.—convoy to the docks. It was cold, dark, and a light rain was falling. My windshield wipers did not work, and since we have only tiny slits for headlights, I felt almost totally blind. Finally we arrived at the harbor, only to learn that once again the hospital ship had docked at the wrong quay and, therefore, was quite a distance from the incoming hospital train. It was our duty to transfer all stretcher cases from the train to the hospital ship. There were two trains, so we did not finish until 11 A.M. Both trains were loaded with Italian prisoners who were to be taken by ship to Turkey and from there back to Italy in exchange for British prisoners held in Italy. All of the Italians were unfit for further service. Most of them were of officer's rank.

All together there were about 120 mental cases, 300 stretcher cases, and an enormous number of walking cases. Their uniforms were nothing but tatters, their make-shift coats made of blankets. When we had emptied both trains, we were dead tired, but after coming home we still had to do maintenance until 5 P.M. A long day!

Alexandria, April 19, 1943

Again I had to fetch prisoners from the docks and take them to the 64th General Hospital. This time they were Germans. I was mad at them because they did nothing but complain. (Of course they were unaware that I understood every word they said.) They did not like it that they were put on stretchers. They should have been grateful because, for us, sitting cases are much easier to handle. Then they talked about my being a girl and said how typically English it was, to let their women do their work and let the blacks do their fighting. I was furious. We are so proud to be able to do our part and they turn it around as if we poor women have to slave for the men! When I related this at dinner, Miss Otto decided to include it in the War Diary.

Alexandria, April 21, 1943

There is a real routine to our work now. When we are on stand-by we hardly have time for maintenance but instead are on the road all day long. Even evenings we are called out on convoy duty. Hospital ships arrive almost daily at the harbor. We unload wounded from Tripoli and Tunisia, load Italian prisoners bound for Turkey and Italy, take our wounded to the 8th and 64th General Hospitals and also all the way to Bucelli. At other times we take them from the hospital ship to the train station or vice versa. Our average day now lasts from 8 A.M. until midnight.

Alexandria, April 26, 1943

Yesterday Miss Otto asked me if I had any objection to going to Daba. I told her that I had none. The original plan was that the six girls would stay for six weeks and then be exchanged for another six, but as it turned out, one of the girls, Pam Mayer, became sick and had to come back. Also Kay and Monica wish to be relieved. I am not quite sure whether I am looking forward to this assignment. It will be hard to live with only English girls. My uneasiness has been reinforced by Wendy Brooks. She is in the hospital with jaundice, and when I visited her today she told me that it surely would not be easy for me in Daba, especially with Pat Hall in charge. Well, we'll see. Most of the other Palestinians are gratified that one of 'theirs' now also has been chosen to go to the Western Desert outpost.

Alexandria, May 4, 1943

My last day off before moving. I have a lot of shopping to do because there will be nothing to buy in Daba. Wendy sent me two books and a very nice letter. Joe came to say goodbye. In the evening Edith and some others bought me drinks in the bar. My heart is getting heavier at the thought of leaving. How will I do, speaking only English? With Edith and some of the Palestinians we have always used German or Hebrew. The latter is still easier for me than English. Then, also, I have never shared a room (it will be a tent in Daba) with only English girls. How will I get along day in and day out with Pat, Jane, and Rowna, whose backgrounds are so different from mine?

Daba in the Western Desert, May 5, 1943

Captain Otto wanted to visit the Desert Detachment so we left Alexandria around noon. The road runs almost parallel to the Mediterranean. There was very little traffic. We passed El-Alamein, saw markers reading, "Forward British Minefield, October 23, 1942," and then "Forward Enemy Minefield." At 1:30 P.M. we met Kay and Monica, who were on their way back to Alexandria from Daba, and we had a picnic together. Arrived in Daba about 4 P.M. Pat Hall, Rowna Powell, and Jane Oldacres, the remaining detachment, rushed out of their tent to greet us. We were taken to the mess tent to drink tea with a few officers. Later I had a kind of wash-up from a one-gallon petrol can filled with luke-warm water that had been heated by the

182

afternoon sun. I felt a lot better after that but smelled faintly of gasoline, our 'desert Eau-de-Cologne.' Miss Otto is staying with us overnight. At 10 P.M. I dropped onto my army cot, and fell asleep listening to the bleating of sheep! The Indians of this Indian Field Ambulance travel with their own food on the hoof, which they slaughter and prepare according to their dietary laws. They are forbidden by their religion to eat most of the regular Army rations.

Daba, May 6, 1943

Today it was my turn to be stand-by. While the stand-by driver has to be properly dressed, ready to go out on any call, the other three work on their ambulances, doing the daily cleaning and maintenance. Until I am called out I'll use the time to describe my new surroundings. The 32nd Indian Field Ambulance, to which the four of us are now attached, is stationed just past El Daba station, about one hundred miles west of Alexandria. The total number of personnel here is about 150. There are some fourteen officers—doctors, a dentist, an MT officer. Most of these are Indians or Anglo-Indians. They are VCOs, Viceroy Commissioned Officers. There are five English officers, who hold their commissions from the King, and a few British NCOs. The Colonel in charge of the unit is an Australian. Indians make up the rest, about eighty percent of the camp. And there are four different messes—for the English officers, for the VCOs, for the British NCOs, and for the enlisted men, who are all Indians. The English class stratification prevails even on the Western Desert!

It is our duty to transport all casualties and sick cases from fifty miles around this stretch of desert—from troops who are on signal and salvage duty and clear mine fields. Serious cases we have to transport to Alexandria. There also are trips to the Field Hospital at Gerawla, sixty-five miles further west on the desert road.

We four girls occupy a corner of the camp a little away from the rest of the tents. Our living arrangement consists of a large square sleeping tent which has plenty of room for four army cots. Each one of us has one corner of the tent. A table and chairs occupy the middle. Our mess tent is much smaller and also lower, but the floor has been dug down about two feet so that we can easily stand up in it too. The bath tent is just a little wigwam with an army canvas bath and a few jerry cans filled with water. After a sort of sponge bath (our average daily allowance is about two gallons), we pour the used water down a gutter made of a piece of corrugated iron which leads outside, where it seeps into the desert sand. The funniest thing is the W.C.—a big wooden crate with three holes in it, surrounded by a low piece of flimsy canvas, with nothing overhead. We will get sunburned in strange places. As personal servants we have two Indians assigned to us. One does the cooking on a makeshift stove constructed of corrugated iron. The other hauls the water, cleans out the tents, etc. The girls appear to be on very good terms with the English officers. The Indians are quite shy, trying to avoid any contact, but if they do talk to us, they address us as '*memsahib*.' As for myself, I don't yet feel comfortable here.

Daba, May 8, 1943

Miss Otto left yesterday. Now I am alone with the three English girls. We live like a small family. Pat, Sergeant Hall, is the head of it. The days pass rather monotonously. We usually get up about 8 A.M. After breakfast we are more or less left to ourselves with our car maintenance, cleaning, washing, writing letters, etc. Our social life is restricted to the five English officers who visit us sometimes for tea. Frequently we go over to the officers' mess tent for a luke-warm drink. Once a week Pat and Jane play bridge with two of the officers, while Rowna and I usually go for walks or listen to the radio. We can walk where we wish but are warned not to touch unidentified objects. There are mines, grenades, and other explosives about. My favorite pastime is to go swimming. The water of the Mediterranean is brilliantly clear and there is very little surf so that I can swim far out. The only thing I dislike is that we always take the Chevy (we have three Austins and one Chevy), which is my responsibility to keep clean, so that after returning from the beach I have to do an extra hour of brushing out sand and general polishing to get my Chevy, the Cinderella among the ambulances, back 'on the road.'

Daba, May 9, 1943

This afternoon Jane, the Colonel, and I went to a cricket match. It was the first I had ever seen and I was delighted with this English national sport. Every day after work we watch the Indians playing hockey, in striped sport shirts, khaki shorts, bare-footed, their waist-length hair blowing in the wind. We have three kinds of Indians—Gurkhas, Sikhs, and Mohammedans. The Gurkhas are small, thick-set, fierce, and strong. They are the guards, standing stiffly with their heavy, curved knives, called *kukres,* as their only weapons. "Stop!" Swish! The knife comes down and bars the way. No one ignores *that* challenge to stop! The Sikhs are handsome, with delicately chiseled faces, fully bearded under their turbans. They carry water supplies and do all our domestic driving. The Mohammedans serve as ward boys, cooks, and servants. Our cook is Buddel, who prepares for us many varieties of curried hash, peppery hot, and other strange dishes.

Before lunch today I was very busy preparing my Chevy for the weekly inspection. Every Monday morning the entire camp is 'on parade.' However, all my efforts will go for naught since I'll have to go on a job tomorrow.

Daba, May 12, 1943

Yesterday I had to prepare my ambulance for work-shop inspection, this without a pit and in a real sandstorm. How can one clean the undercarriage, the springs, and the engine so that there is not a speck of dust anywhere when the wind is blowing sand incessantly? After hours on my back, sweating and trying to keep the blowing sand out of my eyes, I was in a foul mood. It seemed a useless task. No wonder the Indian drivers here think us all half-mad. At last week's unit parade, when they were told to take an example from our ambulances, one of them replied, "But, *Sahib*, the *memsahib*s get *under* their cars!" I took the Chevy to the RASC workshops and am rid of it for a few days. It uses so much oil that they'll probably have to put in a new engine. In the evening Clynton Reed, our Colonel, came over to our mess tent for a drink. He informed us that the 21st CCS is leaving Gerawla to move further west into Libya. The 32nd IFA (that's us) will take over there. We'll move west next week.

Daba to Alexandria, May 14 and 15

I had just finished my tea when Pat rushed in. One serious stretcher case to Alexandria! I drove Rowna's Austin—arrived in Alexandria at 10 P.M. and delivered my patient to the 64th G.H. On the way to our depot I had a flat tire and had to change it, which, with these huge tires, is not an easy matter. Arrived at Rue Fouad at midnight and fell into bed dead tired, but I did not have a restful night. We always have been plagued with bedbugs at the Rue Fouad and pretty regularly the hygiene squad would come and fumigate our apartments. Last night I slept in a room used only for the occasional overnight visitor and here the bedbugs had a feast on me. I hope they'll fumigate before my next visit.

The next morning I did some necessary shopping, saw almost everyone in our unit, was bombarded with questions about our life in the desert, and left around noon, not in the Austin I had come in but in another Chevy. The unfortunate news is that all Austins have been taken away from 502 and been replaced by Fords and Chevys. Everyone is unhappy about this. In the first place, the Austins are far more comfortable for patients than are Fords and Chevys. Secondly, the Austins score much higher in reliability of performance and handling. Thirdly, Austins are the accepted ambulances used at the front. Does this mean that we are relegated to staying forever here in Egypt while the 8th Army keeps advancing?

Daba, May 16, 1943

Today it was Pat's turn to take two stretcher cases to Alexandria. I had a job in the area, another casualty from a mine explosion. We are surrounded by mine fields and many accidents are caused when vehicles veer from the main road. The rest of the day we were busy packing for tomorrow's move. It is fascinating to watch a whole camp of tents come down in no time, leaving the desert barren again with no trace of human habitation.

Daba to Gerawla, May 17, 1943

We prepared everything for our move. The entire morning Pat, Rowna, and Jane grumbled about the loss of their Austins and complained about their Chevys. I went to workshops and brought my own Chevy back with a new engine installed. Around 9 A.M. we sighted three ambulances, two Fords, and a Chevy, coming from the east—Brown, Burgess, and Whichcote. They will take the nurses from the 21st Field Hospital back to Alexandria. Now the four of us will be the only women in the entire Western Desert.

The tents were loaded into waiting trucks, and at 10 A.M. we went with the officers over to the NAAFI in Daba for a farewell breakfast. After that the entire 32nd Indian Field Ambulance moved in convoy formation out of Daba toward Gerawla. We had to drive slowly. I had a new engine in my car and also the road was heavy with traffic. A large convoy was coming from the other direction. At 1 P.M. we picnicked in the desert. By 4 P.M. we had arrived in Gerawla.

As it was rapidly growing dark, nothing much in the way of organization was done that night. Our sleeping tents were erected, and, seeing them, I experienced an odd sensation. We had traveled seventy miles that day and yet, when I looked about me, it was just as though I stood on the sands of Daba. The tent arrangement was identical, the scenery, the sand—all the same. There is, however, one small change which means a lot to us. The 21st Field Hospital, which formerly occupied these grounds, had several nurses attached to their unit, and for them they had built a little wooden shack with an aluminum roof. Inside the shack, neat and private, stood two privies. What a luxury!

Gerawla to Mersa-Matruh, May 20, 1943

This morning a surgical unit consisting of two British officers and four NCOs arrived. Now we are equipped for any emergency. We are much busier since now we are covering the area from the Libyan border to Daba. Most of our discharged patients have to be driven to Mersa-Matruh, which lies fifteen miles to the west. This town has become the official headquarters of the area.

Today it was my turn to make the trip, with four discharged patients. The drive to Mersa-Matruh, I was told, takes half an hour. I had been driving through desert for about twenty minutes when the long, gray ribbon of road took a sudden sharp turn to the right. Ahead was a steep hill, which I had to take very slowly so as not to overheat the engine. Suddenly I was at the top, looking down upon the most breathtaking panorama—a quiet bay, crystal green water which farther out melted into dark blue. Cradled in the bay lay the town of Mersa-Matruh. Most of its buildings were razed to the ground. Slowly I drove through the dead streets. Here and there I could still discern evidence of this once famous resort town—a barber shop sign, a wall left standing from a sidewalk cafe, the ghost of the main hotel, whose registry, I was later told, boasted many a famous name, including that of the Duke of Windsor. The town now is populated by a handful of Arabs, who live among the ruins. There also are large prison camps and barracks on the outskirts of the city. I was amazed at the huge number of Italian POWs walking around freely, driving Army trucks, and walking everywhere without guards. Come to think of it, where could they escape to? No one could get very far without provisions and, of course, water.

Gerawla, May 25, 1943

This morning I found a trench that will make a perfect grease pit!

Gerawla to Alexandria, May 28, 1943

The Deputy Director of Medical Services, the senior RAMC officer in an area, got a posting to Alexandria and needed personal transport. It was my turn. On the way in, he was sitting in front with me. In the back I had a stretcher case for the 64th General Hospital. Now that we are stationed seventy miles farther into the desert, the trip to Alexandria is even longer than before, but with someone to talk to, it's not too bad. Today's drive back, though, was hard. The badly damaged desert road, which prevents speeds over forty miles per hour, the blistering heat, the monotony of the landscape with nothing to look at but sand, made me so drowsy that all the way I had to fight falling asleep at the wheel. The only news I brought back from the depot was that everyone is upset with the requisition of the Austins and their replacement by very old, battered Fords, most of which have over 60,000 miles on their speedometers.

Gerawla to Mersa-Matruh, June 1, 1943

Colin, the Transport Officer, invited me to a picture show. Mersa-Matruh has the only cinema within a radius of hundreds of miles. Upon our arrival, the film became a secondary feature to the audience. The reason was simple. I was the first female to set foot in the theatre tent. Apparently, one of the soldiers had seen us pull up in the staff car and had passed the word along to his eager comrades, for when I entered, the whole audience completely forgot the images on the screen and turned to see a woman in the flesh! They whistled, stamped, howled. Some called for lights—they wanted to get a better look. Others demanded that the reel be stopped so that they could enjoy my entrance and still not miss any of the picture. As for me, I was so embarrassed that if Colin hadn't had a firm grip on my arm, I would have turned and run out of there.

Gerawla, June 2, 1943

The King's birthday! We celebrated with a beach party, which is always pleasant, for the desert beaches are very quiet and secluded. At night we drove to Mersa-Matruh to see an ENSA show. To be truthful, the play was done in a rather amateurish way, but we enjoyed it tremendously anyway. We are starved for entertainment here on the desert.

Gerawla, June 5, 1943

Today I have been on the desert for one month and am as darkly tanned as the others. My English has improved tremendously and I'm beginning to feel at home with Pat, Rowna, and Jane. Colin and I have become really good friends. I have become accustomed to the dry heat, to the *khamsin*, hot winds that cover everything in clouds of sand, to the two-gallon water ration per day for washing, to Buddel, our Indian cook's strange curry concoctions and peculiar sauces, and to being called *Memsahib* by the Indians.

Our work assignments have become routine. For the most part we take discharged patients back to their units. Once a week the train comes to Gerawla and then we take some of the more critical cases from the 32nd and load them onto a special hospital coach bound for Alexandria. Some emergency cases are transported by plane from the nearest air strip. Most of the roads we drive are terrible, full of holes left from the fighting or pounded to pieces by Army traffic.

Gerawla to Buq-Buq, June 12, 1943

The new DDMS does not have a staff car, so today it is my turn to drive him to Buq-Buq, near the Libyan border, about 140 miles from Gerawla. At 8 A.M. I called for him at his quarters in Mersa-Matruh. The route consists of one endless stretch of highway, with sand on either side as far as the eye can see. From time to time one can catch a glimpse of the Mediterranean. Scattered here and there are camps and small airports. Progress is slow because the road is so bad. Not only is it full of holes, but also so narrow that it is very difficult to overtake cars. I was caught in a stream of west-bound ammunition trucks and an east-bound convoy of 8th Army soldiers, probably going on leave. It was amusing to see their faces as they peered down into my ambulance. Apparently they couldn't trust their own eyes. A woman this far into the Western Desert? Impossible! Yes, but here I am.

Up to Sidi Barrani the road was more or less passable. The town is completely in ruins. Its few remaining walls and bits of rubble are all that is left. A little beyond Sidi Barrani the road is so damaged that I had to drive on the sand parallel to the 'highway.' After a five-hour drive we arrived in Buq-Buq—like Gerawla or Daba—tents, soldiers, ruins. At about 3 P.M. my officer finished his tour of inspection and, after a good meal at the NAAFI, we started the return trip. The road was now free of traffic and I made the trip back in four hours.

Gerawla, June 15, 1943

We were just informed that there will be regular trips to Alexandria again. Since we had come to Gerawla it had been decided that the journey to Alexandria was too far for stretcher cases to do in one day. Therefore, we drove them as far as Daba, where they stayed overnight, and then they were taken on to Alexandria by South African drivers, who had replaced us in Daba. However, the patients complained and preferred the trip with us all the way. Naturally, this makes us very happy and also proud.

Gerawla to Alexandria, June 17, 1943

I left yesterday for Alexandria and just returned this afternoon. I was carrying four serious stretcher cases and had to drive very slowly. The trip took me over eight hours. Since we never carry orderlies or nurses with us, the driver has to do everything. I had to stop at least once every hour to see that my patients were all right, to give them water, the urinal, check bandages, etc. By the time I reached Alexandria I was exhausted. Today I drove back empty and made the distance in five hours, fighting sleep every mile of the way.

I feel depressed. I had hoped so much to find a Red Cross letter from my parents waiting for me in Alexandria, but, again, there was nothing.

Gerawla, June 20, 1943

A week ago when I drove to the NAAFI for supplies one of the fellows there offered me a copy of *True Stories*. I have just finished reading the rather primitive love stories in it. Nevertheless, I am thrilled that for the first time I have understood the entire content without the help of a dictionary. It shows how much English I have picked up in the past few weeks. Now I must try to get hold of some better books and maybe by the time my desert duty is over I'll be able to read English as well as German. Then my next project will be to switch from German to English, writing this diary.

I just remembered that yesterday was my birthday. It passed unnoticed. Today, though, thoughts of my parents keep crossing my mind. How I wish I would hear from them!

Gerawla, June 24, 1943

A fine state of affairs! For days we have had nothing but trouble with our "new" ambulances. Rowna's Ford has one flat tire after another. Even when the ambulance is parked overnight, she finds another flat in the morning. (Maybe the South African drivers put a spell on it!) My Chevy has been in workshops in Mersa-Matruh since yesterday. It needs new king-pins, but there aren't any. Pat's car has a broken half-shaft. We are going to take her king-pins out and put them into my car, and maybe we can find a half-shaft and another set of king-pins among the leftover salvage.

Gerawla, June 25, 1943

Now I, too, am off the road. I got my TAB (anti-typhoid) shots and am free of duty for forty-eight hours. Well, without my ambulance there is not much to do anyway. The same, however, can never be said of Pat. She has been out all day rummaging through discarded German and Italian cars hoping to find a half-shaft. So far, no luck.

Gerawla to Daba, June 28, 1943

Pat is on a forty-eight hour leave to Alexandria. Jane has a two-day trip and Rowna is in the workshop with her car. Now it is sand in the petrol pump! I'm holding down the fort alone, and since it is Monday, I am the only one of us 'on Parade.' At three in the afternoon an emergency call came through. A plane had crashed somewhere near Daba. Apparently there are many bad burn cases. We loaded my ambulance with plasma for transfusions and other surgical supplies. Major Cope, our surgeon, and I started off immediately. At Daba we learned that the plane had come down fifteen miles further inland. We arrived there just as the ambulance plane from Cairo landed. It was scheduled to take the wounded to an RAF hospital there. Our major gave first aid, while I listened to an account of the accident. From what I could gather, the plane had caught fire and crashed. Because it was a passenger plane, no parachutes had been issued. What an idiotic ruling! Passengers should be allowed parachutes and, if need be, given a push. There were twelve passengers: six dead, two severe casualties, two light casualties. The pilot escaped uninjured but is suffering from a severe case of shock. The major decided to accompany the ambulance plane to Cairo. I returned to camp alone.

Gerawla, June 30, 1943

We are all excited! Now that Pantelleria, Lampedusa, and most of the other little Italian islands have been taken, where will we strike next? Everyone is trying to guess where the next invasion will take place. I myself hope that it will be soon and that our unit, too, will be posted onto the continent. But so far these are only dreams and connected with the hope of finding my parents.

Gerawla, July 10, 1943

The invasion of Sicily has begun. Two months have passed since Tunis and Bizerta have fallen, two months during which we have waited tensely for new developments. This morning the first communiqué came through. Our 8th Army, the Canadians and the Americans have established a beachhead at the southeast coast of Sicily. The landing itself was apparently simple, contrary to all expectations, and the number of dead and wounded relatively small. Now we sit constantly by our radios, listening.

Gerawla to Alexandria, July 14, 1943

Only a week since my last trip to Alexandria and again it is my turn. Took four surgical cases. On the way back I was just in time to help with an accident that took place twenty miles from Daba. The driver of a lorry had fallen asleep and lost control of the wheel, something that happens frequently in the desert. So I came back with three stretcher cases instead of empty.

Gerawla, July 15, 1943

The news from Sicily continues to be good. The Allies are advancing quickly and meet with little resistance. The Germans, who are probably much stronger than the Italians, are retreating to Catania on the east coast. The civilian population is greeting our troops with flowers, kisses, and general outbreaks of joy. How strange, considering that they are our enemies!

Gerawla, July 19, 1943

Today a few Indians received their commissions as officers and, therefore, a dinner party was arranged. Alas, as soon as we had started to eat the usual curry, an emergency call came through—accident between Daba and Gerawla. I left immediately with Casavulu, the Indian Medical Officer, and one Indian orderly. After a twenty-five mile drive we arrived at the scene of the accident. A jeep had turned over completely, killing the driver and leaving the three passengers badly hurt. Such things happen when drivers who have had only four weeks of training are turned loose to take their place in convoys traveling a thousand miles or more, non-stop, from Alexandria to Tunis.

Gerawla, July 21, 1943

Originally we 'desert rats' were supposed to be relieved every six weeks. I have now been here for two and a half months. Pat, Rowna, and Jane love it here and don't want to be exchanged. I am not as enthusiastic about it, but I feel that I should stay with them. Besides, no one from Alexandria really wants to come out here. It's too primitive and there is no social life, no entertainment except the occasional drink with the officers or a swimming party when time allows it. Among the men, hockey matches have now replaced cricket matches.

This evening we had a discussion with our officers and other ranks. Topic: Women in the Post-War World. I gave my first little speech in English and am very proud of this accomplishment. I was the only one who spoke for equal rights, equal pay for equal work. Naturally, I expected opposition from the men, but to hear from all three of the English girls that a woman's place is in the home and that she should not demand the same remuneration as a man was a shock to me. It made me sad. What kind of a world are we fighting for?

Gerawla, July 26, 1943

Just heard on the radio that Mussolini has abdicated! We can hardly believe it. What does it mean? Will Italy now make a separate peace? We are glued to the wireless. In Sicily our troops are advancing steadily.

Our Surgical Unit is leaving us tomorrow morning. It consisted of two officers and four other ranks. I am sorry to see them go because I liked Major Cope and Captain Gourevitch a lot. In the afternoon the 32nd gave a farewell party for the six of them. Since there were no flowers, the usual garlands were made for them out of bits of colored paper, shells, cigarette packages, and beer bottles! We drank black tea, ate Indian sweets, and listened to Subala Sab's unique and emotional speech, from which I have taken a few excerpts:

Respected Officers and dear members of No. 8 FSU: We, the personnel of 32nd Indian Field Ambulance, have assembled with mingled emotions of sorrow and grief to bid you all farewell on the eve of your sudden departure. Owing to astringencies of time and hard existing circumstances, we are awfully sorry that a grand befitting farewell party could not be arranged. These humble words cannot express the gravity of our sorrows at this juncture . . . No doubt, pangs of separation from loved ones and severage of souls bound together are the bitterest drops in the cup of mortality . . . Your kindness and condescension towards all of us has been marvelous . . . We are losing in you all a team of jolly sportsmen, strict disciples of half nudism, loving brothers and spiritous comrades . . . Major R. W. Cope we found always a loving father, staunch administrator, and ardent disciplinarian. We will always cherish in our memories his grand majestic and philosophical looks, charming smiles, and sweet way of addressing all alike . . . It will not be out of place to pay tribute to Cpl. Stone, who has been all along a fine specimen of all humors and jokes. His clownish gestures and funny humorous profile, appealing movements and talks will be ever cherished in our memories. A word or so for Pte. Turton . . . His dealing with all ranks has earned him a good name of Liberator Bomber, probably based on his huge and monstrous physique and powers . . . We conclude this short yet sincere farewell to you all with heartfelt prayers that may God Almighty pour his choicest blessing on you all and may success and prosperity crown all your noble undertakings. We assure you that our good wishes and praying hearts will always be with you, however distant you may be from us. We are your loving brothers, personnel of 32nd Indian Field Ambulance.

Most of the Indians in the audience understood not one word of this speech and the English were hard put to keep a straight face, but we all applauded mightily.

Gerawla, August 1, 1943

The Arabs have been permitted to return to Mersa-Matruh and the surrounding area. We watch nomads pass by with their donkeys, camels, their women, children, dogs, and swarms of flies.

Gerawla, August 2, 1943

Pat has just returned from Alexandria. The news she brought us is not cheering. Two other Palestinian ATS units are now stationed in Alexandria. One unit, stationed outside the city, are staff car and lorry drivers. The other unit consists of clerks. Miss Otto was offered a promotion to Senior Commander in charge of all ATS, including us, in the area. Typical of Miss Otto, she did not accept before discussing the matter with our entire unit. After lengthy consideration it was decided that she should accept the promotion, with the condition that should 502 get a posting, she would come back as our Commanding Officer. Her office will continue to be located in our building and she will live with us as before.

Gerawla, August 12, 1943

Today Rowna and I have to take a few stretcher cases to the midnight train for Cairo. I try to keep awake and will use the time writing my diary. I have not written for almost two weeks because life has become very routine here in the desert. Sometimes we have a lot to do, at other times less. I have decided to ask for two weeks' leave. It's been nine months since my last leave. I shall spend a week in Palestine and a week in Syria. I'll probably leave at the end of the month—hope to be able to catch a plane from Mersa-Matruh to Cairo and from there one to Lydda in Palestine.

Gerawla, August 18, 1943

The last of the Axis troops have left Sicily. Where will we strike next? The four of us have a bet on: Jane believes it will be Crete, Rowna bets for Sardinia, Pat for the toe of Italy, and I for Italy's heel. Today I feel miserable—the flu or sand-fly fever.

Gerawla, August 24, 1943

I feel a bit better. Am all packed for my leave. Rowna and Jane came back from Alexandria and brought my leave pass. It begins on the 26th. They also brought the news that Pat Curlewis, our Sergeant-Major, will go on leave for a month to South Africa. This means that Pat Hall will have to take her place in Alexandria. My replacement, for the two weeks of my leave, will arrive tomorrow. There will be no replacement for Pat, who is most unhappy at having to leave the desert. In the evening, while we were having a drink in the officers' mess, there was more news. The 32nd is to move to Mersa-Matruh in a few days. Well, when I come back from my leave I'll have to go looking for them.

Alexandria to Tel-Aviv to Beirut to Damascus, September 9, 1943

I'm back in Alexandria after my fourteen days' leave, which began with a round of bad luck. I couldn't catch a plane out of Mersa-Matruh so drove into Alexandria with Pat Hall and then took the train to Cairo the next day. While in Alexandria I discovered that my beautiful radio, my only possession of any value, had been stolen and there is no hope of getting it back. When I arrived in Cairo the next day, where George, an old friend now stationed there, was waiting for me, I found that since I had arrived a day later than planned, I had missed the plane he had arranged for us to take. Instead, we had to catch the train to Palestine and because I didn't have a seat booked in advance, I had to go second class. ATS girls must travel in a specially reserved coach, so George and I could not travel in the same compartment. The trip took another day-and-a-half of my precious leave time and we arrived in Tel-Aviv dead tired. After finding a room for George, I went to Aunt Else's apartment. She made me take off everything I wore in the hall and sent it to the laundry and the cleaners. Probably she carried memories of World War I and was afraid I would infest her house with fleas and lice!

In Tel-Aviv George and I spent the time swimming, horseback riding, going to the cinema, and sitting at sidewalk cafes meeting old acquaintances. All this was pleasant, but, on the other hand, the stupid questions I was asked about my experiences in the Western Desert and the arrogance of officials and sales people got on my nerves. After four days I was glad to leave for Lebanon. George and I hitched a ride in a Polish lorry to Haifa and then by another lorry, packed with French Air Force fellows, to Beirut. Although we couldn't understand each others' languages, we had a jolly trip. George stayed at the YMCA and I with my old friends Fanny and Richard. The next day, while Fanny and Richard worked, George and I went sightseeing. Beirut struck me very favorably and seemed most cosmopolitan. I really like its climate and its spectacular views of the bay, especially at sunset.

One day we traveled to Damascus on the post-lorry. Army traffic between Damascus and Beirut is almost non-existent and the train, which takes twelve hours each way, was out of the question. The drive, however, took only three hours each way, up and down a mountain road. These mountains are not barren, like the hills in Palestine, but green, covered with pines and fir trees. We passed through clean little villages and orchards in which apple trees hung heavy with fruit. The air was cold and I shivered in my summer uniform, but still I felt good and invigorated. We had only three short hours to see Damascus before the post-lorry started back, but the drive through the mountains alone had been worth the trip. We strolled in the famous bazaar of Damascus, so enormous that it seems a city in itself, its dark, cool streets redolent of exotic spices. After much bargaining I bought a pair of sandals and a box made of inlaid wood as souvenirs of Damascus. We also had a quick excursion through the modern part of the city, which is bigger than Jerusalem.

From Beirut we hitched a ride back to Tel-Aviv. George had managed to get us transport on a plane to Cairo, but at the last minute a new order came through that female personnel are not to be given lifts. So once again I had to go back by train, this time, though, with a first class ticket. The trip seemed endless. Then in the middle of the night we heard the great news that Italy had surrendered and the entire train became one loud and happy family. And now I'm back in Alexandria, at the Rue Fouad, my 'home.'

Alexandria, September 10, 1943

I have been working as stand-by, cleaning up our lorry. Nothing has changed here in Alexandria. Our unit is not too busy. The only battle casualties arriving are Australians and South Africans. British and Canadian casualties are sent to England via Tripoli. I'm waiting for an ambulance from Gerawla. Apparently the 32nd has not yet moved.

But I don't mind waiting. I like it here and enjoy being cool and clean, wearing a starched uniform, being able to take a bath every day and being surrounded by friends and the comforts of the city.

Alexandria to Gerawla, September 11, 1943

My replacement in the desert brought in two stretcher cases last night so now I am taking the ambulance back to Gerawla. I really enjoyed the drive all by myself, and when I arrived Jane and Rowna greeted me like a long-lost friend. Apparently my replacement had not been too much of a success. Without Pat and with Jane as 'Acting Unpaid Temporary Lance Corporal,' the atmosphere is much more relaxed and it's fun to be back.

Gerawla, September 23, 1943

Miss Otto (it's Senior Commander Otto now) arrived today for an inspection tour, accompanied by Miss Stewart, who is now acting Captain of our unit, Pat Hall, and, of course, Pandora the poodle. Pat will stay. The others will return Saturday. I'm always happy when Miss Otto comes. We all enjoyed a drink at the officers' mess. Unfortunately, I won't be around tomorrow to spend the day with our visitors since it's my turn to take four men to Alexandria.

Alexandria, September 24, 1943

On my trip to Alexandria I carried one English soldier, one Italian prisoner, his South African guard, and one Indian orderly—four men with four different languages, yet they conversed with each other animatedly! When I reached the city I saw what looked like the entire Italian navy anchored in the harbor. What a beautiful spectacle! The English said that the Italians were so proud of their handsome ships that they preferred to surrender them undamaged rather than scuttle them.

Alexandria–Gerawla–Mersa-Matruh, September 25, 1943

I had to get up early because I wanted to be back in Gerawla in time for Rowna's birthday party, but it was 1 P.M. before I could get started. The drive took six hours so it was 7 P.M. before I arrived, had a quick wash, changed into fresh khaki, and off we went to Mersa-Matruh. "We" means the four of us and the six British officers of the 32nd. Clynton, the Colonel, had ordered a fine dinner at the "Ship's Inn," a kind of Officers' Mess behind the NAAFI. There were drinks before dinner, wine and beer with dinner, and after-dinner drinks. I always had wondered what it would be like to get a bit 'tight' so I tried everything offered me and refused no refills. I don't recollect the rest of the evening too well, except that I felt simply awful! We all went to the cinema after dinner and my condition worsened. When I tried to look at the screen the scenes turned round and round. Poor Colin! He had to take me outside and hold my head while I was sick. It was so dreadful that it is beyond me why anyone ever wants to get drunk.

Gerawla, September 30, 1943

I was in bed for several days. All of our four Medical Officers came to examine me, which they seemed to enjoy doing, none of them having had a woman patient in years! But not one of them could come up with a diagnosis. Was it the flu? Sand fly fever? Some unknown disease? I felt quite ill and had the most awful headache when I moved, but I had no fever. In retrospect, I believe I simply had an old-fashioned hangover, but not one of the doctors who examined me would have believed that I was so naive that I couldn't tell a hangover from an illness.

Gerawla, October 9, 1943

The move to Mersa-Matruh is finally going to take place. Today an advance party of the 32nd has left to prepare our new camp site.

Gerawla, October 10, 1943

Pat is on a trip to Alexandria. Rowna, Colin, Tom and I went for a last picnic at our beach, but it did not turn out well. A *khamsin*, which had started this morning, increased so that it was no pleasure to stay at the beach. By the time we came back to camp we could hardly find our tents in the blowing sand.

Gerawla, October 13, 1943

This is the fourth day of blowing sand. We are at the height of the *khamsin*. It is quite unbearable. The wind howls so that we have to yell to each other in order to be understood. Outside the tent, visibility is cut to zero. Even inside the tent everything, including us, is covered with fine sand. It's impossible to write letters—the sand would ruin the pen. Reading is also impossible because the paper quickly gets covered with sand. My eyes are red from irritation. Hair color is the same for everyone—sandy. I can even feel sand between my teeth! We have been packing our things for tomorrow's move and sit on our camp beds with nothing to do. Our mood improves somewhat when, one by one, the officers come to pay us a visit, probably in the hope that we can raise their spirits. Clynton closed the office and came over. Tony closed his ward—no patients there because we are moving. Godfrey is not going to operate today. Even Pat has closed her 'workshop'—the bench outside the tent where she is always busy doing something.

Mersa-Matruh, October 14, 1943

Moving day! We are up early. The *khamsin* has passed, the sun is bright again, and the desert air is clear. We pack our belongings into our ambulances, take one last look at the old camp site, and are off to Mersa-Matruh. The last thing we see as we leave are Bedouins searching on the now-deserted grounds for anything useful which the 32nd might have left behind.

Mersa-Matruh, October 15, 1943

Sometimes I believe I shall never understand the ways of the British Army. It must have cost hundreds of pounds to move the 32nd Indian Field Ambulance from Gerawla to Mersa-Matruh and there build a new hospital out of former Egyptian Army barracks. We have spent one night here and just received the news that all was probably for nothing and the 32nd should be packed and ready to be posted somewhere else. There is much speculation. Rumor has it that the 32nd may join another Indian Division and perhaps move into Italy. We are very excited. What will become of us? Will another Field Ambulance take over? Will we stay here or go back to Alexandria?

In spite of these uncertainties we are enchanted with our new surroundings. Our camp stretches along the shore of the "Blue Lagoon," so named because of its incredible azure color. The officers and most of the personnel, including us, are now quartered in real buildings. We have been assigned two large rooms, one for sleeping and one as our mess, and another small one for a kitchen. The other three rooms in our building are still empty. All along the front of the building runs a verandah from which we have a magnificent view—white sand below us, then the quiet water of the Blue Lagoon, beyond it the sand hills, and finally the deeper blue of the sea.

Mersa-Matruh, October 19, 1943

Slowly, order comes to the camp, but everyone is wondering for how long. When will the movement orders arrive? Yesterday we went with a few officers to find a new swimming beach. The lagoon, although so close and beautiful, is out of bounds for swimming because its water is stagnant and therefore probably polluted. We finally settled on a beach called "Cleopatra's Bath," where the water was clear and cool. A few hundred yards out was a kind of ruin which supposedly had enclosed Cleopatra's pool. The shoreline in ancient times must have extended much further out. At ebb tide one can still walk out to the ruins on some rocks. On this first day we swam out and climbed into the entrance. Inside there was nothing but a cave-like shell, eroded by centuries of pounding waves.

Mersa-Matruh to Alexandria, October 21, 1943

Yesterday began as just another slow day, but it didn't end that way. In mid morning we got an urgent call from an outlying camp. A soldier had been caught in a mine explosion and had been badly wounded. He was in danger of losing his eyesight. I drove at top speed to the camp and brought him back to the 32nd. After he was examined and had received first aid treatment, it was decided that he needed immediate specialized attention to save his sight. It was my turn to go to Alexandria and since our surgeon was supposed to leave that day to report to his new station in Burg-El-Arab, just this side of Alexandria, he would come along and look after the patient, at least as far as Burg-El-Arab.

The drive turned out to be a nightmare. The major, who must have had quite a few drinks celebrating his departure, was totally useless as a doctor or even as a medical orderly. Here I was, driving a patient who hovered between life and death, with a 'medical officer in charge' who mumbled a lot of nonsense and did not care about the stretcher case at all but seemed only to be concerned with arriving on time in Burg-El-Arab. On top of that it began to rain, and my windshield wipers did not work. I had to lean way out to the side in order to see the road. By now it also was getting dark. With covered headlights, no wipers, and rain driving into my face, I had hardly any vision. Then, too, the road became slick from this first downpour of the season. My patient moaned from time to time, and the Major was happily out of it all! After about seven hours of this I reached Burg-El-Arab, totally exhausted. Here I dropped off the Major, who suddenly seemed to remember 'our' stretcher case and instructed me to drive as fast as possible the remaining thirty miles to the hospital but, for goodness sake, to be sure to avoid any bumps on the road! Speed, he explained, was necessary to save the soldier's life; avoiding bumps meant saving his eyesight. Great advice for me, with neither headlights nor wipers!

By now I was wet through and through, but my bad luck continued.

Shortly after Burg-El-Arab I ran out of petrol. Something was wrong with the carburetor and I had used a gallon for every nine miles instead of the usual gallon per sixteen miles. Luckily, I had two spare tins, which got me as far as Sister Street in Alexandria. But there I was stranded in the harbor quarter, one of the worst sections of town and no place for a woman, especially at night. Finally, a lorry came to my aid and towed me into our depot where I could tank up and continue the last few miles to the 64th General Hospital. I arrived there at 10 P.M. and delivered my patient, still alive. I even had the feeling that through all the difficulties he had regained consciousness and partially participated in my perils, which might have made him forget his pain for a short while. He managed a little wave as he was carried out of the ambulance.

Mersa-Matruh, October 27, 1943

Everyone is still waiting anxiously for decisions. The 32nd thinks that every day here is their last. The latest rumor has it that Geoffrey, our former surgeon, now in command of the 20th Indian Field Ambulance, will take over here from the 32nd. In the meantime, we are settling in. Two Italian POWs have been assigned to us, one to do the cooking, the other to do cleaning, washing, etc.

Mersa-Matruh, November 2, 1943

The rumor was true. Today Geoffrey's 20th Bhopals arrived. All of a sudden there are twice as many people milling around and everyone is in each other's way. There is not much work for anyone.

Mersa-Matruh, November 14, 1943

Finally orders have come through. The 32nd is to leave tomorrow morning for Cairo, where they will be re-equipped. This probably means that they will leave Egypt and North Africa altogether. We had a little farewell party at the NAAFI.

Mersa-Matruh, November 15, 1943

Everyone has been packing all night through. Part of the 32nd left by train in the early morning hours. The rest left in convoy formation at 7 A.M. The entire camp was up to wave a last goodbye. We four felt very low. After all, for almost nine months we had lived, worked, and played together. Isolated in the desert, nine months is a long time. When the last car disappeared from view, I felt that another chapter of my Army life had ended.

Alexandria, November 17, 1943

It has been decided that I would be the first to return to Alex, so, when one of our drivers from 502 brought a Medical Officer to Mersa-Matruh, I packed my kit-bag and returned with her. Would this be the last time I covered the well-known road?

Alexandria, November 20, 1943

Nothing much has changed here during the last nine months. We do maintenance, go on details, drive along the Corniche to the 64th General Hospital, and wait on duty at the hospitals. Sometimes one works very hard, but other days are spent waiting for something to do—a monotonous routine, but that, too, is part of Army life. There are no more details for the 8th General Hospital since they, too, are all packed up, ready to leave, probably for Italy.

Alexandria, November 22, 1943

Once again, convoy duty to the docks and the familiar routine. First the urgent call. Then, after hurrying down to the harbor, the waiting—this time until 5 P.M. Finally we picked up a few seriously wounded cases from a destroyer which had been hit by a torpedo from a submarine. She had made it back to Alex, but just barely, and had settled, half submerged, just outside the harbor.

Alexandria to Kantarah, November 29, 1943

Some amusing incidents do occur to lighten our days, such as the one that happened today when I had to drive four mental cases to the Kantarah Hospital base. My patients were accompanied by three guards and a high-ranking Navy psychiatrist, a Commander. The patients and guards sat in the back of the ambulance, the Commander in front with me. He did not say one word until we were about twenty miles out of Alexandria. Then suddenly he barked, "Please stop!"

I was startled. We were in the middle of nowhere, but, of course, I replied, "Yes, Sir!"

He unstrapped a small leather satchel and removed a kimono covered with dancing dragons. "Dear God," I thought. "Maybe he too is one of the mental cases!"

After pulling on the kimono, he climbed back into the seat beside me. "Friction, you know," he informed me. "It ruins the finish of my uniform. Gets quite shiny, you know." I leaned as far away from him as possible and concentrated on my driving.

At Kantarah, by the Suez Canal, we had to go across to the hospital by ferry. The whole area is closely patrolled by MPs, one of whom strolled over and asked me, "How many in the car?"

The kimono-robed Commander drew himself up and answered in icy tones, "There are four mental cases in the back."

"Quiet, you!" growled the MP, glancing at the dragons. "Blimey, this one's a pip," he said to me, jerking his thumb toward the Commander. "Likes to dress up, I see."

The Commander's face was contorted with rage. Slowly, he drew up the voluminous sleeve of his robe, displaying the three bright gold bands of his rank. The MP gagged and turned pale. "Yes, SIR!" he shouted and leapt away from the car. My berobed psychiatrist said not another word to me until I left him at the hospital.

Mena, December 10, 1943

I took a forty-eight hour leave to visit the 32nd Indian Field Ambulance before they finally left Egypt. At this moment they are in transit, stationed in Mena, exactly opposite from the ATS camp. I was lucky to get a lift right away in a staff car and arrived at 5 P.M. in Mena, where Colin was waiting for me in his brand-new Jeep. What a strange feeling to drive into camp and see all the familiar faces again! I believe that I, too, was quite a sensation since I was dressed in a skirt and jacket. All the Indians had ever seen us in was slacks, bush jackets, or greasy overalls. The 32nd has received all brand-new equipment, and when I saw the new ambulances, trucks and motorcycles, which Colin let me try out, I was green with envy. Will we ever get to Europe, where all the action is now? I was sorry not to see Clynton. He has received a promotion and is already in Italy.

Alexandria, December 20, 1943

Christmas is just around the corner, my second Christmas with 502, and we are still in Alexandria. I do hope that the new year will bring a posting to the continent. Looking back, '43 was an eventful year—the end of the North African campaign, the invasion of Sicily, the surrender of Italy and the invasion of Southern Italy. For 502 it was a year of some achievements, some disappointments, much waiting, and a very uneven work load. Disappointments because we were left behind in the North African campaign and took no part in the campaigns in Sicily and Southern Italy, because our good Austin ambulances were taken away from us, because seven of our old-timers had left us—either had married and gone home to England or had taken commissions and now were serving in other outfits, and because Miss Otto, too, had left us as our Company Commander and was now Group Major. For me 1943 brought a six-months desert experience where I learned to get along with the barest necessities. I learned to appreciate the beauty and solitude of the desert, especially at sunset, but also to respect the menace of it, where sun and heat can be killers and water is more precious than anything else. I learned to live among the English, far away from my own friends. I learned all I ever want to know about cricket, curry, and sandstorms, and best of all I learned to speak English fluently. I made new friends, like Clynton and Colin, and lost some of the old ones, like Joe, who has been posted away, but that too is part of life in the Army. I am especially sad that Wendy has left the unit. Now we don't have a dispatch rider and my hope of ever becoming one is dashed. And 1944? Will it bring the end of the war? I don't think so, but I have not given up hope of getting to Europe and finding my parents.

Outside it is pouring—no weather for maintenance and nothing else to do. That's why I have become reflective, but enough of that. Instead I shall concentrate on Christmas preparations. This year we will not have the elaborate celebrations of last year, since so many of our friends have gone, most of them fighting in Italy, some fallen in action, some far away as POWs. Still, there will be a party on Christmas Eve and a smaller celebration on the 25th with drinks and snacks for our guests.

Alexandria, December 24, 1943

I don't feel much like writing—I might get too melancholy. It is Christmas Eve. I am sitting in the office since I volunteered to substitute for the transport NCO. From across the hall, from our bar, I hear laughter, singing, and toasts. Here in the office it is very quiet. The water for tea is boiling on the little stove, and Pandora sighs from time to time in her sleep. She probably prefers the quiet in here to the noisy bunch in the bar. A few girls have brought me punch and some sweets. I feel sad and am homesick for I don't know what, or where.

Alexandria, January 31, 1944

Almost a month has passed without anything happening. I now live alone in my room. Dora got married on her leave in Palestine. Miss Otto is trying her best to get her a discharge from the Army. Edith has gone to Mersa-Matruh for a month. We are still keeping four ambulances there. We're all somewhat depressed and our general dissatisfaction makes for an unpleasant atmosphere. Our hope is that the second front will open in the spring and then we, too, will be busy again.

Alexandria, February 16, 1944

I was assigned to drive the Deputy Assistant Director of Medical Services from Cairo. On route we began to talk and he let slip that we soon would be posted to Cairo. Of course, he realized immediately that he had made a mistake by divulging this information, but now I begged him to tell me more and promised that I would not repeat a word. He then told me that part of 502 would be posted to Cairo, probably for only a few months. I was terribly disappointed. After all the waiting and hoping, we'll go backwards instead of forwards, inland instead of overseas. But maybe, if we do our job well in Cairo, afterwards we'll go to Europe. One must keep hoping. I feel funny, knowing more about these plans than anyone else in our unit.

Alexandria, February 21, 1944

Yesterday we had a Company meeting and Miss Otto, (now Senior Commander Otto), told us that she had tried to get us out of Alexandria and over to Europe, arguing that we did not have enough work here. Unfortunately, that approach had backfired. Some of the South African ambulance drivers in Cairo are due for home leave and it has been decided to send half of 502 as their replacements. The posting will take place within the next two weeks. We are all very upset and angry. We are disappointed in being sent to Cairo and unhappy about the splitting of our unit. Now we're waiting anxiously for the lists that will tell us who will go where and when.

Alexandria, February 28, 1944

The lists are out! We're leaving on the eighth of March. I am on the list of the first twenty girls. We will stay in Cairo for six weeks and then be relieved by the next group. Now I'm actually looking forward to the change.

Alexandria, March 7, 1944

Everyone is busy packing. No one has a minute to spare. We're taking all our kit with us, and since we can pack all our belongings in our own ambulances, this is not a problem. We're taking all the Fords and the worst of our Chevs because Miss Otto is hoping that in Cairo there may be an opportunity to trade our old cars for Austins. That, at least, would be something.

Alexandria to Mena, March 8, 1944

Up at 5 A.M. We were scheduled to leave at 6 A.M. and, punctually at 5:45 A.M., we were in convoy formation: fifteen Fords, three Chevs, our utility truck with two of our fitters, and Pat Curlewis on her motorbike as convoy leader. Two military policemen guided us out of town. Slowly we headed south to Cairo. I was number three in the convoy and whenever the road curved I could see the entire convoy in the sideview mirrors, one long row of red crosses wending their way over the seemingly endless desert road. I found this view impressive and was again, as so many times before, overcome with the feeling of belonging, of being a small part in an enormous undertaking, of doing something worthwhile. Neither in the kibbutz nor during the years in Tel-Aviv had I ever experienced this kind of satisfaction in the job I was doing, this sense of purpose.

We arrived at the ATS camp in Mena at 3 P.M. The heat was oppressive and we were too exhausted after nine hours of convoy driving to take much notice of our surroundings but just unpacked, checked our cars, showered, and fell into bed.

Mena and Cairo, March 12, 1944

We are attached to the 513 Company ATS and are not too thrilled about it. Now all the kinds of orders to which we paid little heed in Alexandria have to be observed strictly. That means that our uniforms have to follow regulations—no more silk stockings. Goodbye to our beloved scarves, typical of the 8th Army officers. No Achmed serving dinner on white table clothes, but, as in days of Sarafand, we must stand in line with our messkits, knives, forks, and mugs to get the most unappetizing food dished out. Our hut, which houses sixteen of us, is very large and not too bad, after we fixed things up a bit. Sasha and I were given a corner, and since we all sleep under mosquito netting, we feel quite private. We put up a partition at one end of the hut and will use this as our mess. It can't compare with anything at the Rue Fouad, but we did bring part of our bar along. Alas, no men visitors are to be received in the hut. The latrines (not toilets!) are half a mile away. The shower rooms never have hot water, but they do have rats running around the top beams. Meals are served at certain times only, which means that because of our irregular work hours we often miss them.

On our second day in camp each of us was given the addresses of all important stations and camps, and instructions to familiarize ourselves thoroughly with every section of Cairo. In emergencies there is no time to stop and ask for directions. The first thing of interest along the way is Mena House, the meeting place of Roosevelt and Churchill during their stay in Cairo. It is set in beautiful grounds and has a large swimming pool—elegant! Beyond are fabulously rich suburban homes—the kind of opulence one finds a lot in the Mid East. Then, after a sharp turn in the road, the sudden appearance of the pyramids. Entering Cairo, lovely houses, hotels, and cafes line the streets. Where does all the wealth come from in this country of extreme poverty?

To reach the heart of the city one must cross the Nile. These crossings are made by bridge lifts. In camp we were given a schedule which listed the times of day when the bridges were accessible. The river is filled with slow-moving barges carrying cargoes of cotton, corn, and cattle, and traffic is often held up for more than an hour while they pass under the raised bridges. Huge square houseboats are moored along the shore. Some of them are assigned to the nurses who work at one of our hospitals, built on the banks of the river.

Cairo is unbearably hot, with no ocean breeze to bring relief. It isn't the humid heat of Alexandria, but a dry, harsh heat. The noise and the stench of sweat are overwhelming. I think longingly of 'home' and a cool shower. Since Cairo is much larger than Alexandria, it took me til late afternoon to visit all of the base hospitals, MI rooms, headquarters, etc.

Mena and Cairo, March 16, 1944

My first day off I spent with Sasha and two Air Force sergeants we knew in Alexandria. We decided first to look at the pyramids and the sphinx. The pyramids were impressive only in their huge size, each block of stone so enormous that one wonders how the ancient Egyptians managed to lift these massive weights to the top. The outer facing of the pyramids is largely missing. I don't know how or why the granite was removed. The Arab guides probably could have explained this to me, but since I hate their constant begging and cries of *"Baksheesh!"* I will have to remain unenlightened. Someone suggested that we climb the Cheops pyramid, but I refused. The heat was too unbearable for that.

We continued into Cairo proper. The city is more metropolitan than Alexandria. It has the pulse of a big city with its trams, buses, autos, department stores, and cinemas. Not that we didn't find these things in Alexandria, but here everything is on a grander scale, moves faster and louder. Masses of people, smartly dressed Europeans and white-clad Arabs, bustle, push, and linger in the over-crowded streets. There are Bedouins from the desert, tall and slim Sudanese, blacks from all parts of the continent, every language, every costume, every color and religion moving along the streets. Above it all a continuous roar assaults

207

the ears—horns blasting, yelling people, and every few hours the call to prayer from the minarets of the many mosques. The traffic is frantic. Among elegant chauffeured limousines, busses, trucks, taxis, and horse-drawn gerrys, policemen wave their arms, hopelessly out of rhythm with the changing traffic lights.

On boulevards one admires beautiful shops with artistic window displays. Around the corner, in front of the butcher shops, hang huge shanks of meat, exposed to the sun and covered with thousands of flies.

We had coffee on the terrace of Shepheard's Hotel and, tired from the heat and noise, finally hitched a ride back to the ATS camp.

Mena, March 18, 1944

There is much work for us here. We're kept busy every minute of the day. Hundreds of camps in the area have to be served. Each morning we drive our ambulances out to the various MI rooms to act as standbys for camp casualties. We drive soldiers who report on sick parade to the main hospital in town. Our hours are long and unpredictable, but we feel satisfied that we are needed again.

Mena and Cairo, March 20, 1944

A new detail has been added to our schedule: Cairo West, an airport about ten miles from Mena. Three of us are rotating, so that my turn is every third day, from 8 A.M. to 8 P.M. We are to be standby for air evacuation, which means that if wounded come in by plane, mostly from Italy, Tripoli, and Tunis, we transport them from the plane to the hospital. This is different from the routine at the MI room, where we deal mostly with sick men. At the airfield we get seriously wounded stretcher cases only. But the war is far removed now and planes don't come in too often so we spend much of our time waiting and shuttling officers to the mess and back. There are, however, two attractions on this detail. The main one is the bathroom in the sick bay. A hot bath in a large bathtub, under our present living conditions, is the height of luxury. The other attraction is the camp cinema. Since I have to stay here until 8 P.M., I often go and see a film. The sergeant knows where I am and can get me out whenever needed.

Cairo, March 25, 1944

A terrible sand storm at Cairo West. In the afternoon everyone, including me, had to shovel sand, since neither runways nor roads could be identified. The storm lasted the entire day, and by evening I was worn out.

Mena, March 30, 1944

We have a lot of work, especially since we now have to prepare our cars for vehicle inspection without any help. We don't even have a pit or a vehicle ramp so all maintenance has to be done in the sand. In addition, we now have a lot of night work. I am beginning to long for our life in Alexandria and hope to be transferred soon. But, before that, I have requested leave. It's been nine months since my last leave and I feel I need some relaxation.

Mena, April 10, 1944

I haven't written in my journal for an entire week since I've been quite sick in the hospital. On the third of April I was on duty at Cairo West. I had nothing to do, was just sitting and waiting for twelve hours. Then at 6 P.M. a call came through that twelve stretcher cases would land around 8 P.M. We telephoned our depot and asked for three more ambulances. When the plane arrived, the patients were transferred to our ambulances, taken to the sickbay where they were checked, and then put back into our ambulances. By then it was 9:30 P.M. I led our little convoy at twenty m.p.h. since the patients were all very serious cases. It was midnight when we arrived at the 63rd General Hospital, where we had to wait for another hour until the MO 'on duty' showed up. The unloading seemed to progress at a snail's pace. At 1 A.M. we started for home and arrived at out barracks at 3 A.M.—a twenty-one hour work day. I was so tired that my legs felt unsteady and my hands were shaking. The next day was my day off. I felt rotten but attributed this to yesterday's ordeal. I dozed all day, not moving from my bed. Miss Stewart, who has taken Penny Otto's place, had come down from Alexandria for a visit and when she saw me decided that something was seriously wrong. A medical orderly was called and took my temperature, which must have been high because, in spite of my vehement protests, I was taken to the sick bay. Later that day I must have fallen into a kind of coma, and when I did not improve the next day I was taken to the hospital. I was driven in one of our own ambulances and found the ride quite comfortable.

During the next two days I began to feel better and slowly my strength returned, but I was not allowed to get up. My room was comfortable, but the days passed very slowly. The MO did not make any diagnosis. Could it have been another attack of sandfly fever? The MO is old and kind and believes everything one tells him. I told him that I was feeling great, fit as a fiddle, so he said that I could get up tomorrow.

Yesterday Miss Angus, our first lieutenant, and Edith came to visit me. They arrived quite disheveled. Right after lunch, their dress uniforms pressed and polished since it was their day off, they had taken our little utility car and started out to visit me. As they drove through the native quarter, they were suddenly surrounded by about ten Arabs who, gesticulating wildly, accused Miss Angus of having hit a child, an old ruse to extort money. Of course, no child had been hit. Ten Arabs became fifty Arabs, who climbed all over the little car. The fictitious injured child became three dead ones. The Arabs began to pull on the girls' hair, to pinch them, and to spit on them. Miss Angus' cap was stolen and little boys punctured one of the back tires of the car. This uproar went on for a good twenty minutes until, luckily, a patrol of MPs arrived. The crowd dispersed. Two shaken girls gathered their wits together, changed the tire, and completed the trip.

Although I had to laugh picturing their tale, this problem has really ceased to be a laughing matter. Not only are defenseless Army vehicles stopped, but our equipment is stolen right from under us. After a trip through these rough quarters, we often find everything removable, such as blankets, stretchers, and other Red Cross equipment—gone! If the ambulance is parked unattended for just a few minutes, its tires may disappear. However, a counter-attack is now being put into effect. Indian soldiers, mostly Gurkhas, ride aboard lorries, hidden behind the high tailgates. These lorries are piled high with blankets, items especially valued by the thieves. When the Gurkhas see fingers reaching above the tailgates, down come their large-bladed knives, cutting off those fingers. This may seem like a very drastic measure, but apparently it is the only way to deter the constant theft of our equipment.

Mena, April 10, 1944

I left the hospital today. Physically, though, I don't feel well at all.

Mena, April 12, 1944

Yesterday I was on detail but felt so weak that I had to give up work. Today I am a bit better. I'm glad that my leave has come through. I shall be off for Tel-Aviv in a few days. I hope the promised lift by plane from Cairo to Palestine will come through.

Cairo, April 16, 1944

This morning, attired in my best dress uniform, I got a ride with Sasha, who is on duty at Cairo West. We left early because I had been told that the plane was to leave at 8 A.M. sharp. I figured I would be in

Tel-Aviv in time for lunch. At 8 A.M. I was told the plane would leave at 9 A.M. At 9 A.M. they said it would leave at 10 A.M., since some repairs had not been completed. At 10 they said that by 11 we would leave for sure. I was getting a little nervous because, if the plane did not leave, my railway warrant, which was made out for today's 12:30 train to Palestine, would expire. Finally at noon the two pilots, another officer who also was hitching to Palestine, and I climbed into the big Wellington bomber. There were no windows, no seats, just a campbed onto which we both settled. From where we sat we could not even see the pilots. The machine started, the entire plane shook, and after ten minutes these vibrations increased. The noise was deafening and I was sure that we were in the air. (My only previous flight, in a Liberator, had been short and smooth.) After three quarters of an hour I was glad to have half the trip behind me, but when one of the engines started to backfire I began to feel a bit uncomfortable. After all, I do know what backfiring means in a car and I was not surprised when a minute later I could hear only one engine, the other having given out completely. My travel companion paled and I wondered why we were not crashing down. We crawled forward and, to my great surprise, I saw the runway of—Cairo West! Something was still wrong with the plane and all this time the pilot had tried, in vain, to take off. We were told that the plane had to go back to workshops and that there were no other transports to Palestine available for the next few days. Every time I try to hitch a plane, my plans fall apart. Instead of gaining a day I now had lost one. Furthermore, my train ticket was now invalid and I would have to pay for a ticket myself, if I could get a seat, which was questionable. I called my old friend George, the RAF officer. He gave me new hope, suggesting that he might get a lift for me from the Heliopolis airport. I drove into town and met him at the Kas-El-Nil Barracks. He took me to a very pleasant English family, old friends of his, and we all spent a delightful evening at their home. I stayed overnight at the YWCA.

Cairo to Tel-Aviv, April 17, 1944

George called for me at 7 A.M. We had a quick breakfast at his mess and were at the airport by 8 A.M. The first transport to Palestine left half an hour later but had no room for me. The next left at 11 A.M. but could not take me either. The last of the day, at 1 P.M., had, to be sure, one free seat, but at the last minute a WAAF showed up and, of course, had priority over me. By now I was really upset. Another day lost and time was running out for the train too. Depressed, I was about to leave when a pilot came into the office asking if there was anyone around wanting a lift to Palestine. I could have kissed him. He was a flight instructor and now was going back, taking over from another flight instructor who was expected to land at any time. The plane, another Wellington bomber, arrived at noon, was quickly filled with petrol, and by 1 P.M. we were ready to take off. The plane seemed awfully full. There were two instructors, eight flight students, and two hitchhikers besides me. We sat on our kitbags.

Before boarding I was asked if I had had some flight experience, since this was a bomb-instruction flight and might not be too comfortable. "Oh, yes," I said, unsuspecting. We had not been up very long when suddenly I had the sensation that someone had hit me on the head while at the same time an electric shock ran through my entire body—a most unpleasant combination. I noticed the crew watching me to see how I would react to the bombing effect. I tried to smile but only managed a grimace. This falling through the air was repeated at regular intervals, and since there were no windows or doors, I sat wretchedly hunched over, hoping for a quick end to the flight. After two and a half miserable hours we finally arrived at an airport about thirty miles from Tel-Aviv. When I climbed down the ladder I heard the wing commander of the airport, who apparently had witnessed the landing, angrily chewing out our pilot officer. What irresponsibility to take a girl on a training mission! Didn't he know that during the last week they had had three crash landings and a number of casualties? Actually, this had been the first perfect landing in days! I have had enough of flying for a while.

Tel-Aviv, April 20, 1944

My leave is passing quickly. I spend my time looking up friends, sitting in cafe houses, reading, and horseback riding. The latter gives me the greatest pleasure. I am having a good time, yet am already longing to go 'home.' As nice as it is to see old acquaintances, I feel out of place here. Their daily interests, their joys, and worries seem so far removed from my kind of life now that I often find it difficult to communicate. They and I live in different worlds. In theirs I have become a stranger.

Tel-Aviv, May 1, 1944

My leave is over and today my return trip was supposed to begin, but once again the trip is fraught with difficulties. When I reported this morning at the MP station, I was informed that no seats were available on the train. "Come back in the afternoon." Then in the afternoon, "Come back at 5 P.M." Then, "Sorry, try again tomorrow."

Mena, May 5, 1944

Not until yesterday could I get a seat on the train to Cairo. Hardly had I arrived 'home' at our billets—I had not even unpacked—when I was sent out on a job. After sixteen hours on the train and eight hours on duty, I could hardly keep my eyes open.

Mena, May 8, 1944

We have received a few more Austin ambulances and the rumor is that soon all of our old Chevs and Fords will be exchanged for Austins. I, too, have received an old Austin. To be sure, it's not as nice as our previous ones, but it has a good engine and is one hundred percent more comfortable for the patients than my Ford was. Other changes, all for the better, have taken place while I was gone. We are now living in another hut where we have our own showers and toilets and even a little kitchen where late drivers can fix and warm up food. Even the carpark has been greatly improved. Concrete has been poured and a ramp is being built. A roof will be provided over the maintenance area so that we won't have to work on our cars in the burning sun, nor will we have to lie on the sand when we grease and clean the undercarriage. Pat Curlewis has taken over from Pat Hall and is now in charge of our detachment. All these changes make for a much more pleasant life here. Only Sasha and I are left of the original girls who were sent to Mena. I believe it will be our turn next to go back to Alexandria. If it were not for the awful heat, I would almost be sorry to leave here. The fellowship among us is much more evident here than at our depot, where everyone does her own thing after work. Here we depend more on each other for our entertainment. On the other hand, Alexandria is more comfortable, has a far better climate, and I love going to the beach.

Alexandria, May 23, 1944

Two days ago my relief came and I was sent back to Alexandria. Nothing much has changed in our billets, but the yard looks quite different. We have received some new and also a number of older Austins. All Fords, Chevs, and Dodges are to be exchanged within the next week. This means a lot of work for us, but we are excited and dare to hope again. Perhaps this does mean that 502 will go to Europe after all. In addition to our routine work, we are busy preparing the new cars for inspection, checking the equipment, greasing, changing oil, and performing all the other maintenance tasks, then stripping the old cars before their evacuation to Tel-el-Kebir. The 64th General Hospital has left and the Navy has taken over, but only temporarily. The entire area is changing noticeably and rumors abound. Now 502 is split into three different groups: the Headquarters at Alexandria, the detachment in Mena, and still four girls at Mersa-Matruh. We all take our turns.

Alexandria to Mena to Alexandria, May 28, 1944

Day before yesterday I had my day off and spent it at the beach, where I managed to get terribly sunburned. That same evening I was told that the next day, early in the morning, six of us were to drive all the old Chevs to Tel-el-Kebir, where we would meet the girls from our Mena detachment, who also were evacuating their old Fords. Then all of us were to drive back to Mena in a new 1500 weight truck, work the rest of the day checking and stripping the remaining cars, and on the next day (today) take all these old ambulances to Tel-el-Kebir. From there we were to go back to Mena in the lorry and finally drive new Austin ambulances back to Alexandria. It was a gigantic exchange for forty-eight hours. When I first heard of this program and thought of my sunburn, I was sick at heart, but I could not imagine the agony that lay ahead of me. Many times during these last two days I was close to tears. Every mile was torture. Every vibration of the car against my burned skin under the starched bush-jacket caused me excruciating pain. When I arrived in Mena, my back and arms were covered with blisters, but no sooner had Sasha put cream and powder on me than I had to go out into the burning sun to continue with maintenance. There was nothing I could say. In the Army, sunburns are considered 'self-inflicted wounds' and are, therefore, punishable.

Alexandria, June 1, 1944

The yard has a new look—Austins only, some brand-new, some older. All the old-time members of 502, including me, have received a new one. Yes, I am now considered an old-timer. During the last few months 502 has received quite a few new members. Some are replacements, others have been added to bolster our strength. A few are Palestinian ATS, the rest are English ATS, who had served in the Middle East as sergeants and corporals. They gladly gave up their stripes to join 502.

Alexandria, June 2, 1944

I'm extremely proud of my new ambulance and enjoy caring for it with spit and polish, changing the oil, greasing it, etc. My new car's number is 1211768. I call it simply "68." I'm sure it's a lucky number and we'll go to Europe together. I just painted our Unit sign, a Blue Devil on a white background, on its side.

There is one more thing to be proud of. Most members of 502 have received the Africa Star for the part we played during that campaign. I now wear on my uniform the yellowish-brown ribbon with its red and green stripes.

Alexandria, the week of June 4, 1944

Rome belongs to us! In the humdrum of work I have neglected to mention the news from the front. But to have taken the capital of Italy undamaged—that is a great step forward. The struggle for southern Italy has lasted so long. I hope we'll be able to advance faster now.

Alexandria, June 6, 1944

The news we have waited for so long and eagerly is out—the invasion of France has begun and yesterday our troops carried out the first landings in Norway as well. Many believe that the end of the war is near. I, however, do not share their optimism. I believe that the Germans will still put up a hard fight before it is all over.

Alexandria, June 10, 1944

In contrast to the exciting news on both fronts, nothing much is happening here. We do, however, have a lot of work since the area is still full of troops. Our patients are not war casualties any more but sick soldiers, prisoners, and, at times, civilians from refugee camps.

Alexandria, June 14, 1944

General Stone came on an inspection tour today, so this morning we had a vehicle parade for which we had to polish our ambulances like crazy. The engines, the undercarriages, the insides, all had to shine. The entire parade did not take more than five minutes and he did not really look at a single engine—just walked through, nodding his head. Last night I worked until 9 P.M. cleaning my ambulance because I had been on the road all day. In the morning I had taken a child's body from the 3rd General Hospital to Katatba, the Jugoslav refugee camp. (Now we are hearse drivers too!) Many of the refugee children die because most of them are so undernourished that they cannot survive the slightest illness. On my way back I got into a real sandstorm, so that my ambulance was a mess. I arrived home at 6 P.M. and then worked for three hours to get my car ready for today's inspection. One of those fifteen-hour days again.

Alexandria, June 19, 1944

This is my birthday. Will it be my last one in uniform? I received flowers from Miss Stewart, who still is our Commanding Officer until Miss Otto comes back to us. From Miss Angus, our Lieutenant, I received a book and from Geula and Sasha a leather belt and some handkerchiefs. Edith sent me a charming hand-made wooden bowl. In the morning I was on hospital detail with Nicole. (Nicole is the daughter of a wealthy local family and she drives for us regularly as a volunteer.) We talked the Quartermaster into letting us go early in order to celebrate my birthday. The four of us went in Nicole's little sportscar to the beach, where we swam and sunned and made the acquaintance of some American pilots who occupied the beach cabin next to ours. They had been fixing ground meat patties over an open fire and made sandwiches out of them, which they called hamburgers. These were delicious. In the evening we finished the day with drinks at our bar. A real nice day!

Alexandria, June 22, 1944

A few weeks ago we heard that Miss Chitty, the present Commander of the entire ATS-MEF, is supposed to be transferred back to England. Colonel Waystaffe will take over from her, and her first duty will be an inspection tour of all ATS units. Sergeant Major Curlewis informed me that Colonel Waystaffe will arrive tomorrow and will stay three days in Alexandria. During this time Sasha and I will be staff car drivers for her and her staff. I was not enthusiastic about this because I hate driving in skirt and blouse instead of slacks and bush jacket. I also hate all the saluting and holding doors that goes with staff car driving. I am, however, glad about the change of command. Miss Chitty did not like 502. She always resented our special privileges and the fact that she was powerless to do anything about it. Maybe the new Commander will feel more kindly toward us and will leave Miss Otto a freer hand, which would make moving on from here a definite possibility.

Alexandria, June 23, 1944

In two staff cars we picked up Colonel Waystaffe and the accompanying officers from the airport. She seems to be a pleasant person. The day passed with taking her and her entourage hither and yon.

Alexandria, June 24, 1944

Driving a staff car is much hotter work than driving our ambulances. We are dressed up in skirts and blouses and are wearing hose so we look great but are dripping with perspiration. Sasha says that one can get an inferiority complex from staff car driving and she is quite right. One feels like a chauffeur, waiting, saluting, pulling doors open, closing doors. "Driver this." "Driver that." "Yes, Ma'am." "No, Ma'am." One sits erect and stiff at the wheel and listens to the talk in the back. Often I meet Sasha waiting somewhere and we talk about our 'mistresses' like real servants. I hate it.

Alexandria, June 25, 1944

Thank goodness. This is the last day of being a chauffeur. Tonight we'll take them to the airport and tomorrow I'll drive my ambulance again. When I returned from work I found a belated birthday package from Uncle Hans and family, from Chicago. I also had a card from my sister Edith, from whom I now hear quite regularly. She is in a boarding school in Yeovil, Somerset, getting an excellent education. It's hard to believe that she's already a teen-ager. But no word at all from my parents.

Hardly am I back driving my new ambulance when another change is in the offing. Again Sergeant Major Curlewis called me into the office and asked me if I would like to go to Mersa-Matruh for a week in order to relieve one of the girls there who apparently had a nervous breakdown. Why? She told me the following story. About two weeks ago one of the four girls stationed in Mersa-Matruh woke up at night and caught a glimpse of a man running out of the room in which they slept. She woke the other three, but they laughed it off as a bad dream. They quit laughing when the same thing was repeated during the next few nights, and one of them found her panties and bra, which she had left on her bed, missing in the morning. It was impossible to catch the mysterious night visitor or to identify him. He did not do anything to the girls but just sat and watched them and disappeared as soon as one of them woke up. He might have been anyone from the Indian Field Ambulance Unit or from other units stationed nearby. Possibly he was one of the Italian prisoners who worked around there. The girls were told to sleep with closed doors, and guards were posted around their part of the building. Nothing happened for a week and the guards were removed. A couple of nights later three of the girls were out late and the fourth was alone in the room, asleep. This time the man appeared and attacked her. She fought him and screamed until he let her go and fled. Unfortunately, she could not describe him because it all happened so fast and in complete darkness. She thought that he was dark-skinned and of slight build. That description would fit almost anyone. Anyway, 502 did not want to give up the detachment, but it was thought best to replace the four girls immediately. I was agreeable to going to Mersa-Matruh and thought the entire episode ridiculous, probably highly exaggerated by a couple of hysterical girls. A week in Mersa-Matruh again might be fun.

Mersa-Matruh, July 2, 1944

I arrived in Mersa-Matruh with Phyl, Diggie, and Joyce at 4 P.M. yesterday. This morning the other four girls left. We are all laughing about them and their fears.

Mersa-Matruh, July 3, 1944

God, what a night! Yesterday there was a big party for John Webb, present Commander of the 20th Indian Field Ambulance, which had taken over for the 32nd IFA. He and three other officers are leaving the unit. By 10 P.M. I decided to leave the party and went to bed. The others continued their celebration in the adjoining building. When I think of this now, how I was sleeping all alone in our room with doors and windows wide open and how nobody would have heard my screams with all the noise of the party, I shudder. Luckily, though, I slept undisturbed until the other three returned, about 2 A.M., and went to bed too. About an hour later suddenly Joyce's scream woke me. She was shouting "The man! The man! Diggie, he was under your bed!" I saw Joyce excitedly pointing toward the door and Diggie jumping out of bed. Still half asleep, I sat up in bed, closed my eyes, and screamed as loud and as long as I could! What a picture we must have made! After we had awakened the entire field hospital and were calmed down by all the medical officers, we went back to sleep, this time with closed doors. The night visitor did not return.

Phyl left early this morning for Alexandria with some stretcher cases. Joyce took some more cases at noon. A night in Alexandria will do them both good. Diggie and I are trying to explain some recipes to our Italian cook. He is a POW and very nice, but communication between us is difficult. In the afternoon we went with Mac to the beach for target shooting. He is a very pleasant RE officer, who looks after us like a father. I am quite good with the rifle but not too exact with the pistol. After about one hundred rounds with the rifle my shoulder hurts a good deal. In the evening Diggie and I, being all alone, felt quite uncomfortable. We kept the doors closed but had to leave the windows open, for the heat and stuffiness would otherwise be unbearable. It is a very unpleasant feeling to think that someone might prowl around the house or peep through the windows. Neither of us dares to close her eyes so we talked and stayed awake all night.

Mersa-Matruh, July 6, 1944

The SIB—Special Investigations Branch or something like that, has been called in from Cairo. We picked them up in Mersa-Matruh—two men with two of the most vicious looking dogs I have ever seen, a cross between boxer and bull dog. They spent the night in our ambulances, which are parked right below our billet. Again the intruder did not show up.

Mersa-Matruh, July 7, 1944

The officers of the 20th Indian Field Ambulance are doing everything to make us forget our nightly anxieties. Since they have little work and we have hardly any, we go sailing, swimming, and target shooting. The days are fun, if it only weren't for the nights. The SIB men and their dogs are keeping watch, but what good does that do? I am sure that the night visitor is someone from the Field Ambulance and is well aware of all the plans being made to catch him. Last night the two men moved into our room and now 'sleep' in our beds. We moved some campbeds for ourselves into the little corridor behind the kitchen. Again the intruder did not show up. So this morning the SIB left with their dogs, leaving the case unsolved. Sara, my relief, came today, so the next job to Alexandria will be mine and my days here are numbered. If it were not for the nights, I would be sorry to leave because now it is much nicer than in the days of the 'desert rats.' I like the girls here and not having Pat in charge makes everyone breathe much freer and easier. Also, our living conditions are far more comfortable than they were before. No more tent living. The rooms, a living-dining room, sleeping room, and even a kitchen, are nicely furnished. Our two Italian POW servants are an enormous improvement over Buddel, the Indian cook, who did not even have a kitchen and had to prepare our food in the open. We also have enough water now

219

and our laundry comes back to us starched and ironed. On top of all that, we have the most gorgeous view from our living quarters. The blue lagoon with its white beach is right in our front yard, but all of this I already described when we first moved here.

Alexandria, July 10, 1944

Once again I drove the familiar desert route back to Alexandria. I never before had so many passengers and, after a stop in Daba where I picked up two more sitting patients, I ended up with three stretcher cases, four sitters, one orderly and one sister (nurse.) It's such a pleasure to drive an Austin again. One can drive much faster since the springs are far superior to those in the Fords or Chevs and the ride is comfortably cushioned for all the patients. In the evening I had a bit of a row with Pat Hall. She told me that I would have to go to Mena within the next few days. I found this most unjust since there are many girls who have not been to Mena for half as long as I. But no protest helps. One cannot argue with Pat.

Alexandria, July 11, 1944

I arrived in Alexandria yesterday and am packing again because to-morrow I'll have to leave for Mena for who knows how many weeks. I am sick of this eternal packing and moving.

Mena, July 12, 1944

Again the old desert road to Mena. The old camp and our "new" bungalow are still the same, yet again much has changed for the better. Everyone came out to greet me and it was good to see some familiar faces. My bad mood soon evaporated. The girls have planted a few flower beds around our billet. The ramp for working on the under carriage is finished. Also the roof is in place above the poured concrete. That's a blessing because now the days are hotter than ever. I also like working under Pat Curlewis, our CSM. She's lots of fun and full of in-teresting stories. Pat is South African and spent some time in Spain during the Civil War. At one time she owned a hotel in Kitzbuhl, Aus-tria. I love to listen to her recount her adventures. My first day was spent as 'Orderly-Driver.' That means that I was stand-by but had all kinds of barrack duties like watering flowers, making endless pots of tea and coffee, fetching our mail, seeing that the toilets are clean, etc.

Mena, July 16, 1944

Yesterday I was left in charge of our detachment here since Pat Curlewis and three others of the original 502 members had left for Halfway House, which is a camp halfway between Alexandria and Cairo. All our officers and NCOs from Alexandria were meeting them there to discuss our situation with regard to work. There is very little for us to do in Cairo. On the other hand, in Alexandria there are not enough people to do all the work, even though we again have been reinforced with a few new drivers, but all the South African drivers are leaving and we will have to take over duties in the MI rooms in the entire Alexandria area. Probably the detachment here in Mena soon will be disbanded. Today we had a convoy, the first after a long time—all mental cases who had to be taken from the station to the hospital.

Mena, August 3, 1944

Tonight I am transport NCO. This probably is my last day in Mena because tomorrow my week's leave will begin and I'll be off to Tel-Aviv again. Who knows whether I'll ever come back here. The last three and a half weeks were quite pleasant and I'll take with me many good memories.

En route to Palestine, August 4, 1944

Since I did not intend to hitch a plane ride again, I had to get to Alexandria first because the train from Cairo to Palestine already was fully booked. This means that I'll be twenty-four hours longer on the road. However, I was lucky hitchhiking and got a staff car, which took me right to the door of Rue Fouad, where I arrived at 11:30 A.M. My train left at 3:30 P.M. so there was plenty of time to get to the station. I had nice travel companions and in Tel-el-Kebir a few girls whom I knew from the days in Sarafand joined us. At 7 P.M. we arrived in Ismalia, where Rolf was waiting for me with a carton of cookies. Unfortunately, the train stopped there for only a few minutes. My encounters with Rolf are brief, to say the least.

En route to Palestine, August 5, 1944

The night was not too bad—I got about three hours of sleep, stretched out on the floor. At midnight we arrived in Kantarah, the border station between Egypt and Palestine. There we got hot tea and sandwiches. We arrived in Rechowoth at 11:30 A.M. and were 'home' in Tel-Aviv for lunch—a trip of about thirty hours.

Tel-Aviv, August 6-11, 1944

My leave days passed quickly with the usual round of visiting friends. I spent a lot of time with Dora, who has taken to civilian life very quickly. Edith arrived three days after me on her week's leave and brought a sackful of news from Alexandria. Miss Stewart, our Commanding Officer during Penny Otto's absence, and Miss Angus, our First Lieutenant, are leaving 502 in order to join UNRRA. Miss Otto is coming back to us as our CO. Our outlying detachments, that is Mena and Mersa-Matruh, are being disbanded and the entire unit again will be stationed in Alexandria. Maybe, after all, we'll be shipped to Europe before the war is over.

En route to Mena, August 12-13, 1944

My return journey from Sarafand to Cairo was, as usual, long, dusty, and tiring, but I did have pleasant traveling companions, five girls from the ATS camp in Tel-el-Kebir, all, like me, Palestinians originally from Germany. We spent the night singing German songs. What a mixed-up world we live in! We arrived in Cairo on the 13th at 9 A.M., looking drawn and dirty, and decided to have a big breakfast at Groppi's, a fancy cafe in town. Then I said goodbye to my travel companions and hitchhiked to Mena. Only a few girls are left there and they, too, will leave within the next two weeks. I myself received orders to leave for Alexandria tomorrow.

Alexandria, August 15, 1944

The invasion of southern France has begun. This morning our troops landed on the Riviera.

Alexandria, August 30, 1944

Bunty, our Quartermaster, is beginning to issue all kinds of new kit, mostly warm winter stuff, which we certainly don't need here. Does this mean that we will be posted to Europe?

Alexandria, August 31, 1944

Typical Army organization! At 8 A.M. I had to report at 3rd General Hospital to take patients to Kantarah, a full day's trip. When I arrived at the hospital, nobody knew anything about any cases to be transferred to Kantarah. After running from one office to the next, I finally gave up and drove home. There I was told that they had made a mistake. The patients were waiting at the Greek hospital. By now it was almost noon. I could have been halfway to Kantarah. When I finally got started I had two sitters and both sat next to me. We arrived at Kantarah General Hospital at 6 P.M., and after delivering my patients I was told to have my ambulance disinfected since both patients were tuberculosis cases! They had sat next to me for seven hours, had drunk from my thermos, coughed at me, and never were inside the cabin of the ambulance, the part which had to be disinfected. *I* should have been disinfected! I stayed overnight at the Sisters' ward and left next morning with a stretcher case for Alexandria.

Alexandria, September 2, 1944

Had to take five cases to the docks. What a sight! The entire harbor is full of ships of all sizes and classes. I have never seen the docks so busy. Maybe a new invasion? Maybe Greece this time? Will we be part of it? I'm sure we'll be going soon, but personally, I'd most like to go to Italy. Not only have I always wanted to see Italy, but it is closer to Germany and the hope of finding my parents. This evening I had to take a meningitis case to Amariyah. With all these infectious diseases, being an ambulance driver seems more dangerous now than when we had front line casualties.

Alexandria, September 8, 1944

Today I was hit in the face by a stone thrown by an Arab and momentarily lost control of the steering. Thank goodness nothing happened except that the entire right side of my face is badly swollen. I was lucky that the stone did not hit me in the eye. The Arabs are becoming more and more hostile toward the British Forces and we are, of course, completely defenseless. From now on, at least on night duty, we will not drive alone.

Alexandria, September 28, 1944

Worked all day in Dekeila. In the evening we had the long-awaited Company meeting, during which Miss Otto told us that our movement orders have come through. Hurrah! We are leaving the Middle East, but we don't yet know when or where we're going.

Alexandria, September 30, 1944

A new MAC has arrived in Alexandria and is slowly taking over our work. Miss Otto has returned as our Junior Commander. Pat Curlewis has been promoted to 2nd Lieutenant. Things are really moving! I can't think of anything but our posting. I'm really excited at the thought of getting back onto the Continent. It has been eight years since I left home and over two years since I last heard from my parents. Will I be able to find them? Will they still be in Berlin or—and this I don't even want to think about—will they have been deported and suffered the same fate as the Russian and Polish Jews? Surely once we are on the Continent, I can find out more. In the meantime I keep on writing this diary in the hope that one day they'll read it.

Alexandria, October 4, 1944

We had another Company meeting. Orders are to be ready by the end of this month. We are to take our ambulances with us. I'm beside myself with joy. Now I'm crossing my fingers that the destination will be Italy rather than Greece. To me, Greece is still too close to the Middle East and I want to get as close to Germany as possible and as fast as possible.

Alexandria, October 7, 1944

Yesterday was my day off and the first relaxing day I've had in a long time. I spent almost the entire day with Rolf at the beach (he had a couple of days leave). This was probably our last day together for a long time to come. We wonder where and when we'll see each other again. Today I am once again so rushed that there's no time to think of partings or to speculate on the future. Until 4 P.M. I was on details to Dekeila. Then I worked for several hours to get my car ready for workshop inspection and in the evening I had bar duty.

Alexandria, October 13, 1944

Brigadier Bewsher gave a farewell cocktail party for our entire unit. I hate these snobbish parties, but I do my best to master the art of conversing without really saying anything, of which the British upper class seem to be so fond. Glass in hand, smile on lips, I stand. Attentive cavaliers are eager to make us feel that we're going to be dreadfully missed.

"And what part of England are you from?" A favorite ice-breaker.

"Palestine." The ice re-forms.

"Oh. Well, been to the races lately? How did you like the looks of that new filly . . . No? Say, this isn't a bad drink, is it? I say, are you fond of riding?"

"Yes."

"I say, have you ever been to Scotland?"

"No."

"Quite."

Another guest joins us. "I say, old man, haven't seen you at the Club lately. Been playing any tennis? Damned awful hot, isn't it?"

"Like another drink?"

"So you like horses, eh?"

"Yes."

"Good! Jolly well good. Must say, I feel the same way about 'em."

I sip my drink. My English is awkward and this glib Englishman is a depressing reminder.

"Never been hunting, eh?" he muses sadly. I sip my drink. He leaves. Another officer takes his place, smiles cordially.

"Hello there. I say, what part of Britain are you from?"

I take a fortifying gulp of my whiskey and tell him the dreadful news.

Alexandria, October 15, 1944

Another Company meeting. The final movement orders have arrived! We are leaving in ten days.

Alexandria, October 16, 1944

No more details. All days off have been canceled. We have been divided into sections. I'm in Jane's section, which I like a lot. All day long we packed ambulances with MT stores (tools, spare parts, etc.), quartermaster stores, office equipment, and, of course, most of our bar equipment!

Alexandria, October 17, 1944

Pack, pack, pack! I bought myself a new suitcase, which I'll take on board the ship. We all have one kit bag and one bed roll, which go down into the ship's hold, and a second kit bag which goes into the ambulances. My ambulance will carry all the kit bags of our section. A few girls are going on embarkation leave, but I don't want to. I'm too excited and would rather stay and help with all the preparations.

Alexandria, October 24, 1944

Today a platoon of RASC drivers came and took our entire carpark, that is, our thirty-six Austin ambulances, our staff car, the 3-ton truck, the two small utility cars, Miss Otto's staff car, and the two motorcycles. They probably are going to Port Said to be shipped from there. I do hope that nothing will happen to them until we get them back 'over there.' The drivers seem rather inexperienced. How strange the empty yard looks!

Alexandria, October 30, 1944

The last days here in Alexandria passed quickly, assembling our personal equipment. The following is a list of what each of us had to check out. I kept it because I know how my mother would be interested in it—if she ever gets to read this.

2 Blouse B.D.	1 Dressing field (fork, knife, spoon)
1 Cap winter	1 Housewife
1 Raincoat	1 Lanyard
1 Greatcoat	2 Studs
1 Jacket serge	3 Ties
1 Skirt serge	1 Pair titles
1 Shoes plimsoll	1 Wallet
2 Shoes	3 Packets S.T.N.
1 Boots leather	1 Brass cleaning
2 Trousers serge	1 Brush cotton
1 Gloves MT	1 Brush polishing
1 Goggles	1 Brush tooth
1 Knife clasp	1 Brush hair
3 Overalls combination	1 Comb
2 Belts corset	Full issue of mending materials
4 Brassieres	1 Ground sheet
1 Gloves knitted	1 Bottle water
2 Jerseys	1 Carrier water bottle
1 Scarf woolen	1 Brace without bottle
3 Panties wool	1 Brace with buckle
8 Panties cell or knickers	1 Mess tin
2 Pajamas winter	1 Mug
2 Pajamas summer	1 Haversack
4 Shirts poplin	1 Respirator (gas mask)
8 Collars	1 Steel helmet
3 Socks winter	1 Pkt eyeshields, 2 tinted, 4 clear
3 Socks summer	1 Cape
4 Stockings	1 Oz. cotton waste
3 Vests woolen	1 Ointment
2 Towels	1 Torch
2 Kit bags	1 Bag ration
1 Badge cap	4 Blankets

4 Shirts trop. (may be exchanged for wool later)

1 Jerkin leather	1 Bag linen
1 Shoelaces spare	1 Belt sanitary

3 Sets discs identity (2 on person, 1 on respirator)

All this material had to be marked with our identification. We turned in our summer kit—bush jackets and skirts, pith hats, etc.

We held a parade for our Area Commander, Brigadier Bewsher, in our empty carpark and were quite moved by his farewell speech in which he praised 502 most highly. He had every reason to do so. While in Egypt we had travelled over a million miles, carrying over 140,000 patients, often under most adverse conditions. Our 502 truly had earned a reputation for reliability, efficiency, and a caring attitude toward all its charges.

On Board the R.M.S. *Alcantara*, October 31, 1944

I was too excited to sleep much. Breakfast was at 7 A.M. and then came the last packing, folding up beds and emptying all rooms. All dressed in our new winter issue, we perspired heavily. At 12:30 two huge lorries came to take us to the docks, to, of all quays, number 43. How many times had we stood on this very quay, looking up at the hospital ships, waiting for our 'cargo'! Now it was our turn to board and look down on the familiar dockside. We were in full battle dress with our baggage and were dripping wet with sweat. Luckily we didn't have to wait too long to board our ship. We have very comfortable cabins. Ours has nine beds, but since we're only seven girls, there's plenty of room to spread out. Washing is a bit hard because soap won't foam in salt water. The dining room has waiters in white jackets. It's all way above my expectations. In the late afternoon we had drill in lifejackets, which made us even more uncomfortable, our uniforms sticking to our backs. I hope we'll leave soon or we'll die of the heat.

En Route to Europe, November 1, 1944

7:30 A.M., breakfast—what a breakfast! Real English: flaked oats, poached haddock, fresh bread, preserves, tea, and coffee. I'm sure we will have gained a few pounds by the time we land. The rumor is that we'll leave this afternoon. In the meantime, there's another life-boat drill. Then there's time to explore the ship. The R.M.S. *Alcantara* is a rather large troop ship which before the war cruised between England and South America. Besides our group there are only two other women (civilians), with one child on board. The rest are all men, many of them belonging to the Jewish Brigade. One hears more Hebrew than English on board. At 3 P.M. two pilot boats towed us slowly out of the harbor. All of 502 stood on deck, waving a last goodbye. I wondered whether I would ever see Alexandria again. I wondered, too, where we were headed. In the back of my mind is always the thought that each mile will carry me closer to my parents and my old home.

By 4 P.M. we were moving under our own power. I could see two troopships and a corvette following us. The sea was very calm, the air balmy. An hour later, after all ships had taken their positions in the convoy, the air was rent by a deafening noise as all guns on every ship were fired simultaneously—an ack-ack drill. From now on strict black-out would be enforced. After dinner I went on deck, but it was so dark that I couldn't see my hand in front of my face.

En Route to Europe, November 2, 1944

The rolling of the ship woke me up around 3 A.M. I thought we must have encountered bad weather, but I fell asleep again until 6:30. It seemed to me that the rolling had increased and I felt a bit nauseated, so I dressed quickly and rushed up on deck, expecting to see rough water. To my surprise, the sea was calm, the sky blue—a typical Mediterranean postcard-scape. Still, my stomach felt queasy. For breakfast I grabbed a piece of bread and hurried back up on deck. (Two of the girls are already sea-sick.) I lay down on my life-belt (there are, of course, no deck chairs on a troopship), feeling tired and washed out, but as long as I lay down, my stomach behaved. The convoy now consists of four troopships, one destroyer, and one corvette. It is still very warm, ideal cruise weather. At 10:30 we had another drill. By lunch time I had an enormous appetite but afterwards felt again so weak and tired that I slept for two hours. Why am I so tired when all we do is eat and sleep?

En Route to Europe, November 3, 1944

The weather is beautiful, the sea calm, and a refreshing breeze is blowing. By now we are used to the ship's movement, and if it were not for the lifejackets, which we must carry with us at all times, and the strict blackout, one could believe this was a first-class cruise. We read, sleep, eat, play bridge, and promenade on deck.

En Route to Italy, November 4, 1944

After breakfast I went on deck and there, far in the distance, I could make out land—Sicily, Mount Etna, even Catania were recognizable! Around 9:30 one of our troopships, accompanied by the corvette, left the convoy in the direction of the Straits of Messina. Way out we could see a convoy of about fourteen ships waiting for the troopship. The corvette later returned to our convoy. In the meantime we passed

Mount Etna quite close, its peak covered with snow—a beautiful sight. By noon it was only a small dot on the horizon and we were again surrounded by water only. From time to time we could see in the distance other convoys and here and there a single ship. I could feel that we were nearing land. Then I heard: "The ship will land at Italy's heel, at Taranto!" I have won my bet and am delighted.

Taranto, November 5, 1944

We were up at 5 A.M. and packed to be ready for disembarkation. After breakfast I went up on deck and watched the Italian coast slip by. The water was as calm as a mirror, the landscape hilly and green, the sky a pink glow from the rising sun. It was quite cold. By 7 A.M. we had anchored outside the harbor, which is too small for our large ships. The whole of 502 climbed into boats and headed for shore, that is, all but six of us, who were assigned to the 'luggage party.' We had to go down to the ship's hold to supervise the loading of our Company's baggage. This took about two hours. Finally, we were told to climb right on top of the huge net containing the last of our kitbags. The crane hauled us up, swung high into the air, cleared the decks, swung out, and then deposited us on a small baggage craft tied to our ship. Unfortunately ours was the first load out so we had to sit and wait on that tiny boat for five hours until the barge was full. The little craft bobbed continuously, the wind was blowing, and we were freezing. At last an officer on board the ship, looking down at our shivering misery, felt sorry for us and offered some hot tea. Up we went in the net and, cheered by the hot drink, did not mind the waiting so much after that. By 3 P.M. the boat was loaded and we covered the last two miles to shore, where Jane already was waiting for us with several lorries. Two more grueling hours passed with transferring the baggage from the boat to the lorries. By the time we arrived at our transit camp, it was 6 P.M. and we were chilled to the bone, ravenously hungry, and utterly exhausted. Our quarters, a converted house, consisted of dreary wooden planks and straw mats. The water was ice cold. Still, I decided to take a shower, and though my teeth were chattering and my skin turned blue, I felt better afterwards. In the evening there was a Company meeting. Miss Otto informed us that our ambulances had arrived in Taranto but that it had not yet been decided whether we would drive them to Naples or go by train to Naples and drive the ambulances from there to our destination—Rome! We were jumping with joy. How wonderful to be stationed in Rome! Since Rome has been declared an open city, no military personnel are stationed there, except for medical units, service personnel, and those on leave. We have really lucked out.

Taranto, November 6, 1944

We woke up early and washed again in cold water. The weather is really nippy. At breakfast we were told that we *will* drive our ambulances all the way. Our fitters have already gone to check all cars for tomorrow's departure. We, in the meantime, were free to explore the town. Within an hour we found that there was very little to see. The streets are old, the houses and buildings shabby. The townspeople look poor and unhealthy. All morning I saw only one well-dressed woman. Despite the freezing weather, everyone walks without stockings in crude wooden shoes. Shops are empty—no wares. Black markets serve a few choice patrons. Queues stand in front of grocery stores, their ration books in hand, to get their meager share. As we watched we grew more and more depressed. The crowds were unfriendly, unsmiling, looking right through us with complete indifference. If they viewed our well-fed, warmly-clad bodies with resentment, that's understandable. They are the real sufferers of war, who look forward to nothing but a steady diet of hunger and privation. There were no cinemas, no restaurants, no cafes. All morning we searched for a place to sit and drink a cup of tea, but there was no such place. Still, I returned to the transit camp feeling good in spite of everything. This was my first walk on European soil in eight years, the first refreshing cold air I had breathed since I had left Germany so long ago.

Taranto to Foggia, November 7, 1944

A lorry drove us out of town where, on a green meadow, our ambulances were parked, all in formation by sections. It was a great sight. Each of us ran to inspect hers. Some had acquired a few dents during transport, but all were 'on the road.' My own "68" did not suffer a scratch. Since our mechanics had checked all cars, we were ready to start. Our destination was Foggia, about 130 miles away. The weather was, to my mind, perfect—the air crisp and cold but the sun shining. After Taranto the road climbed for about ten miles and our progress was very slow because of the many convoys winding their way northward, mainly from the Jewish Brigade. Later the landscape flattened out. We passed through meadows and forests. I feel as if I can never get my fill of the greenness, the freshness of the land. Every few miles we pass little villages and there the feeling is very different. They all look poor and sad. All bridges are demolished and more than once we had to ford a river, but we made it, had no breakdowns and only three broken springs. My "68" behaved very well.

It was dark when we arrived in Foggia. Each of us was told to take out a stretcher and four blankets from our ambulance and move into our quarters. 'Quarters' was an unfinished construction which possessed neither windows nor doors, only the openings for these. The wind howled through the rooms. The draft was unbearable. I have never been so cold and could not sleep a wink. How much more comfortable it would have been to sleep in our ambulances or even out in the open, away from the draft. But orders are orders.

Foggia to Naples, November 8, 1944

The water for washing this morning, from an outside faucet, was so cold that our hands ached when we used it. After breakfast we checked our cars and by 8 A.M. were again on the road, destination Naples. After about twenty miles my car was not really pulling. I couldn't keep it in fourth gear and it started to knock at fifteen mph. I pulled over and waved my section on. Monica, our fitter, joined me and tried to find out what was wrong with "68," but after an hour and a half she gave up and we limped along, she following me in case I had a complete breakdown. The route was even more beautiful than yesterday. We were climbing all the way. The country seems to me almost like Switzerland and I enjoyed every minute. First the weather was sunny and cold, but around noon the sky clouded over and a cutting wind began to blow. In spite of my winter uniform I felt quite chilled. Our ambulances, designed for desert warfare, have neither doors nor windows in the driver's cab but just a little canvas screen about two feet high.

After lunch we started to descend the mountain. My car would hold going down since I could drive in first and second gear only, but Monica had to brake continually to stay behind me. We stopped and she told me to drive on while she waited a bit and would then catch up with me. She didn't want to brake continually and burn out her brakes. After another hour's drive I was back in flat country and after a while caught sight of Monica's ambulance in my side view mirror. We passed through another destroyed village and suddenly I couldn't see Monica's ambulance behind me any more. I stopped and waited for three quarters of an hour, but none of the passing cars I flagged down had seen her. She must have taken a wrong turn somewhere. Since it was getting dark and we had been told that these roads are not a bit safe (full of bandits and looters), I finally continued on my own.

Miss Otto had said that when we were left behind, an MP would be waiting for us just outside of Naples and would escort us to our quarters, even if it were 3 A.M. in the morning. It was only 8 P.M. when I arrived, but there was no MP. I drove further—no MP. I began to grow worried. How would I find my unit in this huge town? Soon I was in the middle of city traffic, cars honking on all sides, impatient with my slow progress. At a red light I hooted at a motorized MP. Not until the light had changed several times did he realize that I was signaling for him!

"Have you seen my outfit?"

"What outfit?"

"A convoy of fifty ambulances. How could you miss fifty huge red crosses winding through the city?"

"Well, I did, M'am."

"Any idea how I can find them?"

"Go to the MP Headquarters. They'll help you."

"Can you escort me?"

"No, M'am. I'm on duty."

Frustration overwhelmed me. "Well, then, please give me directions." The directions went something like this: "When you get to Philip's Fountain, turn left on Petrillo Street. Go straight ahead until you come to Mona Cafe. Then bear right. Etc., etc." I hesitated to tell him that this was my first trip to Naples and I didn't know whatchacallit cafe and thingamajig fountain from a hole in the ground. I thanked him and drove away from a snarled-up traffic jam!

I finally located Headquarters but found no parking place. Too tired to care any more, I drove up onto the sidewalk, parked next to the entrance, and tore into the MP building. The first person I saw there was Miss Otto. I breathed a sigh of relief and so did she. Monica, I learned, had taken a short-cut not designated by an official Army sign and had arrived an hour earlier. Captain Otto escorted a very disgusted and tired driver to the transit camp outside of town. We parked "68" and an MP drove us to the hostel where we had been assigned a huge dormitory. We were packed like sardines, but still, it was an improvement over yesterday's lodging. Cold showers again. I guess there is no hot or even warm water to be had in Italy!

Naples, November 9, 1944

In the morning we were taken to the transit camp to check our ambulances for tomorrow's trip. It was raining hard and by noon, when we got back to the hostel, we were wet through and through. After lunch the Chief Commander ATS/CMF (we now were no longer Middle East Forces but Central Mediterranean Forces) gave us a most imbecilic welcome address. She talked about our role as a minority of women, outnumbered by hordes of males, long away from home, and how our very presence could cheer them up. She warned us of the dangers of drinking too much Italian wine and the perils of Italian roads. Apparently she was totally unaware of what we had been doing during the last few years! After this ridiculous talk we had the afternoon free. A few of us decided that, rain or no rain, we had to have a look at the city. Mount Vesuvius was covered by low-hanging clouds, which gave Naples a depressing air. The Neapolitans are as despondent and poor as the rest of the Italians we have seen so far. The city, especially near the harbor, is badly damaged. Throngs of people stream through the streets but all seem to be going nowhere. We saw American and English soldiers and sailors everywhere we went and, for the first time, met a few American women in uniform. Again there was nowhere to stop for a cup of coffee, no restaurants either, only Army clubs, hostels and the YMCA. We are glad not to be stationed here.

Naples, November 10, 1944

We departed the transit camp at 9 A.M.—final destination, Rome. The weather had cleared up, but it still was very cold. Again I had time to observe the beautiful countryside because Monica and I were left behind the convoy. My "68" was still limping along. The road was not as mountainous as yesterday, but every village, every little town we passed, was nothing but a heap of rubble. Most of the population seems to have returned, but it is a mystery to me where and how they live in these ruins. By 5 P.M. it was quite dark and again began to rain. Shortly before reaching Rome we caught up with one of our drivers who had had a breakdown. Monica tried her best but finally decided that she would have to tow her in. All this delayed us further so that it was late in the evening when we finally entered Rome. This time three dispatch riders were waiting for us to guide us to our new home, and what a home it is! It far surpasses anything I had expected. I am too tired to write any more today, but I shall describe it all tomorrow.

Rome, November 11, 1944

We live in a student hostel near the University, at the north end of town. The building, five stories high, is managed by nuns who do the cooking, cleaning, etc. We occupy the ground floor for our offices, bar, and reception room. The dining room we share with the students, all girls, who have their own rooms on the second floor. On the third, fourth, and fifth floors are our bedrooms. The building itself, which had been erected in Mussolini's time, is very modern with an impressive marble staircase and wide corridors. Our rooms are luxurious with excellent beds, night tables, cupboards and chests of drawers, built-in desks, and lovely views. There are only a couple of disadvantages. The building is freezing cold, partly because of all the stone and marble, but also because there is very little heating and, of course, no hot water. Furthermore, there are no elevators, and running up and down four flights of stairs all the time is tiring.

I share a room with Edith. Last night we tried to take a shower. The water coming from the tap was so icy that contact was actually painful. We spent the day unpacking and settling into our charming rooms.

Rome, November 12, 1944

Our actual work is supposed to begin in a few days. In the meantime, all ambulances have to be prepared for workshop inspection. We spent the entire day checking our cars, cleaning the undercarriages, the engines, the insides. We didn't mind since physical labor is the only way to keep warm.

Rome, November 13, 1944

Most of us finished our work by noon. Edith and I decided to go into town. Since there are no busses or taxis because of the petrol shortage, we had to hitch a ride. This was easy. The moment we stepped out of the house two Americans in a jeep passed by, saw us and stopped. Could they take us someplace? Oh, yes! We wanted to go to the Vatican. Their faces fell, but we smiled brightly. I climbed into the front seat next to the driver and Edith sat in the back. Then the difficulties began, because these Yanks spoke American and that's a very strange language to me. I asked the driver, in English, where in America he came from.

"Texas, M'am." Well, I had seen pictures and read books about Texas and its cowboys, so I felt on familiar ground. I asked him if he was a cowboy. This he found extremely funny.

"No, M'am. I used to run a drive-in." This was really puzzling. He ran what? Drove what? Did he own an inn called The Drive? Did he mean that he used to run-in criminals? That must be it—he had been a policeman.

"You're a bobby?"

"No, M'am. My name's Hank. What's yours?" I gave up and let him do the talking.

Our drive took us through the busy part of town, past the train terminal, the Piazza Esedra, down the Via Nazionale, well-known for its beautiful shops and right into Via Novembre, where we could see to the left the remnants of the Villa where Nero presumably watched the burning of Rome. We passed the Piazza Venezia with its big 'Wedding Cake'—that's what our troops call the rather ugly monument to Victor Emmanuele. It deserves its name, for in its high whiteness it looks just like an elaborate wedding cake, covered with icing. In my opinion it's the only ugly building in all of Rome. The Palazzo Venezia, next to it, is old and very beautiful. Mussolini was the last 'Roman Emperor' to occupy it. One can see the balcony from which he dramatically gestured to his audiences. The Piazza Venezia is now full of Army personnel. There is a car park right in the middle of the square and opposite Mussolini's former palace is the building housing the Headquarters of the British and American Armies. We drove over the Corso Vittorio Emmanuele until we came to the River Tiber, crossed the bridge, drove another few hundred yards and stopped before St. Peter's, where the Americans let us out. It was obvious that they were not interested in sightseeing. They drove off in search of more exciting companions, perhaps some who spoke better 'American.'

Though there were many worshipers in the cathedral, we felt lost in its vast space. My initial impression was that it seems more like a museum than a church. I'll have to come back more than once, maybe hire a guide, to appreciate this overpowering assemblage of art and history. We then wandered around the main streets of Rome. There are few wares in the shop windows and nothing to buy except for books and some paper goods. I bought an Italian dictionary. Where there are local restaurants and bars, they are out-of-bounds for Army personnel so we ended up at the YWCA, which has a cozy tea room.

In the evening it was our turn, Edith's and mine, to receive the weekly allowance of one bowl each of *hot* water. Of course, we spilled some of it and most of the heat disappeared as we climbed up four flights of cold marble stairs. Still, we were ecstatic with these few drops and all we could use them for—washing ourselves, brushing our teeth, washing our underwear. We felt as if we were living in the lap of luxury.

Rome, November 14, 1944

Our section is on duty today. Edith and I spent the day in the yard cutting wood for our fireplace. In the afternoon I started my Italian studies and wrote letters. Outside once again it is raining hard, but it's not quite as cold as yesterday.

Rome, November 15, 1944

Edith and I drove in her ambulance all around town so that we'll be acquainted with its layout when our work begins. What a beautiful city this is, with its wide boulevards, clean streets, its numerous fountains and its many monuments and historical buildings, which serve as landmarks and make it easy to orient oneself. In the afternoon we visited an exhibit of masterpieces of European painting at the Palazzo Venezia. Of all the originals we viewed, I was most impressed by Raphael's "Entombment of Christ." We spent the evening continuing our study of Italian. I am beginning to realize, though, that I need some help with pronunciation. Maybe I can make contact with some of the Italian students here. I'll have to ask the Mother Superior in charge of the nuns how to effect this. Incidentally, we have all been issued passes, which we must carry with us at all times. They identify us as members of the Rome Area Command and allow us to enter and leave Rome on official business. This is to differentiate us from the majority of personnel, who are here on leave. There are no fighting troops stationed in Rome.

Rome, November 19, 1944

Last Thursday we had our first convoy, transferring patients from a hospital train to nearby hospitals. I had four stretcher cases. Since then we have been meeting hospital trains every day. So far this is the only work we have. It takes all our skill to turn our cumbersome vehicles with their oversized wide tires on the narrow train platforms. We catch many an admiring glance from the men. Usually we finish our work by noon. Then we clean our ambulances, and if we don't have to prepare them for workshop inspection or are not detailed to cut wood, drive to the laundry, etc., we have time to explore our surroundings.

Rome, November 20, 1944

A few days ago Edith and I approached the Mother Superior and asked her if she could arrange a meeting with a couple of students who would be interested in learning English in exchange for teaching us Italian. She introduced us to two of the girls and last night we had our first lesson. Unfortunately, most of the time was spent speaking English, since they speak it quite well whereas our Italian still is almost non-existent. Our two 'teachers' are our age. Both are students, one majoring in Liberal Arts, the other in Law, hoping to become an attorney. I find it fascinating to listen to them and learn about their backgrounds, their experiences during the war, their world, which seems so different from ours. Although they come from wealthy families (how could they otherwise afford this luxurious student home?) at the moment, like all Italians, they are cold and hungry almost all the time. I already had suspected the latter when I saw the food on their tables. We share the same dining room although we eat at separate tables and usually at different times. Their food consists mostly of some unidentifiable soup and hard, dark bread. Since we have more than enough to eat, I resolved to take them some of our rations. I will have to be careful, though, because such fraternization is strictly against Army regulations.

Rome, November 21, 1944

All our ambulances have to be repainted green to cover the old desert brown. Today I took "68" to workshops and helped with the painting. I spent hours on the roof of my ambulance, first applying the green paint, then moving toward the center and applying white paint to the circle surrounding the red cross. (All ambulances display these large crosses as identification in case of possible air attack.) All the time I was moving toward the center of the roof, until I sat in the middle of the red cross, unable to believe my own stupidity. How would I get down now without ruining my paint job? Why hadn't I had enough sense to start in the middle, working toward the edges, instead of the other way round? As I contemplated my predicament, one of the men came up the ladder to see how I was coming along. He took one look and broke into roars of laughter, attracting every fitter in the shop. They all had a great time laughing their heads off at me. I managed to join in, too, and in time, with their help, found my way down from my perch. I would gladly forget this incident, but my unit won't let me. Over and over I am forced to sit through a blow-by-blow account of it. And I always blush.

Rome, November 22, 1944

We still don't have much work, just meeting hospital trains, loading and unloading to and from the hospitals in the area. In the evening Nelli and Maria, our two student 'teachers,' invited us to their room. We brought some food along and met a few of the other students. This time we did have to speak Italian, and we had a great time.

Rome, November 23, 1944

Although the opera is quite expensive, I decided to take advantage of the terrific cultural opportunities which exist here in Rome. I'm twenty-four years old and until tonight I never had been to either a real opera or a ballet! Tonight three of us went to see three ballets by Rossini, Stravinsky, and Ravel. I was enchanted.

Rome, November 25, 1944

For a change I had to take two stretcher cases and two sitters to a convalescent home situated on the outskirts of Rome. On my way to the hospital I took Nelli with me and dropped her near her work in the city. Some students have a part-time job, and since civilian transportation is almost non-existent, the girls have to walk to work. Nelli walks three times a week, three miles each way. Of course, she had to meet me a block from our carpark so that nobody would see her climbing into my ambulance. It is strictly forbidden to give civilians a lift, but I felt sorry for her. Nelli was very much impressed with the way I handled my huge ambulance. How gladly I would have exchanged my skill in driving for her opportunity to go to the university.

On my way back I was stopped by an Italian policeman, who insisted that no cars could pass through the center of town. It was the day of "Italy's Forces Reborn," and a parade of the motorized elements of the newly trained and equipped Italian troops was expected at any moment. I was not about to wait until the spectacle was over so I ignored his vociferous admonitions and just drove on. A minute later, just before reaching the 'Wedding Cake,' I saw people standing three deep on three sides of the square, waving palm leaves, eager for the parade to begin. Then they saw me and assumed that my ambulance was the first of the expected spectacle. I was in the midst of cheering crowds who covered me and my windshield with flowers. As I turned into the Via Nationale the crowd became denser and even more enthusiastic. I received an ovation befitting a queen, but I felt terribly embarrassed. Finally I spotted an opening, a sidestreet, and turned into it. In my rearview mirror I could see the beginning of the real parade behind me.

Rome, November 26, 1944

My "68" finally has come back from the workshops, its engine completely overhauled. In its olive green paint it looks like new. The weather is awful, the rain pouring down. I spent the day with the usual convoy duty, taking stretcher cases from the 104th General Hospital to the train. In the evening it was my turn to be on bar duty. There I heard the most marvelous news. Miss Otto has been very unhappy with our accommodations and has asked for a change in quarters. We work all day in the cold, raw weather, and return to a refrigerator of a house with no hot water to wash off the grease and oil. The Army, however, wants us to stay at the hostel and finally has agreed to provide enough oil for the boilers in the basement to heat the building. Tomorrow we should have hot water in the bathrooms as well as in our own rooms, and the central heating is also supposed to operate. Personally, I'm glad that we're not moving because I do like it here.

Rome, November 27, 1944

This was my day off and I woke up in a pleasantly warm room. No longer did I see my frozen breath in the air. The incessant rain beat against our window—it wasn't a day to go out so I took a hot bath, the first since leaving Egypt, and wallowed in that luxury. Later two of the Italian students came to visit us. Our room has become a language institute. Some in our unit come in to learn German. Edith and I are practicing Italian with the students and they, in turn, want to improve their English, and with most of the Palestinians we speak Hebrew. Edith has just finished sewing some curtains for our room and also has made me a lampshade from the same material for the reading lamp on my desk. What a cozy room it is now! Edith is really a great roommate. I am lucky to have her as a friend.

Rome, December 1, 1944

Our workload has increased. More and more hospital trains are coming in. Fighting in the north must have escalated. The rain continues unabated and keeping the ambulances clean is a Sisyphean task. I just heard that the 45th MAC—these are the ambulance drivers, all men, with whom we have shared the work here—soon will leave Rome. Then we'll be really busy since we'll be the only ambulance unit in the area. Another event soon to take place is Pandora's 'confinement.' Her puppies are expected any day.

Rome, December 3, 1944

We were duty-section today, which meant that we didn't go on convoy but did all the odd jobs around the house, the carpark, etc. The downstairs has begun to look very nice—our bar, a comfortable mess, a reading room, but since now I like my own room, I seldom go downstairs. I would rather spend my free time with Nelli, Franzi, Odetta, and Lydia, our four Italian friends. I wish, though, that I had been downstairs last night. As it was, I only heard about the incident from some of our girls. A detachment of American doctors and chemists (pharmacists) are stationed a few doors down from our building. They had seen English MAC girls coming and going from our building and had decided to pay a get-acquainted visit. What they did not know was that our switchboard is located right at the entrance, and every evening for one hour the Italian students are allowed to receive incoming calls. An excited bunch of girls is always crowded around the nun on duty at the switchboard. 'Our' nuns do not wear habits but simple black street-length dresses and black shoes and stockings. Into this setting walked three quite tipsy Americans. One of them spied the sweet young thing in black at the switchboard, wove his way over to where she sat, planted his cap squarely on her head, and kissed her soundly. The truth must have dawned on him when he heard her cry "Madre mia!" and saw her make the sign of the cross. He blushed, reeled around, and staggered back to the street. The next day a note of apology arrived from the Americans and we sent over a note explaining our living arrangements. The Italian girls giggled over this scandalous event for days.

Rome, December 4, 1944

Once again I had a day off and this time the rain stopped for a little while. Edith and I, guided by Nelli, did a little more sightseeing. One could live in Rome for years and still not see all there is to admire here. Nelli told us that the Via Nazionale used to be one of the most elegant streets before the war, with the most expensive boutiques, inviting outdoor cafes and excellent restaurants. Nothing of this is in evidence now. The store windows exhibit a few inferior but terribly expensive wares. Except for books, paper and postcards, there is nothing to buy. Most of what the civilian population wears must be pre-war stuff. I see many women in fur coats but without stockings. As a whole, the people seem subdued, as if the war years had made them indifferent. I feel sorry for them and have a bad conscience because I am so much better fed and better dressed. Of course, I'm also intensely loyal to 'my side.' This mixture of feelings is hard to explain. I don't quite understand it myself.

Rome, December 6, 1944

Franci and Julia, two of our Italian student friends, have left for home. Nelli will leave next week for her Christmas vacation. Soon most of them will be gone and the house will seem empty without them. Incidentally, none of the other 502 girls have made friends with students here—only Edith and I. I cannot understand this, because we have such a wonderful opportunity to meet Italians, learn their language, get acquainted with another culture, and on top of it all be able to help them in many ways. Almost every evening I load up at dinner with bread, butter, cheese, meat, and whatever else I can hide under my battle jacket, which I then unload in Nelli's room. It is the first decent food these girls have had for a long time. Our own diet also is somewhat deficient, especially lacking in fresh foods. We now have been issued vitamins to take care of the deficiency. Most of us had never heard of vitamins before and we keep forgetting to take them, though a bottle filled with the tablets always stands on the table right next to the salt and pepper shakers.

Rome, December 8, 1944

At 8 A.M., as usual, a convoy went to the station. I had hoped for patients to one of the near-by hospitals but instead got five stretcher cases to the 99th General Hospital. Again it was raining very hard and the road was even more slippery than yesterday. I was also cold. The little canvas shield did not protect me from the wind blowing the rain into the open cab. On the return trip I saw a jeep turn over, and two of our own ambulances had break--downs caused by skidding.

Rome, December 9, 1944

Pandora had her pups! She is the proud mother of six pups and they are adorable. Unfortunately, we can't keep them. Only by having Pandora officially declared our mascot were we allowed to bring her with us to Italy. The Army will not let us have more than one mascot so I suppose Miss Otto will have to give away Pandora's offspring. What a pity.

I am on bar duty, but Hannie took over for me because Hans S., an old friend from Tel-Aviv, came in for the weekend and had tickets for the opera. We had a wonderful evening. I'm really catching up on my neglected musical education.

Rome, December 10, 1944

My day off and what luck—the sun was shining, though it has turned very cold—good weather for a brisk walk. Hans called for me after breakfast and, with the help of a guidebook, we went sightseeing. This time it was the Coliseum and the church of St. Pietro in Vincoli to look at Michelangelo's Moses. Only last week the statue was uncovered. Until then it had been protected by sandbags against possible air attacks. After a good but rather small meal at the YWCA we went to the movies—*Christmas Time* with Deanna Durbin. By the way, the Y's are the only places we can go to for eating, dancing, or just to rest our feet. In Egypt we could go to any officers' club, but here in Italy the division between officer and Other Ranks is strictly enforced so that even in the company of an officer we can't enter their clubs. This is an idiotic rule. Many of our girls have husbands, brothers, or other relatives serving with officer's rank. It's ridiculous that these men can take any Italian girl into their clubs yet not their own wives or sisters if the latter are non-coms in the services.

Rome, December 11, 1944

As I came down to our carpark at 7:30 A.M., I found everything covered with frost and the windshield iced over. It has been eight years since I've seen that! I had to report to the Convalescent Camp and after depositing a few transfer cases I rushed home to say goodbye to Nelli and Franci, who were leaving for their homes today. Nelli lives in Ascoli Piceno, where her father is the mayor of the town. She has invited Edith and me to spend Christmas there with her family. We'll ask for a week's leave to Ascoli and hope that we'll get permission to travel there.

Rome, December 12, 1944

What a day! Again it rained and a cold wind blew. I had to prepare "68" for section inspection and got wet through and through. The cold penetrated from the damp ground on which I lay. So far we have no pits in which to stand but have to clean and grease our undercarriage flat on our backs. After hours of this torture the undercarriage still was not shining, but by 4 P.M. I gave up, tired, dirty and convinced that I would suffer from rheumatism from this day on.

Rome, December 19, 1944

Miss Otto has managed to buy two bicycles for 502, using the money in our Welfare Fund. They will make it easier for us to get around Rome on our days off since it is not always possible to get a hitch and public transportation, what little there is of it, consists of open trucks overloaded with people, even hanging on to the sides. It was my job to clean, grease, and check the bicycles. What fun it will be to use them in our free time. In the evening our unit had invited a few of the American girls stationed here and one of them, a sergeant, gave a lecture entitled "An American Explains America." What a strange and fascinating country that must be.

Rome, December 22, 1944

It has not rained for a few days and has turned very cold, just the right kind of Christmas weather. In the midst of all the festive preparations that are going on around us, Edith and I are packing. We got our passes, permission to be absent from quarters from December 23 to December 29 for the purpose of proceeding to Ascoli Piceno. Pat Curlewis signed the orders somewhat reluctantly. She kept asking us what kind of transportation we had arranged since there are few if any Army units stationed in the hills around Ascoli Piceno, on the other side of the Appenines. We assured her that Edith's friend, an American sergeant from the Red Cross, was going to take us in his jeep. We did not tell her that he only had promised to take us out of Rome!

Rome to Ascoli Piceno, December 23, 1944

At 8:30 A.M. Ray came to fetch us and drove us out on Route 4 just north of the city. From there our adventure began. We had assumed that there would be a good deal of military traffic moving north and that hitching a ride would be no problem. How wrong we were. Ray's disappearing jeep was the last military car we saw for many hours. Pat Curlewis had been right. Route 4, although it looked as good as any other on the map, was not a military route. What could we do? Go back? No, we were bound for Ascoli and we'd get there somehow. But how? As I mentioned before, civilian transportation is almost non-existent and what there is, usually is so loaded with goods and people that there would be no room for us. Finally, though, a little Italian car stopped for us, a doctor who had an out-of-town call. He took us twelve miles north of Rome. Again, we waited patiently. To our relief, a British lorry approached. The driver took us to Riata, which is about a third of the way. We ate our sandwiches on the highway outside of Riata and waited. The rumor must have gone around town that there were two crazy "Inglese in pantalone," for the whole population marched out to stare at us. At 1 P.M. another little Fiat stopped. He took us another few miles, to the crossroads of Ascoli-Aquila.

It was almost 2 P.M. by now and we were right in the mountains far away from any Army camp, any town. There were just a few poor farmhouses. The gray skies darkened swiftly and it started to snow. Would we ever get to Ascoli or would we even find a warm place to spend the night? From the hostile look a passing farmer gave us (he was the only living soul we saw up there), we doubted it. An hour later we heard the huff and puff of an old car coming up the hill. Another kind Italian? The car stopped. We looked inside. Three gangster-types—at least, that's what they seemed like to us! Well, gangsters or not, we couldn't spend the night outdoors, in the mountains. We climbed in. The 'gangsters' became quite agreeable when we offered them our cigarettes, but what a driver! Descending the mountains, he put the little four-seater into neutral, probably to save gas, and drove down the icy serpentine, sliding to the right and the left, missing the edge of the chasm by inches! Edith said she felt so sick she had to close her eyes. I was luckier because I couldn't really see anything with Edith sitting on my lap. Suddenly the car stopped in front of an old, deserted farmhouse. The driver-gangster got out. The other two grinned at us. The setting was one for a nightmare—twilight, a deserted mountain road, a lonely farmhouse, two defenseless girls, and three gangsters. "Have another cigarette!" I whispered.

"*Si, Signorina. Grazie!*"

We puffed at our cigarettes and waited. Then the driver came back. What was he up to?

He opened the hood and filled the radiator with water. Edith and I gasped with relief. The journey continued.

After a while two of the men got out. Apparently they had been hitchhikers too. The gangster-driver had to go to a little village ten miles this side of Ascoli. With many gestures and cries of "*Ma che, Signorine!*" he insisted on taking us all the way to Ascoli. There he found out for us where the Orlinis lived, looked for the house in the darkness, carried our suitcases up the stairs to deliver us into the arms of the Orlini family, and vanished without even waiting for our thanks. The dark mountain road, the unshaven faces, and conversation in a language we barely understood had conjured up for us nonexistent dangers. Those fellows were true gentlemen.

Ascoli Piceno, December 24-28, 1944

The days in Ascoli sped by quickly. We would sleep late, then get up and go for walks through the medieval streets, visiting ancient Roman ruins and picturesque churches. The views are spectacular since Ascoli is surrounded by mountains, now all covered with snow. It was bitterly cold. Everywhere we went we were stared at in kindly bewilderment. We were the first women in uniform the town had seen. I hardly ever saw an American or English soldier on the street, but the town is heavily garrisoned by the Italian Army. Nelli's father, as I mentioned, is the mayor of the town and a lawyer. For his services people generally pay with their farm produce so his kitchen was a place of plenty. We tasted the most delicious Italian dishes. I must have gained ten pounds! The Orlinis also own much land so there was plenty of wood to heat the house. The kitchen was managed by two old but most capable women. They could kill a chicken, bake bread for the family, and chop wood for the stove, but if you had showed them a refrigerator or a gas stove, they would not have known what to do with them. They cooked over an open hearth, blackened by the smoke. They could neither read nor write, but could they ever cook! The Orlinis ate a full meal at lunch and a ten-course dinner in the evening, but nothing in the morning. As a favor to us they brought us each one piece of toast and some kind of ersatz coffee brew into which they poured a generous shot of brandy. Wine is served with each meal and what potent stuff it is! The mayor pressed glass after glass upon us. For the first few days I was in a continuous stupor. Later I thinned it with water and got a bit more used to it.

Being the topic of the town and, at the same time, guests of the mayor, we were invited to several parties. We were the only foreigners present at these get-togethers. Conversation was not too difficult, however. Everyone was pleased with our small Italian vocabulary. Also, Italians are marvelous flatterers and what girl does not enjoy being the center of attraction? The men were good dancers and all of them seriously tried to convince me that Italian men are the best husbands and lovers. Each one of them eventually landed on this topic. They looked at me with sad expressions when I told them that I really wasn't interested in finding out if this was true. "Ah, poveretta!" What I was missing! Although parties and dances are not too much to my taste, I enjoyed myself a great deal. The atmosphere was exactly the opposite of the stiff, boring English cocktail party. Italians are the most hospitable people I have ever met.

There was no Christmas tree and no exchanging of gifts at the Orlinis, but we went with the family to midnight mass on Christmas Eve. Naturally, we sat in the front row, for the Orlinis had their reserved seats for many a generation. Once again the people of Ascoli pushed and pushed to get a better view of us. They appeared far more interested in each detail of our uniforms, our make-up, and our hair-dos than in the church service.

The day before we were to leave it was almost too cold to venture out, but in the evening we went to the cinema and saw a simply awful Italian film. In this respect the Italians lag far behind the Americans and the English. Back at the house a surprise was waiting for us. Alice with her boyfriend and Edith's friend, Ray, had arrived to drive us home. The three of them went out for the evening, 'unchaperoned,' which shocked the Orlinis. I stayed at home with Nelli and her family. It was, after all, our last night in Ascoli and I really had grown fond of all of them. On the 28th we left at noon. The trip back was great. I felt like in old times when I was a child and we toured Switzerland or Austria. Wrapped in warm blankets, we sat in the comfortable car singing all the way home. The scenery was magnificent. Crossing the mountains, everything was covered in snow, until we descended into the flat country. The entire drive back took only four hours, but as far as I was concerned, it could have gone on for days.

Rome, December 30, 1944

I am on duty section. Had to take off the sump under the car, clean it, and put it back. What a filthy job! On top of that, it was so cold that I lost all feeling in my fingers. In the evening I had bar duty.

Rome, December 31, 1944

Now the weather here is just as cold as it was in Ascoli. It is freezing. There is not much work today. Some of the girls played ping-pong, others wrote letters, read, or played bridge. A few unlucky ones had to work outside doing maintenance tasks on their cars. I was glad it was not my turn. In the evening I visited Odetta, one of the few Italian students who stayed here over the holidays. Then suddenly I began to hear shooting and yelling and noticed that it was five minutes to midnight. I hastily said goodbye to Odetta and rushed upstairs to join our girls, most of them already a bit tipsy. We shared a bottle of Asti-Spumanti, toasted in the new year, and whooped it up for another hour. And that was the end of 1944. I wonder what 1945 will bring. The end of the war? A reunion with my parents in Germany or with my sister in England? Who knows.

Rome to Perugia, January 3, 1945

Perugia with its Università Italiana per Stranieri (for foreigners) has become the center of the British Army's education planning. With the eventual end of the war in sight, the Army is interested in retraining and continuing education for its men. At this time many officers are being transferred temporarily to Perugia to learn how to become instructors in the Army's new education planning. It was my duty today to drive an ATS officer, an instructor-to-be, to Perugia. At 7 A.M. I picked her up at the YWCA. Two hours' driving brought us to the snow-covered mountains, and soon the highway itself also was covered with snow. I decided that it was time to put on the chains. When I jumped out of the car I sank knee deep into snow. But what a magnificent landscape—mountains, waterfalls, forests, all blanketed in white. There was no traffic on the road and the stillness around us added to the whiteness of this winter scene. However, I had no time to dwell on the beauty of it. Putting the chains on our huge tires is no easy matter, but the first one went on relatively easily. After trying for half an hour to put the other one on, I realized that something was wrong. The chain was several links too short, probably made for a different sized tire. We would have to do with just one chain. That did not work either. After driving only a few meters we got stuck. Then I took all the blankets we carried in our ambulance, pushed and pried them under the back tire, and tried again. As I gunned the motor, the blankets swished up and over to land a few yards away in a snowdrift. Well, I thought, I needed something heavier. Why not the short chain? With the officer's help I managed to dig it under the back tire, hoping the tire would get a grip on it and I could drive out of the hole the wheel had dug. Again I climbed into the car, revved the engine, and then in my side-view mirror I saw, to my horror, the huge heavy chain flying out from beneath the tire and missing the ATS officer, who was standing behind the ambulance, by inches. If it had hit her, it surely would have killed her instantly. I jumped out to assure myself that she was really all right. Now we started shoveling the snow away and carefully, very slowly, I tried the blanket maneuver again. Inch by inch, shoveling, pushing, and very carefully accelerating, it took us another hour to free "68." I then continued in first gear very slowly, and after about an hour, just when I thought that the poor engine would over-heat any minute, the road began to descend and we were out of the high mountains. The snow began to melt and soon the highway was just slushy. We felt better, but then in the distance we saw Perugia, surrounded by a wall, perched on top of another mountain! Once again we had to climb slowly, carefully, in order not to get stuck, but just before entering the main gate into the medieval city, I had to slow down for a lorry coming toward me, and that did it. We began to slide down and sideways at the same time. I steered the back of the ambulance into the snowbank on the side of the road and so brought it to a halt. By this time I could see no beauty in the white mess around us and longed for desert sand, but only momentarily. A whole platoon of soldiers appeared from nowhere, pushed their shoulders against my ambulance, and with combined effort shoved us through the gate and into the safety of Perugia's walls. Here the entire population seemed to be skiing instead of walking. It was pitch dark by the time we checked in at the YWCA. Seldom have I appreciated a hot bath and a warm meal as much as tonight. Now that I look back, it really was, in spite of the mishaps, a great day.

Perugia to Rome, January 4, 1945

After breakfast I went in search of some kind of Army workshop and finally located an REME unit. They enlarged the tire chain by several links and an hour later I was on my way, this time with both chains mounted on the tires. Once again I traveled through the beautiful white landscape, but only until I reached the main road. Here the snow had completely disappeared and I had to take the chains off again. I arrived home just after dusk, tired, chilled to the bone, but happy.

Rome, January 6, 1945

The Pope now grants daily audiences to all the Armed Forces. I wanted very much to go to one of these so today Edith, Pat, and I decided on a visit to the Vatican. Upon our arrival there, we were guided by the Swiss Guards in their picturesque sixteenth-century uniforms of striped pantaloons and high stockings with halberds in their hands. They led us to a large reception room filled with Army personnel. Since we were the only women in the hall, we were taken right to the front of the room. Behind us the hall began to fill. There must have been about two hundred soldiers in all, patiently waiting, speaking in low voices. We could hear snatches of English, Polish, French, and Hebrew. The guards stood at the entrance, immobile as statues. Then excitement ran through the crowd as the doors opened and Pius XII, followed by several Cardinals, stepped onto the little podium, right in front of us. Although I am not a Catholic, I felt so awe-inspired that I hardly dared to look up. The Pope began to speak. His voice was kind, his English perfect as he welcomed us to the Eternal City. After the short speech, he stepped down from the podium to chat with us informally, pausing here and there to greet and bless. Since we were directly in front, we were among the first to be blessed, and when he noticed the word PALESTINE on our epaulets, he switched to Hebrew, wishing us a speedy homecoming and peace in our land. He continued among the audience, switching from English to French to Polish with the greatest of ease. Then, returning to the podium, he once more wished us all a happy reunion with our families. I was very much impressed by the simplicity of his bearing and his linguistic skill.

Rome, January 14, 1945

A week has passed since I wrote last, but not much has happened. It has been pouring every day. My days are divided among jobs of standby, convoy duty, trips to and from the hospital trains and the convalescent home and the general hospitals, working in the yard, cleaning the ambulance, preparing for workshop inspection, etc. On my last two inspections I received a 'very good' rating, but how I hate doing maintenance in this weather and without a pit! Edith has been promoted to Lance Corporal because poor Jane is in the hospital with diphtheria and probably will have to stay there for quite a while. A few days ago we emptied an entire train of Italian casualties. This time the Italians were in charge of the logistics and was it ever a mess! Everything was in great confusion and took ten times as long as usual. On my days off or free evenings I usually go to the cinema or spend time with the Italian students, most of whom have come back from their Christmas vacations. My Italian continues to improve.

The other day I met the Mother Superior, Sister Constanza, in the hall and had a long talk with her. She complimented me on my Italian, and I found her very pleasant to talk to, although she is somewhat formidable and 502 has had a number of run-ins with her when her wishes have clashed with those of our officers and NCOs. She constantly tries to get some advantage for 'her' house out of our being stationed here. We are quite sure that some of our rations in the common kitchen end up on her nuns' plates. There is neither the humility of a servant of God nor the subservience of one of the vanquished about her. The nuns, on the other hand, are gentle creatures, always cheerful and self-effacing. The order consists of teaching nuns, who are out during the day working in various schools, and those who stay home, cleaning and cooking. There also are a number of lay sisters, young girls, mostly from the country.

Rome, January 16, 1945

I had to see the MO today. A bone on my heel is protruding and has become very painful. He sent me to the orthopedist, who bandaged my foot and mumbled a few Latin words which I did not understand. So I know as little as before, but the trouble probably is caused by the wrong position during driving. I have fitted a piece of wood by the accelerator to elevate my heel and hope this will relieve the pain.

In the evening we had our first art lecture, which I enjoyed a great deal. An Italian professor has been hired to introduce us, once a week, to the art history of Rome. As soon as the weather allows, she will take us on field trips as well.

Rome, January 22, 1945

The Russian offensive, which began a few days ago, is continuing on a gigantic scale. Their troops already are streaming over the Silesian border. Almost all of Poland, as well as part of East Prussia, has been liberated. If the Russians continue this way, the war will be over in two months!

Rome, January 24, 1945

Yesterday I was busy on convoy duty all day. By evening my foot was too painful to walk on so this morning I went to the orthopedist again. He ordered a week of rest, neither walking nor driving. I am really upset because for me to sit still is a punishment.

Rome, January 27, 1945

I am relegated to 'light duty' and have to sit in the office the entire day, helping to fill out forms, file, and do 'busy work.'

Rome, January 28, 1945

No one talks about anything else but the enormous speed of the Russian advance. At this moment they are ninety miles from Berlin! Conflicting emotions assault me. Of course, I am joyful, as we all are, that the end of the war seems near, but in my case a mixture of other feelings complicates this joy. My 'family' has become 502, but one day it will disband and its members will scatter after the war. Most of the girls have a home to return to, but what will I return to—if and when I find my parents? If they are still alive, they are sure to have suffered and it will be my responsibility to help them. But how? I have no special education, no training for a job or a profession. This approaching responsibility weighs heavily on me. Being in the Army has put the future on hold, but soon I'll have to face—what? The old days are gone forever and I can't imagine what will happen next. Of course, I keep all these thoughts to myself, but I find it hard to join in with the others when they talk excitedly about the end of their Army days, about going home.

Rome, January 29, 1945

They do think of the most idiotic work for me! Today I had to sit in the MT office and ask all the girls checking in how many hangers they had in their rooms! In the evening once again I visited my Italian friends. I walked in on a heated discussion concerning women's rights and the right to vote. Woman suffrage—should Italian women be allowed to vote? This is 1945? How strange! Somehow I had taken it for granted that in this day and age all women had this right. Well, I do hope that Italian women will succeed in gaining it. It has been my opinion all along that women everywhere should participate more actively in the political life of their countries. Governments would be far better off if women had more of a say. I am sure that eventually women will be elected as representatives in parliaments, senates, or houses of representatives. Maybe one day a woman will even be a president or a prime minister.

Rome, February 2, 1945

The weather suddenly has turned quite warm—a *sirocco*, I am told. This is a warm wind coming from North Africa, reminiscent of the *khamsin* in Palestine and Egypt, and it makes everyone feel quite washed out. I just heard over the wireless: The Russians are forty-five miles from Berlin!

Rome, February 8, 1945

I am back on the road again. My foot is still a bit painful, but I'm glad to be off 'light duty.' I worked on "68" all morning, cleaning. It really needed it. I hardly had time to wash up after lunch when I was called out for convoy duty.

Rome, February 19, 1945

The weather has been wonderful, cool but sunny. I really enjoy my trips to the Convalescent Depots, of which we have quite a few now. Trains with wounded are still coming in, but not as frequently as when we first arrived here. The only day it rained was last week when I had to prepare my ambulance for workshop inspection. I worked eight hours on "68" and can't understand why we still have neither ramp nor pit for working on the undercarriage.

Our Italian art history instructor, Miss Lilli, took some of us to Ostia, about twenty miles from Rome. We spent an entire afternoon among the excavated ruins. I found it most interesting and, as usual, when I see how the Romans of antiquity used to live, I can't help feeling that, except for the radio, telephone and combustion engine, we haven't made much progress in the last two thousand years. On my days off I continue to do more sightseeing. There is no end to all the churches, monuments, fountains, and art treasures to be admired here. Lydia took me to St. Paul's Basilica, so far my favorite. Afterwards we stopped at a charming little cafe, where we had a cup of chocolate and a teeny little cake, for which we paid two hundred lire! Prices are getting more and more impossible.

Rome, February 23, 1945

Wounded are now coming in by plane and we have regular convoys going to the Aerodrome, about twelve miles outside of Rome. Today I had my first trip on this new job. As we had to wait a while for the planes to arrive, we talked to some American pilots. I enjoy meeting Americans. They are very different from the English, more light-hearted, always fun-loving, somewhat boisterous but always chivalrous and, above all, generous. Somehow, they seem very young, regardless of their age. When the plane finally arrived, I had three stretcher cases, all T.B. patients.

Rome, February 28, 1945

Duty section. Already at 7:30 A.M. I was downstairs for telephone duty until 9:30, when I was relieved. Then convoy—six ambulances to the airport. This time we took sandwiches along, being prepared for the usual long wait. True enough, when we arrived, we were told that the planes would be at least two hours late. As it turned out, those two hours were some of the happiest I can remember. We picnicked next to our cars on a beautiful green meadow. The sun was shining, bees humming around us—a perfect spring day. After eating, we stretched out on the grass, looking at a cloudless blue sky. From time to time we could see a plane landing or taking off in the distance. Once again, the war seemed far away. By 2 P.M. an orderly came over to tell us that the casualties would not arrive today. However, no sooner had we returned home when back we had to go, because the planes *had* come in after all. Amazing that we are winning this war! My load was four stretcher cases, seriously wounded, for the 104th General Hospital. At 6 P.M. I had to go out again, this time as staff-car driver for the DDMS. Did not finish till late at night and didn't have any dinner either. I should mention that we got reinforcements, ten new girls from England.

Rome, March 1, 1945

More wounded are coming in by plane so we have more convoys to the airport now than to the station. Today I had one of the new girls as trainee with me. They all seem to be nice, simple types without the superiority complex of the rest of our upper-class English girls.

Rome, March 2, 1945

My day off. Edith and I spent the time leisurely in our room. In the afternoon Nelli and Franzi came visiting. Later Edith's American friend, Ray, brought one of his pals along and the four of us had dinner at the YWCA. Jimmy, my date, came from Alabama and I understood hardly *anything* he said. Still, we all laughed a lot and had a good time together. After eating, the four of us went to a newly opened American club, an awful place, terribly crowded, noisy and smoky, but I had fun watching all the different types. Americans certainly are a mixture of races and accents. Again it was brought home to me that even in as big a city as Rome, there is no place where Other Ranks (non-commissioned officers) can spend a few pleasant hours quietly.

Rome, March 4, 1945

Work is picking up. Yesterday and today almost all cars were on convoy duty. Tomorrow I am detailed for convoy duty to Naples.

Rome to Naples, March 5, 1945

At 7:40 A.M. we left our depot, six ambulances, Edith in charge. We reported to the 104th General Hospital and by the time we were loaded with patients, baggage, etc., and ready to leave, it was 9 A.M. I had four stretcher cases, all amputees without legs. We took route 7, the same road we had come on our way up to Rome almost three months ago. Again we passed through many destroyed towns and ruined villages. We arrived at 4 P.M., but it took us almost an hour until we found the hospital and delivered our patients. Just as it did on my first visit, Naples depressed me. I am grateful not to be stationed here. Rome is much more beautiful with its clean, wide streets, its impressive buildings, its piazzas with fountains everywhere. Naples, in contrast, gives the impression of an overcrowded, poor, and dirty city. Through traffic-choked streets we finally reached the YWCA, where we spent the night.

Naples to Rome, March 6, 1945

In the morning Edith assigned Trudi and me to bus duty. We were to transport three nursing sisters back to Rome. Trudi took the nurses in her car and I their luggage, which I much preferred. We joined our convoy fifty miles outside of Naples. At lunchtime we spread food and blankets on the grass and anticipated a nice picnic, but it began to rain, a thick, blinding rain. Within minutes we were drenched and running for cover. By the time we reached home our cars were covered from head to tail-light with mud. What a cleaning job for tomorrow! Weary, cold, and hungry, we straggled in, quite willing to call it a day, but within five minutes we were back in our respective ambulances, speeding toward the station and an emergency hospital train, where great numbers of wounded lay waiting. We worked quickly, automatically, until at last a halt was called, at 1 A.M. We chalked up a total of eighteen hours today, eighteen hours behind the wheel without a break.

Rome, March 9, 1945

American forces have crossed the Rhine. The Russians are outside Berlin and also are advancing into eastern and northeastern Germany. Our forces, however, seem to be bogged down in Italy, in mud and slush. From what we hear, the German resistance is still very strong, and casualties are pouring in. We are busy emptying trains and planes of wounded. There is, though, a feeling in the air that the war is coming to an end. As I mentioned before, the Army is trying to prepare its personnel for civilian life. Educating future instructors at the Università Italiana per Stranieri in Perugia is part of this plan. Every unit is to send a representative to this center, where they will learn how to teach in whatever field they might be qualified. Pat Curlewis has informed me that I will be 502's representative. I can use my knowledge of German and after the course come back to 502 as a certified instructor in German. I am not too elated at the prospect of having to go to school for a month, but maybe the experience will serve me well in the future. I am to leave for Perugia on the 19th, in ten days.

Rome, March 11, 1945

A red letter day! Jimmy, my American friend from Alabama, came by this morning and left a dozen big, beautiful fresh eggs for me! What a wonderful gift, more precious than flowers or candy. After work Edith and I locked our door and prepared a feast on our little hot plate—four eggs and buttered bread. These were our first real eggs since we arrived in Italy and they certainly tasted very different from the powdered variety we get in the mess.

Perugia, March 19–April 9, 1945

The trip to Perugia was most uncomfortable. Our transportation was by lorry, the open-backed kind, and, though this time there was no more snow on the road, we—that is, two ATS girls from Naples, four soldiers, and I—huddled close together to protect ourselves from the cold wind. In Perugia we were allotted two rooms at the YWCA. All together there are five girls and five hundred men participating in the courses. The University building is beautiful, a former palace of eighteenth-century architecture, but its rooms are cold and drafty.

The first day we were handed a list of the courses and asked to choose the subject we wished eventually to teach: engineering, radio, electronics, mechanics, English language, history, geography, German, French, and (no doubt added as an afterthought on behalf of the women's forces) Home Economics and Home Management. Since we could choose only one subject, it would be German for me. My room-mates scoffed. Why didn't I take something I hadn't studied before so that I could benefit from the course? But I knew what I was doing. Later, they saw my line of reasoning. The daily schedule for the month was as follows: lectures and study from 9:30 A.M. til 4:40 P.M., with an hour for lunch and, of course, tea-time, observed religiously twice a day. In my class there were five men who also had chosen German as their major field. I was the only woman in this group. Had it been any other subject, I would have felt a little outclassed, but as it was, I was a help-mate to the other students, and my teacher seemed to be developing an inferiority complex. As a rule the Army chooses professors from the officer's corps and sends them to Perugia to teach the future instructors, but apparently they could find no German scholar so they chose instead an Italian civilian who had studied in Germany, Signora Gattesca. She was in her twenties, spoke broken English, and was at a complete loss about how to deal with the soldiers, most of them older than she. The men made fun of her, concentrated on everything about her except her ability to speak German, and caused a general uproar in the class. It was a wonder that she didn't have a nervous breakdown. On more than one occasion she came pretty close to it.

Besides German, we had to attend lectures on "How to Teach," which I found boring. All the things a good teacher is supposed to do I had been doing all along when I was teaching German, informally, to 502, without anyone's telling me how. The only lectures and discussion groups I found interesting were those dealing with problems like rights of women and the future of England and the rest of the world after the war.

One day some British government officials flew to Perugia to view the new educational programs. Signora Gattesca developed a terrible cold. I do believe it was psychosomatic. The CO was frantic, for these officials planned to sit in on ten minutes of each class. He called me to his office and asked how well I could speak German, how I had learned it, and if I ever had taught it. My answers apparently satisfied him because he made me professor for the day! "Listen, fellows," I said to 'my' class. "You must help me! Be as brilliant as possible!" And they were. They paid strict attention, volunteered to recite, laughed when they were supposed to, and asked intelligent questions. The officials stayed for half an hour and afterwards the Colonel urged me to remain at Perugia to take Signora Gattesca's place. He would try to get me an emergency commission. I thought it over, but said no. I longed for Rome and 502. From time to time I had visitors from 502 who brought me the mail and news of the unit. I was homesick. I did, however, enjoy sightseeing in the town with its cobbled streets and ancient brick archways and I liked the beautiful views of the valley below and the sharp, clean air was invigorating. Half way through the course Signorina Gattesca began to let me teach almost the entire German class, help her correct her papers, and make out lesson plans. She seemed much relieved and the fellows liked it better too. Toward the end of the course everyone had 'teaching practice'—a thirty-five minute demonstration in front of the class. Then the class members critiqued the performance. Colonel Nicholsen also observed. My rating: "Lively and interesting teaching. One hundred percent fluency and mastery of the language and its structure. Self-assured, pleasant. Goes a little too fast." If I were not a driver I think I'd like to be a teacher. All the students here studying to be instructors will go back to their units with the rank of sergeant, but it's unthinkable that I'll be a sergeant in 502. We are too small an outfit for three sergeants. I'll just be a part-time instructor in German, which, in effect, I was before. On March 30 we had pay day, or "Pay Parade" as the Army calls it. In

502 this is a casual affair: "By the way, Adi, your pay's over at the office." But here Pay Parade is strictly according to Army regulations, like this: March. Stance. Salute. Stance. Pivot. Stance. Extend pay book (left hand). Salute (right hand). Stance. Wait. Accept salary. Salute. Pivot. March! Five hundred men, standing at attention, paid, however, more attention to us girls going through this routine than to the Paymaster.

Perugia to Rome, April 10, 1945

Yesterday Renia arrived with her ambulance to take us back. We started home at a little after 9 A.M. The weather was perfect—blue sky, bright sun, crisp mountain air, the smell of spring around us. We had decided to go back to Rome via Assisi, about fifteen miles from Perugia. Assisi—the place of St. Francis. There we visited the medieval chapel, the ancient monastery sprawled, large and gray, against the mountains, the old cathedral and atop it, the later church. We climbed endless flights of steps and explored the cool dark recesses of the old basilica where rests the tomb of St. Francis. For me, more impressive than all the churches was the actual situation of Assisi, perched high up on the spur of a mountain with a magnificent view of the Umbrian landscape below. After we left Assisi, Renia and I took turns behind the wheel, and at 1 P.M. we stopped beside a little mountain stream for our picnic lunch. It was an ideal hour. Back at home in Rome everyone seemed glad to see me again. Edith had decorated our room with flowers and a big welcome sign. How good to be back! In the evening we went to opening night to see one of our girls perform in the new show, *Hay Fever.* The audience loved it and seldom have I laughed so hard and so much.

Rome, April 11, 1945

My first duty day after the long absence. Old "68" looks well cared for. I was on detail at the 69th General Hospital. The push in northern Italy has begun. We are as busy as during the 8th Army retreat and later its advance in North Africa. Besides the ten new girls who had joined 502 before I left for Perugia, seven others have just arrived from England. Gone are the days when most of us just sat around, read, sewed, wrote letters, and waited to be called out. Now the wounded are pouring in by plane and train. We work long hours and at night fall into bed dead tired. It is also beginning to get quite warm.

Rome, April 13, 1945

I just read the depressing news that Roosevelt is dead. The Americans here in Rome have declared a day of mourning. A great personality gone. I feel very low.

Rome, April 14, 1945

We received Khaki Dress today—our summer uniforms—four pairs of pants, four bush jackets, three skirts. Nothing fits and every piece is of a different shade of khaki! I have been promoted to Lance Corporal and am busily sewing stripes on all sleeves.

Rome to Naples, April 16, 1945

Convoy to Naples. At 8 A.M. we reported at the 104th General Hospital. Besides mine there were three other ambulances. My load was four stretcher cases, one of them mental, and the latter's guard. The trip was uneventful, yet I felt terribly tired when we finally arrived in Naples and my patients were unloaded at the 92nd General Hospital. We left our ambulances at the hospital and were driven to the YWCA.

Naples to Rome, April 17, 1945

In the morning I fetched a nursing sister and an Indian MO to take them back to Rome. This time we took Route 6, which passes Casino. The hilltop monastery, so long and bitterly fought over, is still recognizable. It is a grim monument to one of the war's bloodiest battles. Seeing it, I can understand why it cost so many lives to capture this mountain. It is a site easy to defend, but very difficult to attack. Beneath tons of rubble the dead still lie. The stench of death still is in the air. I was glad to leave Casino behind me.

Rome, April 18, 1945

I didn't have time to clean my ambulance. At 10 A.M. all ambulances were called out to the airport. Plane after plane landed with wounded, almost like after El-Alamein. When I got back late in the afternoon, Pat Curlewis called me into the office. The final report from Perugia had arrived. I had received the evaluation of "Outstanding" and all kinds of other praise. The letter further suggested that I be transferred to Perugia to teach German at the University, with an immediate promotion to the rank of Sergeant. But I don't want to leave 502 and hope that they will accept my request to stay with my unit.

Rome, April 20, 1945

We heard over the wireless that Russian forces have fought their way into Berlin. Here the wounded continue to pour in from the north. The number of German casualties begins to outnumber our own. The depots seethe with German patients and prisoners. Trains and hospitals overflow. Frequently I am called to translate. Today I took Edith's place as Transport NCO. This means sitting in the office, taking phone calls, receiving all information on how many ambulances are needed and where, how many stretcher cases and sitting cases, and then making out a roster, seeing to it that all work tickets are properly filled out, making out duty lists for the next day, and a thousand other details. There never seem to be enough drivers or enough cars to do the jobs, tickets are not filled out correctly; in short, it is a dreadful job. I'll be much relieved to get back on the road again instead of dealing with forty drivers, their wishes, excuses, the hospitals, the workshops, etc.

Rome, April 30, 1945

Suddenly everything points to a quick ending. Mussolini has been captured and shot. British and American forces have swept into the Po Valley. All organized resistance has broken down. A bulletin from General Mark Clark has come through:

> "Troops of the 15th Army Group have so smashed the German Armies in Italy that they have been virtually eliminated as a military force. This destruction has all been accomplished in the offensive which is now twenty-two days old for the Eighth Army and sixteen days old for the major part of the Fifth Army."

The Russians have occupied nine-tenths of Berlin. I simply can't take it in that the war may be over in a matter of days.

Rome, May 1, 1945

The battle of Berlin is raging. I think constantly of my parents. Where are they? Are they being bombed, killed by our air raids on Berlin? Are they being 'liberated' by the Russians or shot in the streets as Germans? Or—and these are my worst fears—are they among those who were deported to concentration camps? Horrible stories and pictures, dreadful confirmations about these camps are beginning to filter in. I try to learn more in the course of translating for the German POWs, but most of these men are sullen and unresponsive. They dismiss my questions with a shrug or a smile: "Ach, nothing but British and American propaganda."

Rome, May 2, 1945

The German Armies in Italy and West Austria have surrendered. Strange that we have waited so long for this day and now that it has arrived, I can't rejoice. Everyone wonders what will happen to us. Will we stay here or will we be sent somewhere else? In the evening we 'old ones' gave a farewell party for Pat Hall. She is flying home to England to be reunited with her husband, a released POW.

Rome, May 3, 1945

With the cessation of the fighting most of our work also has stopped. I foresee a repetition of our first days here in Rome when we had very little to do. Everyone is betting on the day the war will be over. I have only one thought in mind at the moment and that is how to find out more about my parents. I hope that we won't stay here in Rome until we're discharged but instead will be posted farther north. Every mile toward Germany will bring me that much closer to an answer.

Rome, May 4, 1945

The German armies in Holland, Denmark, and Northwest Germany have surrendered to Montgomery. Miss Otto and Pat Curlewis have left for Caserta, the Headquarters of all Mediterranean Forces, and when they come back we'll have a Company meeting. Maybe we'll move.

Rome, May 5, 1945

A convoy of three ambulances to the airport, but all that came in was one single plane. We were told that it probably will be the last one. The remaining casualties will come in by train.

Rome, May 6, 1945

I wonder where there is still any actual fighting going on and why some isolated German units are still holding on. Berlin has been taken, the cream of the German Army has capitulated, Hitler is either dead or has vanished; Doenitz, the new 'Führer,' admits that continued fighting is senseless. Ninety-nine percent of the 'Reich' has been captured. Still, there are pockets of resistance. Everyone at 502 is very excited about tomorrow's Company meeting.

Rome, May 7, 1945

A sudden announcement on the wireless: Germany has surrendered! We stood around, amazed, unable to comprehend. In the evening, instead of the planned Company meeting, we had a Company party—

free drinks for all! We raised our glasses and toasted the King. Everyone was exuberant. We drank, danced, and laughed until late into the
night. Outside, though, it was comparatively quiet. All military personnel had been confined to barracks. Only a few happy civilians with
a few firecrackers marked the occasion. Tomorrow and the day after
have been declared official V-Days. However, I won't be able to participate in the celebrations. Orders have come through for me to proceed
to Caserta immediately. The purpose of the trip is not clear. All I'm
told is that it's "Official Business." I assume that it must have something to do with the education course I took, maybe another attempt
to make an instructor out of me. I wish that I didn't have to go but
could celebrate with the rest of 502.

Caserta, May 9, 1945

I left Rome for Caserta yesterday. For a change, I was driven on
that trip. The weather was perfect and my spirits lifted. Perhaps it
wasn't going to be so bad after all. When I arrived I registered at the Y,
then quickly changed into dress uniform and headed for the Education
Center, steeling myself against the ordeal of saying "no" to Army
officials. Headquarters are established in the palace of the former
King of Naples. It's an immense building and I got lost. I searched for
over half an hour before I finally found the right room. By that time I
was exhausted, yet my ordeal still was ahead of me. The moment I entered the room an Emergency Commission application was thrust in
front of me. I was half-way through filling out the form before I realized that I was applying for entry into the Army's Educational
Corps. When I refused to complete the form, the Sergeant in charge
was astonished.

"If you don't want the commission, why are you here? After all, it's
voluntary."

"I haven't volunteered!"

"Well, go in anyway. They're waiting for you." He ushered me
through a door. Before me sat seven stern faces—the official reviewing
board. Army officers sat on either side of a shrewd-looking gentleman
who was seated at the center of a long, polished table. He alone spoke
to me.

"Won't you sit down?" He indicated a chair near the table. This
must be the psychiatrist, I thought, who was to determine whether the
candidate was stable, in command of himself, etc.

"Are you Lance-Corporal Bonin?"

"Yes, Sir."

"Regarding your work at the University in Perugia, do you know what the reports say?"

"Yes, Sir." I could not help smiling. There was no cause for alarm. This interview could not affect me, one way or the other. I began to feel more at ease.

"Now tell us a little more about yourself." He settled back in his chair, prepared to listen to a long story.

"Yes, Sir. But first may I ask what this is all about?"

"This is all about awarding you a commission."

"I'm sorry, Sir, but I would like to refuse this honor."

"Oh? Why?"

"Because, Sir, our Army days are almost over, and as I've been with my outfit for over three years, I wouldn't like to leave them now. I'd like to see it through to the finish with them."

"What is the name of this outfit that you don't want to leave, even for a commission?"

"502, Sir. We're all very proud of 502 and our record in the war."

"Have you thought it over very carefully? From Lance-Corporal to Lieutenant is a big boost, both in rank and pay."

"Yes, Sir. I know. But I don't want to leave 502."

"All right. Dismissed."

It was over. As I left Headquarters I heard Churchill's official speech announcing the unconditional surrender of the Germans, ending the war in Europe. It was 11 P.M. by the time I got back to Rome. The house was dark and the streets quiet. The celebration was over and I had missed it. Well, at any rate my future with 502 was secure and I was content. I drank a solitary cup of coffee and went to bed.

Rome to Caserta to Rome, May 10, 1945

Big changes seem to be in the offing. All our ambulances are busy evacuating patients. Apparently all Field Hospitals are being sent to the south, the wounded to be put on ships for home. Today eight of our ambulances were assigned to Naples and four to drive German POWs to Caserta. I was one of the latter. My German passengers, not dreaming that an English soldier could understand them, began a lively discussion about their hospital-prison life. All agreed that the food and medical treatment had been first-rate. About the end of the war they did not seem depressed at all. When I finally told them that I understood what they were saying, they were eager to talk, all of them at the same time. One of them asked me if I knew Cologne, and when I said "yes," he enumerated, his face beaming, all the landmarks there that did not exist anymore but were bombed to rubble. What an odd reaction, to smile while describing how his town was reduced to ruin! Another fellow mentioned with horror what he had heard of Buchenwald and other concentration camps, but his comrades did not believe any of it and attributed the loathsome stories to our propaganda. To my amazement they all had only harsh words for their *Führer* and called him the worst tyrant the world had ever seen.

We arrived in Caserta in the early afternoon, quickly discharged our passengers, had tea at the YWCA, and returned to Rome. On the way back we gave a lift to some American soldiers. At 5:30 P.M. we stopped by the sea for a picnic, sharing our rations and theirs. Their food was a relief from the regular rations that we always take with us on a long drive. We arrived home at 10:30 P.M.

Rome, May 11, 1945

Life continues as though the war were still on, and I often have to remind myself that the fighting is over. We are working under great tension. The day begins at 6 A.M. and ends at 10 or 11 P.M. We are averaging two days' work in one. A constant stream of 502 ambulances travels the road to Naples. Daily, hundreds of men are evacuated from the hospitals and transported to points of embarkation. Today, though, was my day off and I drove with two other girls to a beach about twenty miles north of Rome, a place called Fregene. Before the war it must have been a charming suburb for Rome's wealthy families. Now deserted villas line the path down to the sea. One drives along a road lined with pine trees, then suddenly comes upon the sea. At regular intervals along the road danger signs are posted—the place is loaded with land mines. The water was cold and refreshing, very different from the tepid waters of the Middle East, but the sun shone just as brightly. Shortly before leaving the peaceful beach we were watching two soldiers out on the water, fishing from a small rowboat. Suddenly there was an explosion, a jumble of wood fragments, pieces of bodies, shreds of clothing flying into the air. They had hit a mine. A moment later the sea was calm—no boat, no laughing soldiers. I looked away and was sick. I will not come back to this beach.

Rome, May 15, 1945

I am on details at the 69th General Hospital. The latest word is that the 48th GH will pack up and leave within the next few weeks, but the 69th keeps being filled, now mostly with German prisoners.

Rome, May 22, 1945

Summer definitely is here and it's oppressively hot. I spent the entire day on maintenance, first preparing Edith's ambulance for workshop inspection. (She had to take a convoy to Caserta.) Then I had to help strip three ambulances which are to be evacuated. It was my job to look for the worst tires on ambulances in the carpark, take them off, and replace them with the best tires from the three ambulances that are being evacuated. Dealing with these huge, wide heavy wheels is one of the worst jobs I've ever had to handle.

Rome, May 31, 1945

The last six days have been both happy and difficult for me. Last Friday, after work, I found Clynton Reed, the former CO of the 32nd Indian Field Ambulance, in our mess. He is now a full Colonel. Dressed in his red-striped trousers, he really looked splendid. As usual, he was surrounded by adoring females. I say "as usual" because he does exude a tremendous amount of charm and sex appeal. He's over six feet tall, in his mid 40's, graying at the temples, with a craggy face. His best feature is his smile, which lights up his whole face. Since all the girls quickly fall under his spell, I had always kept my distance. Therefore, I was all the more astonished when he got up, came over to me, and embraced me as if I were the very person he had been waiting for. I must admit that I felt flattered and was not above enjoying the jealous glances from the other girls around us. I was even more surprised when he asked me if I was free to join him for dinner. I was. We had a wonderful dinner at the Hotel Grande. Clynton's rank, as well as his whole bearing, precluded any questions about my being permitted into such august surroundings. But it was not just the good food and elegant atmosphere that made the evening so enjoyable. Clynton's company, in spite of all the reservations I had, charmed me too. Though I had met him in the desert and knew that he was Australian by birth, a doctor (gynecologist) by profession, and also an excellent tennis player (he had been a Davis Cup player), I really did not know him. Now I felt that I very much wanted to become better acquainted with him. Well, I did grow as close to him as one can in five short days.

Every day we spent as many hours as possible together, and for the first time since Laszlo I began to enjoy a closeness that I now realized I had been missing. But this was very different from what I had experienced with Laszlo. It was more light-hearted, with lots of laughter. Clynton, in his gentle, intelligent way, taught me how much fun and pleasure we could find in each other, and I began to wonder what I really felt for this man. Why had I lived such a monastic life for so long and why had I then so quickly given in to Clynton? Of course, the aftermath of my affair with Laszlo had badly frightened me, and, once burned, I had been twice careful. Yet I trusted Clynton immediately. Perhaps it was because he was twenty years older than I. Perhaps it was because he seemed wise, understanding, and kind. Maybe in the back of my mind I believed that a gynecologist would be the epitome of experience and responsibility. Or maybe I was falling in love with him, a little. No, there is no such thing as a little bit of love, but I was certainly growing very fond of Clynton, and I would miss him when he had to leave. I would need him, and that would make me miserable. I thought of the future, but there could be no future for Clynton and me, no commitment of any kind. We came from entirely different worlds. Clynton had chosen the Army as his career. After the war he would go back to India to be the *pukkah sahib*, the privileged British officer in the colonies. He needed a society wife who played bridge and tennis, grew flowers, and was the president of the local bird-watching society. I would not do. I could never fit into this picture. So what must I do? I must take this affair as light-heartedly as it started and look at it as a week of good fun. I must enjoy it and under no circumstances let my heart get involved. I hope I can succeed in this resolve.

Rome, June 1, 1945

Thank goodness, I don't have much time to think. All day I was on duty section. In the evening I had bar duty. It was Clynton's last day in Rome and he spent it sitting at our bar. That made it easier to say goodbye to him because we couldn't be alone together.

Rome, June 2, 1945

Today Miss Otto called me into her office to tell me that she would like me to be in charge of one of our sections. This means a promotion to full Corporal. I will share duties with Edith, who will be responsible for the paperwork, the office part, and I will be in charge of the ambulances, the outside part. This promotion means a lot of extra work and responsibility, but hardly any more pay.

Rome, June 4, 1945

After a long interval we had a convoy to the station. I had four stretcher cases for the 99th General Hospital. In the afternoon Miss Otto called a short meeting and informed us that in all probability we will leave Rome in the near future. Everyone is excited and speculates about where we'll go—Northern Italy? Austria? Maybe Germany? Edith and I are due to go on a week's leave in a few days and would hate to see it canceled because of our move. We're just waiting for a confirmation from the YWCA in Sorrento. All these new developments, more work because of my promotion, the excitement generated by a possible move, and the forthcoming leave to Sorrento give me little time to grieve over Clynton's departure.

Rome, June 5, 1945

It was my day off, and since I want to see as much as possible of Rome before we leave, once again I asked Lydia to be my guide. We spent the morning at the Forum and then intended to see the Capitol museum. We ran around for a long time trying to locate the place, only to find it closed when we finally did find it. We collapsed in a little cafe and ate some watery ice cream. In the afternoon we had an NCO meeting and were told that twenty-five of our ambulances will leave on Friday the 8th. Our new station will be about twenty miles north of Venice at a place called Treviso. All leaves are to be canceled. Naturally, Edith and I are upset. We spent the rest of the day packing. I have mixed feelings about our posting. Of course, I'm glad, as always, to move forward, to see and experience new things. On the other hand, I hate to say goodbye to all my Italian friends and above all to Rome, the most beautiful city I have ever known.

Rome to Naples, June 8, 1945

Today I was in charge of a convoy to Naples, ten ambulances with me in the lead. All the way to Caserta I had to watch my two rearview mirrors to be sure that the last ambulance was following. We made good time and arrived at 2 P.M. After we delivered our patients, we proceeded to Naples, where we left our ambulances and were taken to the YMCA. Unfortunately, there was not enough room for all of us and seven had to go to the ATS Transit Camp. I decided on the latter because, when one is in charge, one should not opt for the best. What a dreadful place that transit camp turned out to be—dirty, messy, and untidy. After we had showered and changed into skirts, we asked for passes, only to be told that without 'gentlemen friends' we could not leave the billets. The 'gentlemen friends' would have to sign out for us and then sign in for us by midnight. I was speechless. Apparently we females could not be trusted unless accompanied by males! We explained that our 'gentlemen friends' were waiting at the YW, our original destination, and since it was still daylight, we finally received permission to leave without a male escort but with the warning that we must come back escorted by a male. We did meet the other girls at the Y and went together to the cinema. On our way back we waved down a jeep with two American officers, who gave us a lift to the transit camp. We informed them of our predicament and asked them to sign us in. I was really embarrassed and quite sure that the two officers thought that we were trying to pick them up.

Naples to Rome, June 9, 1945

At 8 A.M. a car called for us and took us to our ambulances. We had to take a number of orderlies back to Caserta and Rome so it was late when we got home. Edith was waiting for me impatiently to tell me that our leaves have been processed and we are to leave for Sorrento tomorrow. I spent an hour packing before turning in.

Sorrento, June 10–June 17, 1945

Our week on leave was wonderful. We hitched a ride to Sorrento, by ambulance, staff car, and lorry, and found upon arriving that the YWCA where we were to stay must once have been a very exclusive hotel. We had a lovely room with attached bath and a magnificent view of the bay. Below us lay the blue Mediterranean, opposite Mt. Vesuvius with its smoke cloud drifting up into an equally blue sky, and all around white buildings surrounded by gardens. We breakfasted in bed, sunned on the terrace or the beach, went swimming or riding, read, ate, slept, and enjoyed the peace and quiet of the place. One day we took the steamer to Capri, taking a picnic lunch the kitchen prepared for us. We saw the wonderland of the Blue Grotto, where one's voice has a hundred echoes and everything is bathed in a strange blue glow. With a taxi we drove over the entire island and up to the peak, Anacapri. There we stopped at St. Michelle, the home of Axel Munthe, the writer, painter, and collector of fine art. The house is like a museum. His former housekeeper, now the custodian of the place, showed us around. During the last years of his life Munthe went blind, his physicians said, because of the sun and the vivid colors of Capri. I do believe that was true. My eyes, too, ached from the strong sun and the bright colors around us. We returned to Rome well rested and tanned. I wonder if I'll ever return to Sorrento and Capri as a tourist coming from—where?

Back in Rome we hardly had time to unpack before we were pounced upon by the entire outfit with a resume of all the things we would have to do before leaving. Leaving? Yes, early tomorrow morning we'll have to go to Florence with a convoy. All cars not participating in this convoy will proceed straight to our new station at Treviso, twenty miles north of Venice.

Rome, June 18, 1945

My ambulance is already at our new station in Treviso. This morning I am supposed to pack the rest of my belongings and then drive another ambulance to the 106th South African General Hospital where our convoy of twenty ambulances will stay overnight. We will have to transport critical cases to Florence and the ambulances have to be specially prepared with blood transfusion hooks, etc. On the 19th we'll drive to Florence, back to Rome on the 20th, pack the rest of our equipment on the 21st, go back to Florence on the 22nd, and drive from Florence to Treviso on the 23rd. The entire itinerary is crazy. Why go back to Rome and then to Florence again? But we don't have much to say about it so the day passes with lots of work and grumbling.

Rome to Florence, June 19, 1945

Sasha woke me at 3 A.M., pressed a little gift-wrapped box into my hand, congratulated me on my twenty-fifth birthday, and told me that it was time to get up. What kind of a birthday was this, having to go to work at such an ungodly hour! An hour later we were picked up by an ambulance and driven to the 106th South African General Hospital, where, of course, we had to wait for hours. There were four sections in all, each consisting of five ambulances and each ambulance carrying two or three stretcher cases accompanied by either a doctor or a nurse. I was leader of the second section. My two patients had their legs in plaster of paris, held elevated by contraptions fastened to the ceiling of the ambulance. Both had received morphine and were quite out of it. A nurse was in charge of the blood-plasma transfusion during the trip.

Every two hours we stopped to rest our patients. The road was terrible and the constant bumps a source of real pain. The countryside was new to us and beautiful, which here and there took our minds off the serious cargo we were carrying. After Viterbo, we drove along the shore of Lake Bolsena and then the road climbed up to Monte Fiascone and Radicofane. Our top-heavy vehicles lumbered along slowly. Some of the radiators began to steam, but all made it to the summit, only to face a steep descent. I slipped the car into first gear and reached level ground without mishap. Quite a few ambulances, though, suffered burned out brakes. By 5 P.M. we sighted the outskirts of Florence and arrived at the South African General Hospital half an hour later. It took another hour and a half until our patients had been unloaded and we had put our ambulances back into shape. Then we had to get petrol and drive our cars to the overnight parking facility. There Edith had quite an argument with Aideen about checking the ambulances. I agreed with Edith that it was idiotic to check cars when they were that hot, but in such cases I just say, "Yes and amen," and let it be. It was 8 P.M. when we checked into the YWCA. This one, like most others throughout Italy, was quite luxurious, but to our disappointment there was no water to wash up. I finally succeeded in getting a small bowl of the precious liquid from a waiter, who was impressed with my Italian. Dinner was excellent and the room I shared with Edith was charming, though terribly hot, but I was too tired to care. All in all it was not much of a birthday.

Florence to Rome, June 20, 1945

We decided on a different way home, Route I, the coastal road via Leghorn. It is about sixty miles longer but a much better road and leads through flat country all the way. The trip took ten hours. We had a much-needed hot bath and fell into bed.

Rome, June 21, 1945

All morning we were busy loading our ambulances with whatever was still left here. The afternoon we had off and I said goodbye to those I'd grown to like and know so well—the nuns, the Mother Superior, and my Italian girlfriends. I have been very happy in Rome and have made many dear friends here and am sad to leave them. But we're going on to new places, new faces. So, in spite of everything, I am looking forward to Venice and our new surroundings.

En route to Treviso, June 22, 1945

We were ready to leave at 6 A.M. Again I am responsible for the second section of five ambulances. This time, though, I have a second driver, and since we have no patients, the drive is not at all strenuous. By 4 P.M. we checked in at the Y in Florence and this time we even had enough water for our showers. After dinner we four section leaders took one car and drove around town, mainly to find the correct way to lead our convoy out of town, but also to see the cathedral, at least from the outside. It's a very impressive building. It really is a pity that we've driven through much of Italy, yet in most towns all we saw was the petrol-point, the carpark, the YWCA, or the by-pass route.

Florence to Treviso, June 23, 1945

The second day of our convoy. The highway from Florence to Bologna leads through still more mountains. We had to drive slowly for the road was bad. Parts are being repaired but some sections are in such bad condition that we were afraid the car springs would break. No parking on the shoulders. Mines! Danger! The few villages we passed were only ruins. Beyond Bologna the landscape changed quickly. We came into flat country. The further we progressed, the greener the country became. The Germans must have retreated fast here because towns and villages had hardly been touched. Farm houses looked prosperous. We were amazed. People looked better dressed, better fed. Even in features the Northern Italian looks different. Sprinkled throughout the population are tall, blond, blue-eyed types.

We crossed the River Po and the path of war once more was evident. The river is now out of use. It carries no cargo, no passenger boats. Banks and dams have been badly neglected. Part of the river is dried out altogether. Stretches of farmland are flooded. All bridges are destroyed. We crossed over on a pontoon bridge, supervised by Military Police.

The last seventy-five miles of road were great, like peace-time highways. We by-passed Venice and fifteen minutes later were in Mestre. Now on both sides of the highway were beautiful mansions set in parks, shadowed by old trees. We slowed down. One of these mansions would be our home for a while. Five miles later we saw the 'Blue Devil,' our Unit sign. A broad, well-kept driveway led to the house. We had arrived. It is too dark and I am too tired to describe our new home. I still have to unpack.

Treviso, June 24, 1945

Our new home is something special. The property is situated in Preganziol, halfway between Mestre and Treviso and about half an hour by car from Venice. It is surrounded by an enormous park. A gravel path leads to a swimming pool and there is a tennis court and several little summer houses. A small stream winds its way through green lawns and some wooded areas, which also belong to this magnificent estate. The building, the Villa Taverna, also is imposing. I share a room with Edith and Alice, with a view of the park. Adjacent, there's a bath of beautiful sky-blue tile. The only disadvantage here is that there are only two such bathrooms on our floor and everyone who has to use this one must walk through our room, so that it feels a bit like a hall. The rooms are totally empty. Our army cots and kit bags stacked against the richly ornamented walls look out of place. I'll try to find some orange crates and we'll put up little curtains to make the place more homey. The large halls downstairs are being converted to serve as offices, recreation rooms, and mess halls. There are four Italian servants to do the daily chores of cleaning and cooking. This morning before breakfast I put on my bathing suit and took a swim in the pool. What a life! The rest of the day I spent unpacking and cleaning and checking my ambulance.

Treviso, June 25, 1945

After work, which consisted of more maintenance, Edith and I visited Venice for the first time. We rented a gondola. A full moon reflected on the silvery canal. As we glided along the water we became aware of the stillness, disturbed only by the occasional splash of the gondoleer's pole. I was surprised by the absence of honking horns, the grinding of engines, the rush of tires against pavement. Here and there, strains of Italian folk melody floated across the canals. Our gondolier took up the melodies in a light, easy voice. We swept along the narrow canals leading into the heart of the city. One could reach out and touch the wet moss clinging to the sides of the houses on either side of the gondola, so narrow were the passages. As we reached the end of a 'street' our gondolier stopped, hallo'd, and waited. A hallo was returned. Then began the argument over which boat would first make the turn. We lost and waited. Around the corner, with a dexterous twist, the other gondola shot out and passed us. The passengers were hidden from view by velvet curtains. This is romantic, fascinating Venice. I can hardly wait for a return visit. Late at night, after we had returned home, a real thunderstorm broke, such as I have not heard since my childhood. The park looked grand when lightning suddenly bathed the old trees in a kind of violet color. The sound of the rain pouring down, the smell of wet earth and fresh grass—I love it. I fell asleep totally happy and satisfied.

Treviso, June 26, 1945

There is very little work for us here. Each section is on duty every fourth day. For me that means to be transport NCO, detailing my section into telephone duty, as runners, arranging transport to Venice for mail, for dispatches, bar duty, etc. There is no hospital near us. The ambulances are not needed anywhere and we are beginning to realize that we simply are in transit, waiting for a new assignment. From

Venice to Udine near the Austrian border all the properties have been taken over by the 8th Army, to which we, too, belong again, and the entire area is a kind of huge transit camp. I like the idea because there is so much to see and do here and we'll have time to explore. Then there is the additional feeling of anticipation. Where will we go next? In the afternoon the rain came down again in sheets, and there was more thunder and lightning. It is quite cool and I had to put on a sweater. Wonderful!

Venice, June 27, 1945

Edith and I decided to spend the afternoon shopping in Venice. It was still raining, but not as hard, so we put on our raincoats and off we went. The shopping quickly turned to window shopping only. Though Venice does have some very tasteful shops filled with all kinds of luxury articles (silver and glassware, paintings and art objects), the prices are astronomical. Essential items such as soap, fabrics, and shoes, for instance, are extremely scarce. Venice by daylight was free from the spell of the full moon. We hired a gondola again and went in a series of twists and turns to explore some of the more obscure canals. Fruit peelings floated by. The odor that permeated the air was bad. Above, a latticed window opened and a robust woman appeared, holding something in her hand—garbage. Soup bones, cabbage leaves, and other unidentifiable morsels hit the water several feet away from us. Ragged and dirty children frolicked along the canal front, prancing on pieces of decayed wood, shrieking and squealing. Our gondola nosed its way through the water, slowly. Paper, wine bottles, and dead rats floated quietly out to sea. Venice by daylight was not enchanting.

Upon returning home, we heard some terrible news. One of our Palestinian girls had received a letter from her brother in the Czech Army, who had found his brother in Prague. From him he had learned that their parents both were dead. From the concentration camp in Theresienstadt they had been transferred to another camp, where they had died in a gas chamber. I can't sleep tonight. What if my parents shared that same fate? Now that I am so close, am I already too late?

Treviso, June 28, 1945

I can't think of anything but what happened to Helen's parents. Thank goodness I'm on duty today and have to concentrate on my job. In the evening almost all of us Palestinians visited a neighboring villa in which a company of the Jewish Brigade is stationed. The purpose of the visit was to welcome and help Jewish refugees who have made their way from recently freed concentration camps to the first outposts of the Jewish Brigade near Udine. From there our boys had brought them to this outfit. Another Palestinian company will take them to Bari where they will wait at a large refugee camp for shipment to Palestine. All this has to be done secretly because it is totally illegal. It is unbelievable what these fellows do for the refugees, and only now I realize what a blessing the Jewish Brigade is. Our boys are not only transporting the refugees, but feeding and clothing them. They give up half their cigarette rations, half their clothing, half their food, and sleep with one blanket less in order to feed and clothe their future countrymen. Even more than that, if discovered, prison and dishonorable discharge from the Army await them. Now they have asked for our help so we are busily collecting clothes and sewing. Today was my first meeting with a batch of these Nazi victims. I had hoped, and, of course, feared at the same time, to meet someone who could possibly know something about the fate of my parents. But most of this group of refugees were organized Zionist youth groups who had started out from Poland or Lithuania to find the road south, with the eventual goal—Israel. Most of them could speak Hebrew, and the tales of horror they told have made me sick.

Treviso, July 2, 1945

For days I have been watching carloads of Jewish refugees pass by our house. The trucks belong to another Jewish Unit further north, who take their cargo to the Palestinian drivers next door to us. Most of the refugees are clad in Army uniforms so as not to arouse suspicion. It's probably the first decent warm bit of clothing they've worn in a long time. These courageous people, who come from camps in Germany, Poland, and all the other Eastern-European countries, have traveled a route which no one has shown them, which is not marked on any map. They have thronged southward, into Austria and Italy, and finally will land in the big transit camps at Bari and Naples. The thought of these people, who, having lived through horrors, deprived of everything human, have still so much force, will-power, and hope, fills me with admiration. There is nothing attractive about these men and women. They are ragged and dirty. Hunger, privation, and fear are etched deeply into their minds and bodies. The oldsters take their food demandingly and without thanks. But the youngsters are different. They are open and eager to be friendly. Well-organized Zionists, they all speak Hebrew and are looking forward to a full life in Palestine. The Jewish soldiers keep some of these boys and put them into their workshops, teaching them mechanics and driving, trades to take with them to the new land. We vowed to aid them, too, and collected clothes, washed dishes, served food. Even some of the English girls are participating. They, too, spend some free hours collecting and sewing clothes for the refugees. One can never do enough, but we all are grateful to be able to help, if only a little.

Most of the DPs are Poles and Lithuanians. There is not a single German Jew among them. I asked questions: "Have you met any German Jews? Have any escaped?" The answer never varies. It comes with awful finality. "No. None. Nothing. No one is left."

I had a sweet letter from Clynton today. He wants to meet me in Venice. But the timing is all wrong. My mind is full of tales I hear daily from the refugees. I feel almost guilty for not having suffered equally, and I have a need to be with people who understand. Good old Clynton, so British, so upper class. How can he understand my fears, my hopes? We are divided by two millennia of history and at the moment I don't feel that I can bridge the gap.

Treviso, July 3, 1945

Duty section today. Besides my regular duties, I translated a lot of orders from English to Italian for our Italian help. (And to think that I didn't know either of these languages when I joined the Army three years ago!) In the evening we had an NCO meeting. Miss Otto informed us that a decision has been made for our future assignment. We will become part of the occupation Army in Austria and probably will leave here within two or three weeks. To hear this is welcome news. As beautiful as it is here, I'm already eager to see new places, and even more important, the farther north we go, the easier it will be to find out about my parents. Other items mentioned during the meeting concerned upcoming discharges, possibilities of signing on for further Army duty, and home leaves. But there is nothing definite yet about these points. I have applied for home leave to England to visit my sister, whom I haven't seen since 1936. Palestinians are, as a rule, only given home leave to Palestine, but I have asked Miss Otto to help me get an exception granted.

Treviso to Venice, July 6, 1945

I found some discarded boxes and am making nightstands for Edith and me. She is sewing curtains for them. In the evening Emanuel called for me and we went in to Venice. We ate at the Luna Hotel, drank Italian Spumanti, and took a gondola ride. I really can't imagine anything more romantic than Venice by night, and I tried to be good company, but I keep on being haunted by the vivid descriptions and stories told by the DPs [displaced persons]. I believe, though, that Emanuel understands since he is, like me, a Palestinian, a Jew.

Treviso, July 7, 1945

The highest ranking ATS officer, a Major General, is going to inspect our unit next week. All day long we had to drill for this coming event.

Treviso, July 11, 1945

Well, it's over—the Major-General has come and gone. We had arranged to have a motor-bike escort meet the officer and lead her into camp. With snappy salute the escort swung her bike around and came in, the General's staff, MPs, photographers, and reporters following in her wake. At the signal, 502 froze into columns and stood like ramrods. Upon her arrival the General inspected workshops, etc., and then inspected us, stopping here and there to talk to some of us. "How long have you been in Italy?" With a start I realized that she was addressing me and in my excitement I could not remember. I barely managed to stutter out, "Quite a while, M'am!" She gave me a peculiar look and went on her way, convinced, no doubt, that I was rather dim. Then, at a shrill whistle, we jumped into our cars and paraded past the General in first gear. One's position behind the wheel does not free one from the business of saluting. While approaching the reviewing group, one slumps low in the seat and then at the crucial moment straightens up, arms straight and hard against the steering wheel. That constitutes the salute. The driver cannot, of course, remove her hands from the wheel nor her eyes from the road. The parade was very impressive, but we're all glad that it's over.

Treviso, July 16, 1945

I am supposed to be promoted to Sergeant in charge of our educational program, but so far I have only the duties without the actual rank. Today I gave my first official German lesson. Now that we know that we will be going to Austria, all the girls want to learn German. So far, thirty have signed up for the class. I am supposed to give a lesson each morning, even on my day off, and three times a week also in the afternoon.

Venice, July 17, 1945

One of our friends from Sorrento, who is now the ADST, the senior RASC officer of our area, has come to Venice for a short vacation and invited Edith and me to accompany him on a sight-seeing tour. We remembered the Colonel as a somber, studious man, not given to gaiety but with an insatiable thirst for knowledge; in other words, rather a bore. Still, any promise of diversion should not be ignored so we accepted his invitation and after lunch drove into Venice to meet him. This was our second visit to Venice by daylight. The weather was hot and sticky. Again the stench of the canals was sickening and the water was thick with scum and filth. Garbage and refuse lay rotting on the surface. Any breeze would have helped, but there was none. Gingerly, Edith and I climbed down into a gondola, followed by the Colonel and a guide. From a sturdy leather portfolio the Colonel extracted four guidebooks. He opened the first of them to page one and in clipped tones began to read aloud. Two guide books later we still were listening. The Colonel's voice had grown hoarse but still intoned faithfully the printed impressions of Venice. Only once did he look up from his reading, and that was to dismiss our "incompetent" guide, who had sat in stunned silence, unable to get a word in edgewise. The Colonel then hired a new guide. This one climbed aboard and introduced us to the Bridge of Sighs, which we were approaching. The Colonel flicked over a page of his guidebook, scanned it briefly, and with a disgruntled look sat back to listen. Our new guide provided the romantic histories of each building and palace along the canal—tales of love, adventure, and intrigue. The Colonel fidgeted, for he was education-minded and did not find such romantic nonsense enlightening. The guide began to tell us of the amours of a certain countess who lived in the sumptuous villa to our left, but we never did find out how the tale ended because the Colonel, exasperated beyond endurance, interrupted the story to fire the guide. The Colonel then suggested a visit to the Ducal Palace. Half-heartedly, we agreed. To most people the Ducal Palace brings memories of art. Thanks to the Colonel my memories of it will be quite different. I shall remember a hopeless maze of rooms, the clacking sound of tired feet against hard, endless corridors. Not only was the Colonel education-minded, but he also had stamina! He marched us through art-laden galleries, dozens of them. One by one he studied paintings, slowly and carefully supplementing the guidebook information with observations of his own. Edith was polite. I was not, in spite of frequent warning glances from her. I did not care any more. I was tired. Hours behind the wheel, car maintenance, practice drill in the

Sarafand sun—all seemed restful compared to this. I trailed along behind Edith and the Colonel, too tired to talk. As we entered another gallery and his pedantic explanations began again, I spied a large, ornate chair, to which I limped and sat down. What bliss! A placard, propped close by, announced that I was perched on the celebrated seat of the Doge. I wondered if he ever had enjoyed the comfort of this chair as much as I did now. Edith and the Colonel began to explore further and I arose wearily and followed. Edith was beginning to look unhappy, and though her conversation was still polite, it was getting rather shrill. I plunked down on a succession of chairs, antique or no, during the next hour. When I finally refused to walk any farther, the Colonel suggested another gondola! By nightfall Edith and I were thoroughly exhausted. We were invited to dinner at the Luna Hotel but were too cross and sleepy to enjoy it. We shall avoid this guide-book-Colonel in the future!

Treviso, July 18, 1945

Just when I got busy teaching German, we were given more work. Six of us were assigned to give driving lessons to the sisters (nurses) and VADs of the 22nd Hospital near us. My schedule is daily from 2 P.M. to 4 P.M., and since it takes me half an hour each way to go and return from there, I won't have free afternoons any more. Today was the first lesson and I'm sure I must have drawn the two dumbest sisters. It takes all my self-control to teach them, though, as a rule, I am rather patient.

Treviso, July 22, 1945

I have been terribly busy these last days. My German lessons are in full swing, but progress is much slower than I had imagined it would be. Since everyone has a different schedule and the girls constantly are called out on jobs, I must go through the same lessons three or four times. Like most students, many of them think that learning will come through osmosis rather than hard work. I'm not sure how successful this undertaking will be. My time is filled with preparing and teaching the German lessons, giving driving lessons, and being transport NCO. I haven't even been able to find a spare half hour to go swimming.

Treviso, July 24, 1945

Very suddenly we received a dispatch ordering us to proceed immediately to Velden, Austria. We are in a frenzy of packing. Miss Otto already has left to check out our new quarters and the advance party is to leave tomorrow morning.

Treviso, July 25, 1945

All day I was busy packing my ambulance with Quartermaster stores and checking the loading of the other ambulances in my section. We are supposed to leave with the main body of 502 tomorrow. Now that we are going, I begin to look forward to the move. At 6 P.M. Miss Otto returned from Velden. Our departure has been postponed. The house in Velden is not yet ready for us—there is no water, the gate is not wide enough for our ambulances, there are no toilets, etc., etc. How frustrating Army life can be with its hurry, hurry, hurry in order to wait, wait, wait!

Treviso, July 28, 1945

I just came out of the NCO meeting, during which we were informed of next week's schedule: On Monday, the day after tomorrow, the first section will leave for Velden and each day following one section at a time will follow. That is, all of 502 but myself. After all four sections have departed, I will proceed to Florence and from there will drive to Perugia and then from Perugia to Rome. From Rome I will backtrack through Florence, through Venice, and from Venice I'll drive via Udine to Velden. This long trip is necessary because three of our girls are going to take an educational course at Perugia and another girl, a clerk, is being transferred from Rome and will join our outfit in Austria. This means six days on the road for me, six days of solid driving. I would have preferred to go with the rest of 502, but Captain Otto wants me to bring back a report about the new course in Domestic Sciences now given at Perugia.

Treviso, July 30, 1945

I am on duty as Transport NCO. This morning the first section left, with Dee leading the convoy on her motorbike. It's very quiet here. In the evening Edith returned from her weekend off, which she had spent in Cortina.

Treviso, July 31, 1945

Today passed with nothing much to do. We are all waiting for Miss Otto's return. In the evening Joseph and Emanuel, Edith and I had a farewell dinner at a restaurant in Treviso. On our return at midnight we saw that the new timetable was out, so Miss Otto must have come back. Another change. *Everyone* is leaving for Velden tomorrow, everyone, that is, except Miss Otto, Mary, Sheila, Dotty, and I, with my three passengers for Perugia.

Treviso, August 1, 1945

Before the main convoy left, Miss Otto gave a short speech concerning our future work: Our sudden departure to Austria is due to the fact that we are desperately needed there. The Army has decided to evacuate German prisoners from the entire area. We will drive convoys of badly wounded Germans who are being transported to Graz, apparently against medical advice, so that we can expect some of our cases to die en route. What a gruesome prospect!

At 9 A.M. Aideen's section left and shortly after that Edith's. By 10 A.M. the last convoy had passed out of sight. An unaccustomed silence filled the house. I am supposed to leave day after tomorrow, and I'm glad. This big empty place has ceased to be 'home.'

Treviso to Florence to Perugia to Rome to Florence to Mestre, August 3–7, 1945

We had planned to start at 7 A.M. this morning, but we were an hour late. Our cook overslept and I had to wake the girls myself. I drove the first two hours, then let the others take over. This way, the trip didn't become tiring. We were in excellent spirits and sang all the way to Florence. There were no passengers to worry about and no convoy to follow. We made the trip in eight hours, which left us enough time for sightseeing. We hurried over to the Y, secured rooms for the night, freshened up, and set out. As usual, after walking only half a block, a jeep stopped us. Two charming Americans lifted their caps and invited us for a ride. It will forever remain a mystery to me how these boys manage to be everywhere and always seem to have enough time for a joy-ride, a cup of coffee, and a chat! We accepted and were pleased to learn that both of the fellows were stationed in Florence and were, therefore, excellent guides. They took us first to the River Arno, which divides the town into two parts. The river itself is a dull, sluggish brown, but the bridges across it are fascinating. I had seen the Ponte Vecchio, the most famous of these bridges, on my first trip through Florence, en route to Venice, but I hadn't stopped. This time we got out of the car and walked across it. It's more like a medieval shopping street than a bridge, with people living in narrow houses built above shops and offices. Next we drove over the famous square, Loggia dei Lanzi, and visited several palaces full of art treasures and we entered the Duomo, or cathedral. I wish I had had days to spend in Florence. Our guides were not as intellectual as the Colonel in Venice, but I enjoyed this kind of sightseeing far more, especially since we concluded the afternoon with a drive through the countryside. The air was exhilarating, as Florence lies quite high. We had dinner with our American friends and then bade them goodbye.

The next day's journey took us only one hundred miles, to Perugia. There I had to see each girl properly enrolled and check that they each filled out the necessary red-tape papers. By 5 P.M. all of them were settled in their rooms at the YWCA, all had done the necessary paperwork, and I was ready for bed. Sunday morning I left Perugia alone, feeling light and carefree. I drove fast at times, then slowed down simply to enjoy my leisure. At about noon I could hear the peal of church bells. As I passed through the villages I noticed the natives, dressed in their Sunday best, briskly heading toward church. Everything was serene and quiet—until my car developed a loud noise in the motor! Every few feet it backfired. I began to worry a bit, but since the road now was down the mountain, I thought that it really didn't matter. I would have it looked after in Rome. When I saw the faint outline of St. Peter's dome, my heart quickened. I do so love this city. First I drove to the former residence of 502. The nuns and students rushed out to embrace me. I did feel as if I had come 'home.' An ATS group of office workers was now stationed there, and they invited me to stay the night. I gladly accepted. My old Italian girlfriends and I sat up until almost dawn exchanging memories.

Early Monday morning I collected Peggy and we went into town to do some shopping for 502. I had a list an arm's length long. We anticipated that we'd be able to buy even less in Austria than in Italy. After the shopping we took my ambulance to the workshop, where we found two very stupid fellows on duty who apparently knew nothing whatsoever about mechanics. After grubbing around the inside of the motor and underneath the car for over an hour, they announced that nothing was wrong! I climbed in and, in a huff, drove off with a series of backfires. While waiting impatiently for those idiots to locate the trouble, I was approached by three soldiers. Rumor had gotten around that I was going to Austria, and they wanted a lift. I told them to get aboard. So we had plenty of company on our northbound trip. We made Florence in record time, where I left my three hitchhikers at the YMCA, with strict orders to be ready the following morning at 8:15 sharp or I would go without them.

My fifth day on the road took us over the mountains to Bologna and then to Mestre. There I left one of our hitchhikers. Peggy and the other two soldiers I dropped off at their respective Ys, and then I drove over to Emanuel's outfit. He stood just outside the workshop entrance, as if he had been waiting for me. That gave me a warm feeling after my long trip. He saw me safely installed in a requisitioned villa a few doors down from their outfit and told me to be ready for dinner at 7:30 P.M. We had cocktails at the Europa in Venice and dinner at the Luna. The evening was most pleasant. Emanuel also promised to have my ambulance checked first thing in the morning.

Mestre to Velden, Austria, August 8, 1945

In spite of my lovely room, I had an awful night. There was no mosquito net over my bed and the little beasts dive-bombed me all night long. This was my last day in Italy. Outside, it poured rain. For breakfast there was no coffee but Army tea—a dreadful way to start the day. Emanuel came to fetch me at 9 A.M. and took me to their workshop, where my ambulance had been repaired. I picked up Peggy but could find no trace of my other hitchhikers. By 10 A.M. the two of us were northward bound toward our new 'home.' I drove first. The landscape was flat, the mountains in the background and later to our left. I could go no faster than thirty miles an hour because the rain was coming down in buckets and visibility was limited. We passed through Udine and by noon reached Tarvisio, at the border between Italy and Austria. A lonely MP, drenched by the downpour, smiled and waved us on. How simple it can be, at times, to pass a border. Austria. Within half a mile everything had changed, and yet it was so familiar to me—the Gothic script on every sign, the neat houses with their red gables, flowerpots in front of every window. Everything looked clean and friendly and, in spite of the rain, beautiful. Everything, that is, except the people. Because of the weather, only a few were out, but they either looked right through us or averted their eyes. Gone were the happy Italians, waving and smiling at us. No shouts now of "Viva, Anglaise!" No holding out of hands for the expected gifts of chocolate and chewing gum. It took two more hours to reach Velden. My windshield wipers with their monotonous slip-slop hypnotized me and caused my thoughts to drift. Nine years since I left home. Where is home now? I am sure it is not Palestine. I don't think that I'd like to live there forever. Return to Berlin? These few miles and my first encounter with the civilian population show such a gulf between us, 'me' and 'them,' that surely there can be no returning to Germany. England? No, if one is not English born, one will forever remain an outsider. That much I have learned living among the English. More than ever I was aware that I had lost, irrevocably, my roots, my home. Will I ever find a new one?

But no more daydreaming! I passed Villach and saw the first sign—Velden, 8Km. Then Lake Wörther lay before us, framed by wooded hills with the mountains in the background. What an exquisite place! Our house lies directly by the lake. I can't think of a more enchanting place to live.

Velden, August 9, 1945

Today was my day off, which gave me time to settle in. Our grounds here consist of our house, a little above the lake, two caretaker cottages, and below a boat-house and two piers. Our carpark is a bit further up the slope, directly in back of our quarters. The house itself is three stories high. The third floor has three small rooms nestling under the eves, one of which I share with Edith and Alice. From our dormer window we have a magnificent view of the lake. There are some drawbacks, however. The house is a bit small for seventy people, and the plumbing still is not working. Some of the German prisoners are working on the water lines and building emergency toilets, but since these lack any kind of roof covering and it continues to rain, I shall soon be totally constipated. Or maybe I shall expire first from a concussion, because every time I approach my bed, I hit my head on the sloping ceiling!

The German prisoners who work for us as gardeners, cooks, woodcutters, and repairmen seem to be swarming all over the place, talking among themselves, discussing each one of us as we pass. Of course, they don't know that quite a few of us understand every word they say. Still, it is unpleasant to be continually stared at and commented on.

After lunch Edith and I had our hair cut at a beauty salon and then found a dressmaker for some alterations. I am addressed as *Gnädige Frau,* the German equivalent of 'Madame.' Everyone is polite, but not warm. It is confusing—on the one hand, the women in their *dirndls* and the men in their *lederhosen* and kneesocks with their charming dialect that makes their German sound so friendly, their pretty houses, and above all the magnificent landscape. On the other hand, the vacant expressions when they look at us, the empty stores (there is absolutely nothing to buy), and everywhere German uniforms, probably of former soldiers. It is beginning to dawn on me that we are not part of a welcome force here, not friends who have come to liberate, but rather the enemy, who has come to occupy. I—the enemy? Don't I share with them the same language, the same culture? But then, how

are they to know this? I wear the British uniform, I drive a British ambulance, and I have come as part of the occupying army, the army they
fought and which is now the new law of the land. And do I even want
them to know that I have much in common with them? They might
well hate me for being on the 'other' side. And should I not also hate
them for what they have been part of? How much simpler life had
been in Italy!

Velden, August 10, 1945

In the morning I had to see the area MO to get my TAB injection.
The afternoon was taken up with preparing "68" for workshop inspection. We have no pits here for working on the undercarriage and
not even a water hose to wash away the mud and grime. My arm
began to ache from the injection, so I finished early and will do the
rest tomorrow.

Velden, August 13, 1945

6:15 A.M.—convoy. Ten ambulances to Klagenfurt, from where we
are to take our patients, all Germans, to the train in Lienz. I had two
stretcher cases and two sitters, who shared the front with me. One of
the fellows, I discovered, was from Munich, the other from Berlin.
Both were astonished at my German, especially the Berliner, who instantly recognized my Berlin accent. I merely stated that I had studied
there. They plied me with questions about life in England and in the
Army. I could not help myself but began to brag about how free and
democratic Britain is and how well we are treated in the Army. They
were amazed and, in turn, surprised me by the bitterness with which
they spoke of their officers, calling them "cowardly dogs" and worse,
and of how badly they were treated in their Army. Still, these fellows
clung tenaciously to the Nazi theory that Hitler was a truly great man.
Only the big-shots had distorted and misdirected Hitler's beliefs, they
said. When I tried to turn the subject to concentration camps, they fell
silent. Of this they seemed genuinely ashamed. As I thought later
about this conversation it occurred to me that our ability to speak
German really has a great propaganda value for the British.

Velden, August 16, 1945

At 6:30 A.M. we went in convoy to Hermagen, about an hour's drive
on a very bad road. We were supposed to evacuate a German field hospital, taking all the patients to the nearby train station. Of course,
upon our arrival nothing was ready, and we had to wait for three

hours until the loading of stretcher cases began. We did not mind because the weather was perfect and we stretched out on the grass. But why did we have to get up at 5 A.M.? Finally, we evacuated the entire hospital within an hour, since the train station was only a mile away. I had three trips of five stretcher cases each time. Some observations: The smell in and around the field hospital was awful. Maybe the Germans don't have enough disinfectants. The patients look very malnourished. Most of them are amputees. The German medical officers who were in charge seemed very unfriendly, often even rude to their men. I saw one MD kicking a soldier's leg, which stuck out under the blanket of the stretcher. The German sisters, on the other hand, appeared compassionate and careful of their charges. All our patients admired our comfortable ambulances.

Velden, August 17, 1945

Duty section. It's raining hard and I dread having to give "68" her necessary overhaul, lying on the cold and muddy earth, getting chilled and dirty, but maintenance must be done. In the afternoon I drove over to Pörtschach to get the daily dispatches (Army talk for 'mail') and some supplies. When I arrived I found the entire British Headquarters in a frenzied state of excitement. Japan has unconditionally surrendered! Now World War II has come to an end. Peace everywhere, but what kind of peace will it be?

Velden, August 19, 1945

I spent the whole morning filling out questionnaires for our civilian labor. Then Miss Otto called me to tell me that I should start my German lessons again. I'm not too enthusiastic because the girls lose interest so soon after beginning that it's no pleasure to teach them. In the evening we had our own unit V-J party.

Velden, August 20, 1945

At 8:30 A.M. I started my first German lesson again. We'll meet every morning for one hour, and for those on early duty I'll also have a late afternoon session several times a week. At 10:15 A.M. we had an NCO meeting. Miss Otto has succeeded in requisitioning the villa next door to the 'main house,' which suddenly had become vacant. She would like all officers and NCOs to move into this villa. However, there won't be room for all of us. Yet Edith wants a 'two girl per room' so badly that I agreed to move with her, but I'm sorry to leave my garret room with its beautiful lake view.

Velden, August 21, 1945

Moving day. We worked all day to make our new room a cozy habitat. Edith is thrilled, I less so because I see many disadvantages. Our room is on the ground floor and has big windows, but no lake view. We have quite a walk to the main house, which is okay as long as it isn't raining or snowing. There is no bath downstairs either, only a tiny basin in our room and we won't be able to get hot water from the kitchen anymore. At the moment we don't have electric light either since there are no bulbs available.

Velden, August 22, 1945

I like the new room less and less. All the German prisoners who work for us like to peer into our window when they pass by, which they seem to do more frequently than necessary. And there are so many of them—repairing the water lines, installing new plumbing, cutting wood, gardening, helping the cooks, etc. It almost seems as if there are more of them than there are personnel of 502. Edith has promised to sew some curtains. Maybe this will help.

Our workload has now resumed some routine. Ambulances are stationed daily at Villach. Daily trips are made to Udine, Italy, and cars go each day to Spittal and Klagenfurt. The story about driving fatally wounded prisoners and that there was a chance they would die en route was just another crazy rumor. Most of our German patients are sitting cases, except when we have to evacuate a hospital, as we did the other day. I just heard that four girls are to leave in a few days as an advance detachment for Vienna. Later eleven more are to follow. We also are to have a detachment in Graz.

Velden, August 23, 1945

Once again it is pouring rain. I was stand-by and passed the time reading. At the moment I'm engrossed in a history of America. More and more I am thinking of going to the States after my discharge. Uncle Hans, my father's brother, has written to my sister in England and to me that if anything should have happened to my parents we ought to consider going to America.

Velden, August 24, 1945

Workshop inspection. Thank goodness, the weather is good. My "68" was unbelievably dirty, but by 4 P.M. I had finished. In the big house there was great excitement. Everyone is helping in the preparation for the party tonight, a reception for about forty guests—officers and men from the hospitals, the MI rooms, and the RASC, all people with whom we work.

Velden, August 25, 1945

The party was a great success. We had a dance band, free drinks for everyone, and an enormous buffet with all kinds of hors d'ouevres, cakes, cookies, iced coffee, fruit, nuts, etc. Everyone had a grand time, most of them talking about going home and discussing their future plans and looking forward to fulfilling them. I could not share the gaiety and soon left, feeling depressed. My uncle's letter has spelled out what I have feared all along, that in all probability my parents no longer are alive and that I must make some decisions about my own future with this in mind. I realize that the Army times are coming to an end and I will have to take charge of my life.

Velden, August 26, 1945

This morning I talked to Miss Otto and as a result of our conversation I have written two letters. The first was an application for home leave. After so many years abroad, each member of His Majesty's Forces is entitled to one month's home leave. For us Palestinians this means Palestine. However, since I have no close family in Palestine and my nearest relative, my sister, lives in England, I have asked to be granted permission for home leave in England. The second letter was an inquiry addressed to the American Consul asking if there is any possibility of a transfer from the British into the American Armed Forces. A leave to England would make it possible to see my sister again. It has been nine years since I last saw her. Service in the American Army probably would give me American citizenship, and, since I like Army life, perhaps I could stay in the American Army. I know that it is really impossible for me to become British. As I mentioned before, one must be born English or forever remain a foreigner. On the other hand, from what I have seen so far of Americans and from all I have read, they are a nation of immigrants themselves and would readily accept someone like me.

Velden, August 27, 1945

Four girls left this morning for Vienna, but within an hour they were back. At the last moment the entire venture was canceled. A dispatch rider from Headquarters had been sent after them with a last-minute change of orders. The cancellation of the Vienna detail is due to the Russians. Apparently, the streets of the city are too dangerous for women, in or out of uniform. Stories of rapes everywhere have come to the attention of Headquarters and now female personnel can only venture out with an armed male escort. We are all very angry and disappointed, but Miss Otto won't give up and sooner or later we'll have our detachment in Vienna.

Velden, August 28, 1945

My day off. Emanuel came up from Treviso and we drove out to the Millstädter See behind Spittal. There we had lunch at the Officers' Country Club, a former hotel. Afterwards, we hired a boat and went out onto the lake. In the evening we had dinner at Maria Wörth. Emanuel admitted that undoubtedly we were in one of the world's most beautiful spots. Still, he did not like his first venture into Austria. He was experiencing the same feelings we all had when we came here, a kind of unexplainable depression. It isn't easy to be among people who have forgotten how to laugh and whose resentment you can feel upon each contact with them.

Velden, August 31, 1945

Suddenly there is almost more work than we can handle. Fifteen ambulances have left to form our new detachment in Graz. We also have three more details, one in Spittal and two in Lendorf. I now have to spend every fourth day in the office as transport NCO. Once again, there is no time to give my German lessons. In the afternoon I had to take four stretcher cases to Spittal.

Velden, September 3, 1945

Today, Miss Otto told us more about the situation in Vienna. The Russians apparently are even worse than we had been told and the Viennese population is starving. Yet, in spite of all the reports, she is determined to have a detachment in Vienna.

It was my turn to be night-duty NCO, so I had to sleep in the office, which I dislike a lot.

Velden, September 12, 1945

We have been here over a month now and I still haven't grown used to our beautiful surroundings. The days pass quickly now that we have a definite routine again and lots of work. We are the only ambulance drivers in this entire area and take care of all admittances, transfers, and discharges from the hospitals and MI rooms around here.

Velden, September 20, 1945

We have a new cook, a Viennese, and how we came by her is a story worth telling. Miss Otto called two of our German-speaking Palestinians into her office and informed them of a plan she had been hatching. There is an Austrian family living up the hill who look after our property. The wife had come to Miss Otto, begging to get their older sister out of Vienna. She, like everyone else there, was starving and deathly afraid of the Russians. If Miss Otto somehow could help to get her out they would be eternally grateful. Emma, the sister, could live with them, and since she is supposed to be an excellent cook, she surely could work in our kitchen, contributing to an improved cuisine. Now Miss Otto had it all figured out. The two girls would drive to Vienna on official business. There they would call at Frau Emma's address and inform her of their plan to smuggle her out of Vienna through the Russian zone and into the arms of her loving family.

The two drivers started out the very next day, located the address, and found a very frightened Emma. However, once the plan was explained to her, she was all for it. She hastily packed her bag and off they went. Just before arriving at the Russian checkpoint, they had Emma climb onto one of the stretchers in the back, put bandages around her head, and wrapped her in Army blankets. Upon reaching the border the ambulance was duly stopped and inspected. The Russian guard pointed to the trembling body on the stretcher and frowned. "She's a very sick ATS officer, Sir," one of our drivers explained. He waived them across and a shudder of relief swept through Emma's ample body. So Emma was comfortably installed at 502 and the character of our meals changed immediately. She thought up various ways to demonstrate her appreciation, but she often was in doubt about how well her cooking was liked. Now and then I would catch sight of her well-developed bosom peeking around the corner of the dining room as she strained to perceive on the girls' faces some sign that they were pleased. But the English are notoriously undemonstrative. Then she hit on a wonderful idea—Viennese pastry! This the English undoubtedly would rave about. Since she knew that I could speak German and must therefore be some sort of connoisseur of Austrian pastry, she ran after me wherever I was, begging, "*Fräulein* Corporal! Taste, taste! *Ist das nicht wunderbar?*"

"*Ja, Emma, wunderbar!*" I would reply because, truly, it was.

"But do *they* like my cooking?" she would ask, waving her fat arms toward the dining room.

"Of course they do, Emma," I kept reassuring her. Today at dinner she produced her *chef d'oeuvre*, Apfelstrudel. The English tasted it but left most of it on their plates. It was not English trifle. I tried to console the almost hysterical cook, pointing out that the English very seldom like what is not completely English, and I patted her shoulder in sympathy, remembering my first days with 502. She has vowed to find something they *will* like or die in the attempt.

Velden, September 23, 1945

We are very busy. When I'm not on detail driving, there's maintenance and office duty and here and there duty section with household chores such as getting the laundry and mail in Pörtschach. We also have to fetch wood, which the prisoners then cut up and stack in huge piles by the main house and next to our villa, too, all in preparation for winter. All last week the weather was wonderful, sunny and a little cooler, but today the clouds gathered and it began to drizzle. I discovered in a storeroom in the big house boxes full of Hitler Youth pamphlets. On questioning one of the maids, I found out that our billets were former Hitler Youth quarters.

Velden, September 24, 1945

Yesterday I was on duty in Klagenfurt when a truckload of new gray-blue flannel pajamas arrived. The Sergeant in charge gave me two pair as a present. Last night I ripped out all the seams and today I went to the dressmaker in Velden, who is going to make me a suit out of the material. She's going to line it too. Her price: a bit of canned goods, three bars of soap, and six packages of cigarettes. I'll have my first fitting tomorrow.

Velden, September 26, 1945

Miss Otto talked to me last night. Jane, who is in charge of our detachment in Graz, is supposed to be discharged any day now. I am to take over the detachment. I hate to leave Edith and my other friends here. Well, it's probably for six weeks only, and I always like to see something new. So today I packed because I have to leave tomorrow.

Velden to Graz, September 27, 1945

Early departure for Graz. Unfortunately, I could not drive alone but had to pick up a few patients, transfers from the 31st General Hospital, where I had to wait a long time until I was finally loaded. There were two alternate routes and I chose the more scenic one. I was not disappointed, even though the road was very bad. Luckily, my patients all were sitting cases and didn't mind being rocked around a little. The country has begun to look like autumn—the leaves have turned to yellow, red, and brown. The sun was out after many a drizzly day, and the villages we passed looked clean, with their shiny red roofs. Here and there we saw the evidence of war—destroyed bridges and rubble of bombed-out houses. The road led first north and the country was quite hilly. Then we turned east and the farther we progressed, the flatter the land became. At 4 P.M. I arrived at the outskirts of Graz. The hospital is at the other end of town. Although I drove only through the suburbs, it was apparent that Graz had suffered tremendously under aerial bombings. I didn't even have time to unpack. Jane pounced on me with her usual energy and insisted on showing me around immediately and introducing me to everyone—the Colonel in charge of the hospital, the Sergeant in charge of the reception room, the Corporal in charge of the mess, etc. I was by now so weary that I had only one wish—to make Jane stop talking so that I could take a shower and go to bed!

Graz, September 28, 1945

Jane left first thing in the morning, and I was very relieved to see her go. She seems to have taken on Pat Hall's characteristics, pushing everyone to constant activity, useful or not. Now I am in charge here. Our billets are in one wing of the hospital. They consist of two very large rooms and two smaller ones, an entrance hall, and a huge bathroom. One of the large rooms serves as our sitting room with one corner for my office. Six of the girls share the other big room, which looks exactly like a hospital ward. The two smaller rooms have two beds each. For the time being I occupy one of these rooms alone. Since we are part of the hospital, we have the comfort of as much hot water and heating as we need. Each room also has a washbasin with hot and cold running water. Our dining room is located next to the soldiers' mess. The food is typical Army food, not a bit like what we are used to at 502.

On my first day with the eight-girl detachment I won their appreciation by engaging a cleaning woman through the hospital office. She will clean and polish the floors, basins, etc. Jane, with her mania for keeping everyone busy every minute of the day, had assigned this job to the stand-by girl.

Graz, September 29, 1945

Our work here consists of taking the discharged patients every morning and delivering them to their units, stationed in a radius of about fifty miles around Graz. These trips seldom take longer than five hours. After lunch we clean up our cars and then, as far as I am concerned, the girls are free, except for the stand-by driver, who is on call for twenty-four hours, and myself. I have to go to the hospital office every evening to get the discharge list. Then, in my office, with the help of a map, I work out the routes for the drivers. The entire operation seems like a bus service! The drivers report to the hospital office in the morning, each with the list I made out for her, and we call the names for one ambulance to Bruck, another to Loeben and surroundings, a third—the Graz Local, etc. I try to change the routes often so that we can all familiarize ourselves with the terrain. There are no stretcher cases, no more casualties. It's fun to drive young and healthy soldiers, not to have to worry about a bad road and broken spines, not to hear groans during the long hours of slow driving, but to chat with happy men—happy because they're out of the hospital, happy because they're going back to friends, but most of all happy because soon it will be over. Home has become quite near to them. Each one talks about how many points he has and what release group he's in and when he thinks the 'great day' will be.

This morning I sent myself to Bruck, about fifty miles from Graz. The weather was perfect, the countryside beautiful, my passengers happy. On the way back, since I was all alone, I sang all the way. I was home in time for lunch and at 4 P.M., after finishing maintenance on "68," I went riding. The 48th General Hospital has a stable nearby with about thirty horses, for the use of patients and personnel. Di and I went riding for two hours—wonderful!

Graz, September 30, 1945

No discharges on Sunday so I gave everyone but the stand-by the day off. I myself had to work almost all day filling out returns since it's the end of the month and the reports have to go to Velden. Edith needs them to incorporate them into the general statistics.

Graz, October 1, 1945

Today I put myself on stand-by. I really like it here. Of course, I miss my friends, but soon it will be my turn to drive to Klagenfurt, our longest trip, and stay overnight at Velden.

Graz, October 3, 1945

I can't write much today. I just received a letter from Uncle Hans, who had heard from an aunt in Sweden that my parents died on a transport to the concentration camp at Auschwitz. I can't believe it. It isn't 'official' news. I *won't* believe it.

Graz, October 4, 1945

I still can't comprehend yesterday's news. I will put it out of my mind since no one knows for certain what has happened.

There was not much work today. I took the Graz run. Once again it is raining and the temperature has fallen considerably. A cold, gray day—inside, outside, everywhere.

Graz, October 5, 1945

Once again to Leibnitz. It was still pouring. I didn't feel well, probably getting a cold. My chest was very tight and my throat sore, but I didn't want to go to bed. One of the girls suggested that three of us go to the theater to see *As You Like It*. My first reaction was to refuse. I was thinking about my folks all the time and was in no mood to have fun. But then in my mind I heard my father saying, "Life goes on, dear Adeline. You must live it to the full." And I could hear my mother saying, "Of course. Vati is right." So I agreed to go. Since we're not allowed to use our ambulances for recreational purposes, we had to take the tram. From the moment we climbed aboard until we alighted, the civilians stared at us, taking in every detail of our uniforms, our make-up, our hair styles. Being quite sure that we couldn't understand a word they said, they criticized in loud voices that often ended in discussions from one end of the car to the other.

The theatre is a rather provincial affair; at least, so it seemed to me after attending the theatre and opera in Rome. Still, I enjoyed it immensely, especially since I understand the language. The audience was almost as interesting as the performance. There were women in evening dresses next to others dressed in men's slacks and jackets, cast-offs from their soldier-husbands. Fur coats and wooden shoes were not an uncommon combination. The lack of men was quite evident. They are scattered everywhere, in prison camps and in hospitals, or dead on some battlefield.

Upon returning home, I found the girls full of excitement. The hospital office had called. One ambulance with two drivers was requested to take one of the nurses to Vienna. Naturally, we all wanted to go and for the sake of fairness drew straws to settle the matter. Diana and I were the winners. Actually, I should not go because my cold has gone into my chest and, I'm sure, is developing once again into bronchitis. But who can resist this new adventure? The Russian Zone is still a mystery and the source of fierce rumor and speculation. Diana and I are thrilled at the prospect before us and a little bit scared too.

Graz to Vienna, October 6, 1945

I felt groggy with sleep when the alarm rang at 5 A.M. The kitchen had prepared an enormous package of sandwiches for us, and by 6 A.M. we were ready to start—Diana and I and the VAD, our passenger for Vienna. For a while the landscape remained the same as around Graz, hilly and pretty. Later, as we neared the Russian Zone, we began to climb toward the Semmering Pass. It was terribly cold and rained buckets, and since the driver's cabin is canvas-covered only, we did not enjoy the drive. At 2 P.M. we arrived at the border between the British and Russian Zones. The British guard glanced at our pass, waved us through, and hurried back into his warm station house. We crossed a narrow strip of no-man's land. By now we were quite apprehensive because we had heard so much about the terrible Russians and everyone had given us a lot of advice about how to behave and deal with them. Then we were there, at the Russian barrier. Strange that within one country, borders now exist where there had been none before. It was exactly like crossing from one country into another. Men came pouring out at the sight of our Red Cross ambulance. One of them strode over, saluted us in a most cordial yet solemn manner, and requested our pass, an elaborate paper stating in three languages, French, Russian, and English, that we had permission to travel through the Russian Zone for the purpose of proceeding to Vienna. The paper was closely scrutinized by all present, turned this way and that for so long that Di and I began to wonder if any of these fellows could read. After about fifteen minutes and much discussion, they finally seemed satisfied and returned our pass.

We were about to leave when five Russian officers rushed up and demanded that we take them along to Vienna. Since the back of our ambulance was empty except for the VAD, we really had no choice. They would not have let us through otherwise. Nevertheless, we were a little scared. The first thing we noticed in the Russian Zone was the lack of motorized transportation. Until we reached Vienna we did not see a single Russian truck or automobile, only horse-drawn carts, entire convoys of them, reminiscent of pictures I had seen from World War I. Where had all the mechanized equipment gone, with which the Russians had conquered Germany and Austria? Where was all the equipment that America and Great Britain had given them? The Russian soldiers we saw walking or riding on horseback along the road looked rather bedraggled. All, however, were heavily armed, rifles slung across their backs, pistols in holsters, even ominous-looking knives hitched to their belts, and all had ammunition belts hanging from their shoulders. Many of them were Mongol in feature and dressed in heavy quilted jackets, giving the impression that once again Attila's wild hordes had invaded Europe. Every village or town we passed was decked out with red flags, and life-sized pictures of Stalin, Molotov, and Russian generals hung on every prominent building and lamppost. It reminded me of Nazi Germany.

Our five Russian hitchhikers were quite amusing. They didn't understand a word of English but had a smattering of German. There was a child-like quality about them. Eyes and mouths wide open, they studied every detail of our uniforms and make-up. They seemed quite primitive in taste and behavior, meeting each new experience with wonder and disbelief. But they were very friendly, once they had accepted us. However, I would not have liked to cross them. We offered them some of our cigarettes. They were smoking the vilest smelling weed and by giving them some of our Virginias, we had hoped to improve the air in the ambulance, but they insisted on keeping our cigarettes, tucking them carefully into their wallets and thanking us with tears in their eyes. They said they would save them and take them home to Russia. One would have thought that we had given them our most precious possessions! Then cigarette puffing was resumed. They were chain-smokers, and wisps of putrid-smelling smoke once more filled the ambulance. I opened my cigarette case a second time and offered them each another cigarette, this one to be smoked! My kind act started a discussion about women. One officer stated that foreign women surpassed Russian women in desirability because they were more feminine in their ways. They wore make-up and dressed more decoratively. Russian women, he added, were practically like men and looked like men. This recital caused violent objections from several of the other officers, who upheld the loveliness of all Russian women, young and old alike! As the debate continued they were almost at each other's throats, but suddenly the boldest of the men asked me about my private life. Did I have a husband or a boyfriend? Did I still love him? I hastily changed the subject.

After we had passed the border into the Russian Zone, we steadily descended until we reached flat country. The road became worse and worse. What once had been a good highway now was pockmarked with bomb craters, especially as we neared Wiener Neustadt, a city about thirty miles from Vienna. Di was driving at a good speed, spurred on by the pleadings of our Russians, who were in no particular hurry but loved the thrill of a fast ride. They egged her on until we were all in the spirit. Suddenly an enormous bomb crater loomed up before our startled eyes. Too late to brake the car, Di swerved sharply to the side, hoping to clear the deep hole. Our two right wheels slipped off the road and the top-heavy ambulance leaned precariously over to the right. I held my breath, sure that we would tip over, but the ambulance righted itself. Even before we could sigh with relief our Russians whooped with laughter and shouted, "*Wunderbar! Wunderbar!* Do it again!" Happy and expectant, they sat waiting for the next pothole, but we ignored them and drove at a speed not exceeding twenty-five m.p.h. the rest of the way.

Wiener Neustadt was nothing but one enormous pile of rubble. By 1 P.M. we arrived at the outskirts of Vienna. The rain was still pouring down and the city made a depressing impression. The first traffic stop we approached was regulated by a large Russian girl in an MP uniform. When she saw our Red Cross car rolling toward her, she snapped to attention, saluted us, clicked her heels, and gave us the right of way. Di and I felt very important. It was the first time we had been acknowledged with a salute. Our Russians told us that most of their women soldiers were used as traffic police. At the next large intersection they asked us to stop, and, with bows, stamping of heels and more salutes, they bade us goodbye.

We asked our way to British HQ and drove on through the downpour. Everything looked dreary. The wide streets of the city must at one time have been very beautiful, but now they are badly damaged. Street fighting and aerial bombing have taken a tremendous toll—desolation and destruction everywhere. We finally found HQ, situated in the former SS barracks in the Schönbrunner Park. After reporting our arrival, we drove over to the hospital, where we delivered our VAD passenger. There we were asked to have lunch and also were told that we could spend the night in the ATS ward. (A few British ATS girls are stationed here, doing clerical work at HQ.) After lunch Di and I decided to drive a little around Vienna while it was still daylight. Since we had not touched our package of sandwiches, we wanted to give them to a hungry Viennese. Soon we sighted a bedraggled old woman, but as I reached down to try to give her the package her eyes widened with fear and she ran from us as fast as her legs could carry her. The next time, we tried a child, but the poor thing ran off, crying. We tried twice more to give away our food, but always with the same result. Perhaps with our fur-lined goggles, our battle jackets over which we had pulled sheepskin-lined leather jerkins, and our fur-lined flying boots we resembled figures from outer space! If only they had waited to see what the package held they would have fainted with pleasure. We finally opened the package so that the sandwiches were visible and deposited it in the middle of a sidewalk. We drove off, removing our threatening presence, hoping that someone would discover the food before the rain ruined it.

Di and I then drove along the Ring, still a beautiful, wide boulevard. We saw the burned-out Opera House, ruins wherever we looked. Almost every third house is destroyed. There are no stores, no coffee houses, and few people on the streets. The once gay city is now nothing but a starving heap of rubble. The wind blew more strongly and cut more icily than I had ever felt it before. It was growing dark and we were frozen stiff so we decided to return to the hospital, but unfortunately we didn't get back there for another two hours. As we turned a corner we were stopped by a small crowd. A woman had been hit by a streetcar and an MP, seeing our ambulance, requested that we take her to a hospital. We drove to three different civilian hospitals, but all refused to take her since they were overcrowded with typhus cases. Finally, a fourth hospital, quite a way out, accepted her. The poor woman had bled a lot and our ambulance was a mess.

It was quite late when we finally got back to our hospital. We had missed dinner but were grateful for the warm beds. The ATS ward had fifteen beds, only five of which were occupied. One of the girls here was very badly hurt. She had been hit by a Russian car and there wasn't much hope that she would live. All evening long the other four patients related horrible tales about the Russians, which verified the stories we had heard at Graz and Velden. Apparently, any girl is fair game for a Russian soldier.

Vienna to Graz, October 7, 1945

At 6 A.M. I was awakened by the morning Sister, who pushed a thermometer into my mouth! She thought Di and I were two new cases who had been admitted during the previous shift. We set her straight. After a good breakfast we left Vienna at 8:45 A.M. It was still raining, off and on, but nothing like yesterday's downpour. We arrived in Graz five hours later, without further incident. The trip has taken more out of me than I care to admit. I think my cold has developed into a bad bronchitis. I ought to go to bed, but I'm going out tonight, rain or no rain, to see Pucini's *Madame Butterfly*. Graz looks so good! It may be a small, provincial town and its inhabitants not too nice to us, but it's wonderful compared to Vienna.

Graz, October 9, 1945

I have come to know the country around Graz within a radius of a hundred miles—Bruck to the north, Loeben to the northwest, and the Yugoslavian border to the south and southeast. Now, for the first time, I realize Europe's immense problem with displaced persons. Every day when I travel the roads there comes toward me an unending line of people, traveling from the East to the West. Most of them are Yugoslavs who are returning from Poland and Russia. At first I thought that I was meeting gypsies. Using horse-drawn carts, whole families sit atop their possessions, the men wearily leading their horses. Others camp by the side of the road. I never see a smile on any of their faces. When I witness this flow of human misery continuing day after day, night after night, hundreds and thousands of refugees, I know that it will take years to resettle these people. Clearing up the after-effects of a war is as great a task as winning a war.

Graz, October 11, 1945

The sun has been out all week, although it is quite cold. I am feeling a bit better, but my chest still sounds awful. I don't want to see a doctor because he would just order bed rest. I'd rather work. I like it here more and more. The work itself is fun, the girls are easy to get along with, and my hours off are most enjoyable.

Last week at the General Hospital office I met a most fascinating civilian worker, the German translator. She is from an old, aristocratic Viennese family, a Baroness no less. Though such people reputedly were the backbone of Hitler's supporters in Austria, when we met, her manner and culture completely disarmed me. We became friends of a sort, and I invited both her and her sister to tea, which, of course, is strictly against regulations. My platoon did not like this at all and turned up their noses. They are strictly against fraternization. Then today I accepted the Baroness's invitation to coffee and met her brother, still in his officer's uniform, but without the insignia. The conversation around the table was interesting, even stimulating, yet I must admit that I felt uncomfortable and out of place. I shall not continue this relationship. For recreation I'll confine myself to the occasional theatre or opera performance and will stop for tea at the YMCA. There is nothing else here—no stores, and, as usual, the only thing to buy are picture postcards.

Graz, October 12, 1945

The weather is still beautiful, cold but sunny. My turn for the Loeben run, but tomorrow I'll put myself on the Klagenfurt trip and will stay in Velden overnight. It will be great to see everyone again. I've been gone from there for two weeks now.

Graz to Velden, October 13, 1945

Left Graz at 8:30 A.M. This time I took route 118, which is a longer but far better road. Unfortunately, the sun soon disappeared and it began to rain. The temperature fell quickly and the cold wetness penetrated. I had quite a bit of pain in my shoulder and after a few hours, driving became a torture. Arrived at Velden at 2:30 P.M. A few hours with my back close to the fireplace in the office and a little chatting with Edith did me good, but I felt miserable just thinking of tomorrow's drive back.

Graz, October 15, 1945

My cough has become much worse. I know that I have an infection. Still, I took the run to Gleisdorf.

Graz, October 17, 1945

I finally gave in and reported to the MO first thing in the morning and, just as I predicted, he diagnosed bronchitis and prescribed bed rest. After much pleading, though, he allowed me to stay in our billets instead of having to be admitted to the hospital. The girls are bringing my food and I can still do the office work.

Graz, October 18, 1945

One of the Red Cross volunteers came to see me and brought me some wool so now I'm knitting a pullover as I lie in bed. Pat, who is our fitter here in case something goes wrong with our cars, is a great help to me. I can totally rely on her to see that everything continues as usual. I still can work out all the routes, schedules, etc., so between knitting, office work and getting a lot of visitors, including the Baroness, the hours pass.

Graz, October 20, 1945

I am still confined to billets. Miss Otto is coming tomorrow so we are cleaning and getting everything in tip-top shape.

Graz, October 21, 1945

I helped the stand-by girl cleaning house since I'm still not allowed to go out. Miss Otto arrived early in the afternoon and her first remark was that I didn't look well at all and probably should be in bed. I took her on a tour of inspection and introduced her to the Colonel in charge of the hospital and to the Matron, both of whom were very complimentary about our work here. Over tea Miss Otto told me it's most doubtful that the Graz detachment will be kept much longer. Instead, 502 will open a much larger detachment in Vienna. Jane, whose discharge papers still have not come through, will be in charge of the Vienna group, with me to assist her. Then when Jane finally leaves, I am to take over. I'm not sure whether to be glad or sorry. Being in charge of the larger detachment would mean a third stripe for me. On the other hand, I had looked forward to being together with Edith again, but since she's already a sergeant, the two of us will have to be in different places. When I told the girls about the probable closure of the Graz detachment, they were sad. In a way, this pleases me because it shows that they like working with me.

Graz, October 22, 1945

I have had it—cabin-fever, it's called. In spite of the doctor's orders, I took today's discharges to Leibnitz.

Graz, October 23, 1945

To Deutschlandberg on a very nice road. In the evening Renia arrived from Velden and brought me a letter from Miss Otto. Now it's final. Our detachment is to be closed within a few days. The girls all make long faces. I am of two minds. I love change and adventure, but then again, Graz with its peace and quiet, its agreeable work, was, I'm sure, much more pleasant than Vienna will be.

Graz to Velden, October 25, 1945

My turn for the Klagenfurt-Velden trip. Unfortunately, it was pouring again and my shoulder was very painful. When I arrived in Velden I was so tired that I went to bed immediately. Everyone is busy preparing for the move to Vienna and Jane is ecstatic. I shudder at the thought of having to work with her and just hope that it won't be for long!

Velden to Graz, October 26, 1945

I left Velden early and was back in Graz by noon. Once again I was struck by the contrast between our peaceful life here and the noisy activity at Velden. I took a hot bath and played a little chess with Renia. It's all so comfortable here. When I think of Vienna, where we are supposed to be billeted with another ATS company and eat in their mess hall, and then on top of it having to deal with Jane, I feel sick!

Graz, October 28, 1945

Already a new MAC has taken over here—all men. We spent the entire morning packing and after lunch five ambulances, with Pat, our fitter, in the lead left for home—Velden, that is. The three of us who are still here will leave tomorrow.

Graz to Velden, October 29, 1945

Up early. We loaded our remaining possessions, including our workshop equipment. The left-over food rations I gave to the cleaning woman and the Baroness, both of whom were overjoyed to receive such delicacies as coffee, sardines, and cheese. At noon we started back to Headquarters. The weather was cold but sunny and we arrived in Velden, quite frozen, before dark.

Velden, November 1, 1945

I picked up my gray-blue flannel suit from the dressmaker. It turned out beautifully. Wonder when I'll wear it—I hope on my leave to England. A quick visit to the hairdresser for a haircut, a round of goodbyes, a last drink at the bar in the evening, and I'm ready to leave, but not gladly.

Velden to Vienna, November 2, 1945

The first convoy, Jane leading eight ambulances, left Velden at 7:30 A.M. I started half an hour later with the other eight ambulances. Everyone waved goodbye and we were off. The drive was not very pleasant. It rained almost constantly, was terribly cold, and the wind blew through our canvas-covered driver's cabins as if we were driving in open cars. Around noon we passed the border into the Russian Zone. Shortly after that, one ambulance in my section had a breakdown, but our fitter, Monica, fixed it quickly. This time the last thirty miles from Wiener Neustadt to Vienna seemed to stretch endlessly. Finally around 5 P.M., in the pitch dark and pouring rain, we arrived in Vienna. My orders were to report to the 70th General Hospital where I was to meet Jane, who was to lead us to our new quarters. I found the hospital without much difficulty, but nobody there knew anything about us or about any orders for ATS quarters at the hospital. Nobody had seen or heard anything of Jane or the eight ambulances of her section. So, there I stood with my convoy in the pouring rain, the girls all hungry and tired, and no one knew what to do with us. After much telephoning and an hour's wait, the word was that all the plans had been changed. We were to live in Schönbrunner Barracks. An MP led us there. Jane was waiting. Before I could utter a word of reproach (after all, she should have been at the hospital to inform me about the change, or, at least, have left a message) she burst forth with her usual chatter: "Where have you been? Isn't this place dreadful? You poor girls look all done in. Let me show you around! Oh, and get your wet things off! I have to tell you . . ." Well, that is Jane, all right. I was too tired to listen. We unpacked only the most necessary things. Will write more about our new billets tomorrow. Suffice it to say that everyone is in a foul mood.

Vienna, November 3, 1945

The Schönbrunner Barracks are the English Headquarters, situated behind the castle and park. A little apart from the barracks is a row of duplexes in which the ATS are quartered. One of these is ours. It consists of two four-bedroom flats, each with kitchen and bath. The entire complex makes a bleak impression. Everything is furnished in typical Army-barracks style—bed, cupboard, and soldier's box. There is no hot water and the bitter cold seeps through the walls. The mess hall is a ten-minute walk away. Eight hundred men eat in one part of it, three hundred women in the other. Jane, as Sergeant, is not allowed to eat with us but must take her meals in the Sergeant's Mess. She is mad. For the first time since training camp in Sarafand we have to stand in line with our mess kits and get the most unappetizing food slopped onto our tin dishes. We are made very much aware of how spoiled we have been at 502 and what a privileged life we have led. After breakfast Jane called a meeting at which she informed us of all the news with regard to our work here. Apparently, as is usual in the Army, we don't seem to be needed here, although we were almost chased from Velden, so urgent were the orders! In all probability, at least some of the ambulances will be sent back to Velden. I hope I'll be among them. More details will follow tonight.

After the meeting we took four ambulances and drove around Vienna to familiarize ourselves with the layout of the city. Vienna is very large but basically laid out in a well-planned fashion. There still are only a few people in the streets, but this, my second impression of Vienna, is a better one than my first. In the Kärntnerstrasse I pulled over for a minute, consulting my map, when a lorry came careening by, passing so close that it smashed my sideview mirror and then continued at top speed without even looking back. I caught only a glimpse of the driver's Russian uniform. They really do drive like idiots!

In the evening we had another meeting. Jane's decision was that I am to go back to Velden with four others—a total of five ambulances. We five are more than happy.

Vienna to Velden, November 5, 1945

We did not return in convoy formation because three ambulances had to take transfers from Vienna to the convalescent home in Velden. We loaded the fourth ambulance with all our kit and I left as the last one, fully packed with all kinds of stores that the girls who remain in Vienna have decided they do not need. As usual, it was pouring. Nine hours later I reached Velden, weary and chilled to the bone, but happy to be back. Unpacked immediately, hoping that I won't have to pack again for a while, but I suppose that will remain just a wish. Eventually, Jane will get her discharge and I'll have to return to Vienna as Sergeant in charge. In the meantime, for the next two weeks at least, I am to take Edith's place here. She's starting her leave tomorrow. It's too bad that, since both of us are NCOs, we hardly see each other.

Velden, November 9, 1945

Almost every day I spent in the MT office, doing Edith's job. In this cold weather it's really the nicest place to be. However, when Edith comes back I suspect that it will be my job to take charge of our carpark, Jane's former job. That is, I'll have to see to it that all drivers do their maintenance properly and that there always are enough cars in tip-top shape and that those cars 'off the road' are speedily repaired. I don't really care for such duty.

Velden, November 15, 1945

A week has passed since I wrote last and not much has happened except that Miss Otto called me into her office and, as I expected, informed me that with my third stripe I will become Sergeant in charge of the yard. I accepted the job but am not too happy about it.

Velden, November 16, 1945

I woke up this morning to the special kind of stillness that only snow can bring. What an enchanted view when I looked out! A white blanket had been spread overnight on the hills, the roofs, the trees.

This was my last day in the MT office. Edith returns tonight, which means that I'll start my outdoor duties tomorrow. Still, I'm awfully glad that she'll be here again. I missed her a lot. In the afternoon we had a Company meeting, at which it was decided that we have too many ambulances and that five of them should be taken off the road. That's fine with me. It will mean five cars less to worry about.

Velden, November 17, 1945

A very busy day for me. Six of us worked on three ambulances, preparing them for their 'hibernation.' It was hard work, taking off their enormous tires, removing the batteries, etc. After a few hours our hands were so stiff and blue that we had to go inside to defrost. We finished the job by 3 P.M.

Velden, November 19, 1945

Edith was on convoy duty so I was once more transport NCO. How nice to sit in the warm office! To be sure, the hours are much longer, but I do prefer office work to dirty yard work.

Velden, November 22, 1945

Every two weeks we have vehicle inspection of all ambulances, and it's one of my new duties to accompany Miss Otto on these rounds. All went well.

Velden, November 26, 1945

I had a rude shock today. Miss Otto told me that my application for home leave to England had been refused. England was not my home and having a sister there was not sufficient reason to grant me leave to Britain.

What more reason do they want? If it is true that my parents are gone (and I still insist on that *if*, because I can't accept it as a certainty), then my sister is the only close relative I have left, and I haven't seen her for nine years. I'm terribly upset, but Miss Otto consoled me and promised to explore some other avenues.

Velden, November 27, 1945

Jane's papers finally have come through, so either Edith or I will have to take over the Vienna detachment. Since I'm so down from yesterday's disappointment, Edith is going to ask Miss Otto if both of us can go to Vienna. That would, of course, mean that I give up my Sergeant's stripe, but I'd rather do that and be with Edith.

Edith just returned from seeing Miss Otto, who agreed that for the time being we can both go to Vienna and that my promotion will have to wait. We'll leave here within a week.

Velden, November 29, 1945

It has been snowing for days. Yesterday I had to work in the yard and it was miserable, freezing cold. At 3 P.M. it already was so dark that we had to stop working, and I was glad of it. Today I was transport NCO, thank goodness. But every time someone came into the office an icy wind blew in and I was busy in three languages: Please shut the door! *Bitte, mach die Tür zu! Tisgeri bewakasha et hadelet!* The stove, too, took up much of my time. It either got too hot or started to smoke or wanted to go out altogether. The wood is so wet that it needs an expert to keep the fire just right.

Velden, December 1, 1945

It's still snowing. Velden and its surroundings are more picturesque than ever, like a Christmas landscape. But we have more and more trouble keeping our rooms warm because of the damp wood we have to use. Driving, too, is no pleasure. Many of the roads are not being cleared and we need chains. Putting those on and taking them off with fingers frozen stiff is not an easy task. Edith and I are beginning to pack again. Day after tomorrow we'll leave for Vienna.

Velden to Vienna, December 3, 1945

Outdoors it looked as if the sky would let loose. We both started at 8 A.M., fetched four sitting cases from the Convalescent Depot, and were on our way. Until noon, driving was not bad. We kept just ahead of the rain clouds and made good time. At 1 P.M. we stopped for a short picnic. By 4 P.M. the rain finally caught up with us and really came down. Edith wanted me to take the lead since I had made this trip before, but I hated to because by now it was quite dark and I couldn't tell from my rearview mirror whether she was following me. My windshield wipers suddenly gave up and I was almost blinded by the pounding rain. The road seemed endless and looked different from what I remembered. I was afraid that somewhere I had taken a wrong turn and we no longer were driving toward Vienna. We passed no villages and, of course, in this weather there wasn't a soul on the road. I was exhausted from the long hours, the uncertainty, and the eyestrain. At last we saw some lights, a few little houses and a man on a bicycle. He told us that Vienna was about an hour's drive ahead. Thank goodness, because by now both of us were dead tired, chilled, wet through and through, and very hungry. It seemed like an eternity since we had left Velden. Soon we saw more and more lights and just by the underpass before entering the city proper I stopped to make sure that Edith was still behind me. Thirty minutes later we had delivered our patients and then drove to the Schönbrunner barracks. My first impression of our quarters was that everything is far better than when I was here last with Jane. Above all, we now have hot water. Though we were dog-tired, we unpacked immediately and I helped Edith arrange our room. In no time she put up some drapes, we hung a few pictures, put curtains over wooden crates, and within an hour we had turned our barracks quarters into a charming room, thus keeping up the tradition that our room always is the most comfy of all. Most of the credit for this belongs to Edith.

Vienna, December 4, 1945

This morning I was stand-by and in the afternoon Pat Curlewis took Edith and me on a trip around the city to familiarize us with the layout. Vienna has changed remarkably since I was here four weeks ago. Some of the rubble has been cleared away, there are more people in the streets, and even a few shops have opened their doors. In the evening I had my first job. The 70th General Hospital called. I had to take a stretcher case from there to another hospital. I found my way easily, though it was quite dark and, of course, raining. It always seems to rain in Vienna.

Vienna, December 5, 1945

The work here reminds me of the old days in Egypt. Every day each of us is detailed at a different hospital or MI Room, where we sit all day, waiting for calls. We take along our knitting, read a lot, and write letters. From time to time we are called out into the bitter cold to drive a few sitting cases, take an MO home, or bring him back to duty. The days are long, boring, and therefore tiring.

Vienna, December 6, 1945

Jane and Pat Curlewis have left and Edith now has taken over the office. There are ten drivers besides us and we all get along beautifully. We live in our two apartments like one happy family. Most of the time we're free in the evening, but, except for a visit to the theater or opera, we spend our off-time at home. We get only one day off every tenth day, but Edith manages to take at least half a day when it's my day off so we can do things together.

Vienna, December 9, 1945

Stand-by, and I was glad of it. It was so cold outside that everyone hated to go out. An absolutely icy wind is blowing. The windshields freeze over and we have to throw hot water on them to clear them. In a few cars even the petrol froze overnight.

Vienna, December 10, 1945

On duty at Kitchener Barracks. I hate this place. We burn all the furniture we can find in the unused part of the building to keep warm, but just when we get a bit more comfortable, the fireplace begins to smoke so badly that we must retreat to another ice-cold room.

Vienna, December 11, 1945

My day off and Edith found a replacement in the office so that we can spend the day together. After breakfast we searched out the American Red Cross and inquired if they needed people. We would be interested in working for them after our discharge. They were not very encouraging. Vienna is very spread-out and the distances enormous. There is no place to stop for lunch or just a cup of coffee so we made for home, disappointed, tired, hungry, and frozen to the bone.

Vienna, December 12, 1945

Mirah has discovered a bakery nearby and we take turns fetching fresh rolls every morning. Whenever an ambulance arrives from Velden—and that happens almost weekly now—it always brings us boxes of food. The larders in our two kitchens are well-stocked and it is now very seldom that we take the long walk to the awful ATS mess with its noise and miserable food. What I hate even more than the standing in line there with one's mess kit is what happens after the meal. Outside the mess hall stand half a dozen huge garbage cans, into which we scrape the remains of our food. These cans are surrounded by dozens of children and old women, containers in hand, begging for the leftovers—a chunk of bread, a tiny piece of meat, half a potato. The shy ones scrape out the garbage cans without looking at us. Since we pass all this misery on our way into the mess hall, we lose our appetite before beginning to eat. So now we do most of our own cooking.

Even so, there are reminders, incidents that make us ashamed of our full stomachs. The char-woman engaged to clean our two flats is a frail and sad-eyed creature. She goes about her work like a frightened little mouse. Yesterday I was slicing a piece of Emma's bread when she walked into the kitchen. I cut off another chunk and offered it to her.

To my chagrin, she fell to her knees with a sob and kissed my hand. "*Fräulein!* You are too good, too kind!" I could not speak for my embarrassment.

Today I was on duty at Schönbrunn and was called out on a job in the afternoon. In the evening three of us once again went to the opera, *Cavalleria Rusticana* and *Pagliacci*. Excellent! My Army years certainly have given me the opportunity to catch up on my musical and theatrical knowledge. Growing up under the Nazis deprived me of that experience in Germany. In Palestine I had neither the opportunity nor the means, and it was not until I came to Rome that I began to enjoy and appreciate the opera. However, today's performance was not without hazards for us. The stage is enormous and of great depth, curtained off at various points. One by one, as the performance progressed, these partitions were lifted and an icy blast, originating upstage, whistled downstage and circulated through the shivering audience. In spite of our blankets, which we had carried with us, we were sure that we would freeze in our seats. After the final curtain we left the theater, expecting to be met by one of our ambulances, an arrangement we had made before leaving. We looked forward to a hot cup of tea in our quarters. But there was no ambulance in sight. The three of us stood huddled under our blankets, close against the building. One by one the theater crowd thinned out until no one remained except a couple of stragglers, two British officers, and ourselves. Still, no ambulance. A staff car pulled up to pick up the British officers. We approached them and were about to ask for a lift, when off they drove without even a glance in our direction. We looked at each other, flabbergasted. How could our own comrades leave us in the lurch? Then it dawned on us that, covered in our blankets, the officers probably had taken us for prostitutes, lingering around where they could make contact with the Army. The night closed in. Now we were really scared. The tales we had heard about Russian soldiers were present in all our minds. And then they came, seven or eight of them, staggering along the street and very drunk but not so drunk that we escaped their notice. They formed a weaving circle around us and stared. Child-like laughter and the stench of bad liquor poured from their lips. They jabbered in Russian and their huge hands began to reach out to grab at our blankets. Then—the most welcome sound I ever heard in my life, the frantic honking of the horn of our ambulance. In seconds we were into the car and Pat had pulled away. It wasn't her fault. She had been delayed by an unexpected detail, but I feel sure that we had been within seconds of a nasty confrontation with the Russians.

Vienna, December 13, 1945

I'm still thinking about our narrow escape last night. The Russians certainly scare us, yet sometimes one cannot help feeling sorry for them. The other day Mirah related the following incident. On her way from Velden to Vienna she gave a lift to a Russian soldier. Enroute, he unwrapped a dirty piece of cloth and took from it a grimy onion and one small potato, undoubtedly snatched from someone's garden, and started to chew on them, raw. When Mirah turned to him, surprised, he told her in broken German that this was all he had been able to find for the day. Whereas the British, American, and French armies are well provisioned, the Russian soldier is supposed to live off the conquered land. No wonder the Austrians hate the Russians, since neither have enough food. Mirah shared her sandwiches with the poor fellow. It probably was the first time he had seen white bread, with the crust cut off! We have all heard that so many Russian soldiers have been deserting that their officers have orders to shoot on sight any they catch doing so.

Vienna, December 14, 1945

Workshop preparation and inspection for "68." Here we do it all in one day so we don't have to get dirty two days in a row. Of course, in this cold we can't clean our cars as well as usual, but it's good enough for me. Every time I dunk my rag into the petrol can (we clean our engines with petrol) it feels like ice and really hurts. In the evening Miss Otto arrived. We are always glad to see her. She gave us the latest news from Velden and then at the end informed me that she will talk to Group Headquarters about my leave to England. She feels sure that eventually I'll get permission to go. I'm terribly excited, especially since I had quite given up on it.

Vienna, December 16, 1945

This morning Miss Otto drove back to Velden and by evening a dispatch came through by telephone that my leave has been granted and I'll have to be ready to leave within a week! I'm beside myself with joy and already have travel fever.

Vienna, December 20, 1945

On detail at the 70th General Hospital—a very boring day. Not much to do, which is just as well. Driving has become really dangerous. The streets are all iced over and our ambulances slide as if they were on an ice rink. We never drive over ten m.p.h. Still, I'm surprised that there aren't more accidents. A bitter cold wind whistles through the wreckage of demolished houses, of which only the facades still stand intact, like gigantic movie props. Occasionally one hears the creak-creak of weakened masonry as the wind hits it and one feels sure that these walls can collapse at any moment. So devastating is the damage in some sections that whole streets, rubble-filled and impassable, are roped off. Driving is no pleasure at all here.

Vienna, December 21, 1945

Detail at Kitchener Barracks. By noon I had finished my work and went home. Spent the entire afternoon packing and in the evening, as a farewell celebration, Edith and I went to see *Die Fledermaus*. This was not only a goodbye to Vienna but also a parting for Edith and me for at least a few months because she expects her discharge papers any day now. By the time I return from England, she'll be home with her family in Palestine. I loved *Die Fledermaus*. The performance was colorful and exhilarating, reminiscent of 'Old Vienna.' We had excellent seats, right in the middle of the fifth row front. During intermission, as we walked through the foyer, we were surrounded by Russian, American, French, and English officers, most of them, especially the Russians, in their dress uniforms, and this, too, added to the illusion of being transported back to the glorious days of the Austrian monarchy. What a fitting goodbye to Vienna!

Vienna to Velden, December 22, 1945

Dotty arrived last night while we were at the opera. Her ambulance was loaded with food to replenish the detachment's larders and bottles to restock the bar. She is to take me back to Velden, from where I'll depart on my leave. The two of us started out at 8:30 A.M., bundled up in all the clothes we possessed. It again was bitterly cold, with that icy wind cutting right through us, since the driver's cabin of our ambulances is open. After all, they were not designed for this kind of weather but for desert warfare. However, once on the open road, we began to relax and enjoy the beautiful landscape. A broad, thick carpet of virgin snow lay undisturbed on the land, giving it a serene loveliness. It looks peaceful and gets us into a real Christmas mood. By noon, though, both of us were so frozen that we had only one wish, to get to Velden as quickly as possible and thaw out. We took turns behind the wheel, and by 5 P.M. we were home. How nice it is here. I had almost forgotten. Knotty-pine walls, open hearth—what a treat after the inadequate central heating system in Vienna. How dreary Vienna is in comparison with this. From my window I can see the snow-covered mountains, closing us in from the outside world. I'm glad to be home, though it is for a few days only.

Velden, December 23, 1945

I was not put on the duty roster since I'm busy with packing. Not only do I have to pack for my leave, but also all other possessions which I'm leaving here have to be packed. Who knows what room I'll be assigned when I return from England? The depot here looks and smells very much like Christmas. Everybody is busy decorating our big hall, trimming the huge Christmas tree, and preparing for tomorrow's festivities. Emma and her kitchen staff are baking up a storm. We all are in a mood of happy expectation.

Velden, December 24, 1945

I'm all packed and now am only waiting for my movement orders. Winnie's home leave has come through also so we'll be traveling together, which makes me very happy. Christmas Eve—the traditional dinner with plum pudding. Three cheers for the cook, for 502, for Miss Otto. And then, of course, as always, "Ladies, the King!" Everybody was in great spirits. I, as usual on such occasions, became quite sentimental, for was this not our last Christmas in the Army? Where will we all be by next year and what will this new year bring to each one of us? I can't help reflecting on the past four years of Army life. In many ways it was a sad experience, for what else but tragic can a war be? Yet, in many ways for me and many others, these years have been the fullest years, for the war opened our eyes to more than just daily living. It gave many of us, for the first time in our lives, the feeling of doing something important and worthwhile. And where else do you make friends and companions as you do in the Army? Looking at the girls, I feel that each one of them is familiar to me, each with her hopes, her strengths, and weaknesses. For years we have shared everything. Yet, in a few months, each one of us will go a different way, live a different life, and most of us will even speak a different language. Miss Otto, so capable, what will she do? Go into politics or maybe get married and become the lady of the manor? Pat Curlewis—back to her home in South Africa to live the life of the wealthy? Won't it seem strange to her, when she flies her own plane or is driven around by the chauffeur, to remember how she used to cuss when she greased her own ambulance? Ida wants to live on a sheep farm in her native Australia. And the Palestinians—what will await them? A home and security or more fighting? And I—where will I go? Soon, very soon, I must face the fact that where I am going to live no longer depends on my parents. It is time for me to admit that they are among the millions of the lost—victims of the holocaust.

Velden, December 25, 1945

Of course, there is no real work today. I volunteered to be transport NCO, but there's not much to do in the office either. The joyful Christmas atmosphere pervades everything. Our bar, usually open only from 6 P.M., was opened before lunch and drinks were free. Lunch was served in the big hall and Mary, our Sergeant Major, distributed presents to all the servants. Then each of us got a little gift as well. In the afternoon I had an even better Christmas present. Miss Otto informed me that my promotion to Sergeant finally has come through and I shall go on leave with my new rank. I'm really glad about this. Here at 502, rank is of little importance, but in England it will make a great difference. Besides, I can use the extra pay!

Velden, December 26, 1945 – Boxing Day

Today was very special. We gave a Christmas party for the refugee children who live in one of the camps surrounding Klagenfurt. For weeks our girls have knitted, stuffed toy animals, and sewed gift clothing in preparation. Then it was Emma's turn. She, with the help of a few of the girls, baked and cooked all day to have food for these kids, who probably have never had a really full belly. Six ambulances drove over to the camp, where the little ones were waiting. There were about forty of them, ranging in age from four to seven. Most of them are Yugoslavs, Poles, and Hungarians. That meant language difficulties, which we tried our best to overcome. But the children didn't want to speak anyway. They were so shy that they hardly dared to look at us. Seated at the huge table, which was loaded to capacity, they touched not a morsel of food but sat with dead-serious faces, bewildered and completely tongue-tied. We decided to leave them alone for a little while. When we returned after about fifteen minutes, the table was absolutely empty, but none of the kids were chewing, nor were there any crumbs left on their plates. They sat, silent as before, looking just as sad as they had before. What had happened? One glance at their clothes told us. Their pockets were bulging. They had stuffed it all away. Were they thinking of their parents, brothers, and sisters, or were they just used to hiding away their food, like frightened animals, to store it away in a hurry and eat it later in peace? We acted as if nothing had happened and brought more helpings from the kitchen. I believe Emma secretly wished always to cook and bake for such grateful customers. Now you should have seen the transformation! They ate eagerly, eyes began to sparkle, and they began to jabber. An hour later it looked the way any happy children's party is supposed to look and sound. Then the main event. Joyce had dressed up as Santa Claus and gave each boy and girl a present. At 7:30 P.M. we took them back, contented and tired and probably, for the first time in their little lives, really happy.

Velden, December 27, 1945

Now that the holidays have passed, Winnie and I are getting impatient to be off, but no one knows when the next train will leave. The word is that the roads are impassable because of snow. I don't dare to telegraph my sister because who knows when I'll arrive in England. It's a good thing that my twenty-eight days' leave will commence only when I actually have arrived at my destination.

Velden to Udine, December 28, 1945

I'm now sitting at the officers' hotel in Udine. It all happened very quickly. This morning I was working in the office as transport NCO when Pat Curlewis came rushing in and informed me that a train was leaving from Villach at 1 P.M., and we were to be on it. I ran like crazy over to my room and threw the last few things into my suitcase. As on previous moves, we had been told to take only as much baggage as we could handle by ourselves. Yet when I had finished packing my enormous suitcase, aptly dubbed 'The Piano,' I was unable to lift it. On top of that I also had a smaller bag and my haversack. Thank goodness, we don't have to carry gas masks or steel helmets any more! Winnie had just about as much baggage as I. No sooner had I closed my suitcase than Miss Otto and Mary came around in an ambulance to take us to Villach. Of course, after this mad dash, we waited an hour for the train. A Sergeant helped us with our baggage. So far so good. We had a compartment all to ourselves and the train was well heated. The monotonous clickety-clack of the wheels and the warmth of the car, after all the excitement of the last few hours, made us drowsy, and both of us slept almost all the way to Udine, where we arrived at 8 P.M. At the station we were told that the train for Milan, where we would board the actual leave train to England, was not to leave before 10 A.M. the next day. The RTO sent us to the officers' transit hotel. In a town as small as provincial Udine, there were no special women's quarters, but that was all to the good. We spent a very comfortable night at a good hotel.

Udine to Milan, December 31, 1945

The trip to Milan took only a few hours. Passing through the Valley of the Po, the weather was pleasant, warm enough for us to shed our greatcoats. As the miles dwindled, Winnie's impatience mounted, for her husband was to meet her in Milan. Toward late afternoon we chugged to a halt in one of the most magnificent railroad stations I've ever seen. Winnie scampered to gather her belongings, all the while darting glances through the train window for a glimpse of her husband. As for me, I could not get over the size and beauty of the station. I watched, fascinated, as huge luggage conveyers rolled forward and deposited their loads on elevators large enough to accommodate both luggage and passengers. (The station was above street level.) It all was so new and exciting that I scarcely noticed Winnie tugging at my arm when from out of the crowd walked her husband. They fell about each other's necks like long-lost lovers, which, of course, they were. Alternately crying and laughing with delight, she introduced us. I liked him. He was a man of quiet good looks and gentle manners. But poor Winnie's reunion with her husband scarcely had begun when it was over. "Goodbye, dear! See you tonight, I hope," she called over her shoulder as a Sergeant whisked us off to a waiting lorry.

We drove through the city, past the suburbs, on and on, far out of Milan, and finally stopped in front of a dreary-looking villa. This was the ATS Transit Camp. Inside, it was even gloomier. We sat down to a typical Army meal of gray mutton and suet pudding. After dinner—and precious little we ate—Winnie dashed off to inquire about a pass to see her husband. She was doomed to disappointment. "Sorry. No passes issued today."

The entire transit camp is filled with girls going to England on leave or returning for a re-posting. The house is a continuous escalator of comings and goings, which has not helped give it much of an atmosphere. Daily a posted 'travel list' records the names of those scheduled to leave camp. Meanwhile, one has to be content to sit and wait, conform to strict regulations, and put up with bad food. For some obscure reason, Winnie and I were confined to camp all day yesterday. I rushed to the bulletin board to scan the list. Our names were not there. Disgusted, I ate my way through a tasteless breakfast. Winnie was even more distraught than I. This morning I rushed again to the 'travel list' and again our names were not on it. One of the girls told me that she had been waiting here for a week!

Afternoon brought a reprieve. We were granted a twenty-four hour leave to Milan, to celebrate New Year's Eve. Hurriedly, we put on our dress uniforms and hitchhiked into town, where we secured two rooms at the YWCA, one for Winnie and her husband and the other for me. What does one do on New Year's Eve in a strange town, with a couple very much in love who haven't seen each other in over a year? One can't remain with them constantly. I sat in my room, quite alone and lonely. Outside, the streets were alive with gaiety. The Y was giving a dance downstairs in one of the large halls. I stopped there briefly. The lobby was almost deserted. Bright paper streamers were hung across the walls and a tired piano player made tired music for one lone couple circling the floor. There was lemonade, gallons of it, waiting for guests who still had not arrived. It was a completely lifeless scene, while outside the city was ablaze with light. There was a sound of horns blasting, shouting and merriment. Crowds were gathering to drink joyous toasts to the New Year, even as the girls of 502 were doing. I could not sleep but lay in bed wondering what was in store for me in the coming year.

In Transit to England, January 1, 1946

Our orders were to report back to the transit camp at noon, so, of course, we (Winnie, her husband, and I) set out early to sightsee a bit. Our hotel, the Y, was in the center of town. Four blocks away was the Piazza del Duomo, where we saw the second-largest medieval cathedral in the world. We visited also the Castello Sforza, the Scala, and the Piazza Loretto, where Mussolini and his mistress were executed in April of last year. Milan does not show the signs of hardship and deprivation that Austria has suffered. Her shops display quantities of merchandise; high-priced, true, but available. Back at the camp we were relieved to find our names listed for transport this afternoon, but my relief gave way to horror when I saw another notice tacked on the bulletin board: "Sergeant Bonin in charge of eight ATS girls, proceeding to England." Would the Sergeant please report to the office immediately to receive all traveling papers for the said eight girls? I had looked forward to a nice, restful journey. Now I envisioned myself continuously chasing after eight girls, perfect strangers at that! I would be responsible for what they did. I would not be able to begin my leave until each girl had signed herself in at her destination in England. What did I do to deserve all this? I had become a Sergeant!

Grimly I went to the office and spent an hour listening to rules and regulations, checked for final clearance on my eight charges, rounded them up, and left for the station. The subservience of these eight was amazing to watch. They would not budge, do a thing, or think a thing until I had nodded. They completely relied on me and my judgment. How unlike the members of 502, who are encouraged to use initiative and resourcefulness at all times! Milan Railroad Station was jammed with shouting officers and thousands of soldiers queued up, waiting for dispersal. "Don't you DARE MOVE!" I ordered. The girls sat down obediently on their suitcases and I dashed off to see about tickets.

Securing passage for one can be a troublesome chore. Now I had to multiply that difficulty by eight. "Women Services, all aboard!" Scarcely had I completed the arrangements and hurtled my way through the last of the red tape when the loud-speaker boomed its warning. Fortunately, my group still was intact. All eight girls rose as one, took their suitcases in hand, and followed me to the train. We were arranged four girls to a compartment, except for me. I was given a compartment to myself, but I asked Winnie to keep me company. The train was sparkling clean and well-heated. At 5 P.M. we were on our way. At 5:08 my duties as Sergeant began. There came a knock at the door and a dispatch: "All officers and NCOs in charge will report to Commanding Officer of train." I reported. We were handed the following orders (one copy at least to be displayed in each coach and in NAAFI buffet car).

- You will not allow any personnel to detrain except when ordered. You are responsible that no lamps or train fittings are stolen. The NAAFI buffet car will serve tea and biscuits for the whole train. Every man must bring his own mug. When your coach is called, you will see your coach through as quickly as possible.
- The lighting on this train is by battery, giving ten hours light only, which must last the whole journey.
- You will require your knife, fork, and spoon, mug, and mess tins at each feeding halt. Officers require mugs only.
- You will not allow anyone of your coach to use the train latrines when the train is stopped. Adequate latrines and ablutions are available at each feeding halt.
- As thefts have occurred from these trains, you will detail two men from your coach to remain as train guards at all feeding halts.
- Comments on any untoward incident will be reported to OC Train immediately.

As required, I read all this aloud to my girls.

My pocket map indicated that the route headed north, toward Lake Maggiore. What a pity that it was too dark to see anything. We pulled into Domodossola at 8:30 P.M. "Disembark!" a loudspeaker announced. "Bring your knives, forks, etc." Coach '1 emptied for dinner, then coach '2, coach '3, all down the line with perfect precision. When our coach was announced, we swung off with mugs, tin plates, knives, forks, and spoons, leaving two girls behind, as ordered. We walked off the station platform into deep snow and struggled through to the gigantic mess hall. Our dinner was hot, ample, and good. We also were given sandwiches for our knapsacks, to munch on later. The whole thing was so well-organized, so marvelously carried out that I was truly impressed. After dinner we filed into the restrooms, where Italian civilian workers supplied us with towels, soap, and hot water. "Fifteen minutes until train-time," said the loudspeaker. I gave a hurried wash to hands and face. "Seven minutes." I hastily combed my hair. "Four minutes!" "Come on, girls, let's go!" Life aboard a British leave-train is fast.

When we returned to our coach we learned that a Swiss electric engine had replaced the one used prior to this stop. The engine switch was made at Domodossola because it's the last station before the Swiss border. British trains are free to travel through Switzerland only if they abide by the strict rule that no coal-fed locomotive can be used at any point within the Swiss borders. Coal creates smoke and smoke creates soot and Switzerland will not have the fairy-like quality of its land tarnished. Also, for the privilege of traveling through their country, the Swiss require that Britain pay a good sum, per head, for each soldier transported. It goes without saying that we were not allowed to get off the train at any time while we were in Switzerland. After the lights were switched off, I read for a while, using the flashlight Edith had given me for my birthday.

In transit to England, January 2, 1946

I slept well but very briefly. At 4 A.M. the sound of loud cheers and laughter awakened me. The train had stopped in Lausanne, Switzerland. From my window I saw a fantastic scene. Dozens of Swiss policemen were lined up, patrolling the train to make certain that no one got off. Behind them by the hundreds, as many as the station platform could hold, were Lausanne's citizens, men, women, and even children, their arms full of presents for us, food, cigarettes, chocolate, and souvenirs. They talked to us through the windows, blew kisses, and waved. They had given up their night's rest in order to greet us. What impressed me most about these people was their well-dressed appearance. They all seemed to be rich, clad in furs, children also beautifully dressed and healthy-looking. What a contrast to the threadbare and hungry people in Italy and Austria! We were stopped for an hour in Lausanne, then traveled again along the shores of Lake Geneva. The skies were so dim that I could see scarcely anything. I fell asleep again about 5:30 A.M. and woke up on French soil. The train stopped at Villers-Lès-Pots for breakfast. All day long we traveled across France, passing Dijon, Sens, and the River Seine in the late afternoon. We were on schedule, but it was dark by the time Paris came into view. What a disappointment it was to by-pass this great city. All we could see were distant city lights, which grew dimmer and dimmer as we raced along. Our next stop was Epluches, about eighteen miles north of Paris, for dinner and a wash-up. We bolted down our food in order to have plenty of time to clean up. In the wash room a huge hot water boiler and three or four basins were ready for us. As NCO, I thought it only proper that I take my place last in line. There was half an hour left till train-time, ample to strip completely and enjoy a good wash-up—I thought. I had just finished soaping when a voice announced over the loudspeaker: "All aboard! Train leaves in five minutes. Five minutes until train time!" Five minutes! Why, the walk back to the train alone would consume every minute of it! No time for further calculations. If I was to make that train, I'd have to do it sans clothing! Slightly hysterical, I jumped into my greatcoat, soap and all, grateful for its protective length but horrified at its lack of enough buttons. I stumbled into my boots. With battle-dress in one hand, undies, stockings, soap, and washcloth in the other, using elbows and chin to anchor the gaping coat-front, I ran!

Our compartment was, as fate would have it, at the far end of the long train. This was a source of great distress to me and of equally great delight to two or three hundred soldier passengers, who watched with relish my progress along the platform. I ran like the very devil. All along the way, train windows were flung open. "Hey, Sarge, you're losing something!" Indeed I was! I looked down to see one of my stockings fluttering down the platform. To recover it would have been a time-wasting and downright revealing maneuver. I sprinted on. "Sarge, something's showing!" I did not dare to wonder what was showing but got a firmer grip on my coat, this time forfeiting a pair of panties and the bar of soap. "Yupeeee ATS!" They were really outdoing themselves. So was I! Just as the train gave its first tentative chug, I arrived. With my greatcoat, and what undies I had left, I collapsed in

317

our compartment. The girls fell around me excitedly. When I had managed to quiet them down, and myself, too, I bade them goodnight and went to my own compartment, but I could not fall asleep. Something had gone wrong with the heating system. Frost flowers began to form even inside the windows and my feet felt like two lumps of ice.

In transit to England, January 3, 1946

At 1 A.M. the lights went on and we were told to make ready. We would arrive in Calais in another hour. Now I was getting really excited. England and my sister were very close. It was not until 3 A.M., though, that we left the train. It was cold, damp, and uncomfortable and we were starving. For the first time since our trip began, things were not organized. From Calais we are to cross the channel to England, but the ship is not scheduled to leave until 8 A.M. We had to rouse a grumbling Corporal, who in turn had to awaken the Sergeant, who had to call the officer-in-charge before we could be shown to our 'quarters,' a large tent. There we spent the remainder of the night. A few fortunate ones sat on the available chairs, the rest of us on the ground to await morning and some food. At 6:30 A.M. the camp came to life. Speakers began blasting from every corner, directing us from there to here to there. We felt like headless chickens hopping about, trying to keep up with the instructions, but finally we did get a decent breakfast.

Somewhat apart from the happily chattering girls in uniform was a large group of civilian women and children, huddled in a corner trying to escape attention. Most of them were French and Italian war brides. They looked pitiful, frightened, and lost among their future countrywomen who, with their typical English reserve, would have nothing to do with these foreigners.

Now instructions were given again. We had to change our currency, get ration cards, and be checked in and out of at least a dozen departments. At 8 A.M. the ship left for Folkestone. It was gray and foggy, cold and dreary, but luckily the sea was not rough. I had been led to expect the worst. The 'worst' did happen, though, but not in the manner predicted. As everyone began to go aboard, I looked around frantically. Help, someone! I couldn't lift my 'piano' alone. Where were the gallants, the helpful soldiers who had surrounded me the past few years? What had become of them? Oh, they were there all right, at the railing, hundreds of them, looking down at me, teasing. "Wanted to be a soldier, hey? Soldiers carry a kit bag, not a trunk," they jeered. The MP on the dock spoke to me curtly. "C'mon, Miss. We haven't got all day. Get aboard." I looked at him hopefully, but he merely snapped a page from my travel book and walked away. Finally, with great resolution, I lifted my stuff and began to stagger up the gang-plank, wondering which would tumble off first, me, the piano, or both of us? Everyone aboard was making bets on it, all but one compassionate soldier, who finally rushed down to help. From the moment we arrived at Folkestone until I sat on a train bound for Victoria Station, I was utterly and completely confused. Porters (how odd to see Englishmen in that role) circulated like whirling dervishes, snatching luggage and disposing of it, I knew not where. At one moment my 'piano' rested heavily at my feet, then it was gone, whisked away by some madman, who seemed to know far better than I where I was going. A swirling crowd of people pushed me along with them. Where were the girls, my eight charges? Well, they certainly couldn't have gone far. Suddenly, I felt my little booklet being pulled from my hand and then thrust back into it. This booklet I had been given in Calais, along with a ration card entitling me to small purchases of food and clothing. The transfer-officer had explained that when I went to England, one leaf of the booklet would be removed at each checking station. Now everywhere loudspeakers were shouting: "Page three, have your book ready for page three."

From somewhere a hand shot out, grabbed the book, and gave it back again. "Page four, ready with page four!" In a while all the pages were gone and I was left, empty cover in hand, looking at one of the most provincial trains I had ever seen. Narrow and squat, its compartments had no virtue other than cleanliness. From behind me a familiar "hello" sounded—Winnie! Then I was pushed aboard and the train started. "My God! Where's my piano?" I shouted. A porter appeared and threw it into the compartment.

When we arrived at Victoria Station, my eight charges were all there, waiting. They had been on a different coach of the same train. One of them was a Corporal. "You," I said to her, "from now on *you're* in charge. Look after these girls and make sure they go where they're supposed to." I gave her the papers. "Now, providing that there are no gales to prevent our ship from crossing the channel, we'll meet here in twenty-eight days." And so I left them. After all, they were English and knew how to deal with England far better than I did. I saw Winnie and her husband drive off in a taxi. Standing alone amidst the confusion I secretly wished the twenty-eight days were up and that I was on my way 'home' again.

I waited over an hour for my sister Edith to show up. I was just about to head for a phone booth when I heard her call, "Adi, Adi! Wait!" There she was, at long last, looking positively radiant, healthy and happy and quite the young lady. After asking solicitously about my journey, she started a stream of chatter which continued until the end of my visit. And what do sixteen-year-old girls talk about? About soldiers, mainly American soldiers! No matter. It was wonderful to be with her.

Transit Camp outside Milan, February 6, 1946

It's been over a month since I wrote in my journal. The first few days in England I stayed with the Franks. It was Mrs. Frank who had been instrumental in getting my sister out of Germany and placing her with an English family. Since I wanted to spend as much time as possible with Edith, I immediately began looking for a room for the two of us, no easy task in London at this time. But I was lucky and found one, though it had only two cots and inadequate heating, one of those awful little gas heaters that you had to feed with the correct change, for which in return it would roast your knees, if you came close enough, but let your backside freeze. So, my sister and I set up house. We had not been together since she was seven years old and I sixteen. Now she was sixteen and I twenty-five. I guess it was hard for both of us. I wanted a closeness that I had no right to expect. She could hardly remember me, and when she talked of 'her parents' back when she was little, they were two people totally different from the father and mother I had known. She had put her German past entirely behind her and was a typical English teenager, who did not even want to be reminded of her background. She had been to an excellent boarding school, her English was educated, and she was much amused at mine, which, since I had learned it at 502, was upper-class but still colored with a German accent. She had forgotten her German or, understandably, did not wish to identify with it. We had led such different lives, and, though both of us tried hard, the differences were almost insurmountable. Still, we made the best of the four weeks trying to get reacquainted. She brought me up-to-date about all that had happened to her—her school, her foster parents, her church (she had become Church of England), and, of course, Bill, her latest infatuation. Bill was an American soldier and I sometimes wondered whether it was not so much Bill but the entire American Army that she was in love with. She was quite a flirt and I was a bit concerned for her, but since she resented any criticism, we dropped the subject.

As for England, at least as much as I saw of it, it is entirely different from what I had imagined. For almost four years I have, from morning till night, been living with the English and have been fed 'good old Blighty' from morning till night or, as 502 members, being more refined, called it, simply 'home.' England had become some distant kind of paradise for me. Confronted with it, I found London very much like any other cosmopolitan city. The 'cold' Englishman I had heard so much about was nowhere to be found. The people were just like any other people, friendly and hospitable. Nowhere was I conscious of being a stranger, but then, London was full of foreigners. Only twice did I feel uncomfortable. Clynton Reed had written me that he might be in London over the New Year so I went over to his club with the hope of seeing him. The porter, though polite, made me feel my three stripes. What? No pips, no crowns? I was led into a hall which, though well heated, remained the coldest and most snobbish room I had ever been in. I was out of luck anyway. "Colonel Reed left three days ago," the Club's secretary informed me.

The second time I felt ill at ease, at least at first, occurred when I met Barbara Crocker. (She had been discharged while I was in Vienna.) I had called her soon after my arrival in London and we had made a date to meet at a hotel, have dinner together, and go to the theatre. I had much looked forward to seeing her again, good old Barbara, plump, short, and jolly. I arrived at the hotel early and went over to the news-stand, where I began to thumb through a magazine, when somebody behind me exclaimed, "Adi, dear, halooo!" I turned. It took me several seconds to recognize my old comrade. Here was a woman elegantly dressed in high heels, sheer stockings and a fur coat, smart and well-groomed, not at all the girl I had known in the Army. But over dinner we re-established our camaraderie. The theatre was a success too. We saw *While the Sun Shines,* a comedy about an American in London. I accepted Barbara's invitation to visit her at her home in Kent, about two hours by train from London. It was agreed that Edith and I would take the train the following Saturday. As soon as we pulled into the little station, I saw her. Yes, that was the old Barbara again, slacks, babushka, and all. Only the battle dress was missing. And then, of course, no ambulance but her beautiful car. On our arrival she apologized for the accommodations. The big house had been converted into an officers' rest home so the family now lives in a nearby 'cottage.' That's what she called it. To me it looked more like a mansion. Barbara drove us around the countryside. All in all, we had a pleasant day.

I also took Edith on a weekend trip to Birmingham to visit Helen, one of the Palestinian girls in 502. She had married an Englishman while we were still in Egypt. When he was discharged from the Army (we had just moved to Venice) she, too, left the services for her new home. Her husband works in Birmingham as an engineer. During the two days we stayed with them, Helen drove us around a lot and I had the opportunity to see more of England. Then, of course, I spent a good deal of time with the Franks. They took me to some excellent restaurants. I, in turn, invited them to a well-known place in Soho. Edith and I got tickets for a few plays, and before I knew it my twenty-eight days had passed. I'd had such a good time that I didn't want to leave. During my last days I was glued to the wireless, hoping for gale warnings, but Mother Nature was uncooperative. She produced a rain storm, but not of sufficient magnitude to postpone my departure.

So it was that on the evening of February 1st, I once again met Winnie and her husband at Victoria Station. We boarded the train for Folkestone, were driven to the transit camp there, where we slept about two hours, had breakfast at 5 A.M. and left on the boat at 7 A.M. This time the sea was quite rough and nobody was allowed on deck. I slept on a bunk till Calais. Transit camp, money exchange, lunch, and by 2 P.M. we were aboard the leave train. Winnie and I shared a compartment with one other girl. No 'charges' to take care of this trip. What a relief! The train was well-heated all the way. Again we stopped at Epluches for dinner.

On February 3, after lunch, we crossed into Switzerland, and this time we could appreciate the scenery in the daylight. The sun was out. I looked out the window constantly, admiring the magnificent snow-covered mountains, the charming valleys, marveling at the operatic tableaux unfolding hour after hour. At 5 P.M. we stopped at Lausanne and once again were welcomed by its citizens, who shook our hands and showered us with souvenirs. Finally, at 3 A.M. on February 4, our train pulled into Milan and we were whizzed off to the transit camp. That was two days ago. I've spent the time catching up on some sleep. Yesterday Winnie and I caught a lift and spent a few hours in Milan. We hope there will be a train and movement orders to Udine for us tomorrow.

Milan to Udine, February 7, 1946

Last night our names were on the list. Our transport left at 7:30 P.M. for the station. There nobody knew anything about us. How typically Army. In the end we did manage to get on the train but had to share a compartment with five officers. The train was heated, but there were no lights. Crowded, we spent a rather miserable night.

Udine, February 8, 1946

We finally arrived at Udine at 1 P.M., where we learned that the next train for Villach was not scheduled to leave until Sunday, two whole days from now. We were taken to a transit camp and after a good wash and a change of uniform, I decided to investigate the possibility of getting some other kind of transportation. Just as we were leaving the hotel, who should walk in but Dottie. She had come into town with our 1500 weight lorry. We were awfully glad to see her. She promised to take us back to Velden with her the following day.

Udine to Velden, February 9, 1946

We were off to Velden by noon. Sitting atop great stacks of supplies in the back of Dottie's lorry, Winnie and I traveled in silence, teeth chattering, faces stinging with the cold. When at last we arrived home, tired and quite frozen but still eager for the reunion, a rude surprise awaited me. "Adi, your discharge papers are here. You're to leave for Palestine in nine days." I listened stupified, unable to accustom myself to the news. Quite suddenly, Palestine seemed a remote, strange place. I wanted to stay here, here in this life that had become such a part of me, among friends who were, indeed, my family in every sense of the word. I walked across the icy courtyard and into the big house, where happy 'hellos' cut deep to remind me of a goodbye soon to come.

Velden, February 10, 1946

Velden has changed a lot during the time I have been gone. Our Headquarters have taken on the atmosphere of a transit camp. Each day some of the old members of 502 are leaving, some for England, others for Palestine. A few are off on leave, but most are going home for good. New girls are arriving from England to take their places. They seem younger, inexperienced, and of quite a different background. It just isn't the same any more and I don't like it, but maybe under these circumstances leaving won't be so hard.

Velden, February 13, 1946

The last two days were filled with all kinds of odd jobs. I have been taking out three of the new girls for additional driving instruction. Then I prepared "68" for workshop inspection, probably for the last time. Yesterday I packed a box and took it to the RTO. We are all allowed to send two boxes home. The latest information about my discharge is that all the Palestinian girls are to leave for home by the 20th of this month.

Today Miss Otto summoned me to her office. "I must go to Vienna on Thursday," she said. "Would you like to drive me? You'll have a chance to say goodbye to the girls there." I'm delighted to get away for two days. Besides, I always enjoy driving Miss Otto. It's fun talking with her, and I do look forward to seeing the girls from the Vienna detachment once more.

Velden to Vienna, February 15, 1946

Yesterday was a day I never want to live through again. Early yesterday morning orders from the MP station at Semmering Pass came in that all units must stay clear of that area and that under no circumstances were cars to be driven through. Miss Otto, however, objected to making the trip by train and reasoned that our ambulance could easily get through with no questions asked. So, after breakfast, she and I began the long drive to Vienna. Snowed over, completely covered with treacherous layers of ice, the condition of the highway was very dangerous. I could not drive faster than twenty-five m.p.h. My eyes were glued to the tire marks preceding cars had made. It was imperative to drive a straight course to avoid getting stuck in the mountain snow drifts on either side of us. "A straight line! A straight line!" I kept saying to myself and fought against growing snow-blindness. Several miles outside of Bruck the road descends steeply, curves sharply to the right, and then continues to run parallel to a wide, roaring river some hundred feet below. We reached the curve. I saw the river far below and saw the changed angle of the road. I tried to make a right turn, turning the steering wheel to the right, but the wheels didn't respond and we began to skid. What happened then took only a few seconds but seemed like an eternity. We spun around crazily. Straight ahead a broken, unrepaired railing warned of what lay far below—the icy river bed! "Right! Right!" I prayed. With a last sickening skid the top-heavy ambulance did swing to the right, where it hit a milestone buried in the snow and slowly turned over, cushioned by the high snow embankment. Penny and I scrambled out, our faces as white as the snow that engulfed our car. It was impossible to determine the extent of the damage. We were afraid the milepost had ripped the oil sump, in which case the car would be quite useless. While Miss Otto stayed behind, I walked into Bruck, secured a tow truck at the work shop, and started back, hoping all the time that the car's springs would hold up under the strain they were being put to. I was back with the tow truck within an hour. Penny had not been idle. She had shoveled most of the snow aside and after the tow truck pulled us out, we saw that a damaged fender was all that had resulted from the accident.

At 7 P.M., limp with exhaustion, we arrived at Schönbrunner Barracks. I don't know how I had the courage to climb back into that ambulance and drive the rest of the way on that road.

Today I chauffered Miss Otto all over Vienna. At 4 P.M. she dismissed me and told me to return to Velden tomorrow. She will take a late train back tonight. So I said a last goodbye to the girls in the Vienna detachment, not without regret. They were wonderful sports and had been great fun to live and work with.

Vienna to Velden, February 16, 1946

Left Vienna at 8:30 A.M. It had not snowed for the last two days, but the roads were still icy. After we passed the Semmering Pass, driving became a little easier and I didn't have to concentrate so hard. I say 'we' because I had one passenger, Shari Schmidt, one of our Palestinian girls who had just returned to Vienna from her leave. And what a story she had to tell! Like me, Shari was born in Berlin and had immigrated to Israel. She had learned that her father managed to survive the concentration camp and now was living in Frankfurt. Therefore, she had applied for leave to visit him and after several refusals finally had been granted leave to proceed to Frankfurt, Germany, but after a three weeks' visit with her father, she decided to go on to Berlin for a few days. In Berlin she went to her old neighborhood, found some friends, and stayed with them. Two days later she was picked up by the Russian police. A dispatch, something like the following, was sent to Miss Otto from the Russian Zone in Berlin:

A suspicious character has been picked up. Upon being interrogated, said girl stated that her name is Shari Schmidt; that she belongs to His British Majesty's Forces in Austria; that her outfit is 502 MAC ATS; that her commanding officer is P.E. Otto. The above aroused suspicion because of her ability to speak German without an accent. She had been seen wearing the British uniform, yet talking freely to several Germans. Said girl has been living with a German family, who maintain that the suspect had come for a few days' visit. Her pass is not made out for Berlin but for Frankfurt. Will Captain Otto kindly vouch for this member of her outfit, if the above statements are true. Otherwise, the matter will be placed in the hands of Intelligence.

In the meantime, Shari had been detained as a prisoner of the Russians who, she said, had treated her in a very proper manner except that they hadn't allowed her any reading material and she had become quite bored. She treated the whole episode as a very funny joke. She couldn't tell me much about Berlin, as the Russian police patrol had caught her on her second day there, except that the damage in the city was far worse than anything she had seen either in Italy or Austria. Still, she had enjoyed her little adventure. Captain Otto had not. Shari was confined to barracks for a week, not because she had caused so much trouble but because she had traveled to Berlin without proper authorization. I envied Shari in spite of her punishment and wished that I, too, could have gotten to Berlin, but I would never have been granted a pass there since it is out of bounds. Nor could I have gone to any other city in Germany because, unlike Shari, I had no living relatives in the British Zone. Besides, I knew that by now, if my parents had survived the Nazis and the war, they would have contacted Uncle Hans in the USA, or my sister in England. So it still seemed to me that I had done the right thing requesting leave to be together with my sister. I feel sure that this is what my parents would have wanted me to do.

Velden, February 18, 1946

Yesterday I was busy all day with maintenance in the yard, and all the time I was thinking, "This is the last time I'll clean 'my' ambulance, which has already been assigned to one of the new girls. This is the last time I inspect the other cars in the yard." At dinner I reflected on the last time I'll eat Emma's cooking in the company of all that remains of 502. How I hate to have to leave! It's a good thing that today every minute was filled with last duties. In the morning I had a dentist's appointment and later a complete physical. The Army wants to be sure that you are 100 percent fit upon discharge so as to avoid any later claims against the service. The Medical Officer did not like the sound of my chest, but I was adamant that I was healthy. I hated the idea of not being 100 percent fit. He asked me where I was going to live and when I told him Palestine, he felt that that would be a good climate for any residual effects of my many bouts with bronchitis and agreed to sign me out as entirely fit. In the evening the five of us leaving tomorrow were given a little farewell party in our bar. I had a hard time to keep my tears from showing.

Velden, February 19, 1946

The morning passed quickly with driving to area Headquarters, running from office to office to get all kinds of papers signed, and then doing a last bit of packing. At 4 P.M., one of our ambulances drove us to the Villach train station. Just before we boarded our train, each of us was given a handsome leather box engraved with "502 MAC ATS 1942–1946" and also a farewell letter from Miss Otto. It's been less than two weeks since my last long train ride. Then I was so much looking forward to returning home to 502, to being with what had become my extended family. Now once more I'm on the train, southbound this time and in a very different frame of mind, not looking forward happily but sad and totally uncertain of how to shape my future. Yet, deep down, I know I'll find a way.

Enroute to Naples, February 20, 1946

Late last night, about 10 P.M., the train stopped for dinner at Udine. Esther and I shared a compartment, so each of us could stretch out on the bench and had a good night's rest. This morning we had breakfast in Verona, then lunch in Bologna and dinner in Rimini.

Rome, February 21, 1946

We pulled into Rome at noon and were informed that the train for Naples, our destination, would leave in three hours. Shari and the two Hepner sisters were eager to be on it because by now they had become quite impatient to get home. They hoped to catch a plane for Palestine the next day and be reunited with their families that same evening. Esther and I, on the other hand, felt no great urgency to be demobbed. I wanted very much to spend a couple of days in Rome and Esther happily agreed. The two of us went to the RTO and managed to get passes for the Naples train on the 23rd. This was easy to do because our demobilization papers didn't specify a definite date of arrival in Palestine. We got a lovely room at the YWCA, the Hotel Imperiale, and after a good lunch we went out shopping. The stores are stocked again and I purchased stockings, two blouses, and two pairs of slacks. In the evening we took in a movie and finally, well satisfied, called it a day.

Rome to Naples, February 23, 1946

I spent most of yesterday visiting at the Pensionato where we were stationed and met a number of the students, talked to Mother Superior, had coffee with Lydia and Odetta, and enjoyed refreshing my Italian. Today our train left at 1 P.M., and we didn't arrive in Naples until 10 P.M.—seven hours! It seemed an endless journey. Upon arrival we were told that the YW was all filled up and we'd have to stay at the Transit Hotel. 'Hotel' is much too nice a name for this dirty dump. By the way, Shari and the Hepner sisters are still here, staying in the same dormitory with us. They're supposed to leave any day now.

Naples, February 24, 1946

Since it's Sunday today, we slept until 9 A.M. Then we went down for breakfast, only to be told that breakfast is served every day at 7 A.M. only. Great! Last night we didn't get any dinner and now not even a cup of coffee! We counted the hours until lunch, lying on our uncomfortable cots. There aren't even any chairs in these rooms. Then suddenly I pricked up my ears. One of the transients was explaining that the Army can't force any of its personnel to travel by air when going home, that one could insist on being sent home by ship. This, however, would involve a special application and an interview with the appropriate officer, who would try to persuade us to fly home. Esther and I talked it over and decided that we would go this route. Nobody knew when the next ship would leave for Palestine. If we were lucky, it might take weeks. The more I could postpone my final return, the better. As far as Esther was concerned, she was looking for some way to avoid going back at all!

Naples, February 25, 1946

Immediately after breakfast we went to Group Headquarters and filled out some forms requesting transportation by sea and an interview with regard to our refusal to be sent home by air. While waiting, we swore to each other that we wouldn't give in to any threats but would stand firm in our resolve.

"What's this? You don't wish to travel by plane?" A gruff officer was interviewing me privately in his office.

"Oh, no, Sir. Absolutely not, Sir!"

"And why not, may I ask?"

I took a deep breath and injected a quiver into my voice. "Terrible things happen to me up in the air, Sir."

The officer raised a cynical eyebrow. "Such as?" he countered.

"I get awfully sick and dizzy and weak and terribly frightened!"

Somewhere behind the closed door of another office Esther was going through a similar interview, but probably with a great deal more pathos and emotion. She, no doubt, had everyone sobbing by this time. My interviewer was dry-eyed. "You may go," he informed me coolly. "We'll let you know the results of this interview."

I got up from my chair. "Well, that's fine, Sir. Thank you." But I want you to know that I still refuse to fly."

In the afternoon we ran our feet off window-shopping. To keep Esther's mind off her wild schemes to keep from returning to Palestine, I shoved her from store to store. She bought everything she could lay her hands on. We staggered beneath the weight of her purchases. Two Yankees in a jeep, spying our heavy load, pulled over and offered to drive us to our destination. We accepted. They took a circuitous route, plunging into the heart of the city, showing us a part of Naples we never had seen before. Progress was very slow. We drove through a series of archways, around mountainous heaps of rubble. Facing us were towering half-shells of buildings, like gigantic cliff dwellings. A few women in filthy clothing knelt at a fountain, flogging limp gray rags against the scum-covered cement. They were quiet. So were the children playing among the rock heaps. No, they weren't playing. They were scavenging, clawing into the rubble to find something that could be sold on the black market for a piece of fish, a head of wilted cabbage, perhaps. A boy had found something, some kind of tin, but a bigger fellow gave him a blow that sent him reeling against the wall and ran off with the 'treasure.' One of the women approached us. *"Signore,"* she said to the Yankees, ignoring Esther and me, "pretty girl, no?" pointing to a doorway. "My daughter. Very nice girl. Come back tonight to see us, no? With a piece of chocolate? Two cigarettes, no?" One of the Yankees reached into his pocket and flung her a pack of cigarettes. Then we careened off. This is how the people of Naples are living now, if you can call this living.

Naples, March 2, 1946

My last entry was on February 25. The following day I woke up not feeling well at all and decided to spend the day in bed. The room weighed heavily on my spirits—it was gloomy, depressing, and draughty. The next day Esther announced that she didn't feel well either and climbed into her bunk. I suspect that sheer boredom rather than illness prompted her action, but while she sat chatting happily, I began to grow feverish. "Enough of this. I feel just rotten," I told her. "Might as well report sick." The Sergeant in charge said that we must see the doctor. "Fine," I croaked. "Where is he?"

"At Headquarters."

So out into the pouring rain we plunged. An icy wind whipped at us. By the time we reached the MO's office, my head was swimming. One whole hour later I was ushered in.

"You've got the flu. Go right to bed."

Back at the transit camp I reported to sick bay, Esther plodding faithfully at my heels. "How much nicer this is than our room," she said, sinking into bed. If there was a difference, I was too sick to notice it. The next two days I passed in a stupor. Somewhere along the line the Hepner sisters came to bid me goodbye. They were gone, at any rate, by the time I 'came to.' This is my fifth day in bed and I'm really fed up.

Esther, too, has had enough of the sick bay, but, unlike me, she did something about it. Last night, under the protecting cloak of darkness, after the last inspection of the day, she dressed, waved goodbye, and was gone. She promised to bring me my dinner, but the dinner never arrived. Neither did Esther. At midnight I heard footsteps. Esther had returned. Fuming, I watched her climb into bed and fall contentedly asleep. Today both Esther and Shari have left for 'parts unknown.' The sick bay is deserted. There's nothing to read and no one to visit with. I climb out of bed and sit by the window, hoping something of interest will occur. There's nothing to do but count the hours and the rain drops. Both advance with dull monotony.

Naples, March 3, 1946

Esther left the sick bay for good. Now I'm totally alone, with nothing to read, no one to talk to. I'm left to stare at the walls and hope that somebody will remember to bring me something to eat. My temperature is finally normal again, but I still feel very weak. I've decided, though, to move back to our room tomorrow. Nobody will notice anyway since I have seen neither doctor nor nurse around here. One probably could die here and no one would know!

Naples, March 4, 1946

Right after breakfast I reported back to our old room. Shari was there but not Esther. We wondered if she finally had made good on her threat to disappear before being sent back home. Late in the afternoon we were informed that Esther's and my requests had been granted and the next ship for Egypt or Palestine probably would leave on or about March 9th. Shari, too, has received her orders. She has a seat on tomorrow's plane.

Naples to Rome, March 6, 1946

I woke up this morning feeling quite well again and, to my great relief, Esther had come back too. Since both of us dislike Naples and this dreadful billet here, we decided to ask for a pass to spend two more days in Rome. After properly signing out, we left the transit camp at 10 A.M. Right away we caught a lift, and by 4:30 P.M. we had moved into another one of the luxurious rooms at the YW in Rome. I'm really happy to be back in this, my favorite city.

Rome, March 7, 1946

We woke up to a gorgeous day and after breakfast decided to wander around, enjoying our respite from Naples and its awful transit camp. The minute we left the hotel we were surrounded by a group of Italians, each of them trying to outbid the other, offering us so much for our uniforms, so much for our shoes, and didn't we have a coat for sale. These black-marketeers station themselves at all military hotels, and as soon as any Army personnel step out into the street, they swoop down like so many vultures. We fought our way clear, walked down to the Via Nazionale, did some window shopping and bought some souvenirs.

Along the street a photographer stopped us and took our picture. He assured us that it would be beautiful and that we would do well to retrieve it, handing us a couple of stubs. We shopped until we had just enough money left to pay for our lodgings at the Y. We were broke, but it still was too early to go back to the hotel so we went instead to get our pictures.

Inquiring our way, we finally found ourselves in front of a rather old, shabby building. An arrow on the wall directed us up several flights of stairs to the photographer's shop. Our pictures were rather good. We asked the price and then remembered that we had no money left. Would cigarettes do? Oh, yes! Glancing furtively around the room and cautioning us with a finger to his lips, the photographer led us into an adjoining room. My God! I thought myself back at camp, visiting the Quartermaster's store. Neatly stacked on shelves reaching to the ceiling were layers and layers of Army goods—shoes, coats, pajamas, uniforms, socks, and on the far side of the room shelves bulging with food supplies and cigarettes. We were really taken aback. What a brazen display! We made it clear that we would give him only enough cigarettes to cover the cost of the pictures, only that and no more. Obviously, he was disappointed because he had plainly thought himself in for some substantial business in cigarettes.

In the evening we decided to take in an ENSA show. On the way to the theater four Americans in a jeep hailed us.

"Wanna go out, girls?"

"No, thanks. We're on our way to a show."

"Oh." that stopped them, but only briefly. "Wanna lift there?" We accepted and they drove us over. Half jokingly, Esther suggested that they stop back for us after the show.

"O.K.!" and they were gone in a cloud of dust. The show was out at 10 P.M. and, sure enough, at 10 P.M. they were there, waiting for us;

they drove us back to the Y. What nice fellows! I am beginning to like Americans more and more.

Naples, March 9, 1946

We left Rome yesterday morning. Got a lift from two charming British Air Force fellows, had a picnic on the way, and arrived in Naples at 4 P.M. Our two friends drove us right to the transit camp. It was raining, and the draughty building with its gloomy atmosphere depressed us. On top of that, we were informed that the ship would not leave on the 9th, today, but only tomorrow. We could have stayed another day in Rome!

On board S.S. Dunnotar Castle, March 12, 1946

If the authorities had known what a poor sailor I am, they would have *ordered* me to fly home! For the past twenty-four hours I have wished myself on land, in the air, any place but aboard ship! But this morning the sea was calm, and so am I. Our last few hours in Italy were miserable. It was still raining. Soaked to the skin, we stood on the dock waiting to board the *Dunnotar Castle*. She is a trim, good-looking ship. I looked forward to my Mediterranean cruise. Late in the afternoon the last of the luggage and supplies were hauled aboard, and so were we. The gangplank was lifted. I stood on deck watching Naples slip away from my view.

"Nasty weather, eh?" I whirled around at the sound of the familiar voice.

"Emanuel! What in heaven's name are *you* doing here?"

"I'm going home too. I was given my papers very suddenly. It's good to see you!" I was glad too. Strange, how often our paths have crossed through the years.

I went down to inspect the cabins. They're very roomy and comfortable. Esther and I share one with another girl. She, like Esther, does not want to go home. I had better keep an eye on both of them! While, at the moment, avenues of escape seem rather limited, one cannot underestimate the supreme prowess of Esther in this matter. We dined in unique company the first evening. Although this is primarily a troop ship, we have a few high priority civilians on board. Sharing our table are a young Italian couple who have made their home in Egypt, a politician from Iraq, two Red Cross workers from Yugoslavia, two British entertainers hired by the Army, and a Syrian doctor. After dinner we saw two newly released American films. They were good and highly appreciated.

332

I spent all of yesterday, our second day out, in bed. The sea was rough, tossing our sizable ship about as though it were a cork, or so it seemed to me. However, this morning the storm has passed. I ventured out for the boat drill and a stroll around the deck. I saw Esther flirting with the whole ship. Thank goodness, she is out of my hair. Emanuel has just asked me to play a game of chess with him.

Ismalia, Egypt, March 16, 1946

Two days ago we landed in Port Said, Egypt. After our disembarkation, we boarded a train for Ismalia and were rushed pell-mell back into the country of *baksheesh, galabias,* and flies. The transit camp at Ismalia is very pleasant. Situated along the shore of Lake Timsah, with houses surrounded by little green meadows stretching down toward the water, the place looks more like an officers' rest camp than a transit camp. Whole families of soldiers, their wives, and kids people the doll-like houses. Yesterday we were jerked back into the tensions of the Middle East. A curfew was called. No British soldier was allowed to leave the camp—something about an outbreak of violence among the native population. So we sat around idly all day. This morning curfew was still in effect, but a couple of hours ago it suddenly was lifted. Esther and I went off to investigate the town. The hot Egyptian sun bearing down on us could not detract from the charm of Ismalia. What a lovely place, with numerous parks, wide avenues, and a beautiful residential quarter. If ever I had to live in Egypt, I would choose Ismalia.

Palestine, March 18, 1946

Yesterday the train left for Palestine. I had a second-class compartment shared by Esther and another ATS girl on her way home. Today at noon our train pulled into Kantarah, where we had the usual Army lunch. When the train left the station, an English officer accompanied by a Sergeant stepped into our compartment. They looked disdainfully about. Pointing a patrol stick toward our luggage, the officer spoke. "This, this, this and this—down!" We waited for the Sergeant to pull the baggage from the racks, but he only looked out of the window at the passing landscape, not deigning to notice our distress. We waited.

"Well, come on. I haven't all day, y'know." The officer's voice was surly. His eyes conveyed hostility and mistrust. Gone was the gallantry, the warm comradeship we had known these past four years. Vanished as though they had never existed! I was an alien.

"Well?" His stick drummed impatiently against the seat back. I hauled my 'piano' from the rack, and the man leaned over to inspect its contents. After a thorough search of the luggage, we did not know for what, the two men left our compartment without saying another word.

Half an hour later another officer barged in. "Sergeant, your movement orders!" he barked at me.

As I was handing them to him, an idea came to me. "I say, Captain, could we get off the train at Rechowoth before going on to Sarafand? It would help awfully if we could drop our luggage at home instead of hauling it to the camp and back. We'd catch the afternoon train to Sarafand."

He looked at me in a manner which implied that what I had suggested was absolutely criminal. All British soldiers have been warned about illegal immigrants to Palestine so I don't suppose I could blame him for being suspicious. Then he pointed to my discharge papers. "Movement orders are not written in pencil. This is most irregular. Where did you get them?"

I couldn't explain the actions of the officer who had issued the papers, I pointed out. "Here are my pay-book and my identification papers. If these are not enough, then I don't know how else to prove my identity," I said.

He did not answer but stomped out with my credentials. Several minutes later special guards were posted at the door of our compartment and there they remained until the train halted in Sarafand. Was this the victorious homecoming? Feeling quite inglorious, I grabbed my luggage and prepared to alight. "I expect to receive a confirmation of your arrival at camp within the hour," a clipped British voice was saying. "If not, I'll search every corner of this God-damned country of yours for the three of you."

I looked up. It was the officer who recently had visited the compartment. Impeccably groomed, wearing the uniform and the insignia of His Majesty's Army, even as I was, he stood before me. And it was as though I saw him clearly for the first time. He looked quite strange and—foreign.

5. THE NEXT STEP

Nobody in Sarafand knew anything about us. Apparently we had not been given the correct release books and until such time as these documents were received, we could not be discharged. After much confusion we were given a ten-day leave pass with orders to report back to Sarafand on March 28. When I finally arrived at Tante Else's flat, Bärbel, Lotte's daughter, told me that her mother and grandmother (Aunt Else) were on vacation in Tiberias and that she herself was in town for a few days before returning to her duties. I was not quite sure what these duties were but had a vague idea that she was doing her stint in the Haganah or some other quasi-military organization.

The first days after my return were filled with visits to old friends in Tel-Aviv and the constant telling and re-telling of stories about my 'Army days.' Though I enjoyed this, I felt more at ease spending time with Edith and the few former 502 members who lived in Tel-Aviv. The same went for my uniform. Though now I could wear mufti if I so chose, my uniform felt more comfortable. Yet day after day I felt less proud wearing it. It identified me with the British who, as I soon found out, represented to the Jews of Palestine the most unjust, intransigent, and cruel enforcement of an unacceptable policy. During the war we had fought side by side with the British and expected that afterwards our loyalty would be rewarded by relaxing the restrictions on immigration imposed by the hated White Paper. But once again the British were more interested in placating the Arabs (who had been largely Axis-friendly during the war) and protecting their oil and military interests in the Middle East. When the displaced Jews of Europe tried desperately to emigrate to Palestine after the war, the British mustered all their forces to prevent such 'illegal' immigration. A few DPs made it, but the majority were caught, returned to Europe, or detained in camps on Cyprus. Some died there. Some even were killed when they resisted British efforts to turn them back. And these were the survivors of concentration camps and the terrors of war! Was it any wonder that the British now were hated and opposed?

For me and my entire orientation it meant an almost 360 degree turn. At 502, surrounded by and steeped in British atmosphere, I had been unaware of all this. I had spent four happy years as part of the British forces which, almost overnight, now had become my enemy. And nothing could have brought this closer to home than the events of the next few days. On March 25, the eighth day of my last military leave, I had just returned from lunch with the Grossmanns when Bärbel informed me that she was expecting a few friends and would appreciate it if I did not pay any attention to who was coming and what they were talking about. I was a bit surprised at this businesslike reception. I had the feeling that my sudden appearance had surprised her and that somehow it had disturbed some plan of hers, but since I did not know her too well, I did not pay much attention to it. I told her that I was only going to shower, change into mufti, and be on my way. I was going to dinner at Edith's in Ramat Gan. Bärbel, or Bracha as her friends called her, seemed much relieved. While I was in the shower I heard her pals arrive. Then I heard them whisper a lot and later there was much paper tearing. While I was getting dressed the toilet was running constantly. I wondered if they were flushing down what they had torn up. But I was not too curious, and if I thought of it at all I must have considered it a rather childish conspiracy. I do remember that Bärbel told me not to worry, she would not be home until early the next morning.

I spent a delightful evening with Edith, reminiscing and catching up on all the news. It was quite late when I returned from Ramat Gan. Bärbel was still out. When I woke up the next morning she still had not come home. Again, I did not think much about it until about an hour later when the telephone rang, reporters appeared at the front door, and friends began to call. It was hard to get at the facts in all the chaos. Apparently Bracha, our Bärbel, had been shot by the British while guarding a road leading to the harbor. She, like many other armed defenders of the resistance movement, had been on alert, awaiting the arrival of the *Wingate*, a ship full of 'illegal' immigrants. The British must have found out about it and in the ensuing clashes between the military and the Jewish defense forces, Bracha was wounded by a shot fired from an armored car. Someone had heard that she had been transferred to the Government Hospital in Jaffa. Nobody knew how seriously wounded she was since no one had been allowed into the hospital. I decided to go to Jaffa immediately. Perhaps, in my uniform, they would let me in. But when I arrived there I was told that she was dead and no one could see her. Her body would be released the next day for the funeral. The official version was that she had used her Sten-gun against an approaching British tank, which then had opened fire and shot her. But there were still many unanswered questions. It seemed hard to believe that she would have attacked a tank with a gun. Especially hard to understand was the fact that no one, not even her mother later that day, was allowed to see the body. And what had happened to her after she was shot? According to the British Sergeant in command of the armored car, the fatal shot was fired at 11:30 P.M., yet she had not been taken to the Government Hospital until 4 A.M. the next morning. What had they done with her in the intervening hours? The papers were full of speculation. Some said that Bracha died immediately, others that the British soldiers carried her off to prison, bleeding profusely, that there they tried to extract incriminating information from her, and that it was only after they realized the hopelessness of their efforts that she was transferred to the hospital.

Tante Else and Lotte had just arrived from Tiberias when I returned from Jaffa. The next few hours were a nightmare. Again and again Lotte wanted to know everything about her daughter's last hours. But there was little I could tell her, except that I was the last one of the family who had seen her alive. The next day Bärbel was buried. All I remember of the funeral were Lotte's silent tears and Tante Else, on Professor Zondek's arm, looking so fragile, so broken-hearted.

Two days later I reported back to Sarafand. By now my papers had arrived and the actual process of being officially discharged took just over an hour. I had to return all uniform changes except the one I was wearing. After receiving my last pay and getting my paybook duly stamped and declared invalid from that time on, I was given—this is hard to believe—a sort of housedress, a flowered cotton frock. I suppose it was meant to tide me over until I could buy some civilian clothes. So there I stood, the cotton dress over my arm, in one hand an envelope with a few Palestinian pounds, representing my mustering out pay, in the other my battle ribbons. My four years of service in His Majesty's Forces were over.

What now? I had made my rounds, seeing old friends, but after the initial pleasure in these visits I found it hard to relate to them. Fanny and Richard had moved to Jerusalem. Sonya had an entirely new circle of friends with whom I shared little. Hedden Grossmann was suffering so badly from asthma that even talking was hard for her. The girls I had known in the Beth Hachaluzoth long ago had moved out, who knows where. Rolf had been discharged several months before. We met a couple of times but did not hit it off. He wanted to get married, settle down. I could not see that for myself at all. But what could I see? I knew that I had to make some plans, yet I had no clear picture of my future. All I wanted to do was to be with my Army buddies. Closest to me was, of course, Edith, but there also were Myra and Esther, Alice and Tonya, and good old Emanuel from Treviso and Venice days, and later on Joseph, whenever he came to Tel-Aviv. I think most of us felt somewhat displaced. We spent countless hours together, even traveling to Haifa and Jerusalem to meet our former pals and reminisce endlessly.

In the days that followed Bärbel's death I also spent much time with Tante Else. She had moved over to Professor Zondek's house so that he could keep an eye on her. Lotte stayed with some friends for a while, then came back, and once more the two of us shared the flat. Tante Else seemed to take solace in having me around, and soon I became so much a part of the family that my place at the dinner table was set automatically and I was expected to call if I could not make it. On Shabbat, the cook's day off, the three of us, Professor Zondek, Tante Else, and I, would eat out. Often I would accompany them to their monthly concerts of chamber music. It was assumed that I would be 'home' for their Friday night socials. I found myself spending more time with them than Lotte did. Yet, though my days were full, none of these activities was leading to anything. I had to make some decisions, to find a way to earn a living. I went to the Resettlement Office, where I was told that the Army would pay for a six months' typing and shorthand course. I signed up for it and was given the address of a private tutor. Now my mornings were filled with lessons and homework, neither of which I enjoyed much. The second thing I did was to write a long overdue answer to my Uncle Hans' letter from Chicago, where he now was practicing medicine. The letter had been sent to my Army address, then was forwarded, and finally had reached me during that dreadful week of Bärbel's death. I had put it aside because I did not feel I could deal with it right then. The letter concerned the death of my parents and confirmed once more what he had written to me before when I was in Graz, only this time there were exact details from the Red Cross, that is, as exact as could be expected:

Otto Bonin, born 4/26/1886 Berlin, was removed to Auschwitz on the 4th of March, 1943, with the 34th East Transport. Also Lilly Bonin, née Plessner, born 6/7/1889 Berlin, was transported

338

on the 1st of March, 1943, with the 31st East Transport to Concentration Camp Auschwitz. Further information about the fate of your relatives is impossible to ascertain.

Last October, when the news had come via Sweden, I had not wanted to believe it, but deep down I knew it was true. I had just pushed it back. Now I simply had to face it, but I also realized that I must not dwell on it. I had seen and heard of too many who had suffered the guilt of survivors, and I was convinced that this would be the last thing my parents would have wished for me. So it was with their approval in mind that I responded to the second part of my uncle's letter, in which he asked me to consider coming to America. He would like to offer me as well as my sister Edith, if not a home, at least the opportunity of a new beginning in the United States. He would be able to send affidavits for both of us and if I was willing to accept his offer, I should see the American Consul in Jerusalem for further details. I decided to do so. An appointment was set up for the 16th of May.

All the way to Jerusalem I thought about the last time I had travelled this road. Five years had passed since then. How young I had been, how stupid, but above all how lucky that things had not turned out the way I wanted them at the time. Again I thought I must have had a guardian angel watching over me. I shuddered now at the thought of what might have happened if I had not been taken off that train: detection, for sure, at crossing the Suez Canal and an Egyptian prison, and me pregnant! Or, even if I had escaped that horrible fate, years of being held in a camp, married to Laszlo with who knows how many kids by now? When we entered Jerusalem the walls and gates of the Old City shone like gold in the late afternoon light. Again the sight thrilled me. As I felt that elation I swore to myself never to look back on that dreadful period. Instead I must be grateful for the happy years I had spent in the Army, for all the adventures I had experienced, the camaraderie I had shared, and the widening of my horizons that had enriched my life. Indeed, I felt fortunate at that moment.

At the American Consulate I had to show my birth certificate, Army discharge papers, health certificate, etc. I filled out numerous forms and finally talked to the Consul, or, rather, his representative. He told me that I would immigrate to the United States under the German quota. (The Americans don't consider your current passport but rather your country of birth.) Since the German quota, as a result of the war, was at the moment not at all filled, he thought that what used to take years before the war should now be processed within ten to twelve months. I should, however, figure that it might take a bit longer to actually get to the States because there was very little transportation available. Most ships were being refurbished for peacetime use, and no definite schedules were yet in effect. But I would hear from the Consulate as soon as my visa arrived. He stood up, wished me luck, we shook hands—and I was on my way to America.

Or was I? During the next few months, even for the rest of 1946, I was often in doubt about whether I really should leave Palestine. As time passed my life assumed a pleasant routine, and I asked myself more than once why I would want to change it. When my typing and shorthand course came to an end I received a certificate of completion, but I did not feel proficient in either of these two skills. Nevertheless, through a friend of Lotte's, I got a job at "Express Service." They were international forwarding agents who handled customs clearing, transports, warehousing, and insurance. The owner, Dr. Guttmann, a former lawyer from Frankfurt, hired me, although I told him quite frankly that neither my shorthand nor my typing were first-class. On the other hand, when he asked me if I was intelligent and quick to learn, I was very positive on both accounts. So I started work, first half days only, but by June it had become a full-time job. Thank goodness, I didn't have to type too many letters, and shorthand hardly ever was required. My work consisted mostly of issuing insurance certificates, preparing customs entries, taking orders over the phone, dealing with complaints, checking manifests, etc. The atmosphere at "Express Service" was one of easy camaraderie among all employees and I soon felt as if I belonged, something that always has been very important to me.

Tante Else and Uncle Schorsh, as I called Professor Zondek now, had given me 'family.' My job was pleasant and paid enough for all I needed, even allowed me to save some, especially since I did not have to pay rent or much for food either. Between my old Army buddies and the new friends I had met I had as much social life as I could handle. I was enjoying myself and nobody could understand why I wanted to change all this for an uncertain future in a foreign land, far away and among strangers. But it really was quite simple. In spite of the pleasant trappings of my life, or perhaps even because of them, I felt confined. Yes, life was comfortable now, but what about the future? Where was I going from here? Have a 'nice' but not very challenging job? Maybe meet a 'nice' fellow, get married, and have a 'nice' family? Have a 'nice' little apartment and spend the rest of my life going nowhere in particular?

But then there was America, the land of endless possibilities, of unlimited choices. I was neither fantasizing about a 'rags to riches' script, nor did I have any preconceived idea about what I wanted to do there. On the contrary, it was the totally unknown, the new, that fascinated me. It was also the immensity of the country that attracted me. From all I had heard and read, America was described in superlatives. It was in every way the biggest, the richest, with the most of everything. It seemed to brim with energy. I felt its challenge and was impatient to take it up. So here I was, torn between the comfortable, the familiar, and the unknown and exciting. As I weighed all sides of the question it became clear to me that my future was waiting for me over there.

My decision, though, was severely put to the test. What was happening in Palestine in the following months almost made me change my mind. The intransigence of the British government, its absolute refusal to permit the entrance of more Jews into Palestine, was provoking an increasing number of sabotage operations, most of which were attributed to either the Irgun or the Stern Gang. Whereas the Haganah and its commando units, the Palmach, restricted their activities mostly to helping the 'illegal' immigration, the terrorist groups began to wage guerrilla warfare, setting fire to British ammunition and oil dumps and harassing British convoys. Though the Yishuv in general did not approve of such terrorist methods, most of us felt that we had waited patiently for too long, always expecting the British to keep their promises and act fairly. Now more and more Jews were advocating the necessity for the creation of a Jewish state, which would allow us to control our own immigration so that the pitiful remnants of the Holocaust could finally settle in a homeland.

Palestine was fast becoming a police state as the British, reacting to these acts of violence, practically declared war on the Yishuv. A hundred thousand British soldiers and two thousand policemen broke into kibbutzim and searched Jewish institutions, looking for weapons and 'terrorists.' They imposed curfews in the cities, the first of which took place on June 19, my birthday. Soon the curfews became part of our life. I would wake up to the rumble of a tank and then hear the loudspeaker announcing the hours of the curfew. Sometimes it would start at 6 A.M. and last for twelve hours, at other times even longer. Sometimes the curfew was lifted for an hour around noon, usually only for women, so that we could quickly run to the corner store to buy the most urgent supplies. Often curfews were declared after sundown, lasting through the night. This meant that stores and businesses had to close early to allow employers and employees to get home in time. When the Irgun blew up the King David Hotel in Jerusalem, killing

341

about eighty British, Jewish, and Arab civil servants, the British declared a four-day curfew on Tel-Aviv. During that time all buildings were evacuated and all of us, block by block, were taken to large squares in the city where we had to show our identity cards and were searched for weapons. But as the Battle of Britain had united the English and instilled in them a fighting spirit, so did these curfews unite us in defiance of the British and, as the armed uprisings continued, so grew our sympathy for and cooperation with the forces engaged in sabotage and illegal immigration. During the curfew hours we became acquainted with our neighbors next to us, above us, and below us. We had houseparties, played cards, shared our food, and when curfew was lifted for a shopping hour, we divided duties among us to help the ill, the elderly, and the handicapped. Out of this sharing, the bad as well as the good times, the feeling of belonging that I so valued grew. It tugged at me and threw me into doubts about where my allegiance lay. I thought of Bärbel, who had laid down her life for what the Yishuv was fighting for, of Tante Else and Uncle Schorsh, who wanted me so much to stay, of all my friends and buddies.

But then I thought of my sister Edith. Every letter I received from her bubbled over with the excitement of going to the States. At the American Consulate in London she had been told that her papers would be ready by spring. She was counting the days and had, of course, no doubt that I would join her as soon as possible. In the meantime, she would stay with Uncle Hans and his family. Neither he nor my sister had any idea of the doubts that assailed me.

It was around September that I ran into Irene G., who had been 'the other driver' at the Sarafand training camp and who then also had been posted to Egypt, though not to my unit. I always had thought of Irene as very sophisticated and independent and had enjoyed listening to her relate her many experiences. I knew she had been to America before the war and now I wanted to know all about that period in her life. I had a thousand questions, which she patiently answered over the next few weeks, because after our first meeting we saw each other frequently. What Irene told me began to tip the scales. I had, of course, heard that a healthy young person with a lot of drive and energy and a little luck could get ahead over there. But what I did not know was that there was free education for anyone and second chances for those who had not finished high school. Were there many of the latter and how did they manage to live while going to school or to the university? They worked in the daytime and went to school at night or on weekends. High school classes at night? University lectures on weekends? Weekends! I had forgotten that in America you worked only five days instead of our six-day week. It must be wonderful to have two whole days free every week! But far more important, I could finish my interrupted high school education. Who knows, I might even get into the University, and who knows what opportunities that might lead to? Irene was right. I'd be a fool not to try. The scales had tipped.

The rest of the year and well into 1947 I spent a lot of time preparing for my new life. I tried to work as much overtime as I could and I gave English lessons, all in order to earn a little extra money to see me through my first few weeks in the new homeland. I also needed to buy a new wardrobe. Under no circumstances did I want to arrive looking like a poor immigrant. I wanted to start on the right foot, looking prosperous and expecting to be successful. In this my girlfriend Edith helped me a great deal. What fun we had trying on hats, choosing fabrics, going to the dressmaker. It all seemed a wonderful game, until some innocuous remark would remind us both that this time we were preparing to part for a long time, perhaps forever. Still, even with the occasional heartache, the sadness that tinges all departures, my last months in Tel-Aviv were good ones and passed so quickly that I was almost surprised when, in March, 1947, I received a note from the Consulate telling me to pick up all documents for immigration to the United States of America. Once more I went to Jerusalem, probably for the last time. At the Consulate the official immigration visa was stamped into my British-Palestinian passport. I could now enter the United States as a permanent resident. All I had to do was wait for transportation. Since there was still a dearth of passenger ships, this could take another few months, but as soon as passage was available I would be informed. All these formalities took less than an hour so I had plenty of time to visit Fanny and admire her new baby. Richard was at work. I then stopped to say goodbye to some other friends and had a last lunch with Esther, who was working as a civilian employee at British Headquarters. She was the same exuberant, happy-go-lucky girl I had known in the Army and she kept me in stitches telling me about her adventures at the switchboard. We reminisced, especially about our last weeks in Naples, Rome, and our return home. Then I was ready for a last dinner with Joseph. This did not work out too well. He was the only one of all my friends who blamed me for abandoning 'my country.' I did not answer his criticism. He would not have understood anything I might have told him.

I took a few days off to go to Haifa for a last meeting with some Army friends from that area, and when I returned home there was a letter from Jerusalem telling me to book passage on the *Marine Carp* leaving Haifa on June 13, 1947. The last weeks in Palestine passed by very quickly. Everyone was giving me a farewell party, a last gift, and much advice for my future. Here and there I shed a tear, especially when I said goodbye to Edith, but on the whole I was growing too excited to dwell much on the sadder aspects of leaving. I had my ticket, my passport, and had exchanged all my Palestinian pounds and piasters into American dollars. Express Service had taken care of my large trunk, which was to go into the ship's hold, and early on the 13th of June, Martin, my boss, drove me to Haifa. Lotte, who had left a few days before to stay with some friends, met us at the harbor. The *Marine Carp* was in, loading cargo, but before boarding I had to report at the shipping office. There a nasty surprise awaited me. Though I had paid for a second-class ticket (there was only hold or second class), I was told that only female passengers over forty years of age were to be given a cabin and that I had to be satisfied with a bunk in the hold. The *Marine Carp* was one of those small 'liberty ships' designed to carry troops and supplies during the war. There were only a few cabins available. I protested, but the clerk just shrugged his shoulders and counted out the refund due me—in Palestinian pounds. This was a terrible blow for several reasons. First, since I had had to pay my passage in dollars, I had, of course, already lost in the exchange. On top of getting back fewer pounds than I had paid originally, I now had to change the money at the bank, back into dollars. In these three exchanges I had lost more than I had been able to save in months! The other reason was my new bunk assignment in the hold. I remembered the 'accommodations' on the ship that took me from Marseilles to Palestine, and, knowing that I was not the best of sailors, I was nonplused, but there was nothing I could do at that moment.

Lotte, Martin, and I had a last drink together, they toasted to my future in America, and then it was time for boarding. One last goodbye and I followed the Arab porter, who had whisked my suitcase away. We descended into the hold, and every time we turned down another staircase I was surer that this must be the bottom of the ship. Finally he put my suitcase down, pointed to a huge dormitory, *salaamed*, and climbed back up. How can I describe what I saw, smelled, and felt during the next few minutes? I was standing by the staircase in a small hall, off which four dormitories opened. The bunks were in clusters of four, two uppers and two lowers, the mattresses of each two so close together that they appeared as one. At a glance I could not tell how many bunks there were in each dormitory—perhaps eighty to one hundred. Two of the holds were filled with Arabs, mostly women and children, hoards of children running around, playing on the floor. Food, flies, fetid air from unwashed bodies and dirty diapers, mixed with that peculiar smell so typical of mid-Eastern villages and markets. Someone said that these passengers had boarded the ship in Beirut. I wondered if they, too, were immigrating to the States. The other two dormitories now were filling up quickly with Jewish passengers, one assigned to the men, the other to the women. Many of them, like me, were very unhappy at having been relegated to holds instead of the expected cabins. I felt more and more claustrophobic and wondered how I could stand a three weeks' journey in this sweltering, crowded, and unaired atmosphere. But worse was yet to come.

When I looked at my berth number, I realized that my bunk was not in the hold with my compatriots, which was at least clean, but with the Arabs. My first thought was that by the time I arrived in New York I would smell like them! My second was, what would happen in this dormitory if the sea got rough and everyone got seasick? The smell, which already was overwhelming, would become unbearable. Vomit, excrement, stench! No, I would under no circumstances stay here. I had to do something. Back up I climbed, looking for the Purser, but when I finally located him he was too busy to talk to me and waved me off. Any complaints, changes, or problems would have to wait until we were at sea. We weighed anchor around noon. I stayed on deck, filling my lungs with good sea air. As soon as the shoreline disappeared I looked again for the Purser. This time he *did* talk to me, but very curtly. No, there was no chance whatsoever that I could get a cabin. The few that were not filled yet were reserved for passengers boarding in Athens. At least, until then, nothing could be done. When I asked him why, then, could I not have a cabin bunk until Athens, he yelled at me to leave him alone. So far this had not been an auspicious beginning, but I had decided that there was no way that I would sleep in that fetid hole. If the Purser would not listen to me, I'd look for the next in command, or better yet, go right to the top, to the Captain.

I looked at the bridge. It seemed very high from where I was standing, but I began to climb. On the top deck an iron chain with a sign "No Admittance" barred my way. I hesitated only a moment, then climbed over the first of these obstacles. There were two more such signs, but I disregarded them too. A lanky young fellow was sitting on the railing of the bridge, watching my progress. Finally, a little out of breath, I stood in front of him. "I would like to see the Captain, please."

He took the pipe he had been chewing on out of his mouth, looked at me, half smiling and half disapproving. "Do you know what 'no admittance' means, Ma'am?" he countered.

I wasn't going into that. "I must speak to the Captain. It's urgent," I repeated.

"I *am* the Captain. So, speak."

I was so astonished that for a moment I was struck dumb. This young fellow in khaki pants, a short-sleeved shirt, with no insignia and an old, soft-billed cap was the commander of our ship? I had expected an older man in Navy uniform with gold stripes on his sleeves and gold braid on his cap. Somehow this Captain's informality intimidated me more than if he had behaved in the stiff British manner I had expected and was used to. Still, I was not going to be deterred. I told him how I had booked a berth in a second-class cabin but, without being asked, had been switched to a hold, where I was supposed to share accommodations for the next three weeks under absolutely intolerable conditions.

"Why so intolerable?" he asked.

For an answer I simply asked him, "Sir, have you been down there, seen the filth and smelled the stink?"

He laughed. "No, and I don't want to."

Then he became serious and asked me why I had not seen the Purser. After all, this was under the Purser's jurisdiction. I recounted my appeal to the Purser and his quick and unfriendly dismissal of me. The Captain became even more serious.

"You say he yelled at you?"

"Yes, Sir."

The Captain called the Purser to come up and asked him, in front of me, if at this moment there were any empty cabins available. There were, answered the Purser, at least to Athens, but he had not yet checked the manifest to find out how many passengers were coming on board in Athens.

"Well then, go and check it out immediately."

The Purser was back within ten minutes, and if looks could have killed, I would have dropped dead for sure. Yes, there were two four-bed cabins with one bunk available in each, but the difference between hold and cabin was quite expensive, he added, looking at me contemptuously.

"Are you willing to pay?" asked the Captain.

"Yes, of course," I answered, without hesitation.

"Take the lady to her cabin and then come back to see me."

The Purser was furious. He probably was going to get a further dressing down by the Captain, but I didn't care. I had won! The price, though, was steep, more than I had expected—two hundred dollars, the Purser announced gleefully. Two hundred dollars represented more than half of what I owned to begin life in America. But, at least, I now was assured a comfortable passage. The cabin was an outside one and my berth was the upper one, by the porthole. There were two wash-basins in the cabin with nice, clean showers and toilets only two doors down. The other three bunks would not be occupied until Athens. By the time I had unpacked and changed my meal tickets from cafeteria to dining room, it was time for dinner. I shared a table with seven other passengers, most of them the "over 40s" who had been able to hold onto their cabins. Opposite me sat two American ladies who had been working in Beirut, then done some sightseeing in the "Holy Land," and now were on their way back home. The poor women hardly had time to eat, so beleaguered were they by our many questions, which they answered patiently, smiling at our eagerness to find out as much as possible about our new country.

I was so tired that first evening that after dinner I went straight to bed and slept until I heard the breakfast gong. It was a beautiful day. The sun was out, the sea was a deep blue, the sky a hue lighter, and when, after a good breakfast, I got up on deck, I inhaled the fresh breeze and felt great. I hunted for a deck chair, then saw the two American ladies already settled in theirs. They waved, inviting me to sit with them. A Mr. S. from Tel-Aviv and his son joined us later, and that was the way it remained for the entire voyage. We would meet at the same place and spend most of the time between meals on our deck chairs, talking, reading, or just dozing. The first day out everyone talked about Athens, where we were going to dock early on the 16th of June. Nobody knew how much time, if any, we would have for sightseeing. After lunch we found out. We would arrive at Piraeus around 7 A.M. and would leave again by noon. I was terribly excited at the prospect of seeing Athens, the Acropolis, and whatever else we had time for. Two days later we did dock shortly after 7 A.M., but it took forever until all the formalities were completed and we could disembark. There weren't enough taxis to take us all, so some of us, I among them, had to make do with the horse-drawn carriages waiting at the foot of the gangplank. I remember the ride from Piraeus to Athens and then up to the Acropolis as one of my great disappointments. Not that it was the fault of either Athens or the Acropolis but rather the fault of our mad driver. What should have been a highlight of our journey at our only port of call turned into the wildest ride ever. Over a terrible road, with potholes the size of washtubs, he drove his two nags at speeds almost beyond their capacity, urging them on with shout and whip. By the time we reached the Acropolis we were so dust-covered and frazzled that we had lost all enthusiasm for sightseeing. We scrambled around the ruins and then it was time to climb back into that awful contraption for our equally mad dash back to the ship.

When I entered my cabin again I met the other three passengers, two women and a girl about eight years old. They introduced themselves quite formally. One of the ladies—she was apparently the spokeswoman for the three of them—was the mother of the little girl, the other woman either her sister-in-law, cousin, or perhaps some other kind of relative—I never did find out. She acted more like a governess or maid to the intimidating, rotund Mrs. K., originally from Indianapolis. (I had no idea where that was.) She told me that she was the wife of an UNRRA official. I had the feeling that, the way she phrased it, she meant to convey that her husband held the equivalent of at least a major's rank. They were on so-called 'home leave.' She paused. I took advantage of that moment to introduce myself. "I am so glad to meet you," she said. "English, aren't you?" And without catching her breath, "You don't know how relieved we are that we don't have to share our cabin with any of those Jewish refugees." I was stunned. I also was speechless. How do you answer such a remark? If I told her right then and there who I was and what I thought of people like her, at best we would have two unpleasant weeks ahead of us. At worst, she could go to the Purser and ask for a change of cabins. I could just see the Purser rejoicing at my humiliation. So I did not say anything at that moment, but I mulled over the problem all that afternoon. Then it came to me. I would behave extra nice to them all the way, so that they really would come to like me, but then, on the last day, just before we disembarked, I would tell them that this ever-so-pleasant girl of whom they really had become quite fond, was one of 'those Jewish refugees.' As usual, when I had made a plan, I felt better.

The weather held all the way through the Mediterranean. We passed through the Straits of Gibraltar during the night. I woke up, feeling that the movement of the ship had changed, and from the moment we hit the Atlantic I always felt a bit queasy. I never became really seasick, but I never felt quite right. Many times I had to forego dinner. Sometimes I would sit down for a meal, only to rush out before even touching it. It felt as if the ship were doing figure-eights, rolling from side to side and dipping up and down at the same time. It had, of course, no stabilizer or air-conditioning either. But we were lucky. The weather was good most of the time and the sea was not too rough. An occasional rainstorm would confine us to our cabins since there were neither lounges nor any other kind of common room on board. When the waiters were not setting up the dining room, we could retreat there. I felt sorry for the passengers in the hold. During good weather they shared the decks with us, but when it turned too cold or rainy outside, they had to return to their airless bunks down below and their cafeteria was open during meals only. I made friends with one of the women from 'down there' and introduced her to our little deck group. She, too, enjoyed the two American ladies, who, I soon found out, did not have to be prodded much. They loved to talk about America and enjoyed waving the flag. They could not have found a more receptive audience.

The days passed. We had left Haifa on June 13 and were supposed to arrive in New York on June 29. And so we would have, but our Captain received orders on June 28 to slow down. The *Queen Mary* was scheduled to arrive on the 29th also and, for some reason—I believe it had to do with overloaded customs and baggage facilities—we had to wait until she was berthed and her passengers had disembarked. Late in the afternoon I was standing on deck waiting to see land when the *Queen Mary* sailed by us. She was so huge that our ship seemed a nutshell in comparison and I found it hard to believe that we had been able to cross the ocean on her.

On the morning of the 30th, the 30th of June, 1947, our ship sailed into New York harbor. I saw the Statue of Liberty on my left and on my right, growing bigger and bigger, the skyline of New York. I had never seen a skyscraper and now suddenly there they were, truly scraping the clouds. I was awestruck, overwhelmed by the sheer size of the city. I had seen Berlin, London, Rome, Vienna, but none of these had exuded the sense of power conveyed by the immensity of this city. For a moment I felt panic rising, but I fought it. I thought of my parents and their confidence in me. I heard my father saying, "You'll find your way!" I straightened up. Yes, he was right. I would find my way here.

An hour later, with all the others, I disembarked and stood in the customs hall under that same flag which years ago, as a child, I had chosen for my bicycle because it seemed to me the most beautiful. Now it stood for something far more than beauty. It stood for infinite opportunity. Still later, my passport stamped "Admitted" and my few possessions collected, I stepped out into the whirling, noisy, and confusing excitement of my first day in my new country.

EPILOGUE

Many years later I was teaching at a community college when one of my students lamented the fact that the streets of America no longer are paved with gold. "But they are," I told him. "Gold comes in many forms." For me it came in the form of education. Not right away. I held a number of different jobs. I moved out West. I went to a community college, then to the university, and finally to graduate school. There were many ups and a few downs in my life, as there are in everyone's, but I never doubted having made the right choice in coming to America, nor have I ever had a moment's regret for having chosen teaching as my profession. The college, its faculty, and, over the years, thousands of students have strengthened my belief that there is no better way to declare allegiance to one's adopted land than to teach, to help in passing on a world-wide cultural heritage which all of us share.

GLOSSARY OF MILITARY INITIALS

ADST	Assistant Director of Supply and Transport
ATS	Auxiliary Territorial Service (women's branch of the Army)
CCS	Casualty Collecting Station
CMF	Central Mediterranean Forces
CO	Commanding Officer
CSM	Company Sergeant Major
DDMS	Deputy Director of Medical Services
ENSA	Entertainment National Service Association
FSU	Field Surgical Unit
IFA	Indian Field Ambulance
MAC	Motorized Ambulance Corps
MEF	Middle East Forces
MI	Medical Inspection
MO	Medical Officer
MT	Mechanical Transport
MTC	Mechanized Transport Corps
NAAFI	Navy Army Air Force Institutes (similar to American PX)
NCO	Non-commissioned Officer
OC	Officer Commanding
RAF	Royal Air Force
RAMC	Royal Army Medical Corps
RASC	Royal Army Service Corps
RE	Royal Engineers
REME	Royal Electric and Mechanical Engineers
RTO	Railway Transport Officer
TAB	Anti-typhoid shots
UNRRA	United Nations Relief and Rehabilitation Administration
VAD	Voluntary Aid Detachment (nurse's aids)
VCO	Viceroy Commissioned Officer (an Indian officer not directly commissioned by the King)
WAAF	Women's Auxiliary Air Force

The ATS's official term for the rank of Lieutenant was Subaltern; for Captain—Junior Commander; for Major—Senior Commander.